ELVIS
WE LOVE YOU
TENDER

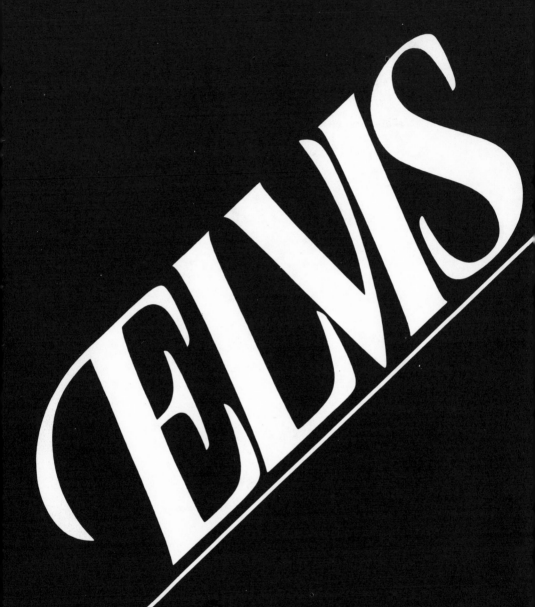

ELVIS

WE LOVE YOU TENDER

A DELILAH/MIKE FRANKLIN BOOK
DELACORTE PRESS/NEW YORK

DEE PRESLEY, BILLY, RICK,
and DAVID STANLEY
as told to MARTIN TORGOFF

Published by
Delacorte Press
1 Dag Hammarskjold Plaza
New York, N.Y. 10017

A portion of this book first appeared in *Ladies' Home Journal*.

Manufactured in the United States of America

Third Printing—1980

Designed by Giorgetta Bell McRee

ACKNOWLEDGMENTS

Grateful acknowledgment is made for permission to quote from the following copy-
righted material.

"Old Shep" Words and Music by Red Foley: © 1935 by Duchess Music Corporation,
New York, N.Y. Copyright renewed. Used by permission. All rights reserved.

"Johnny B. Goode" by Chuck Berry: Copyright © 1958 by Arc Music Corporation.
Used by permission.

"Heartbreak Hotel" Words and Music by Mae B. Axton/Tommy Durden/Elvis Presley:
© 1956 Tree Publishing Co., Inc. Reprinted by permission of the publisher.

"Loving You" by Jerry Leiber & Mike Stoller: Copyright © 1957 by Elvis Presley
Music. Copyright Assigned to Gladys Music (Intersong Music, Publisher). International
copyright secured. All rights reserved. Used by permission.

"Trying to Get to You": Copyright—Slow Dancing Music Inc./Motion Music Co.,
world rights assigned to and administered by Slow Dancing Music Inc., 1978, 515
Madison Avenue, New York, N.Y. 10022.

"Steam Roller" by James Taylor: © 1970 by Blackwood Music Inc. and Country Road
Music. Used by permission.

"Come On Everybody": Every effort has been made to locate the proprietor of this
property. If the proprietor will write to the publisher, formal arrangements will be made.

"Trouble" by Jerry Leiber and Mike Stoller: Copyright © 1958 by Elvis Presley Music.
Copyright Assigned to Gladys Music. International copyright secured. All rights reserved.
Used by permission.

"U.S. Male": Copyright © 1966 Vector Music Corporation, 1107 18th Avenue South,
Nashville, TN 37212. Used by permission.

LIBRARY OF CONGRESS CATALOGING IN PUBLICATION DATA

Main entry under title:

Elvis, we love you tender.

    "A Delilah/Mike Franklin book."
    Includes index.
    1. Presley, Elvis Aron.   2. Singers—United States
—Biography. I. Presley, Dee. II. Torgoff, Martin.
ML420.P96E47   784'.092'4 [B]   79-20830

ISBN: 0-440-02323-8

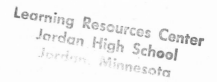

Psalm 121:1
   "I will lift up mine eyes unto the hills,
   From whence cometh my help"

When I was a small child, my mother died leaving only a few memories and a lonely little girl always dreaming of faraway places, a beautiful home, children, a handsome husband, and a perfect marriage. This all happened but still, sometimes, the loneliness never left. So to her memory I dedicate this book. My life has not been exactly what I would have planned, but I have had the happiness and the heartaches.

To my beautiful mother who gave me life, Bessie May Heath Elliott

To my three wonderful sons, Billy, Rick, and David, who are my great loves

To William J. Stanley, Sr., the father of my great loves

To Vernon Presley, I loved him.

To Elvis Presley, we will always remember you fondly.

DEE PRESLEY

To my mother, who made everything possible

BILLY STANLEY

To my mother, there's not enough words to say how great she is and express how much I love her.

DAVID STANLEY

To the two influential and beautiful women in my life, my mother and my beloved wife, Robyn

I Corinthians 13:11
   "When I was a child, I spake as a child,
   I understood as a child, I thought as a child:
   But when I became a man, I put away childish things."

God has changed my life now, and I am living for Him.

RICK STANLEY

We have a natural fascination with individuals of extraordinary talent, achievement, or power. We are drawn by their glamour and curious about the special abilities that make it permissible, indeed essential, for them to enact upon the public stage the hopes and dreams we all possess but fear or do not choose—or simply have no opportunity—to carry out ourselves.

> John E. Mack, *A Prince of Our Disorder:*
> *The Life of T. E. Lawrence*

I don't know what it is. . . . I just fell into it, really. My daddy and I were laughing about it the other day. He looked at me and said, "What happened, El? The last thing I can remember is I was working in a can factory and you were drivin' a truck." We all feel the same way about it still. It just . . . caught us up.

> Elvis Presley, to C. Jennings Roberts of
> *The Saturday Evening Post,* 1956

And the priestess spoke again and said:
Speak to us of Reason and Passion.
And he answered, saying:
Your soul is oftentimes a battlefield,
upon which your reason and your judgment wage
war against your passion and your appetite.

> Kahlil Gibran, *The Prophet*
> "On Reason and Passion"

CONTENTS

Author's Note: A Family Portrait *xiii*

PART ONE • **DREAMS** 1929–1969 1

Chapter 1 • Wild in the Country 3
Chapter 2 • Bright Lights, Big City 15
Chapter 3 • Trying to Get to You 43
Chapter 4 • The Rewards 63
Chapter 5 • The Brothers Stanley 83
Chapter 6 • Cuttin' Loose 93

PART TWO • **"BOSS"** 1969–1971 105

Chapter 7 • TCB 107
Chapter 8 • Rock Me, Lord 141
Chapter 9 • U.S. Male 161
Chapter 10 • Never Been to Heaven 185

xii

PART THREE • FALL FROM GRACE
1972–1975 195

Chapter 11 • I Can't Stop Loving You *197*
Chapter 12 • Lisa Marie *211*
Chapter 13 • Ups and Downs *215*
Chapter 14 • Sing Away Sorrow, Cast Away Care *229*
Chapter 15 • Fight at the Airport Lounge *243*
Chapter 16 • Going Down the Tubes *251*
Chapter 17 • Southern Belles *267*

PART FOUR • THE FINAL CURTAIN
1975–1977 277

Chapter 18 • Taking It to the Limits *279*
Chapter 19 • Daddy and Dee *293*
Chapter 20 • *Elvis: What Happened?* *317*
Chapter 21 • "And Now the End Is Near" *329*
Chapter 22 • Mother and Child Reunion *333*
Chapter 23 • The Legacy *361*

INDEX • 387

AUTHOR'S NOTE

A FAMILY PORTRAIT

What follows is the story of a family whose path happened to cross with the ever-ascending star of Elvis Aron Presley. At that precise moment in time, the lives of Billy, Rick, and David Stanley, who became his stepbrothers, and the life of Dee Presley, their mother, were all transformed. They remained within the firmament of that star until the very end of his life.

Much of what Elvis Presley was all about is today embodied in the lives of those who were closest to him, and many of the mysteries and paradoxes that shrouded his life are made comprehensible by an understanding of Elvis's impact on their lives. Somewhere between the experience of knowing and loving Elvis and the pain of his loss, his legends become human. This book seeks to reveal the human face of Elvis Presley.

Although this is essentially a very personal book based on primary source information, a great deal of background information has also been necessary. Therefore, I must gratefully acknowledge several writers who have all, at one time or another, written eloquently and authoritatively on Elvis's life, xiv music, times, or related subjects: Jerry Hopkins, whose biography *Elvis* (1970) remains the seminal and most scrupulously researched work on his life and which was an invaluable source of information on his early years; Greil Marcus, rock and literary critic, whose work throughout the years—particularly 'Elvis: Presliad,' the concluding chapter of his excellent book *Mystery Train: Images of America in Rock 'n' Roll Music* (1976)—contains the most passionate and insightful prose on Elvis to date; Peter Guralnick, expert on the blues, rockabilly, and the early years of rock, for *Feel Like Going Home: Portraits in the Blues and Rock 'n' Roll* (1971), a delightful and touching personal journey, and for his excellent magazine pieces; Dave Marsh, for his thoughtful commentaries on rock in *Rolling Stone* over the years; Jonathan Cott, aficionado of too many things to even mention; and, finally, David Dalton (the writer as rock star) for simply being himself and for helping me understand how truly "supernatural" Elvis really was.

Finally, because so many of our common dreams, values, problems, and fears are contained within this story, this has become not only a book about Elvis, but also the chronicle of an American family. As a writer, I have tried to paint a picture of a way of life, of different ways of life, of lives both with and without Elvis. To do so, I have played the role of the journalist; other times, I have felt more like a storyteller sitting on a veranda and telling the story of four interesting, complicated people.

We begin with Davada Elliot Stanley Presley, affectionately known as "Dee." She glides in and out of the narrative in the same manner that she was taught as a little girl to enter and leave a room—with a polished grace that demands your attention. From there the tale weaves, spins, backtracks, stumbles headlong into tragedy, and ends in hope.

MARTIN TORGOFF
Georgetown
February 1979

PART ONE

DREAMS

1929·1969

Sow a Thought and you reap an Act;
Sow an Act and you reap a Habit;
Sow a Habit and you reap a Character;
Sow a Character and you reap a Destiny.

Authorship Unknown

CHAPTER 1

WILD IN THE COUNTRY

The very first time that she saw him was at the Warwick Theater in Newport News, Virginia, so long ago that it now seems like a dream.

So this *is what the fuss is all about, she thought, as women around her crawled over the seats to get to him, screaming, jumping up and down, crying and whimpering, filling the theater with a rising, caterwauling roar that all but drowned him out even though she sat in the front row.*

Her three young boys slept peacefully at home that night, and she was able to get away, just for the night, far from the stifling routine and gnawing anxieties of her life, and had come to the theater to see this man that everybody was talking about. And they watched him up there—drap suited, his hair gunked high into that sweeping, preposterous pompadour and trailing back into the ducktail, the nose flaring away, the lips sneering as the heavy-lidded blue eyes smoldered and closed, batted, then rolled back into his head as he belted out the song. His legs were bent and cocked like pistols about to fire; the hips swiveled as he bump-thumped a high-slung guitar.

4   She couldn't quite put her finger on what it was, but she was vaguely aware of a feeling of prescience that night, some remote sense of kinship that she felt for the figure on the stage. Fascinated, she watched him closely as he kicked up a whirlwind and souped up the fantasies of his audience. He seemed to be looking right at her as if to acknowledge the feeling himself, and their eyes met again and again. In the years to come, even before she became his stepmother, she would recall that evening to him, and he would graciously flatter her: "Of course I remember you from that night, Mrs. Stanley," he would say. "How could I evah forget someone so beautiful?"

Elvis . . . so long ago. Time passes, but the images come rushing back in torrents and his life seems more indelible than ever—the gospels and the rockers, the garish flash and homespun funk, the faces of the people he loved, the kindnesses, the cruelties, the endless backwash of titillating gossip. She can see him now emerging on the front porch of Graceland—resurrected, lean and handsome again, yawning as he strolls nonchalantly down to the front gate where he might sign a few autographs, flatter a doting matron, or kiss a young girl. Or she thinks back to that night at the Warwick, before she even knew him.

"Have you heard the news!" he yelped, as they bopped and boogie-woogied in the aisles: "There's good rockin' tonight!"

If some Hollywood honcho of the thirties like L. B. Mayer had decided to make a movie about Dee Presley's youth, Shirley Temple would surely have been cast for the part.

She was born Davada Elliot on a small tobacco farm outside of Clarkesville, Tennessee (about forty-five miles northwest of Nashville), on the morning of June 19, 1925, near the sleepy country hamlet of Palmyra. Her father, James Wright Elliot, was a sharecropper who had managed to purchase a small amount of land for himself before his marriage to Bessie May Heath. Each had been married and divorced before, bringing a son from the previous marriage. William Elliot was six when Davada (Dee) was born and Bessie's boy, Richard Neely, was ten. The blond, blue-eyed child was named Davada by her

mother, and for the first four years of her life—before Bessie   5
May "took sick"—the child was cuddled endlessly by her
mother, much fussed over by her brothers, and pranced daintily
about the small farmhouse in clean gingham dresses, her
blonde ringlets bouncing behind her.

James Elliot had the reputation of a ladies' man around those
parts. He was a handsome devil—wiry, moustachioed, with
sharp, angular features and keen blue eyes—and when Bessie
became bedridden with a cold that she was never to recover
from, he recruited a young woman as a live-in housekeeper.
While poor Bessie May languished in bed, her health deteriorating, little Davada could hear James kicking about the house
at night, drinking and frolicking with the young woman. The
giggling and drunken laughter were sounds that she never
forgot.

James was really more of a romantic than a born hellraiser. A
gambling man, he liked to step out and have a good time, and
like many Southern men, his temper spoke like a double-bar-
reled shotgun when it was triggered. "My father frightened me,"
remembers Dee, "but he would give me anything I wanted."

There was an air of violence and mystery about James that
little Davada never understood, particularly when he went riding off into the balmy Tennessee nights with the white-hooded
local vigilantes to dispense "justice," sometimes not returning
for days on end.

If there was one thing that Davada remembered about the
night that her mother passed away, it was being lifted up by a
neighbor to say good-bye and kiss her mother's delicate hands
for the last time. She also remembered the solemn oath that
Bessie May managed to extract from James before she breathed
a deep sigh and passed into another world. "Never break up the
family," she heard her say, "and never let another woman
touch Davada."

James would only keep the latter part of the promise. After
the death the boys were sent off to neighboring farms and Davada began spending her time with a favorite aunt in nearby
Waverly, returning home at nights to sleep in her father's room.

6 But when he thought his daughter asleep, James would sneak out to spend the night elsewhere, leaving the child alone to contemplate the darkness and cry herself to sleep.

When James brought in another live-in housekeeper, Davada was six, and she resented Ollie Crafton almost from the moment she arrived. She disliked having to share her daddy with a woman who wasn't anywhere near as pretty as Bessie May, and Ollie also brought a daughter along—a gangly, freckle-faced redhead named Margaret.

James just went along his merry way, drinking, working his land by day, bird-dogging women at night. His conscience, however, soon began to bother him. "Father was beginning to realize that I was getting old enough to know what was going on," recalls Dee. "He knew that he wasn't setting a good example." Perhaps James also remembered his oath to a dying wife. It's hard to say what was really going on inside him except that one day, when he was out working in the barn, he heard the voice of the Lord whispering in his ear, and he resolved then and there never to take another drink (for it was *surely* the Devil's brew), to make an honest woman of Ollie Crafton, and to bring his daughter up properly. Thereafter he quickly moved from the backsliding, hedonistic ways of the natural-born sinner, right to the self-righteous existence of the newly reformed puritan.

Without demeaning James Elliot's redemption in the eyes of the Lord, it now becomes necessary to shift the focus of attention some one hundred eighty country miles to the southwest, over rolling fields, through blue woods and small towns, past that great city on the banks of the mighty Mississippi, Memphis, and finally down into the bottomlands of Lee County, in northeastern Mississippi, where the community of East Tupelo is situated.

There, in 1933, a well-built blond farm worker named Vernon Elvis Presley, then only seventeen, was courting a dark-haired, sultry-eyed woman four years older than he was. That year, as James Elliot remarried and Davada turned nine, Vernon married Gladys Smith.

The young couple eked out a meager living between them as 7 Vernon hoed cotton, corn, and peas, and Gladys worked as a sewing-machine operator for the Tupelo Garment Company. They lived with in-laws at first while Vernon drove trucks, sorted lumber, and continued to work crops, but Gladys had to quit her job when she became pregnant. Things were bad enough in the deep rural South during the Great Depression, but with Gladys out of work, money became scarcer than ever for the Presleys.

Fortunately a benevolent dairy farmer named Orville Bean had loaned Vernon enough money to build a small, shotgun style house in East Tupelo, which was completed before Gladys was ready to give birth. The house, raised on stilts to protect it from overflowing creeks, was small, drab, but theirs, and was called "shotgun" because it was small enough to open the front door and blast a shotgun clear through the house and out the back door without hitting anything.

Unusually large during the last months of pregnancy, Gladys kept telling friends and in-laws that she was carrying twins, but nobody seemed inclined to believe her until shortly after noon on January 8, 1935, when she went into labor and gave birth to identical twin boys. The first child to be removed was Elvis Aron. The second child was stillborn. Jesse Garon Presley was buried in Priceville Cemetery the following day in an unmarked grave.

A ruthless tornado, one of the worst in history, whipped right through Tupelo during the first year of Elvis's life, taking many lives and sweeping whole houses into its black vortex of destruction. In the years to come Gladys and Elvis would reminisce about that tornado and consider themselves lucky to have escaped with their lives. Elvis would also remember his twin brother, Jesse Garon. Some people firmly believe that identical twins are joined psychically, like the fabled Corsican brothers, and Elvis would later ponder a sense of incompleteness at having lost a part of himself he could never know.

From Elvis's first moments on earth until his mother's death some twenty-three years later, Gladys Presley never stopped worrying about his every waking moment, and when she discov-

8   ered that her boy was a somnambulist, she worried about his sleeping moments as well. Many of Elvis's fans assumed that Gladys's fear for the safety of her son was a natural overreaction to the loss of his twin brother, but that still doesn't take into account the fact that she was an unusual woman to begin with, unusually intuitive about her child, and several people who knew her in those days and in years to come would call her "psychic" about Elvis. Her love for the boy was a fawning, all-consuming emotion that never stopped growing or allowed her a moment's respite. When he turned five and started school, Gladys began walking Elvis to school and never stopped until he entered high school, and even then she insisted that he take his own silverware to school so he couldn't get germs from the other students.

Through all of the hard times that the Presleys faced, Gladys would always go out of her way to make her boy feel that he wasn't as poor as his circumstances would make it seem, and that even if his surroundings were humble, he was as good as or better than any man.

Elvis heard his first music when Gladys took him to the small, rickety First Assembly of God Church on Adams Street, in Tupelo, and it was the rousing gospel hymns heard there and at revivalist meetings that Elvis first began to sing. When his elementary-school teacher discovered the boy's voice to be strong and remarkably clear, his principal took him to the Mississippi-Alabama State Fair of 1945. There, standing on a chair in front of hundreds of people and unaccompanied by music, he sang "Old Shep," an old sentimental ballad about a boy and his dog. "Old Shep, he has gone where the good doggies go," sang the skinny ten-year-old, his voice quavering with emotion, "and no more with Old Shep will I roam. But if dogs have a heaven there's one thing I know . . . Old Shep has a wonderful home. . . ."

Elvis was awarded second prize, which allowed him to go on the rides for free. It was the very first time in his life he ever got anything for just singing, and while it sparked in him a lifelong love for amusement parks, it's also safe to assume that the boy

learned a simple but important object lesson that day: He could   9
call attention to himself with his voice, and singing could make
fantasies come true.

Elvis asked his parents for a bicycle the following year, but
Gladys was afraid that he might fall off and get hurt and persuaded him to get a guitar instead. Vester, Vernon's brother,
taught the boy a few chords, and before long he was listening to
the radio, tuning in black bluesmen, country pickers, balla-
deers, and gospel singers, while he tried to pick out melodies.

Elsewhere around the country other young boys were also
learning how to play the guitar. One day they would become
part of a very unusual brotherhood. Way up in St. Louis, one
of them, a seventeen-year-old named Chuck Berry, was also
doing some picking when he wasn't getting into trouble or trying to learn about the cosmetics business. Later he would write
a song that would become their anthem. "Johnny B. Goode"
would tell the story of a country boy strumming his guitar in the
backwoods and come to epitomize the rockabilly glory of Elvis
Presley. "Maybe someday your name will be in lights," it would
go, "saying Johnny B. Goode tonight!"

While Gladys Presley worried about Elvis playing along the
muddy banks of the Tupelo creeks and the boy strummed his
guitar at nightfall accompanied by a symphony of crickets and
the croaking of frogs, Davada Elliot was blossoming into one of
the prettiest flowers of Montgomery County, Tennessee. Indeed, she was a striking little girl, standing about five feet, three
inches with peaches-and-cream skin, long blond tresses, a
slightly upturned nose, eyes of languid blue, and all the drawling mannerisms of the Southern coquette.

James Elliot had become stern and uncompromising in his
religious beliefs, and he raised his daughter accordingly. She
was forbidden movies, the company of young men, and all of
the trappings of the bobby sox culture that swept America during the forties. But the young girl had her dreams. "I liked excitement, and I always got bored very easily," reflects Dee. "I
don't think that I could have ever married the local high-school

10 boy and settled down in my hometown. I wanted to travel, and there were so many things I wanted to do. All my life I knew that I was going to be something."

The years passed uneventfully. Oh, there were plenty of farm boys close at heel during her years at Lone Oak Central High School, but Davada wanted nothing to do with a bunch of guffawing local yokels in dirty denim overalls. She wanted the kind of man she read about in books, and she did not really need her father's harsh admonitions to stay clear of trouble.

Matrimony, of course, was the ultimate goal, but it was the circumstances of marriage that really mattered. Everyone got married young because in those days, it was better to be safe than sorry. Davada's friends seemed content to marry their high-school sweethearts, settle down, and have a bunch of kids before they had a chance to do much else. James Elliot, well aware of the worldly danger that would be waiting to tempt his beautiful daughter outside the Montgomery County line, had a nice local boy all picked out for Davada to marry. He was a nice enough fellow from a respectable family and would come over on Sundays to sit around and make small talk with James while he grinned sheepishly at Davada and shuffled around clumsily on the porch. What a *clod*, she thought, and resisted the idea as if her life depended on it. Why, the very sight of him dredged up an image of life on a farm—a life of boring, suffocating routine.

To make herself attractive, she cultivated in herself all of the classic traits long associated with that most revered of southern institutions—Womanhood. Like Scarlett, Davada was also a changeling, a consummate actress in the pursuit of a goal. The man to have her would have to pay the price of her dreams. Pay to play.

Davada looked around Clarksville and didn't like what she saw. Women were at a distinct disadvantage in the scheme of things and had to compensate for it in other ways. "When a young lady gave herself in those days," she remembers, "it was the only thing she had to give and was supposed to be the greatest thing in the world. I could never let a man take me lightly and just go to bed with me. It was going to come very high."

Davada resolved to bide her time. Her husband would have
to be, at once, a gentleman, a good breadwinner, master of the
household, a good father to her children, and, on top of it all,
one handsome stud. At the same time he would always have to
be susceptible to the feminine charms of Davada, to her beauty
and respectability. "Actually," she says, "the best way for a
woman to exert her strength would be to let him believe that
she had no strength at all." A strong woman, she believed,
could get what she wanted without even opening her mouth.

She looked for strong virile men to control her, as her father
had, yet these were the very men that she feared and resented
the most and the men least likely to indulge and shower her
with all of the fine romantic trappings that she craved—the
hand-kissing, the flowers, the genteel manners of the noblesse.
Love was at the root of her search, but what drove her, propelled her forward, and gave her strength and identity was a
compulsion to have all of the things promised by the American
Dream—love, a family, a nice home, good friends, and beautiful things. The fulfilment of her dreams was, in her mind, her
destiny. "I was convinced that if there was ever a woman in the
world destined to be happy," she says, "it was *me*."

It was clear that she wasn't going to get these things in Clarksville, Tennessee. But where to go? Her two brothers had both
found work with the Ford Motor Company and invited her to
stay with them while she looked for a job. It seemed as good
a place as any, so, following her high school graduation, she
packed her bags, hopped a bus, and headed north to the bright
lights and big-city life of Detroit, Michigan. It was the summer
of 1942.

By the time she returned to Clarksville to visit her father, she
was no longer Davada Elliot, but "Dee," a woman of considerably more style, substance, and sophistication. If the adoption
of the name was meant to signal the changing of Davada from
country to city girl, it was also a perfect metaphor for all that
would remain young and breezy about her—a perfect sobriquet
for the child-woman that she would always remain.

When Dee returned, her friend Jean Elrod arranged a double

12 date one evening with a couple of soldiers who were stationed at Fort Campbell, Kentucky. At her very first glance Dee's date appeared to be the very incarnation of everything her schoolgirl fantasies told her a real man should be.

A definite variation on the theme of Clark Gable, Bill Stanley was tall (six feet two), moustachioed (a vital entree for all subsequent men in her life), with a strapping chest full of battle ribbons and decorations for valor in combat. In Europe he was General Patton's personal bodyguard; needless to say, he was quite a sight, representing all of the forbidden fruits of Dee's strict, religious upbringing. He was worldly, dangerous, and sexy; he was also married, but he fell in love with Dee on that breezy summer night as they played the games and rode the rides together at the small country carnival that had pitched camp several miles outside of Clarksville. They saw each other again before Bill had to return to Europe. "I'll be seeing you soon," he said after a long good-bye kiss. "Someday, when you grow up a little, I'll marry you."

Back in Detroit, where Dee modeled and worked for the Ford Company, she waited for his letter to arrive. After no word from Bill arrived for a long time, she went ahead with plans to marry another young man who was courting her and wrote Bill to inform him.

In 1948 Dee returned to Clarksville once again to tell her father about her plans. James seemed strangely satisfied. "Well, Dee," he said, "I'm happy that Bill Stanley is out of the picture forever. He's in the States, you know. You got a letter from him."

The feeling that overcame Dee was like the first, sharp dip of a rollercoaster, when the heart leaps right up into the throat.

"Father . . ." she stammered, "where *is* it? The letter."

"I burned it," he said casually, avoiding her eyes. "I didn't think you'd be needing it anyway."

"I can't believe you *did* that to me!"

More than the anger she felt toward her father, Dee felt frustration at the possibility she might never know the contents of the letter, at the uncertainty that would always linger in her mind.

Suddenly she remembered his serial number, seeing it clearly

in her mind as it was stenciled on his duffel bag. She calmly sat
down and wrote him a letter, telling him what had happened, and addressed it care of Camp Pickett, Virginia. She hurried into town, mailed it, and prayed that it would find its way.

It was a long shot, but it worked. The reply was almost immediate; the message as clear as a mountain stream. *I'm free now. Come.*

The wedding, held against James Elliot's wishes, took place at Camp Pickett on February 1, 1949. It was a military affair. Dee looked beautiful in her bridal gown, and Bill was resplendently handsome in his dress uniform as they emerged, arm in arm, under a row of crossed, gleaming sabres.

The Presleys had hit rock bottom back in Tupelo. Like many other rural southerners, they would soon also be moving to where opportunities for work were more plentiful. Southern blacks and whites either migrated north, like Dee, or else gravitated to the larger southern cities. After it became almost impossible for Vernon Presley to find work around his hometown, he was forced to look for work in Memphis, some one hundred miles to the northwest. His family moved out of the small shack that Elvis was born in and into another one next to Shakerag, Tupelo's black shantytown. For Vernon Presley life was reduced to that rawest and most basic of struggles to put food on the table and a roof overhead.

One night in 1948 he packed his family and all of their belongings into a 1939 Plymouth and headed for Memphis. "We were broke, man," Elvis would later remember. "We just left overnight. Things had to be better."

They were almost penniless when they arrived, moving into a one-room apartment in one of the shabbiest sections of the city. Gladys Presley wasted no time getting a job as a waitress in a cafeteria. Vernon drove a truck for a while, then landed a job packing paint cans into wooden crates at the United Paint Company. He earned eighty-three cents an hour and would hold the job for five long years.

Elvis, then thirteen and about to enter high school, was completely bewildered by his new environment . . . shy, and ner-

14   vous, but always polite. Gladys taught him to say, "Yes, sir" and "No, ma'am" to everyone (like a young gentleman), and always to stand when a woman entered the room.

At L.C. Humes High School, where he was enrolled, he remained shy and unobtrusive. With no money, little confidence, and few friends, about the only thing he did have was acne. He loved football, of course, but was neither big nor good enough to be a player of consequence on the school team (Gladys also worried about him on the football fields), so after school, he strummed his old guitar and occasionally wandered down to the Mississippi, to Beale Street, where they played the blues, past sleazy beer parlors and honky tonk joints, past crap games and high-heeled hookers, through the smell of frying chicken and potatoes to the Lansky Brothers clothing store on the corner of Second Street, which sold the kind of clothes country musicians liked to buy, and where Elvis admired the pink sports coats, the Stetson hats, the white alligator shoes.

Man, he was thinking, leaning against the windows with his hands in his pockets and his eyes opening wider to drink in the slick duds, *I sure would like to get me some of those. . . .*

CHAPTER 2

BRIGHT LIGHTS, BIG CITY

Bill Stanley was a rugged, two-fisted sort who could clear out an entire barroom if he had to and certainly lay out any man who smarted off to him or glanced at his wife in a forward manner.

The novels of James Jones are populated with men like him—Sergeant Warden and Private Robert E. Lee Prewitt in *From Here to Eternity* come immediately to mind. He was part Cherokee, a born foot-soldier who had joined up as soon as he was seventeen and old enough to work his way up through the ranks. The army had become his only home.

After distinguishing himself in combat, Bill became General George S. Patton's personal bodyguard during the invasion of Germany and the race for Berlin. He was a war hero and patriot—the classic noncom. His youngest son, David (who would grow up to be most like him), remarks that he was a man "who would just as soon kill you as look at you." Billy, his oldest boy, calls him the "baddest sonofabitch walking in the valley."

A single month of marriage was more than enough to disabuse Dee of any romantic notions about her husband being a

16   sentimental man. He was always most comfortable in the company of men like himself—prideful, violent, self-sacrificing, ul-
tramasculine—and his main interests in life were weapons, tactics, athletics, running his platoon, and some very hardnosed
drinking.

Dee did not settle easily into army life at Fort Monroe,
Virginia. Easily bored to begin with, she found life on the post
dreary and monotonous. In the evenings Bill returned home for
dinner, and they would sit around, listen to music, talk, and go
to bed. Dee couldn't quite put her finger on exactly what the
problem was, but she felt something lacking when she and Bill
made love. She knew that her sexual experience was limited to
one man; perhaps the long wait had stoked the fires of expecta-
tion to unreasonable heights—she didn't know. Bill went about
introducing his young wife to the sexual realm of things with
patience and verve, as if everything was perfect, and Dee never
discussed her feelings because she had been taught not to emphasize the importance of that part of life anyway.

What was important to her was having children, which she
wanted desperately. Motherhood, to Dee, was the ultimate aspi-
ration of a woman, and Dee looked forward to it more than
anything else in life. Unlike Elvis, she had never really experienced a mother's love herself and planned to give her children
all of the love that her mother's death had deprived her of.

During the first month of her marriage she succeeded in getting pregnant, but as her stomach swelled in the succeeding
months, she began to feel the first nagging twinges of dissatis-
faction with her marriage.

As Dee began to realize, Bill Stanley drank more than the
average beer-swilling soldier who enjoyed sitting around the PX
drinking and laughing with his buddies. The experience of war
had lodged itself too firmly in his mind; he drank to dull the
images of mangled bodies and amputated limbs that still burned
in his brain, and to remove the stench of charred flesh from his
nostrils.

"Bill never drank or even smoked a cigarette until he went
through seeing his very best friend in the war get killed," Dee says.

"His head was completely blown off, and Bill was right there. It 17 made him start drinking."

The pregnancy did not go smoothly. Dee has RH negative blood, Type A; the RH factor could complicate childbirth in those days, making every pregnancy a painful, uncertain struggle. One day during her seventh month she was stricken with acute appendicitis. Bill was nowhere to be found, and she was rushed to the base hospital, writhing in pain, for an emergency operation. The operation was successful, but the baby was lost. "My husband wasn't the one who waited outside the operating room," she says bitterly. "It was my friend, Chaplain Jackson. I had the appendectomy and I lost the baby the following day, and my husband didn't even know until after it happened. When he came, I just wanted him out of the room because he had been at the officers' club, drinking. I could smell it on his breath, and I was just disgusted. He should have been there, was the way I felt."

Dee and Bill patched things up, but the seed of loneliness had been planted. That next year, 1950, Dee lost another baby due to an early miscarriage and became despondent, thinking that she would never be able to have a child. Her tears and remorse were cut short by the North Koreans when they crossed the Thirty-eighth Parallel and drove deep into South Korea. Suddenly Bill was hurrying his outfit into combat readiness, preparing to ship out, astonished at the outbreak of another war but, like the professional soldier, stoically accepting the dark call to combat. Within months he found himself once again in battle. Korea seemed even bloodier than Europe. For months, without respite, he fought his way up and down the country, watching his men die. Then, on furlough in Japan, he busted his guts on long drinking binges before being shipped right back.

With Bill off fighting in Korea, Dee faced the distinct possibility of never seeing him again. It suddenly seemed childish to spend her time sitting back in the States, lamenting her unsuccessful pregnancies, and she lifted the veils of self-pity and began making plans to move to Japan so she could be with him on his

18 leaves from the front. It was late in 1951 before she could get
there, and by that time she hadn't heard from him in months.
Feeling hopelessly lost, lonely, and confounded by the language
barrier, she settled in the port city of Yokahama and waited.

Like a man returning from the dead, Bill finally appeared one
day at her door. Before he left, Dee became pregnant for the
third time and spent the next nine months in mute fear, certain
that the baby would never see the light of day. An army surgeon
kept her under close observation and a kindly Japanese "mama-
san" helped her through the most difficult moments of the pregnancy.

The child, William Job Stanley, Jr., was born on January 18,
1953 (a Capricorn, like Elvis), and in Dee's words, "You would
think that he was the only baby ever born in the world." Cra-
dling the child in her arms, she thanked God for finally allowing her to know the sublime joys of childbirth and motherhood.
The baby bore a strong resemblance to his father, then stationed
back in Japan and out whooping it up with a couple of war buddies. Bill Stanley was behaving like a man who had once again
come through the meatgrinder. He drank hard and sowed the
seeds of life in his wife's womb. Two months later Dee was
pregnant again, and she and Bill were preparing to head home.
Bill Junior was a strong and healthy infant, and Dee was
happy to be going stateside. She went about the preparations
gleefully, hoping this time for a girl.

The Memphis Housing Authority accepted Vernon Presley's
application for public housing after Elvis completed his first
year of high school, and the Presleys, after over a year in Memphis, moved into a two-bedroom apartment in the low-rent
project called the Lauderdale Courts at 185 Winchester Avenue. It was a welcome step up the economic ladder, but the
Presleys weren't out of the woods. Elvis later remembered picking through garbage pails for useful things to bring home during
those lean years, and if the family had moved up a step, one
step was all that they were allowed: The rules of the Housing
Authority stipulated that if ever Vernon and Gladys's combined
income exceeded the income ceiling set for their family, they

BRIGHT LIGHTS, BIG CITY

would be forced to move. Bitter and frustrated, Vernon felt trapped—damned if he could make a little more money for his family and damned if he couldn't. Several times during the next few years when they were fortunate enough to improve their earnings only slightly, the threat of eviction hung over them like a dark cloud.

Gladys was working as a nurse's aide at Saint Joseph's Hospital and Vernon was packing crates when Elvis got his first job. In November of 1950 he was hired as an usher at Loew's State Theater, where he spent his evenings in the dark, watching stars like Tony Curtis and Robert Mitchum act out his own fantasies on the screen. He liked the job but was fired soon for taking a poke at a fellow employee who snitched on a candy girl for giving Elvis free food.

Some of Elvis's earnings went to the household, and with the rest he made a beeline back to the Lansky Brothers and purchased himself the slick duds he admired in their window. As soon as he was old enough to shave, he began growing his sideburns long, in emulation of the tough truckdrivers who ambled around Memphis. He also grew his hair long—outrageously long, for those days—and combed it back with so much gunk that even though it was dirty blond, it looked dark and lacquered. (He was so absorbed in the way it looked that he had it cut at the local beautician's shop instead of at the barber's.)

With his loud clothes and long hair, Elvis looked like a Beale Street pimp crossed with a country musician, but to the tough, crewcut redneck kids at school, he looked like something from outer space, or worse, like a fairy. During those years ridicule cascaded his way quite often, coming from his classmates and his football coach. (Years later Elvis would reminisce about this in front of a Las Vegas audience: "I tell you it got pretty weird," he would say. "They used to see me comin' down the street and they'd say, 'Hot dang! Let's get him; he's a squirrel! Get him! He just come down outta the trees!'")

The harassment got Elvis into numerous scrapes, and several times he came to within an inch of getting his young behind kicked in, which he would later recall to his stepbrothers. "Whooo!" exclaims Rick Stanley, thinking back on some of El-

20   vis's tales. "Can you imagine the way he looked, being around all of those tough redneck skinheads? Man, you had to be a brave dude to do that—either that or just plain crazy!"

Actually, Elvis was a little of both, but his appearance was also a part of a plan to consolidate a sense of his specialness in a world of overwhelming conformity. He was an outsider even then—the new kid in town seeking acceptance and a sense of belonging in the community of his peers—and he sought admittance by proving his individualism, by setting up his own terms. Elvis wanted to be accepted both because he was different and in spite of those differences, and from the very beginning he saw that the way to be a part of what was going on was to be "himself"—an unusual approach for someone so seemingly shy and insecure. Nevertheless, it was a hard road. His interests like football, shop, and ROTC kept him in close proximity to the very guys who were most likely to scorn him. Except for one instance when he played and sang in the school auditorium, Elvis remained a nonentity at school even with his clothes and hair. He worked odd jobs to make a little money, helped out at home when possible, played his guitar off by himself, and graduated in June of 1953, one of the most forgettable members of his senior class.

Stateside once again, Bill Stanley's good moments mixed with his bad. Dee had hoped that the birth of Billy would shake him out of the bottle and wake him up to the joys and responsibilities of fatherhood. Like all recidivists, Bill would profess reform and then go back to his old ways, hitting the bottle harder than ever. At the Red Stone Arsenal in Huntsville, Alabama, Dee began to recognize the hopelessness of expecting real and permanent improvement. Slowly but inexorably they became estranged.

At least Dee had kin in Huntsville to see her through the pregnancy. Richard Neely, her half-brother, lived there with his wife, Edith, and it was Edith who saw Dee through another difficult birth. The child, another boy, was born in December of 1953. Because she had wanted a girl, Dee was slightly disap-

pointed, but this baby looked more like her than Bill. Richard
Earl Stanley was "almost too pretty to be a boy," says Dee, and
just as Bill Stanley had already determined that Billy Junior
would one day attend West Point and serve his country, Dee
looked at her newborn son and decided right there that he
would be the doctor of the family and save lives instead of take
them.

In 1954, while Dee attended to her two infant sons and became pregnant again, history began to run its course in Memphis, Tennessee. That year Gladys Presley's birthday precipitated one of the most extraordinary musical careers of the
twentieth century.

Elvis's first job out of high school was with the Crown Electric Company, delivering supplies out to job sites where the
company's electricians were working. He was a conscientious
employee, driving through the streets of Memphis in a Ford
pickup (the sideburns fitting right in). During the evenings, he
was studying to become an electrician so he could one day
collect union wages, but he was also thinking quite seriously of
becoming a Tennessee state trooper when he turned twenty-
one.

On his way out to jobs Elvis would drive by the Memphis
Recording Service at 706 Union Avenue. There, for a nominal
fee of some four dollars, the service offered cheap recordings
which they would transfer directly onto ten-inch acetates for
their customers. Elvis planned to stop in one day and record his
mother a birthday present. One Saturday afternoon he stopped
his truck, got out, and strolled in with his old guitar. The place
was busy, and Elvis approached the young woman who seemed
to be in charge. Marion Keisker, a former Miss Radio of Memphis, was then in her early thirties.

"I'd like to make a record for my mother's birthday, ma'am."

"Sorry," Marion said, "but you'll have to wait your turn.
There's people ahead of you and I'm busy now."

Elvis took a seat and waited patiently. Marion approached
him when his turn came. "Well, who do *you* think you sound

22 like?" she asked conversationally. Everybody who came in thought they sounded like somebody famous, and she was used to answers like Frank Sinatra or Eddy Arnold.

Elvis looked pensive for a second. "I don't sound like nobody."

He then cut two songs, the titles of which, ironically, sum up the best and worst of how that day would change his life. The first was the Ink Spots' "My Happiness"; the second, a ballad called "That's When Your Heartaches Begin."

Marion looked at Elvis out there in the studio, completely self-absorbed, crooning the songs in his unusual, unrefined voice, and decided to record him for her own purposes. She managed to put the first tune and part of his second song on some extra tape. There was something about the kid that she liked. She was thinking of her boss, Sam C. Phillips.

Though Sam Phillips also owned Sun Records, his recording service was what paid the bills. A genial man of medium build, dark, wavy hair, and a well-groomed appearance, Sam was an Alabama boy, raised on his daddy's plantation. His childhood had been musical, and legend has it that he first heard the blues as a very young child, sitting on the knee of an old black field-hand. True or not, when Sam became tired of his broadcasting job in Memphis, he opened up a small studio of his own—Sun Records with the immortal orange-and-yellow label—and began recording some of the greatest bluesmen of the Deep South. At that time there was nowhere else for them to go except all the way up North, to Chicago, and before Sam ever met Elvis Presley, he had the distinction of first recording such blues luminaries as B.B. King and "Howlin' Wolf" Burnett, among many others. His recording service over the years had become the destination of scores of musicians and singers who hoped to make a name for themselves in the segregated world of "race music," or what became known as "rhythm and blues." While Sam would manage to sell some of his masters to places like Chess and Checker in Chicago, his business had remained small and barely profitable. But he had one bold ambition. "If I could find a white man who had the Negro sound and the Negro feeling, I could make a million," he said to Marion on many occasions. The words kept Marion on the lookout for just such a singer. Much to the teenager's surprise, she took down Elvis's name and address and later played his tape for her boss. Sam was moderately impressed, but not enough to call.

Elvis was spending his nights singing gospels at the Memphis Auditorium (they were all-night, public sings), and by the time he returned to the recording service, his mind was more on music than ever before. This time he walked in and encountered Sam instead of Marion. They spoke briefly after Elvis recorded two more sentimental ballads. Sam was amiable and encouraging but promised nothing, least of all recording time, but he was sufficiently impressed to at least take down Elvis's name again. "I'll keep you in mind if something comes up."

During the following months, whenever a tune came up that might be right for him, Marion Keisker, for some unfathomable reason, never ceased to champion Elvis's cause to her busy boss. In April something came up. It was a mildly successful ballad by an unknown black singer that Sam had managed to acquire—"Without You."

"What about the kid with the sideburns," she asked again.

Sam shrugged his shoulders indifferently. "All right," he said after thinking a moment. "Might not be a bad idea."

Elvis came running when he got the message from Marion. He entered the studio out of breath and perspiring, his hair falling down over his forehead.

"All right, kid," Sam said. "What is it you think you can do?" Again the question was ordinary enough; most of the hopefuls that Sam saw had some speciality.

"I can do *anything*," Elvis said.

Unfortunately, the kid's performance didn't even come close to his bravado. His rendition of the ballad was bad, but his attempt at another song, "Rag Mop," was even worse. They spoke briefly after the recording, and Elvis told Sam all about his idol, Dean Martin, and about the country and blues singers he admired. Then, Sam had an idea. There was a young guitarist named Scotty Moore hanging around the studio who also liked country music and the blues, and Scotty had a friend named Bill Black, who played string bass. He would call Scotty and get

24 the boys together. Maybe, if they worked at it, he could get something usable.

Elvis stopped by Scotty's apartment, Scotty later recalled to writer Jerry Hopkins, wearing "a pink shirt, white shoes, and that ducktail—I thought my wife was going to go out the back door!" The boys ran through all of their favorite country tunes, ballads, and blues and soon started practicing with Bill Black.

On July 5, 1954, they got their shot.

Bill, Scotty, and Elvis were in the studio that night while Sam busied himself in the back room with the controls. The music was pedestrian and uninspired. Sam first recorded "I Love You Because," a country ballad, the original of which was to surface some twenty years later.

The Moment came during a Coke break. The boys had been fiddling with a blues, Big Boy Crudup's "That's All Right (Mama)," and during the break, in a moment of sublime spontaneity that had more to do with "cuttin' up" than anything else, Elvis, in one outburst of inspired mimicry and frustrated energy, started bounding about the studio with his guitar, banging out a string-snapping, souped-up version of the song. It was an action only a boy willing to make a fool of himself would take, and it was funny. Laughing, Scotty and Bill joined in, picking up the tempo.

Sam's ears pricked up at the first sound of it. The emotion and feeling of the blues were all there, but it was hopped up and countrified coming out of Elvis—it sounded easy and natural. It was powerful. And fun.

"Damn!" he exclaimed out in the studio. "I don't know what it is you're doin', but keep doin' it!"

He went into the control booth and set the levels, switching the machine and mikes on when the boys broke into a slightly more self-conscious attempt. The playback left them all amazed. It pulsed, jumped, and flowed; it sounded black.

"God, they're gonna run us right outta town when they hear this!"

Sam and Dewey Phillips had the same last name, but the only kinship they shared was a passion for the blues. Sam knew

that Dewey was the only white DJ in Memphis who would give
the record airplay; his *Red Hot and Blue* show was widely listened to by a white audience that was more receptive to the influence of rhythm and blues, so he hustled over to Station
WHBQ as soon as the dub was finished. Dewey listened once
and liked it.

The very first night that his voice carried over the airwaves of
America, Elvis was at the Suzore #2 Theater, too nervous to
stay at home and listen, couched in darkness, slumped down in
his seat, not knowing what to expect. The song crackled from
the transmitters at WHBQ and cut through the Memphis night
like a razor, creating a palpable excitement in the humid air as
it poured forth from radios in living rooms and enveloped the
imaginations of listeners throughout the city. Phones began to
ring at the radio station, and Dewey kept cueing up the song,
over and over again. "Who *is* he, anyway?" his listeners kept
asking.

Gladys and Vernon had no telephone in their apartment, but
their radio was tuned to WHBQ. They hurried to the theater
and walked up and down the darkened aisles, looking for Elvis,
and found him sitting there, surprised to see them, oblivious to
the rumblings and stirrings about to break open his life like an
earthquake.

"You best get over to the radio station, son," said Gladys
Presley. "They been lookin' for ya."

Elvis arrived at the station breathless, nervous, excited, yet
strangely confident. The two men sat alone in the small booth
stacked with records and tapes.

"Mr. Phillips," he confessed, "I don't know nuthin' 'bout
bein' interviewed!"

"Jes' don't say nuthin' dirty, son," said Dewey, switching on
the microphone.

It was July 6, 1954, and to use a shopworn but wonderfully
applicable cliché, Things Were Never the Same.

Elvis cried at the sight of his first record and after his first appearance at the Grand Ole Opry, but for different reasons. By
the time the record was ready for release, Sam already had

26 orders for five thousand copies. Despite the flat-out refusal of most white radio stations to take it on, it went on to sell twenty thousand copies, and Elvis began making his first public appearances in and around Memphis at places like the Eagle's Nest and the Airport Inn, developing a small following.

The boys eventually picked up a drummer named D. J. Fontana and months of hard work in the studio followed. The music that emerged was a unique synthesis of the musical style of rhythm and blues with that of country music and came to be known as "rockabilly."

Musical influences flowed into Memphis, Tennessee, like tributaries to a river, and it was possible in such a city for the outer fringes of white musical culture to commingle with black and produce such a musical miscegenation as rockabilly, which would become "rock 'n' roll" as the music became more popular. Elvis was the synthesizer. He could draw upon anything—jumping black boogie and honky tonk, Mississippi delta blues, white country music like bluegrass and romantic country ballads, and then roll them into his own white hillbilly boogie. The music exploded in Sam Phillips's studio. He painstakingly recorded it and gave it a distinctive and full sound with his own technique of clean reverberation.

Elvis was able to integrate the power and uniqueness of his developing musical identity with the blues sound, which was what gave his music such substance and dynamic force. He may have grown up in Mississippi, the spiritual home of the blues, but he wasn't merely aping a black form of music. The music had come naturally enough in the tempo and style of the spirituals, but the harsh terms of his boyhood had also created in him a natural empathy for a style of traditional black folk-music that was all at once intensely personal, emotional, and romantic. Elvis made his blues a vehicle for transcending those harsh terms, for freedom, power, and acceptance, and, ostensibly, for success.

But the style of the music itself was undoubtedly black, and the boys worried about audience reaction to "That's All Right (Mama)" for very good reasons: The blues were considered "sinful" by the white southern culture in those days because many

blues lyrics were bawdy and bespoke a lusty life apart and outside of society—a life of hard times, pain, knifefights and gun-
play, transience, cheap whiskey, lost love, floozies, wronged
women, chain gangs, cottonfields, and freightyards. The blues
was a music of social bonds and their constraints and the desire
for release.

Elvis was not the first white man to sing the blues but one of
the first to take flight in the risk and challenge of outstepping his
bounds by doing something different, making the music an
emotional expression of everything he ever had been and hoped
to be. The results, songs like Roy Brown's "Good Rockin' Tonight," Sleepy John Estes's "Milkcow Blues Boogie," and Junior
Parker's "Mystery Train," resonated with an emotional power
and intensity and a musical integrity because they had the very
special distinction of being "firsts." Breaking rules, refusing guidelines and limits, Elvis was learning how to become "successful." The handful of records he cut for Sam Phillips would
stand taller in significance than much of what he would later
accomplish in his career. Musically, at least, these were Elvis
Presley's wildest and most pagan days and a period of remarkable innocence and spontaneity. This was Elvis B.C.: before the
Colonel.

Quitting his job at Crown Electric, Elvis burned his bridges
behind him and played his first big audience at the Overton
Park Shell in Memphis. The "All Country" show that night fea-
tured Marty Robbins and Webb Pierce, two established country-
music stars. Elvis was nervous as a cat and walked out to perform "Good Rockin' Tonight," trying to give the song everything he had. But the voice alone wasn't enough to consume
his sizzling ambition to make good that night, so he threw his
body into the music almost unconsciously: His feet began shuf-
fling, the knees bent and shook, the hips swiveled and pumped
in time to the music. Compared to the rest of the show, the
song stuck out like a sore thumb and so did Elvis—it was raw
and lowdown, its beat infectious, and all of a sudden Elvis was
sexy up there—sensuous, dark, dangerous.

The audience, at first amused or shocked, was finally stunned.

28 There was that electric anticipation of the making of an
event in his performance, of something unprecedented and por-
tentous. The women in the audience began squirming excitedly, the men seemed excited and curiously insecure as some
women swooned and others began moving toward the stage and
idle screams sounded from different parts of the crowd. For the
first time Elvis sensed his power and began to understand how
to tap it, and the more he shimmied and wiggled, the more
people reacted to him. They seemed like a sponge to be filled,
wrung dry, then filled again. Best of all, he was learning to sing,
projecting his voice and commanding attention by dramatizing
himself, overtaking the music, dipping low and sexy, growling
from the back of his throat, teasing with it, wailing hard, crooning gracefully like a movie star.

The place was coming apart when he left the stage. Webb
Pierce wasn't so enthusiastic. Slated to come out next, the old
pro was seething backstage at the nerve of this kid to pull a
cheap stunt like that and upstage the show's headliner. He let
Elvis know about his feelings as he passed. "Sonofabitch!"

The next month, September, Elvis arrived for his first appearance at the Grand Ole Opry to be broadcast from the Ryman
Auditorium. Pumped up from his performance in Memphis,
riding high and thrilled to be appearing on a show that he had
only dreamed about for years, he was once again ready to lay it
all out there. He walked around all day, amazed, at first, at how
rundown the legendary building was, and as show time approached, he paced around backstage, thinking about the thirty-
five hundred people out in the audience. Hank Snow, then
red hot on the country charts with a hit record, was the show's
host.

"What's your name?" Snow asked.

"Elvis Presley, sir."

Snow just looked at him. "No, I mean, what's the name you
sing under?"

"Elvis Presley, sir."

Elvis then walked out and sang "That's All Right (Mama)"
and the flip side of the record, "Blue Moon of Kentucky," a

_____

bluegrass tune. The audience, used to the straight country-and-western acts, didn't know how to react. When he finished, there was only polite applause.

Elvis felt disappointed and awkward enough backstage, but then he was approached by the Opry booking agent, Jim Denny. Denny had booked Elvis on Sam's recommendation, and he wanted to give the kid a bit of advice.

"You ain't goin' nowhere with *that*, son," he said, contemptuously. "You ought to go back to drivin' a truck!"

Heartbroken, Elvis cried all the way back to Memphis.

Several weeks of low spirits followed before Elvis lifted himself out of his blue funk. Now with an official manager, Bob Neal, he started garnering a reputation for himself on the country music circuits as the "Hillbilly Cat" and the "King of Western Bop"—such strange names that serve to illustrate just what kind of trouble people were having making heads or tails out of Elvis Presley, for they conjure up hybrid images of rednecks and beatniks, of cowboys and hipsters.

In 1955 Elvis's first Sun releases received the favorable attention of *Billboard* magazine, and he then met Colonel Thomas A. Parker. Tom Parker was a manager of talent who handled such stars as Eddy Arnold and Hank Snow. Shrewd, fast talking, and colorful, he wore rope ties, Stetson hats, rumpled suits, and always had a large cigar rolling happily around in his jowly face. A carnival barker in style and speech, the Colonel had spent a good part of his life around that rarified world of the Fast Buck. In his heart of hearts he was a smooth, horsetrading businessman; an uncannily effective combination of high-rolling gambler and con man. Never loved but always respected and admired, the Colonel was also legendary for his rodomontade: Tom Parker could shuck and jive better than most men walking God's green earth, but underneath it all he was one of the most astute managers and businessmen in the music business, having built up a sterling reputation for his hard-sell promotion and for delivering exactly what he promised. He could spot talent a mile away. When he heard about Elvis, his money glands must have begun to salivate. The Colo-

30 nel had the vital connections to get Elvis a contract with a major record company as well as the most lucrative bookings on the country-music circuits.

Through Bob Neal, he began booking Elvis more steadily, taking him further away from the schoolhouse dances, small clubs, and open-air spots he performed on flatbed trucks. Slowly he wooed Vernon and Gladys Presley away from Neal and Sam Phillips until, in November, he gained exclusive control over Elvis's career and began shopping around for a company to buy out Elvis's remaining contract with Sun records. He also plotted a step-by-step strategy to make "his boy" a household word in America.

"You listen to the Colonel, son," Vernon and Gladys would say. "He knows best."

"Ahm sorry but you'll have to speak to mah manager, the Colonel," would be Elvis's polite but firm response to all business offers and queries from the press. "Ah nevah do anythin' without his knowledge."

"When I first knew Elvis he had a million dollahs worth of talent," the Colonel would soon enough be able to say. "Now he has a millions dollahs!"

The Colonel first gave "his boy" the Keys to the Highway, booking him on a series of long, grueling junkets throughout the South and the Southwest. Elvis packed his band and their equipment in a 1951 Lincoln and set off for his rendezvous with America. He also took along a high-school chum named Red West. A strapping fellow, quick with his fists, Red became Elvis's first bodyguard and helped protect him from the increasing numbers of jealous men who decided that they wanted to break Elvis's neck when their girl friends and wives went gaga at his performances.

The road tasted good to Elvis. He burned up the highways of the South in his car, jumping from gig to gig and hardly ever sleeping in the same place more than once, often waking to dewy mornings parked along roadsides in Texas, Mississippi, and Arkansas, sometimes blowing the engines of his cars and abandoning them on the side of the road. In the evenings he performed, leaving a trail of bedlam wherever he went, working hard but playing just as hard. He shot pool and rode motor-cycles with a vengeance and decided to see how many chicks he could bang just for the hell of it. His buddies would later re-mark that he didn't do too badly.

Later that year Elvis caused his very first riot, in Jacksonville, Florida. Droves of hysterical women stormed the stage. They rushed and surrounded him, trying to tear the clothes from his body.

Elvis retaliated. He bought a pink Cadillac.

While women clutched, pawed, and tore at Elvis's body in Jacksonville, a child was born in Fort Eustis, Virginia, who would one day grow up to protect him from such dementia. David Edward Stanley, the last and largest of the Stanley litter, weighed in at a hefty thirteen pounds and three ounces, prompting the nurses in the maternity ward to call him "Samp-son." Dee was horrified to learn that he had a slightly deformed right heel, but corrective surgery and the temporary wearing of a brace helped him.

Bill was chief warrant officer on the post when his orders for Greenland arrived. Their marriage was sliding downhill, but Bill knew that Dee was fed up with moving and babies, and his instincts told him that she was reaching that critical point when a woman decides that a marriage becomes untenable and starts looking for other alternatives. He resigned his commission and reenlisted as a noncommissioned officer to prevent the transfer and save the marriage. What he didn't know was that Dee—emotionally and in her mind—was already on the way out, preparing herself for the inevitable.

Like the little girl who had lost her mother and so loved and feared her father, she once more sought refuge in her dreams. Now, she dreamed for her boys, and the more nightmarish her anxieties became, the more she insulated herself into their world, becoming selfish and picayune and escaping the unpleas-antness of her life by filling herself with them during those long

32   days alone and the nights when her husband never came home.
"Nothing was ever going to hurt them or go wrong for them,"
she says. "I had everything planned."
Then she saw Elvis Presley.

As Colonel Parker started translating Elvis's talent and ambition into greenbacks, Vernon and Gladys Presley began to taste the first fruits of their son's success. Their standard of living began to improve drastically when the Colonel persuaded RCA to cough up a then unheard-of sum of forty thousand dollars for Elvis's Sun contract. The bidding for the contract, which received a great deal of publicity, had been spirited. The Colonel knew that he had aces in the hole so he played his cards accordingly, but the size of the pot was beyond anyone's wildest dreams.

"Heartbreak Hotel," recorded in RCA's Nashville Studios on January 5, 1956, was the record that metamorphosed Elvis Presley into a myth at the age of twenty-one and cast his fate to the winds of history.

A sexy blues number with plenty of echo and a wrenching guitar break, the song came to symbolize the growth pangs of a whole generation of young Americans coming of age during the era of Ike, the Cold War, television, and rock 'n' roll. Slickly produced and packaged, it began soaring up the national charts after Elvis performed it live on CBS before the end of that month.

While the "Hillbilly Cat" may have been raging throughout the South and Southwest, very few people up North outside of the music business knew he was alive yet. It was the life-and-death struggle for ratings that consumed producers even during those incipient years of TV's live "Golden Era" that brought Elvis's face to millions of unsuspecting Americans when Jack Philbin, who produced Jackie Gleason's half-hour variety special, decided that Elvis was the "guitar-playing Marlon Brando." (There would be hundreds of comparisons in months and years to come between Elvis, Brando, and James Dean.) Later that month, on a cold night in New York City, where Elvis was

never to feel at home, he entered CBS's studio in the theater
district for his first television performance.

With their chins tucked down and their collars turned up to
ward off the bitter cold, the passersby paid the unlikely name
"Elvis Presley" on the marquee very little mind. The theater
was virtually empty inside. Finding the cameras unintimidating,
Elvis, onstage, glowered right into them as if to arrogantly convey to the viewers, *"Yeah? So what!"* With his legs spread apart,
he struck what was becoming his classic pose and lurched easily
into the number, twitching, undulating slowly, his eyes hurt
and vulnerable, his face screwed up with emotion.

"Waaal since mah baybeee left me . . ."

He sang high, carefully drawing each syllable out onto a
high-tension wire.

"Ah found a new place to doowell . . ."

The beat between lines, a thudding BAHDOMP of guitar and
drum, jolted the length of his body as he passed easily into elec-
tronic transmission, rematerializing for the first time into cath-
ode rays and instantaneously popping forth from screens. With
the passing of each millisecond of air time, as the voice trailed
low and pumped out the emotion and the spasms flailed the sex
and power out from the studio and into living rooms, women
fell desperately in love with him and kids saw their world more
sharply delineated into Cool and Square. . . .

"It's down at the end of Lonely Street . . . It's Heartbreak
Hotel."

And Elvis, no longer mere flesh and blood, became an
image, an archetype, a multidimensional object of culture and
history, unleashing a force that would liberate others, liberate
himself, yet sweep him among those very forces and make him
forever a prisoner of that moment.

He got rich quickly. With "Heartbreak Hotel" number one
on the charts, the RCA studio in Nashville became his factory
with RCA's Steve Sholes the foreman of the operation and Colonel Tom Parker the ever-present consulting overseer. Tasting
the Big Time at last, Elvis brimmed with energy in the succeeding months, driving his team to perfection, spewing out hit after

34 immortal hit, moving away from the rockabilly format toward a pop style identifiable as "rock 'n' roll." Using compositions by Otis Blackwell, Leiber and Stoller, Ray Charles, Carl Perkins, and others, and backed by the Jordonaires, his songs exploded like concussion bombs—"Hound Dog," "Blue Suede Shoes," "All Shook Up," "Don't Be Cruel."

The dreams and fantasies materialized with breathtaking speed. Back in Memphis he took forty thousand dollars and plunked it down for a ranch house at 1034 Audubon Drive.

Vernon Presley packed his last paint can sometime before Elvis signed his contract with RCA, and he and Gladys then moved into their new home, taking the giant step from Lauderdale Courts to one of the most respectable upper-middle-class neighborhoods of the city. Their circumstances had changed with such dizzying speed that it didn't seem real at first. . . . Their standard of living changed drastically; they didn't. Gladys hung the family laundry out to dry in the yard, perhaps demonstrating that you can take the people out of the country but not the country out of the people; anyway, some of her more staid neighbors got uppity about it and complained. Elvis, of course, was incensed: "My mother can do anything she damn well pleases!" he told them.

Now idle, Vernon started taking an avid interest in his son's career, steeping himself in the wherefores and aforementioneds of his business affairs. Together, they still maintained their friendships with the people back at the low-rent project, only now they drove around to see them in Elvis's growing fleet of cars.

The cloudburst of Elvis's instant fame brought people to their house who rang the doorbell and wanted to chat, walked around the house, camped out on the lawn, and peered unabashedly right into the windows. Reporters by the carload showed up at the front door to ask every sort of question about Elvis and about their lives, leaving no stones unturned. This state of affairs was upsetting enough to Gladys, but it was only compounded by her loneliness and worry when Elvis was away, which was more and more often those days.

Gladys Presley was an intuitive and superstitious woman, and her dreams were beset with premonitions of disaster for her boy.

She still anguished ceaselessly for his safety, and there were instances when her anxieties became monumental, as when Elvis collapsed from exhaustion after a tour, and after he had a close brush with death when a small plane he was flying in nearly went down. (She made him promise never to fly again.) Once she dreamt he perished in a fire, and bounded awake. Elvis called soon after and she learned that his car had caught fire that very evening. In her heart she would have preferred that he quit right then and there to settle down, open a business, and raise a family, but she realized that her intuition about Elvis had all been for a reason—hers was a child of destiny, and she wouldn't stand in the way of the dreams she'd helped him to nurture. "Be careful out there, son," she would entreat Elvis whenever he had to leave home, taking his hand like a little boy and kissing his cheek. "Don't worry, Mamma," Elvis would say, calming her. "Everything's gonna be okay."

To Elvis, the true blessings of success were to be found in the simple satisfaction of knowing that his mother would never have to work again.

Nineteen fifty-seven, which Dee Stanley spent in Fort Eustis, Virginia, tending to her three sons, was the Year of the Pelvis. Roundly denounced by parent, press, and pulpit as the corruptor of the young Americans who had adopted him as forever theirs, Elvis, within that one year of intensive national attention, became both Teen Idol and Devil Incarnate. He was rock 'n' roll's first outlaw.

The music that Allan Freed dubbed "rock 'n' roll" was creating a storm of controversy, and the uproar centered around Elvis Presley's gyrations. One of a small handful of leaders in the vanguard of rock 'n' roll, Elvis had no more "invented" the music than Fred Astaire had tap dancing. Nevertheless, as its most successful, visible white practitioner, he was being held accountable for it and raised up as its perfect living symbol. As quickly as kids deified him, making him a folk hero, parents vilified him.

36   Rock 'n' roll was bouncing across the country like an out-of-control slinky coming crazily down an endless flight of stairs. Suddenly it seemed everywhere. Chuck Berry was skipping merrily across stages, grinning puckishly and wreaking havoc with his guitar, and Little Richard Penniman was flying off his piano possessed of the demon that made him scream "A WOP BOP ALU BOP A WOP BAM BOOM . . . TUTTI FRUTTI!" Buddy Holly and the Crickets were making their historic recordings in Clovis, New Mexico, and everywhere else rock 'n' roll's founding elite was defining itself and its young audiences. Jerry Lee Lewis, Bo Diddley, Fats Domino—the styles were as unique as the individuals themselves, but to so many grown-ups, it all reeked of wildness, rebellion, sex, perversions of the soul, atheism, violence, anarchy, and even that ultimate evil of the fifties, communism. Somehow it seemed that the duck-tailed, gunk-haired southern boy had given advent to these youthful seances of sexual energy—this strange voodoo called "rock 'n' roll"—and Elvis was blamed lock, stock, and barrel. He was called everything from tasteless and talentless to dangerous and disgusting. The kids held him up as everything Cool they could aspire to and their parents (who had fought a war to make the world safe and secure!) saw him as that insidious agent of social destruction that would unglue western civilization and be the ruination of Everything They Held Sacred.

Faced with the overwhelming adulation of hero worship and the dark onus of the villain, Elvis just shrugged his shoulders and drawled his sparse but famous comments to the national press. Most of these comments were innocuous, self-effacing, polite, charming, and oh so soft-spoken, showing the world that while he may have been the whirling dervish of sex onstage, offstage he was really every mother's son.

History had bestowed an unusual and electrifying momentum behind Elvis's career. He appeared on the cultural horizon like some kind of long-awaited messiah to breathe life and energy into the bland and stodgy atmosphere of the conformist fifties, but in doing so had further separated the generations. Before long he would have the parents securely in his pocket as well, but while rock 'n' roll was being nationally debated and even banned in some cities, the ironic dichotomy of being so good to so many while he was so bad to the rest embedded itself deeply into his psyche and emotional experience. So many people who would later wonder about Elvis's last years, when the good and bad in his life all blurred together, would do well to harken back to this period of contradiction in his life.

At the height of this madness, when Elvis could provoke riot conditions by his mere presence, he appeared on *The Ed Sullivan Show*, coast to coast, cut off from the waist down by the television camera, singing "Hound Dog" while the theater erupted in pandemonium.

Soon after, Hollywood, which had been nosing around cautiously, started biting. The Colonel, orchestrating Elvis's career like a multimillion dollar sideshow, was concluding deals for Elvis as easily as he could spin one of his yarns. Elvis's face and name started showing up on pens, clothing, and everything else the Colonel could get it on, and when America was all but saturated, Hollywood decided that it was about time to sign the boy up.

Famous, wealthy, sought after everywhere, Elvis could now indulge himself everything that he could never afford as a kid. He stocked his life with clothes, cars, and new friends, renting out the rollerdome and amusement park in Memphis for his all-night parties. Among the guests were all of the kids from school who never knew he existed.

On August 22, 1956, production began for *Love Me Tender*, his first film. On January 4, 1958, four days before his twenty-third birthday, he took his army physical.

Bill Stanley received transfer papers for Orleans, France, at about the same time that the national press was obsessing itself with Elvis's draft board.

"We went to my hometown," remembers Dee, "because my father was sick and because he never had a chance to see his grandsons. We got there and Bill hardly spent a single night there because he was drinking so heavily by then."

The visit with James Elliot lasted about a month, and during that entire time Dee tried to keep her unhappiness from her fa-

38 ther. James had only to see her to know that her spirits had been crushed.

One bosky spring afternoon as they sat on the porch together talking, it all came out. Dee was staring into the outlying fields thinking about leaving for Europe when she turned to her father. He suddenly looked so old and frail on the sun-dappled corner of the porch that she realized she might never see him again and began to cry.

"Daddy," she cried softly, hanging her head, "I'm afraid I won't be able to stand it there. Bill and I haven't been gettin' along now for a long time and . . ."

James Elliot listened carefully to Dee's tales of Bill's drinking. She expected the stern words of reproach her father was always certain to offer.

"Now, honey," he said gently, stroking her hair and brushing away the tears. "You've gotta be strong, girl. You married Bill knowin' what kind of man he was. You know you can always come home if'n you need to. Let me know and I can send the money."

When Dee and Bill made their final transoceanic crossing together, she felt that there was a way out. James Elliot had given her light at the end of the tunnel. Orleans saw the nadir of Dee's marriage. Their quarters were cold and drafty and the hot water didn't work properly. Within several months Dee began to think more and more of her father's offer. Then, one day in the cafeteria, sitting there with Billy, Ricky, and David, having a cup of coffee, she made her decision to leave. She would take the boys back to Clarksville with her, get a job of some kind, and hope for the best.

"Mrs. Stanley?"

It was the base chaplain standing over her. She could tell immediately from the serious, compassionate tone in his voice that he was there on official business, and from the expression on his face that her father was dead.

"I'm afraid I have some bad news for you. . . ."

Bill was transferred to Frankfurt, Germany, when the company commander decided that the nature of his responsibilities there would probably allow him less time to himself and keep him off the sauce. Dee packed their things and readied the children for still another home. Nothing mattered now except the boys. The transfer didn't dismay her. She felt only resignation, having, after all, nowhere to go.

When fans lined up outside of theaters across the nation to see their boy for the first time on the silver screen in *Love Me Tender*, it became instantly clear to the Hollywood establishment that Elvis Presley was indeed "bankable." A smash hit at the box office, the film was panned by critics everywhere, setting the trend for all of the thirty-one subsequent commercially successful but mostly critically disastrous Elvis Presley films. Elvis and the Colonel cried all the way to the bank but Elvis still wanted to take his acting seriously and be accepted as a legitimate artist; it was never easy for him to swallow his pride after being savaged by film critics everywhere. But if the movies couldn't put him across as an actor, at least they would make him millions. When one reporter asked his reaction to the bad reviews after the release of *Jailhouse Rock* in October of 1957, Elvis curled his lip sardonically, paused, smiled good naturedly, and said, "Well, that's the way the mop flops."

That year Elvis made a sizeable investment in his future. For one hundred thousand dollars he purchased Graceland, an elegant estate of thirteen rolling acres in Whitehaven, then a suburb of Memphis. From U.S. 51, which ran past its iron gate, the two story, twenty-three room mansion with its four graceful pillars looked like an antebellum plantation house sitting atop a hill and couched by oak trees. To the world, Graceland told the story of Elvis's success. The fans who began flocking there to gawk at the mansion and hopefully glimpse their hero began to truly comprehend that the journey from shotgun shack to mansion was complete, and that Elvis *was* the modern Horatio Alger who proved to the entire world that, yes, folks, America was *still* the Land of Opportunity, still a place where talent, hard work, and faith can make a poor country boy into a millionaire.

What Elvis remained ignorant of during the first two me-

40 teoric years of his career was his mother's poor health. Vernon Presley, knowing Elvis's strong attachment to his mother, managed to successfully conceal Gladys Presley's true condition, which had steadily deteriorated. The long years of night work, overtime, and poor nutrition had left Gladys in poor health to begin with, but the pressures created by Elvis's explosion had only exacerbated it. The fans, reporters, and concern for Elvis had taken its toll, and his increasingly long absences from home left her feeling empty and anxious. She channeled much of her nervousness into eating, but the foods she ate—starchy dishes, eggs, fatty meats, and sweets—only bloated her. The weight problems she developed upset her greatly, because she did not think it was appropriate for the mother of a national celebrity to appear unattractive and fat; she wanted Elvis to be always proud of her, so she took diet pills, but only built up a tolerance. The more she took, the less effective they became, and she grew despondent. In her unhappiness, she began drinking. With deep, dark circles under her eyes, a double chin, and ballooning weight, she appeared terrible in her photographs, but then only drank more. As it became worse, she was frequently ill. When Gladys and Vernon accompanied Elvis to Fort Hood, Texas, for his advanced training, Elvis could see that his mother was in poor health and began to worry. Still, he had no idea how bad the situation was.

Her death from a heart attack triggered by acute hepatitis on August 14, 1958, was the shock of his life.

Elvis Presley's life can be seen as one long and dramatic unfolding of tragic ironies. You can combine them into a list, a "List of Ironies" which contributed to his career, his divorce, the last devastating period of his life and, finally, his death. The cruelest and most profound irony on that list is that the most important person in his life died at the very zenith of his success and at the threshold of his manhood, when he was in more of a position than ever before to take care of her and give her everything.

Gladys's death came only several months after Elvis received the very first good critical notices for his performance in *King Creole*. The good reviews had filled him with a deep satisfaction

and sense of accomplishment which stayed with him right up   41
until his mother's sudden death, and the contrast of the happiness against the shattering tragedy only jarred him more.

From that moment on Elvis Presley's entire life was shaded by an inconsolable grief that would make itself felt in virtually everything that he did, in his greatest successes and most abysmal moments of despair. Everything that he was to accomplish in the years to come would be fraught with a feeling that it was somehow transitory and fleeting, that it could just as easily be taken or thrown away.

Now that Elvis was a public figure, his mother's death and funeral at Forest Hill Cemetery became a public event to be exploited by mass media and flashed around the world like any other news item. Dee remembers reading about it in Germany and thinking about how she lost her own mother, wondering if Elvis would bear emotional scars that would plague him in later years. He would, of course, and their effect would be profound. Everyone who knew Elvis then or would come to know him understood that Gladys Presley was the most sensitive subject in his life and stay well away unless Elvis brought it up. He never discussed his mother with anyone except his daddy, and for the rest of his life he would refuse to watch his second film, *Loving You,* in which she appears in the audience. "I will spend my whole life through . . . loving you," he sings in the film. ". . . Winter, summer, springtime, too."

Elvis then receded into whatever anonymity the ranks allowed him, becoming an exemplary GI. When the press learned that he was to sail for a tour of duty in Germany, the Colonel informed them that Elvis would surface in Brooklyn, at his point of embarkation, for a brief press conference. On a sunny day in September, amid much hoopla, Elvis, dressed in khakis, deftly fielded questions, flanked by Colonel Parker, army brass, and a large contingent from RCA who had arrived to record the event for an LP entitled, simply, *Elvis Sails.* The troopship *General Randall* stood by waiting to transport him to Bremerhaven, Germany.

"One of the last things Mom said was that Dad and I should always be together," Elvis had said. He confirmed it at the ship-

42   yard: "My father and grandmother are following me to Germany in a few weeks; they'll be livin' in a house near the post where I'll be stationed."

"I was an only child," Elvis then said to the reporter who asked for a comment on his mother's death. "She was very close. More than a mother. . . ."

CHAPTER 3

TRYING TO GET TO YOU

As the phone began to ring, Dee stood there, wondering what she was going to say. The clerk at the Grünewald answered and she asked for the Presley room. The connection was made.

"Hullo?"

"Uh, hello, uh, is Elvis there?" she asked uncertainly.

"This *is* Elvis." The voice was deeper than she expected, but the lilting drawl was unmistakable, making her think of home. To her astonishment, she had the real McCoy.

"Yes, hello there," she said sweetly now, leaping right in. "You don't know me, Elvis, but perhaps you know my husband. He's an officer at the base. My name is Dee Stanley, Elvis, and I was just calling to welcome you to Germany. It isn't too often that we get celebrities from home out here."

"Well, I do appreciate that, Mrs. Stanley," said Private Presley. "Thank you very, very much, ma'am."

Dee fumbled in the short silence that followed, wondering if she was saying the right thing.

"I also wanted to tell you how very sorry we all were to hear

44   about your poor mother," she said solemnly. "Please accept our condolences." She paused for a second, then brightened up the tone of her voice. "Now, how would you and all your family like to have supper one night with me and my husband out here at our place? I'm sure you'd enjoy a little home cookin' after all that slop they feed you out at the base!"

"Oh, the food out there isn't so bad," Elvis laughed. "Well, thank you very much for the invitation, ma'am. It's sweet of you to think of us, but I have to go on maneuvers next week. Why don't you call back this Monday, and I'll speak to my daddy about it?"

Just then one of Dee's friends entered. "Who are you talking to?" she whispered. Dee put her hand over the phone and whispered back, "Elvis." Her mouth dropped open and she started jumping up and down, screaming.

"I'm sorry, Elvis," said Dee over the wail in the background, embarrassed. "One of my friends just walked in, and I guess she's a little taken aback that I'm really talking to you on the phone. I'll call back Monday."

"Fine, Mrs. Stanley," he said, restraining his laughter. "That'll be just fine."

The phone call that changed Dee's life was a whim; she has often pondered what made her do it in the first place. Her boredom was certainly a factor, as were her problems, along with a simple desire to extend some southern hospitality to some fellow Tennesseans far from home. Of course, she also wanted to meet Elvis Presley. Who wouldn't?

It would prove another irony that Bill had tried to surprise her several days earlier by taking her out to the base to meet him. Since his arrival in Germany, people back at their quarters had talked of little else, and Bill thought she might get a kick out of seeing him. Dee was caught completely off guard because Bill Stanley, like many husbands at the time whose wives liked Elvis, wasn't exactly crazy about him. Dee was even worried that Bill would pull rank on him and embarrass her, and she was both disappointed and relieved when they learned that he wasn't on the post that day. According to army regulations, Elvis was

allowed to spend his evenings and weekends offbase if he wasn't
on special duty. Before moving into a four-bedroom house on
14 Goethestrasse, Elvis, Vernon, and Minnie Mae Presley,
Vernon's mother, had all rented rooms at the Hotel Grünewald,
in Bad Nauheim. Several days later, after thinking about it,
Dee, a woman known to be remarkably direct sometimes in saying what she means and doing what she wants to do, picked up
the phone.

When she called back on the designated Monday, Elvis invited her to coffee at the hotel. She found herself driving over to
Bad Nauheim, past small farmhouses, quaint roadside cafes,
and rustic inns that lined the way into the village. Accessible
from both Freidberg and Frankfurt, Bad Neuheim was a popular spa because the influx of money and tourists had not marred
its unique, provincial charm. The Grünewald was a small, two-
storied, white-brick building fringed with black trim and colorful awnings—one of those buildings that looked much better on
the outside than on the inside. Dee approached it dressed
casually in black silk and black high-heel pumps. Her
ash-blond hair, then shoulder length, was brushed back, swept
off her forehead, and the black of her outfit accentuated her
blue eyes.

She entered the lobby of the hotel. It was red carpeted with a
large crystal chandelier hanging overhead, and she fixed her
eyes on the balcony where she expected Elvis to appear behind
the balustrade. A voice behind her said, "Mrs. Stanley?"

She turned to confront Vernon Presley, dressed nattily in a
tweed sport coat, with his wavy graying hair brushed back. For a
brief interlude they stood in stunned silence, unable to move or
say anything, while everything else inside the hotel seemingly
stopped.

"I was completely aghast at how handsome he was!" remembers Dee, laughing. "I just didn't expect him to look like
that! It was a funny feeling because I felt very vulnerable, and I
was afraid of saying something foolish, but I must say, it was an
immediate physical attraction. The same way it was with Bill."

The coffee that followed in the main dining room passed in a
whir of dizzy glances and giddy small-talk while Minnie Mae

46   Presley, an earthy and good-humored woman then in her sixties, looked on curiously. They conversed without taking their eyes off each other, and Dee carefully studied Vernon's face. There was a sadness that rimmed his eyes and furrowed his brow which Dee attributed to the death of Gladys Presley, but his blue eyes burned and seemed to reach right across the table and caress her. She found herself responding to him almost involuntarily. To her, he was engagingly handsome ("I still think that Vernon was the real looker of the Presley men," she says)— handsome in a completely different way from Bill. Vernon was approaching his mid-forties and his blond hair was graying fast, so he cut the image of the "older man," which Dee found instantly appealing. His manner was simple and there was something gruff about him, but he had a quiet dignity and self-respect which she found assuring. Like the first night she met Bill, the attraction brought about a gusty sexual feeling in her, but this time she was worried.

When the coffee was over, Vernon walked her out to her car, and before Dee stepped in, he slipped his arm around her waist and looked her deeply and earnestly in the eyes. "I'm so glad we met, Dee," he said. "I'm sure we'll be seeing each other again soon. I feel it."

Dee said nothing. Driving home, she realized that she hadn't even thought about Elvis once. He had been out on maneuvers and unable to be there, and Dee wasn't the slightest bit disappointed.

Never a man to mince his words or waste time beating around the bush, Vernon Presley called back the very next day. A date was arranged, but this time Bill would be there, which made Dee more comfortable. Bill thought the idea was a perfect way for Dee to be able to get out a bit more and have some fun. The truly strange thing about the month that followed was the speed with which the two men took to each other. They befriended each other almost immediately. It probably explains why Bill never even had an inkling of what Vernon Presley had on his mind, for Bill Stanley was not a naive man.

"We just started going around together like good old friends," says Dee. "Sometimes at night we would all go to the *biergarten* and sit around and talk. Then when they became better friends, Bill would call Vernon to take me shopping when he was too busy, and Vernon started coming around and playing with me and the boys. The feeling between us was growing and growing, and then came Ricky's birthday party. I couldn't find any balloons, and then the doorbell rang and someone was bringing balloons and a beautiful sled. It was from Vernon. He just kept doing all of those sweet and thoughtful things for me that my husband never had done."

Having observed the situation in Dee's home firsthand, it didn't take Vernon long to realize that the quickest way to Dee's heart was through her boys. The more things he did for Billy, Ricky, and David, the faster he endeared himself to their mother. Vernon also began to understand that Bill was a problem drinker. His benders had increased in length and frequency, and his absences from the house only encouraged further the burgeoning relationship between his wife and Vernon Presley.

Within several weeks Vernon was pursuing Dee ardently, and they could be seen together in Elvis's MG, racing around the German countryside, laughing, picnicking, or stopping at cafes for wine and coffee. Bill Stanley had never seen his wife so radiantly happy, and he kept calling Vernon up, expressing his appreciation, further encouraging the friendship.

That first month was a step-by-step study in storybook seduction (Dee's guilt increased commensurately with each new step taken). Baptized into the Church of Christ at a very young age, she was abundantly aware that adultery was a sin. Her growing feelings for Vernon Presley frightened her, and yet they compelled her to keep going back. The handholding and gentle caresses quickly led to kisses so nakedly passionate that it seemed, after only weeks, they were meant to be together. After about a month she and Vernon were at the breaking point, and one afternoon in Vernon's room at the Grünewald, a single kiss broke down the walls and tumbled them into bed. The trees swayed gently outside their window, and the hours passed away like minutes until the entire room was cast in the soft, shadowy

48 tones of the late afternoon, and Dee had discovered, to her guilt-ridden delight, what a wonderful lover Vernon Presley really was. Like father like son, they say. If the prodigious nature of Elvis's sexuality was legendary during his prime, he certainly got it from his daddy, who knew how to please a woman. Unlike Bill, he was gentle, lingering and dallying, exploring all of the nuances and subtleties important in the sexual awakening of a woman. When it was over, Dee felt like she had been loved by a man for the first time in her life. Overwhelmed by her happiness and her guilt, she cried.

Over the next few weeks Dee and Vernon continued to see each other often. They would disappear for hours on end, and Dee would return home with a glowing pallor and a bubbling countenance but fraught with fear and guilt. The mere sight of her three sons was reproach enough. Bill suspected nothing. He was rarely home, and when he was, he and Dee slept in different bedrooms, but Dee became more self-conscious as her feelings for Vernon grew. "I felt so guilty for feeling that way," she says, "because even though Bill and I did not have a good marriage, he was still my husband and the father of my children. The phone would ring all the time, and it would be Vernon and I couldn't speak. My husband would be there, and I'd have to say, 'Sorry, wrong number,' and put the phone down. I began to feel cheap."

It was Dee, in the end, who could no longer tolerate the sordid feeling of having to deceive Bill. One afternoon, after Vernon had dropped her off, she decided to break it off with him and either try once again to live with Bill as his wife or else head home alone to make it on her own. She had returned that day to find her three boys playing with their babysitter. It was the day of her tenth anniversary, and her mixed emotions about Bill and Vernon were churning inside of her when the phone began to ring. She picked it up and drew in a deep breath. It was Vernon Presley.

"Vernon," she said slowly, carefully measuring her words, "I don't want to see you anymore. I feel terrible about this whole thing. I want you to get out of my life. Don't ever call me again."

The words stung and a silence followed, but Vernon wasn't
taking no for an answer.

"This isn't what you're saying it is, Dee," he said. "This is
not cheap, because I want to marry you. I know you're not
going to stay with Bill forever. I want you to fly back to the
States and begin divorce proceedings. I'll be there, Dee. I love
you, baby."

Elvis Presley knew exactly what his daddy was up to. From
the first time that Vernon brought Dee Stanley around to the
house on Goethestrasse, it was evident to him that there was a
special woman in his father's life. Almost from the outset he
captivated Dee with his charm and manners. Dee asked if he
remembered seeing her that night at the Warwick Theater. "Of
course I remember you, Mrs. Stanley," was the reply. "How
could I ever forget someone so beautiful?"

Elvis was just beginning to adjust to his identity as US
53310761 and spent most of his time worrying about inspections
and driving his "scout" Jeep on maneuvers. Except for the ten
thousand or so fan letters he received each week, his life was no
different from any other soldier's on the base. He had received
no special treatment because of his celebrity status and the men
in his outfit were developing a strong respect and sense of loyalty for him.

Several of his old Memphis buddies had come over to make
themselves useful, and it made Elvis more comfortable to surround himself with some familiar faces. Lamar Fike, originally
just a crazy fan of Elvis's, had come to see him one day at his
house in Memphis and had never left, all three hundred pounds
of him. Red West, Elvis's bullnecked high-school chum, was
invited along after his discharge from the marines. Elvis had
also made some new buddies. Charlie Hodge was a diminutive
recruit from Decatur, Alabama, who had sought Elvis out on
their transatlantic crossing, producing an acoustic guitar. The
two boys just sat and sang together and got acquainted below
decks on the *General Randall*. Joe Esposito was the only Yan-
kee in the bunch. Small, dark, friendly, and quick witted, he
and Elvis met at the base. Elvis took an immediate liking to

50 him because Joe was sharp and fun to have around and they became close friends. After Elvis's discharge, the boys would form
the nucleus of the so-called "Memphis Mafia," and except for
Red West, who turned against Elvis after being fired in 1976,
would all remain loyal and work for him for the rest of his life.

At nights when Elvis was off duty, they would all gather at
the house on Goethestrasse to horse around, sit around the
piano and sing, or play records (Jerry Lee Lewis and Marty
Robbins). Vernon would occasionally bring Dee over: "They
would sometimes just sit around with Cokes all night long,
smoking and playing records," she remembers. "Vernon and
Elvis would sometimes reminisce about Tupelo, about the hard
times and some of the funny things that happened. I remember
them talking about this cat fight between two women they saw.
These two women once had a fight in front of their house, and
they were tearing and screaming at each other and rolling
around on the ground. Whenever they even started talking
about it, it would break them up."

Dee enjoyed herself at the house but often remained self-
conscious because she was married. There was, at times, an underlying tension between her and Elvis that could pop up and
just as rapidly subside. Elvis knew how Vernon felt about Dee
and never cautioned his father about the possibility of adverse
publicity should the newspapers get wind of what was going on,
but Elvis nevertheless had emotional adjustments to make when
they began seeing each other. For one thing, he had to get used
to the idea that Vernon Presley was a single man again, a man
who needed and would be looking for the companionship of
new women.

Dee could sense an almost fraternal feeling developing between father and son during this period. As an attractive man
and the father of an international celebrity, Vernon was a natural target for all kinds of women. Elvis fancied the idea of his
daddy having fun, but the emotional intensity of his relationship with Dee, which came only months after Gladys's
death, was something else.

Dee knew how sensitive he was about Gladys; Elvis couldn't
help but feel that Dee was somehow trying to replace her. Of

course, she also knew that a woman like Gladys Presley would always be irreplaceable to the son who had worshiped the ground she walked on. She wondered if Elvis thought it was disrespectful or indecent for his father to fall so much in love with her and worried that he held it against her, even though Elvis always made it clear to Vernon that he only wanted his happiness in whatever he did.

Elvis was careful to keep his feelings bottled up and well concealed. Ever the gracious gentleman, he went out of his way to make Dee feel as comfortable as possible. In her heart, she blessed him for it.

One night after she and Vernon entered the house in Bad Nauheim, Elvis was sitting at the piano, dressed in his fatigues. He was sitting there alone, tinkering on the keys. He looked up as they entered, and smiled.

"Daddy," he said, "here's a song for you and Dee."

He broke into "Trying to Get to You," one of his oldest Sun tunes.

Dee remembers him sitting there as his rich, bluesy voice easily filled the living room and took hold of her. With his eyes shut and his head tilted upwards and his shoulders hunched over the keyboard, it looked like a scene from a movie. He sang sweet and high and curled his voice gracefully down almost to a husky, mellow bass register:

> "I've been travelin' over mountains
> Even through the valleys, too
> I've been travelin' night and day
> I've been runnin' all the way, baby
> Tryin' to get to you. . . .
> Lord above you knows I love you
> It was He who brought me through
> In my waveless darky night
> He would shine as bright as light
> When I was trying to get to you."

"Thank you, Elvis," Dee said when he was finished, "for giving us a song."

52   Whatever awkward feelings Elvis may have had about Vernon and Dee, they were put aside when he met Priscilla.

Priscilla Beaulieu was not quite fifteen when she was introduced to Elvis by Currie Grant, then a liaison with the army's Special Services. Like the Stanley boys, she was an "army brat"; her stepfather was an air force captain stationed up in Weisbaden. According to Dee, who met her soon after Elvis did, Priscilla was, even then, unforgettably beautiful: "She was as cute as a petite Dresden doll," she says. "Her hair was one long, brown mane of curls that hung down her shoulder and she had a little button nose. She was a very well-mannered girl, very sophisticated for her age, but not pretentious."

When Elvis met her, it was obvious to Dee that he liked her because he behaved funny around her, like a high-school kid trying to impress his date with his funny antics. They began seeing more of each other, riding around in Elvis's BMW and spending time at the house on Goethestrasse. Dee remembers Elvis's Christmas party that year and how attracted to her Elvis seemed. The place was filled with very sophisticated women, many of them trying their best to attract Elvis's eye. Dee and Vernon had gone to pick up Priscilla to bring her to the party. "Cilla was dressed very simply in a print dress with a high collar," Dee recalls, "and all of the other women were in low-cut things. She was the prettiest girl there, and Elvis couldn't take his eyes off her the whole night!"

The attraction isn't hard to understand. Elvis found Priscilla (he would call her Cilla) entrancingly beautiful, but the infatuation went far beyond physical attraction.

Aside from his mother, his emotional intimacy with women had been scant. His years on the road and the sexual aura surrounding Elvis had left him an avid—if still somewhat shy—womanizer. He liked to have his fun, yes, and those exciting times gave rise to an endless procession of attractive Next-in-Lines, but he kept an emotional distance from the women in his life. Gladys always wanted her boy to find a nice girl and settle down and gladly opened her doors to any of his girl friends.

Elvis's high-school sweetheart, a raven-haired little girl

named Dixie Locke, had called it quits after Elvis took to the road with D. J., Scotty, and Bill in 1954. His next steady girl friend had been Anita Wood, a blond, pretty, and very charming Memphis television personality several years older than he. Anita and Elvis had spent time together at Graceland, and Gladys Presley thought she was a sweet girl and good for Elvis. When Elvis was drafted and sent overseas, she was the "girl he left behind" whom his fans presumed he might one day marry, but Elvis was too young and having too much fun to settle down. His image as a sex symbol kept him from settling down at that point in his life. Also, in later years, Elvis would admit that even though he cared deeply for her and they dated for six years, he wanted a woman "sharper" than Anita. He simply let their relationship fall away.

Sex-kittenish Hollywood starlets would abound in his life in the years to come. His costar in *Loving You*, Yvonne Lime, had also come to Graceland, sparking rumors of impending marriage in the gossip columns, and while in Germany, Elvis did his sightseeing with a beautiful seventeen-year-old named Margit Buergin and also with Vera Tchechowa, a dark, sultry young film actress in Berlin. And, on Elvis's trip to Paris, he was photographed in nightclubs with any number of French delights.

But then Cilla was very young and radiated a wholesome, unspoiled quality that Elvis would always seek in a woman. It was her youth that made him feel so secure with her. He could tell just by looking at her that not only would she grow up to be exquisitely beautiful, but she would also have plenty of another quality he would insist on in his women: class—plus intelligence, a graceful poise, social adroitness, and a sense of self-awareness. Whether or not he was conscious of it at the time, he saw in her the possibility of the Real Thing—the kind of love between man and wife evinced by Gladys and Vernon and something that he would, for many reasons, find very elusive in his life.

Dee was wrestling with her own elusive love life. As the years wore on in Germany, pressure mounted on Dee to make a

54 decision about Vernon and her marriage to Bill Stanley. The next move was clearly hers. Dee's choice seemed clear, but she was still wracked with indecision. Her sons contributed to her dilemma because she knew that any decision she made would be a crapshoot with *their* lives as well as hers. "I lived in fear of something happening to my sons if Bill's drinking continued," she says. "You just can't do that kind of thing in front of children. I wanted them to have the best of everything."

And then there was Vernon Presley: "Everywhere I went, I knew that the phone would ring and it would be Vernon calling. There wasn't anything fancy about what he said—just simple, beautiful words. 'Dee, you're my life. I cannot live without you.' I didn't need any violins playing when Vernon talked to me."

The three of them still continued to socialize, and Bill suspected nothing: "Can you *imagine* all of us together at parties and at dinner, with Vernon and I feeling that way about each other?"

Dee needed to get away and think. Vernon was trying to make up her mind, asserting his feelings for her, proposing marriage. Dee loved both men in different ways. Confused and anxious, she decided to take the boys back with her to Virginia and visit with relatives. She packed her bags and readied her boys. On the day of her departure Bill and Vernon both drove her to the airport in Frankfurt. Billy, Ricky, and David, then seven, six, and four, giggled and roughhoused in the car, excited about their trip. Bill was behaving strangely. He was quiet and melancholic. Vernon was silent. The scene at the airport was difficult for Dee to manage without breaking down. They boarded the plane and Dee strapped her three sons into their seats. Then she went back to the door for one final look.

There they were, standing side by side by the fence, each thinking completely different thoughts about her. Bill suddenly looked lost and bewildered, and Dee felt a great sympathy for him. Vernon looked determined, his jaw set stubbornly. The Presley men were alike in one respect: When they made up their minds that they wanted something, nothing short of the apocalypse would stop them from getting it.

Dee waved good-bye and lingered for one more moment. She   55
knew at that precise second that she would leave Bill Stanley.
She felt neither cold blooded, guilty, or happy about the decision; it was just the way it was.

Vernon had already called by the time Dee arrived in
Virginia, anxious to fly to the States to get the ball rolling. It
seemed that after the takeoff of the plane, Bill had invited Vernon back to his house. The two men entered the apartment and
Bill cracked open a bottle. "I've lost her, Vernon," he said de-
spondently. "I've lost Dee." He then asked Vernon to try and
help him get her back. "You're my dearest friend," he said.
"You took her shopping and gave her so much that I didn't. She
loved you, you know. She'll listen to you. . . ."
Suddenly the deception became too much for the speechless
Vernon Presley. He couldn't tell Bill that he was determined to
marry his wife, but he resolved to get back to the States to settle
it as quickly as possible. He knew that the most important way
of reassuring Dee would be to show her how much he cared for
her and what her life would be like with him.
In April, when he flew home, Vernon invited Dee to Memphis and picked her up at the airport in Elvis's red Cadillac.
They reached Graceland just after nightfall. Vernon stopped the
car at the outside gate. The white limestone mansion with its
four stately pillars sat up on a rise about a quarter of a mile off
the road, and the driveway meandered through the finely mani-
cured lawn up to the ornate front door. Tastefully lit with criss-
crossing spots and porch lights, the mansion shimmered like a
jewel in the Tennessee night. There was a faint hint of spring in
the air even though the night was crisp and cool, and the leaves
were beginning to appear on the magnolia and oak that covered
the grounds. Standing there, Dee suddenly began to realize the
implications of what she was doing. The beauty of Graceland
provoked in her a heady comprehension of what it would mean
for her, but especially of what it would mean for her sons.
"From the very beginning," she says, "I knew that someone was
going to make it possible for them to have everything, and for
me to never leave them." At a glance the image before her

56 represented all of the security and style that her life had lacked. "You wouldn't have to be around me very long to pick up how much I loved beauty—the clothes and the glamor and the wining and dining. It's quite obvious; even Bill must have known right away that that's what I wanted out of life." In Dee's mind the finery of her new life would always remain secondary in importance, but the wonders of a permanent home for her sons, and good schools, church, financial security, friends from respectable families, and college were paramount.

The man who would make it all happen stood by her with his arm around her waist. Dee was sure that Vernon Presley truly loved her. "I was very relaxed and confident about the way he felt about me," she says. "You don't take a chance seeing a married woman like that, when the publicity might present such a problem for your son, unless you are in love."

She still wondered how he really felt about her sons, however. Before the week was over, Vernon would also put all of her apprehensions about that to rest. The boys would live at Graceland, he promised, and they would never have to worry about anything. To show his sincerity, he would open a bank account in their name and deposit in it a considerable amount of money to assure Dee that she could take care of them during the divorce proceedings. There would also be an engagement ring.

"Come on, baby," said Vernon, gently nudging her forward. They went around back, where the pool was glistening in the lights. The back door then opened to reveal Alberta, Graceland's indomitable maid. "Oh! This must be Miss Dee!" she exclaimed, drying her hands on her apron. "Lawdy mercy!" she said, her eyes opening wide, "Mr. Vernon's done gone and got hisself a movie star! Ain't she just the purdiest little thing. . . ."

When Vernon flew back to Germany sometime in May, Dee found herself with the painful and unpleasant task of having to tell Bill Stanley that it was all over. Bill had hurried home but when he arrived in Virginia, Dee just couldn't find the heart to tell him until one day a cable arrived from Vernon in Europe. "Will be arriving soon," it read. "Can't live without you."

"I'm not even going to ask you about this," he said to her on the afternoon it arrived. Dee came home to find him waiting for her, brandishing the telegram in her face. "I probably made this happen, didn't I?" he asked sadly.

There was nothing left to do but tell the truth. Faced with divorce, Bill made one last desperate attempt at dissuading his wife from leaving him. They would move to Hawaii, he promised; he would retire from the service and stop drinking. It was the most painful day in Dee's life, but her mind was made up, and she was sticking to her guns. She became frightened as things then became tense and uncertain.

Vernon hurried back to Virginia when he found out that things were getting sticky with Bill. He arrived to find Dee worried about the boys. Billy, Rick, and David were then taken to Breezy Points Farm in Virginia where they would remain until everything was settled.

Breezy Points was a private home-school for children. The three young boys were bewildered. They could sense that something important was happening but remained completely in the dark. Billy Stanley, the oldest, remembers it even today: "It was some kind of home for rich kids while their parents were gone for the season," he says, "but we thought it was an orphanage. We spent a Christmas there and saw all these parents come to pick their kids up, and we'd wait for our mother to call from Germany." I remember Dee explaining where we were fixin' to move to—to Memphis, to a house with a big gate and everything. Then the other kids started telling me who my new brother was going to be. They said 'Elvis Presley.' Who? *Elvis Presley?* What does he do? That's when they started making guitars with Elvis's picture on them and one of the girls had one. That was the first time I ever saw him."

Dee may have passed the critical point of no return with Bill, but the matter of Elvis Presley's reaction still remained in question. "I called Elvis one night and told him that I was in love with his father," Dee remembers, "and he said something very

58 sweet to me. He said, 'Dee, you have a way of making people love you.' I thought that it was very necessary to discuss it with him in person because I know how he felt after losing his mother. It was a very big step for Vernon to take. I had three sons myself and had they been older I would have certainly discussed it with them. Vernon wasn't going to ask his permission—he wanted to *share* it with him, but I felt that the only way I would go through with it was with his approval. I wasn't going to push Elvis into liking me. I wanted him to, and I was a little nervous when we went to see him in the hospital in Frankfurt. He had tonsillitis at the time. He made me feel completely at ease."

When they arrived at the hospital, they found Elvis sitting up in bed, happy to see them. The conversation that followed was simple and direct. Once again, to Dee's heartfelt gratitude, Elvis was the gentleman.

"Mrs. Stanley, I want my daddy to be happy," he said. "He was a wonderful husband and father, and I've always wanted a brother. Now I guess I'll have three. We can just add another room onto Graceland."

"From that moment on," says Dee, "I knew that I would marry Vernon Presley."

It was settled.

When Vernon and Dee arrived home it seemed Bill was not going to let her go without a struggle. He was threatening to make legal trouble. Dee was beside herself at first, but then collected her feelings and decided to reason with him. She had made a decision and she had to make him understand why. "I had to make him stop that," she says. "I was leaving somebody that I loved. I'd wanted the marriage to work, but I was doing what I had to do. When he made sure that I wanted Vernon Presley—when he saw that that was what I really wanted (or thought I wanted), he knew that it was time to get out. He handled it. I almost died to divorce him."

Vernon took care of all the necessary legal papers, which were waiting for Bill in the study at Graceland when he arrived. It was, in essence, a fait accompli that gave Dee custody of the children; there was nothing that Bill could do unless he wanted to plunge everyone into messy, acrimonious litigation.

The signing of the papers was done privately. Bill Stanley couldn't have felt much better than the French generals who signed the papers of armistice in the railway car at Compiègne, yet he remained the stoic gentleman to the very end. During his time at Graceland, he only permitted himself two displays of emotion, both of which remained firmly etched in everyone's mind.

"Vernon, I'm going to tell you something," he said dolefully, picking up his glass. "You have her now. You took her from me, but if it wasn't for *this*, you or any other man couldn't have taken her from me."

Then he was silent. "Always love her," he said, getting up to go. On his way out the door he picked up Billy, his firstborn son. "I want you to listen to me, Billy," he said softly. "Mr. Presley is going to be your new father. I won't be here anymore. I want you to say 'yes, sir' and 'no, sir' to him and remember to always take care of your mother."

And with that he was gone.

The Memphis press quickly picked up on Dee. She was spotted entering and leaving Graceland, and everyone was wondering who the "mysterious blond" was—whether she was connected with Vernon or was perhaps a German girl that Elvis may have met. As Vernon's relatives began to catch on, particularly Gladys's side of the family, Dee began to experience the first waves of jealousy and mistrust that would hover over her for years. Some of Vernon's relatives thought it was shameful for him to be considering marriage so soon after Gladys Presley's death. Dee was suddenly cast as a wily opportunist, out to get at the Presley fortune. To know that people were saying those things about her without even knowing her was painful for Dee, but it was something that she would learn to ignore.

In Germany, Elvis neared the date of his discharge. By January of 1960 he had been promoted to sergeant and put in charge of a three-man reconnaissance unit. Colonel Tom

60 Parker was busy whipping up the recording and movie industries for the return of his boy, and the national media was in a frenzy. *Jailhouse Rock*, which had grossed close to four million dollars its first time out, was being prepared for rerelease. Recording dates were being set up and producer Hal Wallis was preparing production for Elvis's next film, *G.I. Blues*. Nary a single recording star had emerged to challenge or overtake Elvis's stature or popularity during his absence, and Frank Sinatra—Mr. Showbiz himself, who had once called rock 'n' rollers a bunch of "cretins"—was negotiating with the Colonel to get Elvis for a television special after his discharge.

Priscilla accompanied Elvis to the Frankfurt airport on the day of his flight back to the States, and the two were photographed kissing good-bye. In the months to come Elvis would realize how much he missed her.

Elvis arrived at Fort Dix, New Jersey, during a blizzard. He was discharged from there on March 2, 1960. During his train ride home, the stations in every town he passed through were mobbed with his fans. Elvis, riding on the back of the train like a president campaigning or a returning conqueror, waved, smiled, and signed autographs. When he reached Memphis, it seemed like the entire city turned out to greet him. The streets were lined all the way from the railroad depot to the gates of Graceland.

Elvis relaxed at Graceland before leaving for Miami to tape his special with Frank Sinatra. During this period he stopped in to say hello to the three young boys who were to be his stepbrothers. He found them busy downstairs, playing. Billy, Ricky, and David were then eight, seven, and five years old, still not aware of the importance of the man who approached them. He introduced himself as their brother and picked each of them up. "I like you boys," he said gently. "I like you very much."

"We had just come from Virginia," remembers Rick Stanley, "and that was the first time we met him or talked to him. Of course I was so young, but I remember how cool he was when he picked us up and expressed his love for us."

The following morning, when the boys awoke, they found

three of every imaginable kind of toy and even pets strewn across the downstairs—sleds, bicycles, kittens, and puppies—everything. "That just blew our minds for sure!" Rick laughs. "That was the first thing any of us remember about him."

Rubbing their eyes in disbelief, Billy, Ricky, and David just looked at each other and wondered if that guy Elvis might be Santa Claus.

As preparations for the wedding were made, Dee pondered the possible consequences of her actions. Had she done the right thing? She felt sure that she had made the right decision for herself. In a religious-scriptural sense, she did not feel at fault because of Bill's infidelities during the course of their marriage, but she had a reservation about her boys that she would never be able to shake. "I worried that I had deprived them of the most important thing in their lives—their natural father. But at least now I could bring my sons up right, the way I always dreamed of doing."

She couldn't possibly have known that it would one day all blow up in her face.

Adverse publicity and family reaction mounted as the wedding date approached. Vernon Presley was disturbed but unwavering in his determination to marry Dee. Vernon, Elvis, and Dee stood on the lawn at Graceland one day before the marriage. "Elvis," he said, gesturing toward the mansion. "This whole thing don't mean a damn to me if I have to give up Dee."

"Come on, Daddy," comforted his son. "You're talkin' foolish."

Vernon and Dee were married in Huntsville, Alabama, at Richard Neely's home, on July 3, 1960. It was a small wedding and reception described by the press as "sudden" and "secret." Although he phoned that night to offer his congratulations, Elvis remained in Memphis. His excuse for not attending was that his presence there would have distracted from the ceremony, but it was tacitly understood that he wanted to abstain because he felt his presence there would have been emotionally

62 awkward. Looking back, Dee remarks that "I think what hurt Elvis most at the time was feeling that the closeness between father and son was going to be less because the father was getting married, and married *before* him. I knew it was going to take time for him to accept me even if I was never going to try to take his mother's place. But I didn't worry about it because I was marrying Vernon Presley, not Elvis."

The decade of the sixties was breaking over America in the waves of energy and optimism occasioned by President John F. Kennedy's new administration in Washington. Dee Elliott Stanley Presley, newlywed and now "official" mistress of Graceland, approached her new life confidently but with a watchful eye and strong tugs from her past. Elvis Presley had just released a song appropriately entitled "It's Now or Never."

". . . tomorrow will be too late," it went. "It's now or never, my love won't wait."

CHAPTER 4

THE REWARDS

When considering the life of Elvis Presley and his impact on those around him, it is convenient to divide his life into four major periods, all beginning and ending with major events and each with a distinct flavor of its own. The first period could easily be called *The Dream* and cover the entire span from his birth up through his youth and into the years of his first astounding successes, past the death of his mother, into and out of the army. The second major period, spanning the years 1960–68, might be labeled *The Reward*, embracing the Hollywood years, his marriage, the birth of his daughter, and ending with the completion of his last feature film and his return to live performing. The third phase, *The Comeback*, begins with the first years of his hugely successful road tours, and ends with his divorce. The final period, *The Decline*, would comprise the final five years of his life.

Home again from the army, Elvis relaxed, contacted old friends, and began assembling the group of people who would make up his inner circle. Putting his affairs in order after his

64 eighteen-month absence from Graceland, he had ample time to reflect upon his life. He was twenty-five years old, and it was time to embark upon the second phase—*The Reward*. He had worked hard and paid his dues as an entertainer. Having served his country faithfully, he was now legitimized as a superstar, accepted by the cultural mainstream of his country instead of considered an underground hero on its fringes. Elvis, the Colonel, and the people around him knew that it was time to reap the harvest of Elvis's hard work, but despite the optimism and promise of the future, the mansion seemed sadly empty without Gladys Presley.

Elvis devoted the period 1960–67 almost exclusively to amassing an incredible fortune by churning out an average of three motion pictures a year. The list of film titles and the characters he played go on and on; suffice it to say that some were better than others and the more notable things about the films were their stifling uniformity, the steadily deteriorating quality of the scripts and musical scores, and the fact that it didn't take too long until they bored Elvis out of his wits. Today, if nothing else, they remain a monumental tribute to Elvis's remarkable box-office power, for what other star could have made turkeys like *Harum Scarum* and still walked away with a small fortune?

In later years Elvis would cringe with embarrassment whenever one of his movies was on television and flatly refuse to watch, but with a guarantee of a million dollars plus fifty percent of the take per picture, they made Elvis (and the Colonel) fantastically rich. He made no public appearances during this period because a large portion of his income was now contingent upon his fans' willingness to keep paying to see him on the movie screens. Thus the Colonel kept their desire for more of the celluloid Elvis stoked to a high level by keeping him under wraps as much as possible, and Elvis spent most of his time between Hollywood, Palm Springs, and Graceland, honking straight through on Route 66 in a caravan of Cadillacs or in the mobile homes that he loved to drive, keeping to himself and the private little world he created with the help of his faithful retinue.

Graceland was the personification of Elvis Presley's world,
and virtually everything and everyone there somehow revolved
around his existence. For Elvis, his family, and their friends, it
was more than just an estate; it was a living symbol of security,
privacy, power, wealth, and a way of life. Graceland was very
much a part of Elvis's reward.

Autumn brought cooling winds and welcome relief from the
blistering heat of Dee Presley's first Memphian summer. After
Labor Day the humidity that enveloped the city and swallowed
its inhabitants all summer long began to dissipate; usually, so
did the crowds of tourists and fans of Elvis that congregated outside Graceland's music gate. As her three boys romped over the
estate and began Graceland Elementary School—driven there
in the same pink Cadillac that Elvis had bought for Gladys once
the floodgates of success opened over him—Dee focused on
her new life.

In those days being "official hostess" at Graceland was a
polite title for the woman of the household and tantamount to
doing as much as one wanted in a social capacity. Different
women would give the title different meanings in years to come;
for Dee it really didn't amount to much. She planned menus
but only rarely cooked the Sunday dinner for the family, and if
Elvis was home and wanted to have a party, she would help organize things and be there in a beautiful dress standing alongside Vernon to greet his guests. Even so, Elvis hardly ever had
"official" parties. When he was back from Hollywood, his entertainment usually consisted of having friends over, playing
records, drinking Cokes around the pool, motorcycle happen-
ings—in short, the Teen Dream realized. When he returned
from filming, life at the mansion, as Dee put it, consisted of
"Elvis's guys sitting around the television set with their wives or
girl friends, waiting for Elvis to get up and come down. And
when he did, everyone jumped at the same time to be the first
one to him.

"I really felt like an outsider when I first came there," Dee
reflects. "Gladys's clothes stayed in the closet of our bedroom,
and her picture was everywhere. I felt as if she was hovering
over me." For many reasons the adjustment to life at Graceland

66 was difficult. Dee couldn't feel at ease there and a part of the life because she usually preferred her own ways and the space to lead her own life. For one thing, she couldn't feel comfortable about having the mansion redecorated. To the residents of Whitehaven, Graceland may have looked like the elegant antebellum mansion, but on the inside, with its dark blue walls and garish red carpets, it resembled a New Orleans brothel. Elvis sensed Dee's sense of alienation and one day approached her.

"Dee, I want you to consider this your home, too," he said, taking her hand. "You've made Daddy very happy and this place belongs to you and the boys now as much as it does me and Daddy. No matter what anybody says, you remember that, 'cause I don't want anybody makin' you feel bad. There is nothing that needs to be left here for sentimental reasons. We can discuss any redecorating you want to do."

Time wore on and Dee learned to enjoy her notoriety as Mrs. Vernon Presley. Her relationship with Elvis became less and less standoffish and grew into one of genuine warmth and affection, although the closeness in age between them remained a barrier to a true intimacy. "Dee, it would have been much better between us if I were four and you were forty," he often said to her.

"I could never put my arms around Elvis and just hug him and kiss him," she says. "He had to grow to like me. You love little boys, you know, so it was different with my sons. They idolized Elvis from the beginning, and he loved them from the moment he laid eyes on them. I didn't feel Elvis liked me at first, but then there were things about Elvis that I didn't like, either. His temper, for instance, could frighten me. If I would have rushed in there and just gushed all over him, that would have been a very tacky overreaction to the situation. I had to get to know him as a human being first, and I had to earn his respect—I really don't think that he felt I could handle it all. It was 'Here I am, Elvis; if you like me, fine, if you don't, I'm sorry, but I married your daddy anyway.' Soon we grew to like each other fine, and then it grew into real respect and love,

until one day Elvis told me that it was destiny that brought me
and my sons into the family."

Destiny or happenstance, the more Elvis and Dee got to
know each other, the more sensitive and considerate Elvis became to his stepmother's needs and problems. Soon they could
read each other's moods beautifully, and it became apparent to
them that they had much more in common then than they may
have realized at first. As Dee sees it, "We were both very set in
our opinions of things and both very vain and self-centered and
perhaps a little afraid that someone might hurt us. It was strange
how we began to develop such a feeling for each other. If something was bothering me and Elvis saw me, he could pick it out
immediately, and sometimes I wouldn't want to discuss it with
anybody else because they couldn't understand it the way he
could, especially those things that a woman usually goes
through that make her feel insecure. If my hair wasn't looking
good, it could just about make me ill and I wouldn't even go
out; Elvis was the same way. Neither of us were ever going to
get old or fat, and we would drive Vernon crazy. 'You and Elvis
have got to be the two most difficult people in the world to deal
with, Dee,' he would say, and he was right." Elvis and Dee
were alike in their pride, egos, frenetic energy, a shared flair for
the flamboyant, and an endless mania for new fads, styles, and
projects.

Even with the growing intimacy between Dee and Elvis, she
still yearned for a home of her own. The image of life at Graceland may have seemed glamorous and romantic to the fans that
clamored outside the gate, but there were practical problems that
began to grate on her. First and foremost were the limitations
imposed on her by the presence of the fans. Life at Graceland
was like living in a fishbowl. Even birthday parties for her boys
became complicated affairs involving guards and the embarrassment of having to clear invited guests before letting them
through the gates. There was also something unreal and sycho-
phantic about the atmosphere in Graceland with Elvis's entourage in attendance that Dee sought to keep her boys from.
Somehow she felt that if her sons grew up in Graceland, they

68   would grow up into the entourage, and she certainly had other plans for their futures.

The uselessness that Dee felt inside Graceland was another problem. As the new bride she was catered to and waited on, and she began to think about her purpose there. Apart from her boys, there was really nothing much to do. Breakfast would be served, and she and Vernon would take a walk over the grounds. Lunch would be served, and they would sit by the pool, take a ride, or watch a movie in the basement. Within the self-contained, self-sufficient miniworld of Graceland, everything they could possibly need was inside the gates. Alberta would pick the boys up at school, and they would play together, have dinner, relax, and get the boys ready for bed. But whatever they did, Vernon and Dee would be together virtually every minute of the day. The only vacations they took were to visit Elvis on location for a film or else at one of his homes in or around Los Angeles.

At home Elvis was quite careful not to upset the delicate sensibilities of his new stepmother—unless, of course, he was playing one of his numerous practical jokes. Surrounded by his cronies, life around Graceland became filled with slapstick humor, buying sprees, wild shenanigans, and always the kind of macho roughhousing that Elvis and his boys loved to indulge in. Elvis kept Dee well protected from the antics, except when *he* wanted to frighten her.

In those days Scatter, Elvis's famous chimpanzee, was traipsing freely around the halls of the mansion. The chimp was as cute as Bingo on the Abbott and Costello show, except much crazier. Always nattily dressed, he had a penchant for looking up pretty girls' dresses and grabbing at their behinds, fondling himself in public, and riding in Elvis's cars (Elvis would have him chauffered as he rode in the back seat of a Cadillac or Rolls). He also drank bourbon and sat at the dinner table, where he ate with a knife and fork! Dee reasoned that at least if he had to sit at the table, he should dress for the occasion, so one Christmas she tried to put a little sport jacket on him. To her horror the chimp put her hand in his mouth and started biting her thumb harder and harder. "I started screaming," she re-

members, "but Vernon and Elvis were falling on the floor because they thought I was laughing!" Dee was rushed to the doctor eventually.

At times the hordes of fans that Elvis attracted throughout his
career made life at Graceland a little too hectic. Women came
from around the world to camp out in front of the gate just to
catch a glimpse of Elvis and hope for a kiss, a date, a memento,
anything. Most of the fans were sweet and sincere in their intentions; others were bizarre, some even malevolent. Dee remembers the middle-age woman who would write Elvis ten-
page letters filled with raunchy sexual propositions. One night
Vernon and Dee bounded awake when the buzzer from the
guard shack sounded, and the phone began to ring urgently.
Vernon grimaced and sleepily picked it up.

"My God, Uncle Vernon, there's a crazy woman on the
grounds! She broke through the gate!"

Security at Graceland was run by Vernon's brother, Vester
Presley, and Gladys's brother, Travis Smith. It was strictly a
family affair, especially since Vester had married Cletis,
Gladys's sister. One of Travis's sons was on duty that night.

"Well, get that damn woman out of here!" thundered Vernon into the phone.

Dee drew back the draperies, and, right there, standing right
up against the glass, looking like a frazzled bug-eyed witch just
plugged into a wall socket, was the strangest looking woman
imaginable. Dee panicked. Vernon was frightened, too, but the
woman was soon dragged from the grounds. She remained outside the gate, flagging down traffic and saying that *she* was really
Elvis's wife, hiking her skirts and throwing moons at the passing
cars. The next morning, while Dee was telling Alberta about
the excitement the night before, the doorbell began ringing.
"Lawdy mercy, Miss Dee! I hope that ain't her, loose again!"

Sure enough, there she was, jumping up and down. Travis
came up in his Jeep and removed her, but he was having trouble handling her outside the gate. The woman was saying how
she had willed Gladys's death and would do the same to Dee.
Finally Vernon called the police, who told her to leave. Dee
shakes her head when she recalls what happened next: "Vernon

70 and I were out on the front lawn, and we look down and see the woman walking down Highway Fifty-one. Every so often she stops to take something off, but we couldn't see what was happening down there, but all of a sudden, my God! All of her clothes were off, and there she is, in broad daylight!"

That's the last anyone remembers of the mysterious, demented woman—skipping down the highway, naked as a jaybird, until the police picked her up. The tale has a truly bizarre footnote: The woman had threatened one of Travis's sons with a horrible death, which she forecast for him. Sure enough, the hapless fellow fell into a vat of boiling acid shortly thereafter.

Eventually Vernon Presley also began to recognize the necessity of moving his new family into a home of their own. Elvis had been spending most of his time in California and asked Vernon if he would be willing to move the whole family out there permanently, but when Dee protested, Vernon began looking for a house in Memphis. They moved before Dee had a chance to do much redecorating at Graceland, into a house on Hermitage while Vernon had a house built for them at 1266 Dolan Street, which runs right alongside Elvis's estate. The house on Dolan, a two-story five-bedroom, Dutch-style dwelling built with white brick, had Elvis's seven-acre pasture as its backyard and suited everyone's needs perfectly: It kept the family in close proximity to Elvis when he was home but still offered all of the privacies and accommodations of their own place.

The house cost twenty-five thousand dollars to build initially, and Dee went to work on it immediately. "I had every wall knocked out," she remembers, "because it was small. It had a pool outside, a sauna inside my bedroom suite, glass sliding-doors coming into my bedroom where I had a white marble pool installed, which was gold-lit from the bottom. Everything was mirrored, and right at the corner, there was a beautiful golden statue of a woman."

The new home gave Dee a chance to breathe. In changing husbands, she had gone full circle, from one extreme to the other. Bill Stanley was never there; Vernon Presley wanted to be there every minute of the day, and she began to feel "smoth-

ered" and "locked in." "Vernon has said to me that I brought
him back to life after Gladys's death, and that he had a real
worship for me. He would say things like he didn't think it was
possible for someone like me to love someone like him. I didn't
even know what the man was saying, then."

Vernon Presley had enmeshed himself into Elvis's business
affairs. He now had power of attorney for his son and a small office out in back of Graceland, where he took care of Elvis's personal financial affairs. He would go into his office at noon, and
at three he would be back for coffee or lunch. The new home
gave Dee a chance to involve herself in PTA and church activities, but they were still with each other almost constantly.

"I had to always be in the house when Vernon Presley walked
through that door," Dee says. "Always. And that's exactly where
I was, waiting for him. There was never a time when he didn't
want me with him. He'd serve me coffee in bed and tuck me in
every night, and if I had to get up to go to the bathroom, he
would always check on me to see if I was all right, as if he had
some kind of fear of losing me. There were times I didn't want
Vernon to be with me, but it wasn't to be with another man. It
was to be able to breathe for a while—to be free. To read. Anything."

Although their romance had been so overwhelming, there
were many things that Dee did not immediately understand
about her husband. To virtually all of the people who came to
know him, Vernon Presley was, like his celebrated son, replete
with contradictions of character and paradoxes of personality,
many of which are traceable to his dirt-poor beginnings. He was
an easygoing man with a rollicking sense of humor who could,
in a second and with only the slightest provocation, explode and
become as mean as a rattlesnake. Some have said that he was an
absolute tyrant to work for and many have remarked the bitterness about him that seemed to have lingered on from his youth
and the relentless struggle he had to wage just to make a living
for his family.

Vernon's mother, Minnie Mae, was an earthy, strong southern lady who had taken over the Presley family in Tupelo after
her husband, Jesse Presley, had abandoned the family by run-

72 ning off with another woman. According to what Vernon told Dee, Jesse Presley was a "cruel man—Vernon knew nothing but a cruel father. If he ever disciplined him, it was very harsh. His father hardly ever provided clothing for Vernon and his brother, Vester, and Vernon went barefoot until he was quite a grown-up boy. His education never went past the fifth grade."

What Dee and the rest of the world did not know about Vernon Presley was that he had served time in the Mississippi State Penitentiary, allegedly for forging a check to feed his family during the first year of his marriage. When Elvis entered the public arena, it was hushed up and became one of the family secrets to be kept from the press at all costs. In the year after Elvis's death, the story was published by the sensationalist *Midnight Globe*, much to Vernon's unhappiness. "If only I had known what he was carryin' in his heart," Dee says, "everything might have been different."

Vernon Presley was an unflinchingly caring and loving man who sought to protect and shelter his people—an extremely paternal man, a devoted father and husband. "He would never let the people he loved worry about anything," remembers Dee, "and wanted to protect Elvis and I with his life."

Elvis was much like his father. Both men were able to project tremendous strength and confidence, but lurking beneath their fortitude was always a profound sense of insecurity. "They really couldn't help their insecurity considering their background," Dee says, "which made it strange because they were such strong, assertive men, too. Of course, they were both so handsome and they knew how to handle women. To their special women, they always meant what they said, although"—she chuckles—"I know they could say the very same things to women and not mean it. Elvis and Vernon were the kind of men that wanted their women right at home most of the time where they could put a finger on us."

Dee and Vernon didn't agree on many things and one of them was sex. The early days of their marriage were blissful, but Dee felt that Vernon was "overdoing" sex. The sudden abundance of it in her life—so markedly different from what she had known with Bill Stanley—rubbed against the grain of her

priggish upbringing, and if Dee knew how to make Vernon feel
like a king, her aloofness and reticence could also make him
feel very small. "For the first few years of our marriage," she
says, "I felt used, like a possession—a mistress in my own bedroom."

Most of the time Dee simply wanted to do something else ("It
gets boring to spend all of your time with a man holding your
hand, making love to you, with nothing else to do"), but soon
Vernon began to see each man who came near his wife as the
potential one to turn him into a cuckold. His fears and feelings
would well up inside of him until—like the safety valve that lets
the steam out of a pressure cooker when the critical point has
been reached—he too would blow his top. Then, all of the
venom would come pouring out of him, cascading over Dee.

"He was harsh in words," she says, "but it wasn't from the
heart—and it was only for the moment when it happened. Just
words, but words that could break me down. He could be so
harsh one moment, and then almost on his knees, begging me
to forgive him the next."

The possibility that Dee was unsatisfied with her marriage
shattered Vernon Presley and only inflamed his jealousy. "For
the first year," she remarks, "it was really bad. We'd all be at
the table together, and I'd get a flash of Bill and start thinking
that I had robbed the boys of the most important thing—a father. I felt like I had so much to do to make it up to them, to
buy them, and to make sure that nothing ever happened to
them. My sons were more important to me than any other
man."

Nothing that Dee could have said or done could possibly
have made Vernon feel more inadequate, more incapable of living up to Dee's lofty expectations. What made matters even
worse was Vernon's fear that Dee was attracted to Elvis. "That
was a very serious thing from the beginning," she remarks. "It
made me feel very uncomfortable, and I think Elvis felt it too.
Of course, I found Elvis attractive. He had the most beautiful
smile in the world, and there was something lonely about him
that made you want to care for him, but I never even thought
about Elvis and I; Vernon did. Elvis and I had the sort of rela-

74   tionship where we could sit and discuss a book he was reading, or religion, which he loved to talk about. He used to compliment me a lot, though, even more than Vernon did, and he bought me beautiful things—mink coats, cars, very expensive jewelry—and he knew exactly how to flatter me when he wanted to. He would say things like 'Dee, you *are* a beautiful woman, and love is what you want.' And I would just melt. But it got to a point where Elvis and I couldn't sit and have a word together without Vernon thinking about it."

But despite the jealousy that pervaded their marriage, Dee wanted Vernon Presley's child. "I always wanted a little girl," she says, "and a child would have been so loved by Vernon and Elvis and my boys. It would have been something that I could have given to everybody." Like women in days of yore who bore children to "royalty," bearing Vernon's child—a half-sister to Elvis—would have no doubt entrenched her more solidly in the bosom of the family, but after five pregnancies and three children, it wasn't to be an easy task. First she had to have surgery because the three births had distended her uterus. At least this time, she thought, she wouldn't be traveling around the South from one army post to another with a husband who was sure to be drunk should she need him.

When Dee and Vernon took Billy, Ricky, and David down to visit Elvis in Florida, where he was filming *Follow That Dream* at the Crystal River in 1961, Dee suspected that she was pregnant. When she was out on a boat with Elvis during the vacation and he asked how she was, she decided to tell him.

"Well, I think I'm pregnant, Elvis," she said, studying his face.

Elvis's face went blank for a second, as if the words went right past him, and then, as they sank in, his eyes opened wide.

"Oh, my goodness," he stammered happily, "you mean I'm going to have a baby sister?!"

Elvis was thrilled. Dee went to the doctor the very next day, and he confirmed the pregnancy. She looked forward to telling Vernon as soon as they returned to Graceland but didn't bargain on his reaction. Vernon Presley was in one of his jealous moods when she told him.

Staring at her icily for a moment, he said, "Well, that's fine, Dee. Who does it belong to?"

The unexpected shock of his cruel words sent her reeling back, horrified.

"I don't even want it if it's going to be like this!" she screamed at him before she turned to run from the room.

"It was like being slapped in the face," she remembers. "I felt like I wanted to die. I ran out of the house—I didn't even want the baby after that. I had wanted to see our baby more than anything else in the world, and Vernon wanted the same thing. One thing we always said to each other was that we would never hurt each other intentionally. It was so strange. The man gave me everything, and I felt so much love and gratitude for him. I don't think we ever meant to hurt each other, but we did."

Several months into the pregnancy Dee was taken to the hospital. The doctors no longer felt life stirring within her, and the dead fetus was removed. Back in Los Angeles, Elvis had already made the announcement to friends and associates. "Elvis never found out what really happened," relates Dee. "It was all too painful."

While the Colonel continued his Hollywood hard-sell of Elvis to his public and Elvis kept his mind off the growing tedium of his movies by horsing around with his buddies, his romantic life became a constant source of speculation for the media and fans alike. He kept it all very much to himself but could be spotted around the Hollywood–Beverly Hills–Bel-Air vicinity in one of his cars with any one of the pretty starlets from his films, playing tackle football on weekends with his boys, or blazing loudly through the Bel-Air hills on a big Harley chopper. By now he was pushing thirty and still unmarried; his was one of the most publicized bachelorhoods in the history of Hollywood.

But even with all of the Tuesday Welds that Hollywood had to offer, Elvis was unable to forget Priscilla Beaulieu. Letters were exchanged (Elvis *never* wrote letters!), and his thoughts would often drift back to the precociously beautiful teenager. He revealed his feelings about her to Dee once during a stay at

76   Graceland. Elvis had just received a snapshot from her that he wanted to show Dee.

"Check this out, Dee," he said, smiling as he pulled it out of the envelope.

"My, she is beautiful, isn't she?" Dee said, admiring it with him.

"You know, Dee, I've been to bed with no less than a thousand women in my life," he said candidly, enjoying her shocked expression. "This is the one, right here."

Almost as soon as Elvis had returned from Europe, he had invited Priscilla to spend Christmas at Graceland, and her parents had consented. Vernon and Dee had gone to pick her up in New York, and it was obvious from Elvis's excited anticipation before they left and from Priscilla's warmth at the airport how much they had missed each other. She didn't seem at all flustered or perturbed about having to meet all of Elvis's friends or by any publicity she might receive from the visit. All in all she stayed for two weeks, and Elvis took her to the movies and the amusement park and had several get-togethers at Graceland while she was there. "Everyone was impressed by her," Dee remembers. "She was a darling girl and quite a young lady. It was obvious to all of Elvis's friends and relatives how well brought up she was. She didn't drink or smoke, which Elvis liked, and she had a very easy way about her. She also never made a big fuss about Elvis being a star, which he loved."

After her departure Elvis decided that he wanted Priscilla to become a permanent resident at Graceland and called her father to discuss the matter. It was an unusual request coming from the movie star–sex symbol, and Elvis pulled out all of the stops to get his way, promising to one day marry Priscilla, to take care of her and put her through school while she stayed in Memphis. Colonel Beaulieu relented only after Vernon and Dee consented to become, in effect, her guardians. She was to live in their home during her stay.

When Priscilla arrived with her bags, accompanied by her stepfather, she was enrolled at Immaculate Conception High School in Memphis and moved in with Vernon and Dee on

Dolan Street. Whatever shyness she may have felt at first 77
quickly passed, and to the small community of people that lived
or worked at Graceland, her presence was like a spring breeze.
"Priscilla made friends quickly and easily," says Dee. "She did
the things that most normal teenagers do, except when Elvis
was home, when she would do the things that he would like to
do—parties, movies, riding. But she wasn't in any way a normal
teenager because it was always assumed that one day she and
Elvis would get married."

But even if Priscilla was, in Elvis's mind, the girl that he
would one day come home to, her presence at Graceland did
not noticeably alter his Hollywood life-style. According to Dee,
"Elvis would always come home after a film was finished, or we
would go out to Los Angeles, so they would hardly miss a
month without seeing each other. She would wait for his phone
calls every day, and Elvis would very often call, but if he didn't,
I could tell how let down she was the next day. At that time
Elvis was filming *Viva Las Vegas* with Ann-Margret, and I
believe that she's the only one of Elvis's leading ladies that Priscilla ever worried about. After all, Ann-Margret was a beautiful
and very sexy woman, and Priscilla was still in high school at
the time!"

In a way Elvis was clearly testing Priscilla to see if she could
stand up to the kind of pressure that she would one day encounter as Mrs. Elvis Presley. "That was the deciding factor,"
Dee says. "She had to come to Graceland and see how we lived
and what he really expected. She proved that she could stay
there with the family—stand the test, so to speak—and she did
that real well. Everyone really got to love Cilla, which was the
clincher. She was everything he wanted."

So, while Priscilla attended high school, Elvis showered her
with gifts and remained very protective of her when he was
home. While she waited for him, she kept herself busy with a
great many projects, modeled, studied dance and drama,
sketched and palled around with Elvis's cousin Patsy Presley
Gambil. Her relationship with Dee was warm but more sisterly
than anything else, and she became close with Billy, Rick, and

78 David. The sight of her sashaying about the mansion or the grounds dressed in pants and her ballet slippers was sure to bring a smile to everybody's face.

To Colonel Beaulieu and the public, Vernon and Dee may have been portrayed as Priscilla's erstwhile chaperones during her stay in Memphis, but the truth of the matter was that they didn't do much actual chaperoning at all. For all intents and purposes, she was quite on her own, and she moved into the Graceland mansion about two months after her arrival. Though the outside world might have been shocked to find out that Elvis was "keeping" a high-school girl in his house, Vernon and Dee accepted it matter-of-factly. "Cilla was a mature young woman," Dee points out. "She knew what she was doing. She'd be in the room with Elvis or anywhere they wanted to be. I didn't watch her. Nobody did. That's one thing you *never* did to Elvis. You just never tried to keep tabs on him."

While Priscilla had her own life and interests at Graceland while Elvis was away filming (no boyfriends, of course), it was evident to his friends and relatives that she was being "groomed" to be his wife and she never lost sight of that during the years of their courtship. True, she may have worn her hair and dressed the way Elvis liked her to and refrained from eating tuna fish around him (Elvis's aversion to seafood of any kind was well known), but even though her love for Elvis was beyond question, to all who knew her it was obvious that Priscilla was not the kind of girl to be "molded" into anything that she did not want to become. She intended to become a good wife to Elvis in a traditional sense, but she still had a very strong sense of herself and what she was all about. She was a strong-willed woman who never hesitated to stand up for the things she believed in ("That's another thing that Elvis loved about her," notes Dee. "He admired anyone that stood behind their beliefs."), and her interests—art, modeling, dance, riding, fashion, and design—bespoke a multitalented woman who could have been successful in any number of careers had she never met Elvis Presley. She was also the type of person who needed to justify her actions with her inner feelings and beliefs.

In the miniworld of Graceland, it was sometimes more important to be respected than to be liked. Priscilla was both, which made her a sure shot as Elvis's wife. She had the perfect blend of qualities that Elvis sought in a woman: She was, in some ways, very hip to the ways of the world; in others, as fresh and untainted as a virgin snowfall.

From the time of her arrival it took Elvis about six years to get around to popping the question—by that time she had spent approximately one third of her life around him. Nobody that knew or worked for Elvis knew exactly when he would propose, but Dee, who was perhaps more excited than they were, remembers the night very well. It was Christmas of 1966: "They called me upstairs, and I had no idea of what was going on. They were sitting side by side on the couch and Elvis was holding her hand. She was wearing the ring. I was so happy I kept saying, 'Oh my goodness! Is this what I think it is?' And they were laughing. Of course, they were married in the spring, and I had to wait all that time and not tell anybody!

"Priscilla started making arrangements for her gown soon after, and when the day arrived, we all flew out to Palm Springs to stay a couple of days. The press was everywhere, and we had to sneak out to the airport to fly to Vegas for the wedding."

The crafty Colonel handled all of the arrangements and orchestrated the press masterfully throughout. The wedding itself, which took place on the morning of May 1, 1967, was very private and intimate. There were only fourteen people in attendance, and some of Elvis's companions had been conspicuously not informed of what was going on. Joe Esposito and Marty Lacker were co-best men, and Richard Davis, Charlie Hodge, George Klein, and Jerry Schilling, all old friends and associates, were also there. The wedding, held at the Aladdin Hotel, was followed by a lavish bash to which the press had been invited. After a press conference Elvis and Priscilla flew to Palm Springs for a honeymoon. "Elvis was decidedly 'fidgety' that day, but overjoyed," Dee recollects. "Priscilla was just radiant in her white organdy dress. Nobody could take their eyes off of her."

As news of Elvis's marriage spread, letters from his fans began to pour into Graceland. They ranged from hearty congratulations and best wishes to weepy, tearful professions of undying

80   love and a few suicide threats. When Elvis and Priscilla returned to Graceland, they threw a party to invite everyone that had to be excluded·from the wedding party, and most of the wounded feelings were assuaged.

Many of Elvis's followers as well as people within the film and recording industries wondered whether Elvis's marriage would help or hinder his career and how it would affect his image as the slick but wholesome sex symbol. Nothing was changed by it. The news that Priscilla was expecting likewise only added to the public's impression that Elvis had indeed grown up: Not only was he married, but he would soon be a daddy.

During Priscilla's pregnancy, life remained unchanged at Graceland except that Elvis tried to get home as much as he could. Everyone waited anxiously for the birth of the child. Though people behaved as though the czar and czarina were expecting, Priscilla herself remained very much active during her pregnancy, hating to be confined. Dee remembers a winter night right before the birth when it snowed in Memphis. Priscilla and Elvis were out building a snowman with Billy, Ricky, and David, and a fire was roaring in the yard. When her boys came home, Dee asked them if they had had fun. "Oh," they said. "Cilla fell." Dee gasped in horror, afraid that she might have hurt herself or injured the baby. "Gee, Mom," they said. "It was OK. We just all picked her up!"

Elvis stayed around Graceland the entire last month of the pregnancy, and on the morning of February 1, 1968, exactly nine months to the day from their marriage, Priscilla was taken to Baptist Memorial Hospital by Elvis and Charlie Hodge, followed in another car by Jerry Schilling and Joe Esposito. Reporters began swarming outside the hospital once they got wind of Priscilla's admission. Inside, Elvis's friends and relatives began to gather. At 5:01 that afternoon Dr. T.A. Turman informed Elvis that he was the father of a six-pound, fifteen-ounce baby girl. Dee remembers walking down to the maternity ward with Vernon and Elvis for their very first look at Lisa Marie Presley. The three of them stood there for a moment, the two men dazed, as Dee began rapping on the glass and cooing, "Well, hello there, little girl. . . . That is your daddy!"

"She just picked up her head a little and looked at us with those blue eyes," says Dee, "and Elvis's face lit up like a beacon. I've never seen him look like that in all the time I've known him."

Then they went to see Priscilla. "Cilla was still groggy from the anesthetic," Dee remembers. "She couldn't believe she really had a baby girl—it wasn't sinking in. Once she began to grasp it, she just sighed and looked so peaceful."

While Elvis sent the boys out for cigars, Dee and Vernon made their way downstairs to announce the birth to the waiting members of the press. The reporters began firing questions at Vernon, never a man at ease in such situations. "Tell us, Mr. Presley, how does it feel to be a grandfather?" "Well, uh . . ." he stumbled, "this is all so new to us, you know."

Four days later Lisa Marie was in her new home. Calls, telegrams, gifts, and candy arrived from around the world. Elvis was soon off again to film *Live a Little, Love a Little*, one of his all-time worst films. Back at Graceland, Priscilla fell into the routine of caring for her child. Lisa had her father's slightly spread nose and pouting lips as well as the blond hair of his youth, but in temperament there would be the unmistakable influence of her mother. "She was a frisky baby," says Dee. "She was just like her mother in many ways. Her mother really knew how to take care of her and not spoil her, like Elvis did. She was headstrong, too—strong willed just like Cilla. Now Graceland was filled with strong-willed women—Mother Presley, me, Cilla, and Lisa."

Lisa grew to be a healthy child with a finicky appetite and an irrepressible fondness for cats. She adored rides in the golf cart with her daddy and visits to Vernon and Dee's, where she loved to play with her three uncles, Billy, Ricky, and David, then growing into young men.

CHAPTER 5

THE BROTHERS STANLEY

Let me tell you about my brother
A brother like no other
His father married my mother
But he's more than a brother to me

Wherever I go
The people keep asking me
What it's like to be the brother
Of a celebrity. . . .

Two stanzas from a song
by Billy Stanley

Billy, Rick, and David Stanley had a natural father in Bill
Stanley, a stepfather in Vernon Presley, but a surrogate father
and big brother in Elvis Presley. Boys growing up always need a
male role-model to admire, love, and emulate. Even with the
hodgepodge of different masculine influences upon their lives,
Elvis, in essence, was always that shaping force.

84   Rick Stanley's face breaks into a broad, infectious grin whenever he recalls signing the first autograph in his life. "I was in
the first grade," he laughs, "when Dee and Vernon would come
to pick us up. All the girls in the school would come around to
ask for their autographs and one day I started gettin' a little
cocky, so I asked these 'big' seventh-grade girls if they wanted
mine, too—you know, *Elvis's little brother*. They all looked at
me and said 'Sure!' so I got me out this crayon, and . . ."

It was, for all of the Stanley boys, fun, strange, exhilarating,
and sometimes frightening to suddenly find themselves thrust
into Elvis Presley's golden aura, even if they were still too young
to grasp it all. "As the years went by, it became more evident to
us what a heavyweight Elvis really was," Rick says. "To us he
was always just a guy that we loved, but people would freak out
over him everywhere he went; over *us*, too! It took us a while to
realize his power and magnitude."

The newfangled notoriety that the Stanleys experienced as
stepbrothers to "the King of Rock 'n' Roll" could never be all
fun and games. "When it came right down to understanding
what was going on," David says soberly, "it could get serious
very quickly. Hell, man, people were watching us!"

Nobody was more concerned about the effects of Elvis's extraordinary wealth and fame on her boys than Dee Presley. If
the loss of her own mother at such a young age made her ul-
traprotective with her own children, her lingering guilt about
her divorce from Bill Stanley caused her to watch her sons with
a sharp eye for any "personality disorders" that might have en-
sued. "My boys hardly ever showed emotion," says Dee, "because if they fought or were upset I would want to rush them off
to a child psychologist. If anybody said something like 'I hate
you' I would start thinking, 'Oh, my God—my son's going to
grow up with a warped personality.' I just didn't know what the
boys were all about."

In the years that followed she carefully ushered her boys into
a rational, ordered world of services and Sunday school at the
Whitehaven Church of Christ, summer camps, swimming
pools, and a group of screened friends. Wanting so desperately
for her boys to lead conventional lives in the face of such un-

conventional circumstances, she became the classic example of   85
the overbearing mother. In pursuit of normalcy Dee's apron
strings stretched far and wide. "It was a pretty strict life," remembers Billy. "We had a lot of limitations placed on us because Mom knew what was going to happen to us. We just
couldn't understand why we had to be so sheltered."

As the disciplinarian of the family, Vernon was Dee's
sergeant-at-arms, meting out the punishments when they got
out of line. Elvis was always amused to see his father in that
role once again. He would stand by and roar with laughter as
David rubbed his rear after a paddling and cried, "Damn that
Daddy!"

Vernon let Dee set policy for her sons, and he abided by her
gospel, but he was very careful to instill in the boys an acute
awareness of their situation as Elvis's stepbrothers. Lesson one:
Never, under any circumstances, reveal anything about Elvis to
the public or the press. This was the Golden Rule, and the boys
grew up extremely close mouthed, security minded, and press
conscious in everything they said or did outside Graceland. "If
we ever got into trouble," Billy recalls, "it wasn't just Billy
Stanley, but 'Billy Stanley, Elvis's brother,' and it was made
into a big deal. Vernon pushed us to be extra careful, which
was kind of hard for a kid growing up. There were certain things
that kids just like to get out and do that we never felt comfortable doing."

Elvis loved being able to offer the boys the role-model upon
which to found their identities, and the boys looked forward to
his returns to Graceland. For one thing, Elvis Presley was always, first and foremost, in the minds of his stepbrothers, a *gas*.
Now *there's* a guy who knows how to have some fun! they
would think whenever they saw him get wild.

Naturally, because of the age difference between them, there
were times when Elvis simply didn't want the boys around—
usually when something was going on up at the house—and the
boys learned how to be aware of these moments, staying well
away and respecting his privacy even though they longed to be
up there. Then, suddenly, without warning, he would show up
at their house, ready and rarin' to go, even if he had to wake

86   them up (which was sometimes the case, considering Elvis's nocturnal existence). Vernon, who knew his son's unfetterable enthusiasms as well as his wife's dire apprehensions, would protest, but to no avail.

"Ah, come on, Daddy," Elvis would cajole, smiling mischievously at the boys as they scrambled out the door to him. "I'll take good care of 'em!"

The boys always knew that adventure awaited whenever Elvis called. He played with his brothers the same way he did anything else in his life—all out, passionately, to the maximum, until he was tired and didn't want any more. He rode motorcycles, played music, shot pool, spent money, and dated women the same way, and his brothers came to understand this simple fact very early in life: Elvis *was* Elvis, and he was going to do what he wanted. When they were all together, he ran his brothers ragged, and they loved every minute of it.

Their times together included a flurry of activities. There were midnight rides in his fleet of cars around Memphis or out into the countryside and all-night horse rides under the beaming Graceland floodlights and long forays into Libertyland, the Memphis fairground; there were all-night movies when Elvis rented out the movie theater from Paul Shafer, a family friend who worked for the Malco chain of moviehouses, and sledding when it snowed, and go-cart races, and ripping around Elvis's pasture on motorcycles at breakneck speeds. When they got a little bigger, they were included in Elvis's football games— serious affairs in which they were always the smallest but expected to play like the Green Bay Packers, and Elvis starred as a speedy, sure-handed flanker. "David and I would always line up against Elvis," Ricky remembers, "and, man, he would knock the hell out of us!"

As both big brother and father figure in their lives, Elvis was in a unique position to offer the boys advice when they needed it, which he enjoyed doing. When he did it, however, he tried never to seem dogmatic or authoritarian. "He would never give you advice unless you went to him first," Billy says, "because then he knew that you really wanted to listen to what he was going to say. He wouldn't tell you what you *ought* to do either

but just give you his opinion and make sure that he explained
why he thought it was right. Then he would leave it completely
up to you to take it or leave it. Usually he was right on."

In the matter of self-defense, which any lad needs to reckon
with when growing up, Elvis came in handy. Jealous kids and
school bullies would stick to the Stanley boys like flypaper.
"Yeah, we took a lot of shit from kids in the school," Billy
remembers. "You know, from the type of kids who would say,
'Here comes Elvis's little brother—let's whip his ass!' "

Elvis was no stranger to that kind of harassment himself, particularly during his high-school years and the years of his early
successes. He taught the boys never to back down from such
confrontations, and how to be tough; in short, when it was right
and when it was wrong to kick somebody's ass.

On the whole the boys were grateful recipients of the Complete Elvis Presley Method of How to Be Cool, which included
ways, means, nuances, and subtleties of Cool as Elvis understood it and applied it to walking, talking, behaving socially,
wooing chicks, and just about anything else one could think of.
The boys drank it all in thirstily.

Elvis also took particular pleasure in exposing his brothers to
a rich, vast world of gospel, country and western, rock, swing,
folk, and opera. "That's all you ever saw around his house,"
relates Billy, "music everywhere—in the basement, the music
room, his bedroom upstairs. Every imaginable kind of album
and instrument all over the place." One morning the boys
woke to find, set up in their basement, all of the necessary
ingredients for a rock 'n' roll band—drums, bass, and guitar.
Billy began learning bass, Rick the drums, and David drums
and guitar. Steeped as they were in Elvis's music and with the
means now at their disposal, the music in their world became
part of the integral bond between them all and a language they
learned to speak fluently.

It was no small wonder that the boys idolized Elvis and
sought to imitate him: Each facet of his life that he shared with
his brothers only enriched their lives and endeared him to
them. As the boys grew older, Elvis began to recognize how
very different they were from each other and tried to cultivate

88   what he saw as each boy's individual qualities. As a result each brother shared a different relationship with him.

Billy was the oldest, and because he was very sensitive to his mother's divorce and remarriage (he remembers the most), he remained the closest to his mother and the most dependent on her for emotional sustenance. In Dee's eyes he was always the most obedient, trusting, and the easiest to manage, and he grew up quietly withdrawn, gentle, good natured, compassionate, and shy. Yet, at the same time, there was a quiet intensity about Billy—an intentness of concentration and activity, a wildness that lurked beneath the surface of his cool. He was always careful to control himself in all situations.

Within the familial scheme of things, it was always incumbent upon Bill to seem the most grown up of his brothers, and his deep love for his mother kept him closely in tune with her values and beliefs. One by one Dee Presley had her sons enrolled in Harding Academy in East Memphis, a private school under the auspices of the Church of Christ, where teachers, coaches, and virtually everyone else is religious, and where the three R's are combined with Bible classes and Christian theology. The school was academically demanding, and Billy wasn't interested enough to maintain the requisite "B" average. He then transferred to Hillcrest High, in Whitehaven, where he encountered his first cigarettes, liquor, and loose girls. Around Elvis, Billy was more likely than his brothers to lie back, wanting to be sure that his big brother really wanted him around, that he was not imposing in any way, for he is considerate. When they were all together, racing, karate, and music usually formed the basis of their relationship and the topics of discussion.

David Stanley, the youngest, resembled his father in looks and also in temperament. Every family, class, or group of boys needs one "problem child," one maverick or black sheep; that particular individual who turns left just for the hell of it when everybody in the squad is supposed to turn right. Well, that was David. In his mother's words, "David is big, always was big, and because he is large like his father, people always want to try him. It's all they need to do, because he is very short tempered.

He's a gentle person, but he can become angry and violent at
times. You have to know that David's there, because he's going
to let you know about it one way or another."

David was the lover-fighter. He was cocky, swaggering, wise-
cracking, handsome, self-confident, emotional, and rowdy. He
ran away from school after he ran into a nasty teacher who
once roughed him up; then he slapped a few teachers himself,
which made him the perfect candidate for military school. Dee
and Vernon tried Castle Heights Military Academy in Nashville, but it didn't work. "David didn't like to submit to authority," observes his brother Rick. "He just didn't like it." Elvis
would learn to use that trait in David, to cultivate it and make
David proud of it.

To David, his aggression and wildness was less a product of
juvenile delinquency or psychological disorders and more a
product of the rugged individualism he picked up from Elvis.
Elvis loved David's energy, his humor, his compulsive ambition, and his willingness to be different and take chances. He
encouraged these qualities in David, as well as instilling in him
a deep curiosity to experience life and all of its variegated thrills
and spills. "Mom didn't have that much influence on me at
all," he says. "She just had no persuasion. Elvis had complete
control."

Rick Stanley was altogether a different story. With ash-blond
hair (his mother's), wiry, angular features, and the long-
muscled, toned build of a runner-swimmer which falls right in
between David's brawniness and Billy's scrappiness, his looks
are as sharply different from his brothers' as are his personality
and outlook. If you saw him on the beach, bronzed by the sun,
he would seem the absolute epitome of the California surfer,
but his drawl and slow shuffle gave him away for the true child
of the South that he is. His father's Cherokee blood was perhaps
responsible for his prominent, almost Roman nose and the high
cheekbones.

As the middle child, Rick was in certain ways the best ad-
justed of his brothers, and in other ways the most unusual. It
was his peculiar lot to be the scholar of the family, for one
thing, always receiving the highest grades and the academic

90 honors. Dee Presley recognized these qualities in Rick. Whether he liked it or not, she had determined that it would be Rick who would, in the end, be the one to live up to her lofty expectations. She rode him and drove him harder toward those goals than she did either of her other sons. "I was always harder and stricter with Ricky because I knew that he was the one who could do it all," Dee says. But just as Rick could be studious and conscientious, he also had that hellraising streak in him.

Like Elvis and his two brothers, the boy liked to have fun, and woe betide him if he ever made a bad grade or got into trouble. When he did, it was the firm, unflinching hand of Vernon Presley that let him know about it. In fact, Rick even got in trouble when his brothers messed up, becoming a sort of family whipping boy. "Mom always leaned toward Billy and David but Elvis leaned toward me," he says. "I got the butt end of everything and caught the flak. Finally, when I got older, Mom admitted it and so did Vernon. But I had Elvis there, and that made up for it all."

Elvis singled Ricky out as his favorite. It's a sensitive topic among the boys and something that they don't talk about because they don't think it really matters, but Billy puts it aptly and honestly: "Elvis kind of sensed that Ricky was different, that he was kind of a wild one, and he took care of Ricky. Everywhere Elvis went, Ricky was there, and they were close—very close."

There were things about Rick that reminded Elvis of himself when he was younger, but his interest in Rick went deeper than that. Had he been able, Rick was exactly the kind of kid that Elvis would have chosen to be in high school—state decathlon champion, class president, "A" student, successful with pretty, popular girls, and not stuck up about it. Elvis loved the idea of taking Rick under his wing because they had a lot to offer each other.

"Elvis was really like a teacher to me," Rick says, "and we talked about everything. I just sat and listened and observed, and he would just tell me things that would better me in some way. I'd put it into effect automatically because I had that much trust in him—he wouldn't tell me anything wrong. Elvis taught me how to handle just about any situation that might arise with people. After all of his experiences, there was nobody more hip to people than he was. We'd cover financial things, spiritual things, emotional things, everything. Elvis was the one who made me understand that if you're a man and something touches you, there's nothing wrong or nothing to be ashamed of if you show your emotions and cry. Things like that really changed my life."

As long as it didn't interfere with her control over the direction of her son's life, Dee wholeheartedly supported Elvis's relationship with Rick. Elvis may have become Rick's mentor, but his mother still remained a powerful influence in his life. As Rick puts it, "Those two people were the most influential in my life. Elvis was a strong man. He spoke what he meant, and my mom was the same way, so the two of them would clash, but there was a lot of respect between them. Elvis wouldn't push Mom. If you pushed Mom too far, she'd let you have it. Elvis knew that, and he admired Mom for bringing us up in a Christian family. Besides his own wife, I've never seen Elvis treat a woman with as much respect as my mother."

So, while Rick's relationship with Elvis gave him the latitude he needed to consolidate his identity outside of Dee Presley's ken, Elvis never tried consciously to undermine her control. For the most part all of the legends about Elvis's great love for motherhood were true. "Always stick to your mom is what Elvis told me," Rick remembers, "because when your mother goes, your world is gone. Even if you committed a murder, he said, that's the one person who will stand there and say, 'No, my baby's innocent.' "

Certain incidents in the boys' lives were kept from Dee; Vernon handled them. Once Rick and his girl friend were surprised by a couple of overzealous cops while they were parked along a street in Whitehaven. It wouldn't have been all that bad if only they had their clothes on, but unfortunately they didn't.

The police ordered them out of the car, stark naked, and behaved as if they had just captured the two most notorious desperados in the annals of modern crime. God Almighty, thought Rick in back of the police car, envisioning headlines in the

92 Memphis *Commercial Appeal* like **PRESLEY'S LITTLE BROTHER NETTED IN SEX SCANDAL—FAMILY DISGRACED.** Man, it's all over. . . . How am I ever going to face Mom, Elvis, and Vernon? Russian roulette seemed the best way out. Rick resolved to leave home, hoping that the cloud of shame would go with him.

The squad car pulled up in front of the house on Dolan, and the party of Rick, his girl friend, and the officer approached the door. Vernon had already peered out the window, noticed the police car, and told his wife to wait upstairs. Rick waited, his heart skipping and pounding, as the policeman explained the crime.

"What's the matter, buddy!" Vernon suddenly exploded into the officer's face. "Didn't *you* ever do it with a girl in a car when you were a kid? Damn! Is this something you have to bring him home for and humiliate him and embarrass the girl?"

Aghast, the police officer fumbled for his words.

"Hell," Vernon added, disgusted with him, "or is it that you've never had a shot yourself, and you're just mad?"

"Daddy was all for his boys," Rick says, recollecting that evening. "He really wanted us to know what life was like and not to be sheltered. He knew that if you live in a bubble, you'll get your feelings hurt every time that somebody says something to you. He wanted us to know what was going on and learn how to roll with the punches. I think he did a good job bringing us up. He was a down-home guy, and he had a way of breaking everything down to where you could understand it easily."

Vernon Presley may have periodically intervened on behalf of the boys, but Dee Presley would remain the vigilant custodian of her sons' lives until, quite simply, she would lose all control to Elvis Presley.

It was the stunning power of Elvis's return to live performances in 1969 that unglued and rearranged the fabric of their lives, sweeping everyone before it like an awesome tidal wave.

CHAPTER 6

CUTTIN' LOOSE

The year nineteen hundred and sixty-nine was a frenetic period in everyone's life when past patterns were broken and new ones established. Elvis Presley cut loose from the professional patterns of his Hollywood years, and his brothers, one by one, began cutting their mother's apron strings to go off on the road with him.

The years in Hollywood may have made Elvis wealthy, but the stultifying commercial formula of his low-budget movies had also hurt him by removing from his life the single most important element in the growth and productivity of any true artist—a sense of challenge. Risk, challenge, and the possibility of loss were always the best motivations to change in Elvis's life. When the profits from his last films dipped, it became clearer than ever that change was in order.

Sure, there was still a vast army of dedicated fans who would pay to see their boy on the silver screen and pick up his latest album, but Elvis hadn't been in front of a live audience since a raucous benefit performance he'd done for the Memorial Fund

94 of the U.S.S. *Arizona* in March of 1961. Since then he had
ensconced himself in Hollywood, Palm Springs, and Memphis,
while all around him the climate of the times had changed
profoundly. Suddenly, the Hollywood Elvis seemed obsolete,
eclipsed by the advent of a youth culture that Elvis had helped
to spawn, and its high prophets who had grown up influenced
by him—Bob Dylan, the Beatles, and the Rolling Stones. The
war in Vietnam was raging, student protests rising, racial ten-
sions peaking, and America seemed to be slipping into a dark
period of street violence and assassinations. It was a time of
commitment, polarizing passions, and dynamic change. Elvis
felt cut off and removed from what was going on, as if suddenly
discovering that he was painted into a corner. He had only to
turn on the radio, check out his brother's long hair, or drive
down Sunset Boulevard and observe the psychedelic garb of the
freaks to feel it. It was time to step out.

Elvis couldn't just announce a tour or series of live engagements. The Colonel wanted him to build slowly to a commercial crescendo and then, as he would put it, "take it to the
max," and decided on a carefully orchestrated plan that could
provide him sudden and striking visibility and get people thinking about him again.

Elvis's television Christmas special of 1968 proved to be exactly what he needed. More than anything else the show gave
people a chance to see that he was trying out new styles and directions as well as getting right back to his musical roots. With
the help of Steve Binder, a young and talented director, Elvis's
willingness to experiment turned the program into an incredible
coup, plunging him into a period of remarkable determination,
nervousness, and restless energy that pushed him hard to once
again establish himself on top of the rock pile.

The live videotaping was done on June twenty-seventh to be
aired on December third. Bleachers had been constructed in the
sound stage around a small square stage upon which Elvis was
to perform. The Colonel fringed the rim of the stage with pretty
girls, and some of Elvis's closest buddies like Charlie and Lamar
were on hand to play off of Elvis's stage banter.

But the people were real this time and not the professional

groovers hired as extras to stand in the singing and dancing scenes of his films. If Elvis had that to be nervous about, he also knew that everybody would be watching when the show aired—friends, family, fans, critics of one kind or another. As he always did during his most crucial moments before live audiences, he came out edgy and uncertain and shot everything he had into the experience. It was a gamble and the stakes were high, but this only heightened the tension and the emotional satisfaction of the triumph. Elvis couldn't help but show his nerves—his hand shook when he reached for the microphone—but the display only brought him across as more accessible—not some celluloid strip of a remote Hollywood fantasy.

Dressed in black leather, Elvis appeared sinister, sensual, like a rock 'n' roll hoodlum or a dark, avenging angel, moving across the stage catlike in perfect syncopation. Binder taped over four hours of his greatest hits and when it was over, Elvis was so exhausted that he had to be helped from the stage. The segment was edited down to a fifteen-minute opening for the show, and the effect was like a right cross to the jaw: There was a raw lust to make good in Elvis's performance that seized the nationwide audience. Everywhere critics began writing of his "rebirth" and "resurrection."

Back at Graceland everybody huddled around a television set on the night of December third, aware that the night would be one of the most important in Elvis's life. "Man, it was the most incredible thing to just see him suddenly there looking into the camera with that sly look and say, 'If you're looking for trouble, you've come to the right place,' " remembers Rick. "Everybody laughed when he said that, and then he whipped into his songs, and it seemed we were right back there with him; we were movin', man. When the show was over, everybody just looked at each other and knew it was going to happen exactly as Elvis wanted. Daddy just smiled and slapped his knee and shouted, 'Mah boy!' "

In the months that followed, Elvis was infused with a sense of renewal and Graceland was ablaze with activity. He recorded an album in Memphis for the first time since his famous Sun recordings fourteen years earlier. The results, the album *From*

96 *Elvis in Memphis,* contained some of his most vital, substantive music in years. He then released "If I Can Dream," which Earl Brown had written for the television special, and Mac Davis's classic, "In the Ghetto." The songs were a departure from anything in his repertoire and topical in the context of the times, the first a plea for brotherhood and harmony in a time of chaos and the second a moving ballad of black urban despair. "In the Ghetto" was his first successful single in years.

With the completion of *Change of Habit,* Elvis's thirty-first film, his contractual obligations for films were filled and the road to Las Vegas cleared. By that time live concerts had become the pot of gold for entertainers, largely supported by a whole new generation of long-haired, dope-smoking, music-loving kids.

Colonel Tom Parker may have been a born conservative when it came to sticking with the most effective commercial strategy for Elvis's career until the bitter end (i.e., until it was no longer hugely profitable), but the man was also a born gambler. His deep roots in the traveling carnival and country-and-western music enabled him to quickly gander the successes of a whole new breed of promoter—men like Bill Graham, for instance—to best figure out how he and Elvis could most easily get at the big booty of live performances.

Elvis's staunchest fans were, like Elvis, now in their thirties and above, and the dynamic interest in rock 'n' roll nostalgia and the root years of the music played right into the Colonel's hands. Chuck Berry, Dion, and Jerry Lee Lewis were all making comebacks, and the Colonel only needed to package Elvis as "instant nostalgia" to the vast majority of his fans. He needed a place where he could get maximum money for his act at the best possible terms and quickly, where he would also reach the broadest cross section of people, and he naturally chose Las Vegas.

For Elvis and everybody around him, it was certainly to be a moment of truth, but there was never a question of Elvis disappearing should he fail, never a question of his becoming washed up, a has-been, a flash-in-the-pan; Elvis or the people around him just never thought in those terms. The real question—the big "if' in everybody's mind—was whether or not he could reemerge brilliantly as the recognized, uncontested "King."

"There was doubt in his mind about getting out there night after night and doing it again," says Rick, who began spending more and more time with Elvis during that period. "Sure, he was nervous, but he always disguised it well to everybody around him. He was always questioning himself. In his heart, he knew he had it, but after laying off for so long, he was jumpy."

Elvis prepared for his Vegas opening like a man obsessed. The people around him marveled at his discipline and determination. Every resource that he had at his disposal, every spare bit of energy, and all of the emotions of his friends and family were concentrated on that first moment when he would walk out to the lights and let fly. First, he dropped close to fifteen pounds to make sure he would be as lithe and sexy as ever. "He went on a real strict diet," Rick remembers, "which was tough for Elvis considering how much he loved to eat. Green vegetable, no fatty foods or starch, a hamburger or a steak, and that was it."

He then began assembling a solid and very versatile rock 'n' roll band and rehearsing some one hundred songs, many from other composers that he admired and had never had a chance to do, others from his own past. A stage wardrobe was designed that included karate *gis* and tight-fitting, gold-inlaid jumpsuits—stone studded and slashed down to his navel.

When everything was set, Elvis, Priscilla, Vernon, Dee, and the boys took off for Hawaii. Elvis needed a breather before final rehearsals, but he also wanted to get a rich tan for his opening. His mind, as the boys remember, kept drifting toward his rendezvous with the stage as they lay on the beach or around the pool; he seemed distant, glad to be away from it temporarily. "You knew he had a lot on his mind," Billy says, "and everybody tried to talk about other things." Elvis left early to get back for rehearsals, and the family followed, flying in the night before the opening. At the same time, Colonel Parker was air-lifting in journalists and music critics so that they would all be there when the curtain went up.

98   Landing in Las Vegas for the very first time, the Stanley boys understood why it was the perfect environment for Elvis Presley's Great Gamble. The life of this city, smack dab in the Nevada desert, in a timeless atmosphere of sunshine, neon, golden promises, and busted dreams, revolved around tables of chance, women of ill repute, and show business. The hotels on the strip rose into the cloudless summer skies like phallic monuments to a life they would come to know intimately with their stepbrother. "Vegas" was a uniquely American shrine to the frontier values of hellbent free choice and unlimited resources, a place where Elvis Presley would feel at home in the years to come. Everywhere chicks in bikinis and sunglasses cruised, slot machines sang, people laughed, lounged, and drank, money talked, and things seemed to come only in bunches. Around the brand new International, the only major hotel located off the strip, there hovered an aura of electric anticipation. The boys walked around stupefied, immersing themselves in the sights and sounds as press, celebrities, and fans gathered from around the world and women passed them naughty notes that read, to their mother's heartfelt consternation, "Psst . . . if you introduce me to your brother, I'll . . ."

Inside the Showroom, Elvis drove his team of people like a charioteer, running through three dress rehearsals with his new band, his vocal back-up groups, and the hotel's full-piece orchestra. He knew that his audiences would be as diverse as America itself; in Vegas, he could play to the fantasies of girdled ladies from Hoboken, to mod groovers from New York and Los Angeles, to braless, beaded teenybopper girls and toupéed businessmen in polyester leisure suits, to highrollers, lowrollers—to the vast milieu from which he would once again spring forth, full grown, larger than ever.

The Showroom filled early on the night of July 31, 1969. Vernon, Dee, Priscilla, and the boys had their booths up front, off to the side, where they could see everything close and not be caught in the crunch should people rush the stage. Goldengaudy, plush, and plasticized in the style that Las Vegas is famous for, the Showroom sat some two thousand people comfortably, but twenty-five hundred people had been packed in for the opening. Crystal chandeliers hung from the ceilings and Cupid figures adorned the sides and ceilings. Elvis would call them "funky angels" that night.

He waited backstage, knowing that everything was set, drumming nervously, surrounded by his friends, as his entire world focused and intersected emotionally with the task at hand. The lights dimmed and everybody squirmed through sets by the Sweet Inspirations and a comedian until it was time. Then the band broke into an up-tempo, cook-em-up rhythm, the gold lamé curtain rose, and there was Elvis, dressed in a black karate *gi*, strolling to the mike at centerstage where he stopped, smiled uncertainly for a moment, hit his classic pose, and looked as if he was ready to swallow everybody in one gulp. Suspended, for a moment, in time, the audience, standing on chairs and cheering wildly, wouldn't even let him sing. The place was exploding. The power seemed to seize and shake the chandeliers. Then Elvis sang "Blue Suede Shoes," moving hard, snapping the song out at the audience like the perfectly aimed stroke of a bullwhip. When it was over, bedlam prevailed.

In their booth the boys looked at each other incredulously. "Holy *shit!* Did you see that? He kicked *ass! Golleeeee!"*

For the three stepbrothers, it was a moment that changed their lives. They were seeing a new side of their brother—one that they had never really understood. Song after song filled them with his power, and they sat there mesmerized. "It was like seeing a different person," David says. "Elvis was just a guy we loved, our brother, someone we always just hung with and had a lot of fun with. His music was great, sure, and some of his movies were okay, but suddenly it was like 'That's Elvis Presley! *That's* why all these people go nuts over him!' " "That's when we all became fans," agrees Rick, "when we saw the man onstage. That was it. We were hooked."

Backstage after the show the scene was unforgettable. Relatives, friends, members of the band, and other celebrities rushed in, milled about, stunned, buzzing and vibrating with the performance. Dripping wet, spent but euphoric, Elvis was receiving their congratulations when the old Colonel rushed in. Rick remembers the scene well. Never a man given to such public

100 displays of emotions, Tom Parker threw his arms around Elvis and lifted him clear off the ground. The gamble had paid off once again. "Colonel," Elvis said, grinning slyly, "I've been wrong for so long but I was right tonight!"

On the whole, nineteen sixty-nine was a landmark summer, one that remains vividly etched in the American mind. Men walked on the moon for the first time. Half a million young souls gathered on Max Yasgur's farm in upstate New York for three days of peace, love, and music, an event dubbed "Woodstock." In Los Angeles, Charles Manson orchestrated a series of bizarre, bloodcurdling murders. And back in Memphis, Tennessee, Elvis Presley once again had the world at his feet.

Billy, Rick, and David frown on the use of the word "rebellion" when referring to their leaving home and going off on tour with Elvis (even if it was the age of the so-called "generation gap"), because there is something disrespectful to their mother about it. "When the eagle grows up, it's got to spread its wings and fly," is the way Billy puts it. "I just hung around the nest a little longer."

Rick was only sixteen when Elvis asked him to work for him. "Even before I started working for him," he says, "if I saw his glass empty, I'd get him a glass of water. He noticed things like that. It was out of respect, because I really didn't want anything. I just grooved being around the guy. People used to say to me all the time, 'Why do you call him *sir*? I mean, he's your brother.' And I would say, 'Well, I love the man and I respect him.' And I did. Elvis would turn to whoever said it and say, 'That's why he's gonna work for me.' "

Elvis wanted Rick around for several reasons. He was smart, dedicated, and socially adroit, young, trainable, and apt to appreciate the experience. Elvis liked the idea of having family around, someone whose trust and loyalty grew from a lifetime relationship, who he knew would not just be there for handouts. When Elvis had a falling out with Richard Davis, his long-time valet and personal aide, Rick was asked to fill in.

Rick's eyes lit up at the possibility, but his mother's jaw

dropped open. She had never wanted the boys to spend too much time around Graceland to begin with, but this was taking things too far. Now, Dee Presley wasn't the sort of woman to wrangle and haggle about these things; she simply refused. What followed was an intrafamily power struggle of sorts, not actual open warfare with maneuvering armies and decisive thrusts, but more like the protracted siege of a city, with Dee being the city and Elvis the commander of the besieging forces. Dee wasted no time trying to use her husband for leverage, and fought like a mama bear whose cubs were in mortal danger.

"It put Vernon in an embarrassing position," she says. "I asked him to make Elvis understand how I felt, and Vernon told Elvis how badly I wanted them in school. Vernon said, 'Please, Elvis, don't do this to Dee; you know how she is about those boys.' Elvis understood, but he was thinking more about himself than he was me. He always felt good having the boys around him. I was outnumbered."

Vernon Presley may have tried to intercede on Dee's behalf, but in his heart of hearts—shaped and calloused, as it was, by the experience of poverty and then redeemed by the self-made fortunes of his son—he also believed that there is no education like life itself, no classroom better than the street. He also felt that Elvis needed Rick, and Elvis's wishes and needs were, to Vernon, always paramount.

In the end Vernon's divided sense of loyalty to his son and his wife left him somewhere in the middle, in no-man's-land, certainly not the tactical support Dee had hoped for. Dee turned next to Priscilla. "Cilla understood it very well," Dee says. "She thought it terribly cruel to take Ricky, and she begged Elvis not to." It didn't work, either; what Elvis Presley wanted, he got.

As the siege wore on and Dee's resolve weakened, Elvis appeared at her door one day to have a heart-to-heart talk and to deliver the *coup de grâce*. On his face he wore one of his most earnest and sincere expressions.

"I really want him with me, Dee," he said, gazing deeply into her eyes. "He's so much like you."

The opening salvo, flattery, caught her completely off guard,

102 as Elvis knew it would. "Well," Dee said, folding her hands primly in her lap, "that's a compliment, Elvis, but . . ."

Sensing the weak spot in the defenses, Elvis followed it right up. "Anybody that has ever known you can see that Ricky's got your looks; he's got your personality and memory, too. That's why he's gonna make it—'cause he's like you."

"Ricky needs to be a doctor, Elvis," she shot right back, stiffening. "I want him to study medicine. He can't just be wasted; he's got to be a very intellectual young man. He's got too much and . . ."

"If you'll just let him come with me," he promised, "he'll have a private tutor on the road. He'll have Bible classes, and I'll have that limousine ready to take him to church every Sunday. I'll pay him good money and always take care of him, Dee. If he wants to, he'll always be there, right by my side. He can do anything else he wants, or I'll send him to college. He can travel or I'll even get him into the movies."

He looked at her sweetly and smiled. "I'll always take care of your boys, Dee. You *know* that."

She was silent. Elvis could be irresistible when he wanted something, but she still knew it was wrong. Finally she relented for the same reason that a parent does after a child's endless haranguing.

"I know you so well," Elvis said, his arm around her. "I know it'll take time, but if you let him go, I'll prove it to you."

"Well, it's like I'm fightin' a loosin' battle," she sighed reluctantly. "I'm gonna trust you, Elvis, 'cause he's beautiful. One day, I'd like him to be able to walk through the doors of any college. If that's taken away from him, he'll be the loser for it, I can tell you that. I trust you won't let me down."

Rick Stanley was still sixteen when he stepped onto the plane with Elvis Presley. The nearest age of anyone else in the entourage was twenty-eight. "I was pretty impressed when I heard about the teacher and everything," he says. "Mom wasn't going for it, but there wasn't much she could say."

When they were on the plane, sitting next to each other, Elvis turned to him and laughed. "*I'm* the teacher," he said.

For Dee Presley it was the beginning of what she indignantly calls "living in a fool's paradise," during which everything that her son did on the road with Elvis was carefully concealed from her so as not to upset her.

"I could never get Ricky back after that," she says resentfully. "Each time he came back, I knew that he was more beyond me. First Billy went, then David too. Elvis bought cars for them; he bought them Hondas, horses, and expensive gifts that took them away even more. I wasn't ready for my sons to be introduced to that life—to the women of the world. I had no idea to what lengths women would go to get to Elvis! Everything that I taught them, every belief that I held to be necessary was taken away. They were introduced to life and sex by two pros—Vernon and Elvis Presley!"

For Rick and his two brothers, it was the beginning of a unique education and a once-in-a-lifetime opportunity to see the world through the eyes of the man who was a big brother, surrogate father, and now "Boss." The highs with "The Boss" would be the highest imaginable, the lows the most abysmal, and they would also witness, sadly, Elvis Presley's destruction, to which they bear unique and heartbreaking testimony.

The Stanley boys may have been young and a little naive when they left home, but they were very much aware of being in search of an educational experience quite different from what they would have encountered at Vanderbilt. Instead, they were looking for that one-time, all-out, sometimes lethal course only available at that well-known University of High Times and Hard Knocks—The Road.

"Well," their mother says regretfully. "They got it. They damn sure got it. All the way."

PART TWO

TWO

"BOSS"

1969·1971

The King's business required haste.

Samuel XXI : 8

CHAPTER 7

TCB

One frigid night in Washington, D.C., after Elvis had played the Capital Centre, Rick's first call to duty arrived—his first assignment. It was four o'clock in the morning. Outside the temperature flirted with zero. Bitter winds whipped down the streets and snow fell, but the orders came through loud and clear: "Man, I'm *starvin'!*" Elvis said, looking at him. "*Cheeseburgers, now!*"

Rick was off in a flash, but, being inexperienced in these logistical matters, he never thought to pay the hotel bellman to get a cabbie to undertake the mission. No, instead he bundled up and trudged off himself, cutting a strange and solitary figure running through the snow and sleet of Connecticut Avenue and K Street at that hour, his long blond hair—now past his shoulders and creeping toward his butt—streaming behind him. Entering the first all-night diner he came across, he made the score, stuffed the goods into his coat where they nestled against his chest ("I knew they better be warm when I got back!"), then beat it back to the hotel where he burst into Elvis's suite, red nosed and panting hard.

108   "Oh, I'm not hungry anymore," said the Boss nonchalantly, studying his fingernails. "I was just checking to see if you could handle it."

Rick, still winded, stood silently for a moment, eyeing Elvis. "Sure, I can handle it!" he exclaimed. "I'll go out and do it again if you want!"

Elvis frequently tested the loyalty and abilities of those around him, and now that Rick had passed his acid test, it was time for his initiation into the TCB group (aka Memphis Mafia), that fraternity of men that lived with, worked for, and seemingly lived for Elvis Presley. It was an unusual fraternity, to say the least, but the initiation ceremony turned out to be the same time-honored ritual that men have always used to celebrate the burgeoning manhood of younger men; only this time considering that Elvis was involved, it was, might we say, somewhat more grandiose. The scene is best portrayed as an X-rated movie that goes something like this:

Fade In: Las Vegas, night, the Imperial Suite of the Hilton. The camera slowly pans to reveal Elvis's entourage all assembled in the plush room. They are all smiling in anticipation of something. The door opens to reveal a startled Rick Stanley, who stops dead in his tracks as he looks to the far end of the suite where, to his goggle-eyed delight, are seated no fewer than eight—yes, count them, eight—high-priced, sleek U.S. Grade A Choice Las Vegas callgirls. There is tittering and much guffawing in the background as the camera dollies in closely to reveal several brunettes and lanky blondes, a statuesque redhead and a beautiful Eurasian, all dressed in slinky gowns and heels and looking like showgirls from downstairs. "They're all for you—every one of them," says the Boss, laughing, his hand on Rick's shoulder. "Go for it." *Extreme Close-up:* Rick, flabbergasted. His eyes roll around in his head deliciously for a moment, then dart back and forth as he scans the assortment to make his selection—a voluptuous brunette with large, almond eyes. He heads for the bedroom. The camera remains stationary for the next three hours, revealing nothing of the activities going on in the room, but remaining fixed on the door of the bed-

room. Each time he emerges from the bedroom grinning like
the Cheshire cat, it follows him to the end of the suite where he
picks still another. "Haw, haw!" comes a gutteral laugh from
the background (not from Elvis, who is no longer there): "That
little son of a bitch is gonna be just like us!"

Rick never told his brother that he had been making it with
girls since the tender age of fifteen, not wanting to spoil *his* fun.
He settled comfortably into his job with Elvis, and within the
next two years got both of his brothers on the payroll.

"Before they could even get in," he says, "I had to get them
hip to the way Elvis was. I was responsible for them and didn't
want any freakouts once we were off. I said, 'Hey, you know, if
you don't like it—that's just the way it is. That's Elvis.' "

Billy's initiation into life with Elvis came on tour, in 1972.
Elvis was booked into Madison Square Garden. People
thronged Seventh and Eighth Avenues, looking for tickets, and
hawkers, winos, hookers, pimps, and freaks milled about the
thousands of concertgoers, lending the scene an authentic New
York air.

"God," he recalls, "the only thing we knew about New York
was what we saw in movies, which made the place look like the
craziest town in the world! I was scared to death, man."

He may have been initially intimidated by the Big Apple, but
after the show Billy met four girls from downtown, all beautiful,
their hair in ponytails, dressed in long skirts, bobby sox, and
saddle shoes for Elvis's concert and looking like record-hop
queens, straight out of a fifties fantasy, on their way to a platter
party. "From then on," says Billy, "I said, man, you know, this
is it—this must be the place!"

David also came on as soon as he graduated from high
school, and he came on like gangbusters. He worked in Nashville for a short time with Sunberry-Dunbarr music publishers,
but the siren song of the road beckoned and he followed du-
tifully. His initiation came in Tulsa, Oklahoma, in 1974. The
whole affair was perfectly in keeping with his character and
what Elvis loved about him: He got in trouble on his first day.

The boys threw a party that night intending to get the
"rookie" tanked to the gills. There he was on his first night—

110   well toasted—when he noticed through the window that a bevy of girls were sashaying up the road toward the hotel.

"*Hey ya'all,*" he blurted out into the street. "*Yeah, you!*"

The girls stopped to listen to the pitch. They liked the half-crocked boy leaning drunkenly out the window, but mother was coming up the road behind them.

"Here," David yelled, "I'll give you some of my cards!" He threw a whole handful of his newly printed cards out into the street. They fluttered down like ticker tape.

The next morning, hung over and cotton mouthed, David found them waiting for him in the hotel lobby. His head felt as large as a prize hog, and the harshness of the morning light quickly brought down his nighttime fantasy. He told them he didn't remember them. When they persisted, he told them to bug off.

Well, the incident made the Tulsa papers the very next day. **PRESLEY'S BROTHER BELLIGERENT TO FANS,** read the headline.

"What the hell's your goddamned brother doin'!" demanded Elvis and the Colonel when they collared Rick. "He's actin' like a fool already, and he's only been on the road two days!"

Rick took the shot for his brother, but he passed on the message. "Damn, I didn't know," David says. "That day was my first lesson. I learned a million of them working for Elvis."

Life on the road with Elvis stretched far to every horizon in the continental United States. Engagement led to engagement, one tour blended into another, and cities, faces, places, and parties passed into a ceaseless, swirling blur—a merry-go-round of hard work, hijinx, booze, dope, and women, with rock 'n' roll, the blues, and gospel music providing the soundtrack.

No stranger to the road after his veteran years of the fifties, Elvis was now "King," that most exalted nobleman of rock, one of the highest paid acts in the business. The old Lincoln packed with equipment and Scotty, Bill, and D.J. were nostalgia now. The Boss soared through the skies of America in customized luxury jets, high above the roadsides he had slept along, the gigs

Davada Elliot, a country girl, Lone Oak High, Clarksville, Tennessee *(last row, far left)*. Her strict upbringing was filled with solitary treks through the pinewood and magnolia that surrounded her father's farm. Left: "Dee," age twenty, before her marriage to Bill Stanley.

Elvis Aron Presley with his first bicycle (the one his mother finally let him have) in Tupelo, Mississippi, sometime before his father moved the family to Memphis, Tennessee. Left: Graduation picture from L. C. Humes High in Memphis, 1953. (Printhouse Ltd.)

Sgt. Bill Stanley, the dark, handsome stranger of Dee's fantasies, with his three sons, Rick *(left)*, David *(center)*, and Bill junior *(right)*, in Hampton, Virginia, 1956. By this time the marriage had long been sliding downhill and Dee was weighing alternatives.

Bedlam prevails in Long Beach, California, as Elvis croons, swivels, snaps, shakes, and pops. This photo was taken in June 1956. (Wide World)

Above: The man in the gold lamé suit is escorted to a stage in Chicago, 1957. (Wide World) Right: Elvis wows them with a ballad as Bill Black plucks his bass and Scotty Moore strums behind him.

If you don't think Elvis had fun during those years, examine the expression on his face in the taxi cab. Colonel Tom Parker sits in the front seat, shooing away the girls so they won't get hurt. (UPI) Left: Elvis smooches with an unknown motorcycle friend.

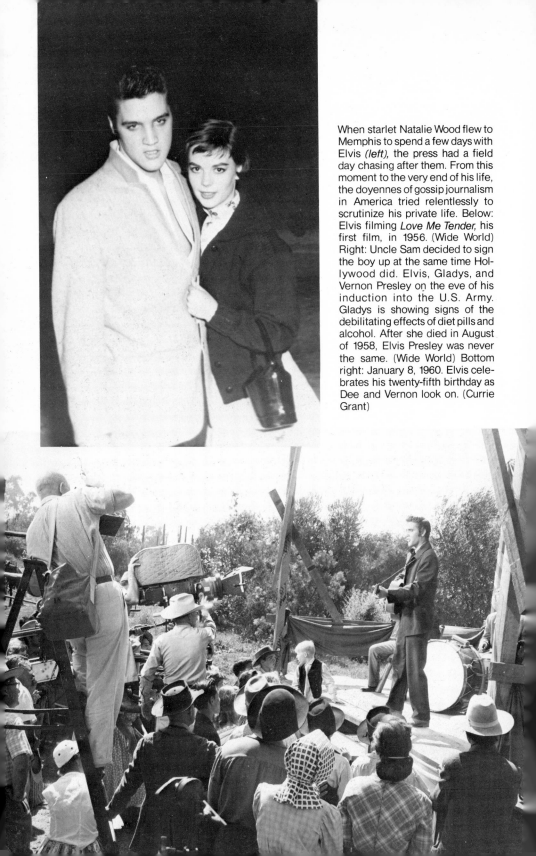

When starlet Natalie Wood flew to Memphis to spend a few days with Elvis *(left)*, the press had a field day chasing after them. From this moment to the very end of his life, the doyennes of gossip journalism in America tried relentlessly to scrutinize his private life. Below: Elvis filming *Love Me Tender*, his first film, in 1956. (Wide World) Right: Uncle Sam decided to sign the boy up at the same time Hollywood did. Elvis, Gladys, and Vernon Presley on the eve of his induction into the U.S. Army. Gladys is showing signs of the debilitating effects of diet pills and alcohol. After she died in August of 1958, Elvis Presley was never the same. (Wide World) Bottom right: January 8, 1960. Elvis celebrates his twenty-fifth birthday as Dee and Vernon look on. (Currie Grant)

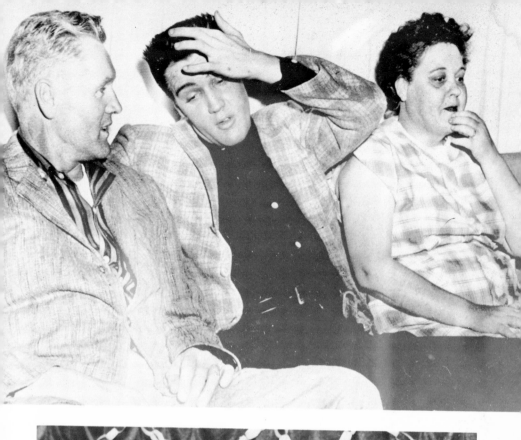

Wedding bells chime
as Dee Elliot Stanley
becomes
Mrs. Vernon Presley.

March 7, 1960, Memphis, Tennessee: Sgt. Elvis Presley is back from the army and greets wellwishers through the iron fence at the rail depot. (Wide World) Below: The Graceland mansion as it looked in September of 1960.

The brothers Stanley growing up. In France *(top left)*, 1957, and with their new daddy, Vernon Presley, outside Graceland in 1960 *(top right)*. Left to right: David, Billy, and Rick *(above)* inside Graceland, and David, Rick, and Billy on Dolan Street in Whitehaven *(right)*.

Elvis goes back to pass *(top)*. A love of football was only one of the many things he imparted to his stepbrothers. As the years went by, he became big brother, surrogate father, teacher, and finally "Boss." (Printhouse Ltd.) Above and right: Elvis believed in getting the boys started young in everything they did. It began with Hondas and led to everything else. (Photographer unknown)

A portrait of Priscilla Beaulieu *(opposite page, top)* and Cilla with Dee *(bottom)*, both taken at the shower Dee Presley threw before the marriage. Insert: Cilla *(left)* and Dee's niece Theresa in the house on Dolan Street, March 1963. Top: The wedding at the Aladdin Hotel, Las Vegas, in May 1967. Above left: Rick, Vernon, Billy, Dee, Cilla, David, and Ernie Borgnine. Above right: Elvis and the boys at the reception held at Graceland for everybody who didn't attend the wedding in Las Vegas.

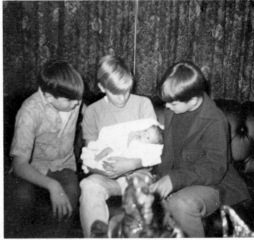

Lisa Marie Presley with Vernon Presley and Colonel Beaulieu *(top);* with Priscilla at Graceland *(middle left);* cuddled by her uncles Billy, Rick, and David *(middle right);* and playing with Rick in the Graceland yard *(above).*

in supper clubs and theaters having long since given way to huge stadiums, civic centers, and luxury hotels in Las Vegas and Lake Tahoe.

The manifold problems and monumental pressures increased to levels commensurate with the volume in dollars and cents involved. However you looked at it, life on the road was something vastly different from any nine-to-five reality: The longer you did it, the more it took out of your hide, until it became more than just a life-style but a separate reality-fantasy of life that kicked on while the rest of the world slept. With Elvis Presley, it became a consciousness of southern-fried funk and flash with a backdrop of sleepy-toned voices, complete with a special lingo, a code of behavior, and morals all its own.

"It was all like a constant blow of coke that just suddenly ended," Rick says.

Sometimes, for the Stanleys, it seemed awesome. Billy was the first to be put off by the nature of the job and life-style. Elvis delegated huge responsibilities to his brothers, knowing that their work would speed up the process of maturation. "It's your baby," he would say when he gave them a job to do. "Now rock it!"

"I knew how strong Elvis was," says Billy. "I knew that after I went to work for him my life would never be the same because that's the way he was. Everybody around Elvis was changed by him. Here I was, eighteen years old, behaving like a thirty-five-year-old man. You were made to think, 'Come on, you're not a kid anymore; you're doin' a man's job now.' That's what scared me about the whole thing."

Elvis picked up on Billy's feelings of uncertainty and gave him some helpful advice. "Once you find out that *you're* a nut," he said, "then you'll get along in the world perfectly, man, 'cause *everybody's* nuts."

It all boiled down to a philosophy of Universal Insanity and the Absurdity of Life. Billy thought hard about it; it made all the sense in the world. Thenceforth, he adopted Elvis's live-and-let-live philosophies. Elvis started calling him "Charlie

112   Manson" because of his long hair, beard, and piercing blue eyes, and his job was to carry Elvis's briefcase that included the payroll and all of Elvis's personal valuables.

Working for Elvis Presley did not offer Blue Cross, pension plans, or unemployment insurance, but there were nonetheless quite a few fringe benefits to be enjoyed by the Stanley boys. The distinction of being Elvis's brothers was first. "He didn't call us 'stepbrothers,' asserts Rick. "Everywhere we went, he would express his love for us—'These are my brothers,' he would say. That meant a lot to us. It was strong, and we were grateful." Elvis's experience and his constant readiness to share it also continued to be a source of great help to his brothers. Says Billy, "Elvis was the only person I could sit down with and bring up the shittiest problem I had in the world, who had the friendship and loyalty to help me work it out."

With cash in their pockets, plenty of good times rolling, mobility, women, interesting people to meet, things looked just fine for the Stanley boys, but on top of it all, they knew that Elvis was always there. They did not take advantage of his good nature, but life around Elvis was a cornucopia of "mellow hits." The phrase is Rick's. He used the word "mellow" a lot, and because of his cool demeanor when things got hectic, it became his nickname.

"Whenever Elvis would do me a great favor," he says, "I would say, 'Man, that's a mellow hit,' so if something exciting happened to him or he had good news, he would look at me and say, 'Rick, that's commonly known the world over as a mellow hit, baby.'" A good example of a mellow hit was unlimited credit established at the gaming tables in Las Vegas. When the Boss no longer needed him, Rick could make his way downstairs and wade through the gamblers to the crap or blackjack games. "In the morning," he says, "I'd come in after a whole night of drinking and running up an outrageous marker. Elvis would just look at me and shake his head. We were his little brothers, man. He loved that big-brother image and being able to do things for us."

From time to time the Boss would find the need to bring his little brothers down to earth, and he could do it as easily as

snapping a finger. "We were all sitting around one time, talk- 113
ing," remembers Billy, "and I was saying, 'Well, here I am,
eighteen years old, traveling around the country, first class, not
paying for anything, driving a brand-new car, making a good
salary, having a good old time. . . . Man, I've got it made in
the shade.' "

Elvis turned to him, a sardonic smile on his face, and said,
"Yeah? When I was your age I was making four million dollars
a year!"

What can you say to something like that?

Rick's job with Elvis never stopped branching out. He was
becoming a general-utility aide, working as valet, in communications and public relations, security, transportation, and
in the entertainment end. It was an opportunity to get to know
Elvis intimately and familiarize himself with all ends of his
business, taking stock of how the machinery of his organization
operated.

As valet he was personally responsible for the Boss's clothes.
Elvis's wardrobe was enormous, filling an entire room back at
Graceland. Elvis liked Rick's taste in clothes, so Rick began
coordinating both the Boss's onstage and offstage wear. Sometimes they disagreed.

"Man, that just doesn't look good," he would say when Elvis
put on something unbecoming and studied himself in the mirror.

"How the hell do *you* know?" the Boss would flash, turning
to him with an irritated sneer on his face. "I've been doin' this
for twenty years, Ricky. I know what the hell looks good!"

"Look, you pay me to tell you what looks good and what
doesn't," Rick would retort. "Are you gonna listen to me or
not?"

In the end Elvis would always do what he wanted. Usually,
after consideration, he would heed Rick's advice. In general he
respected his opinions, and the two of them became insepa-
rable.

As Elvis's personal aide, Rick had to be around more than
anybody else. He got to know every aspect of Elvis's life, within

114 the family, the organization, with his women, every-where—what he liked and disliked and why, his opinions, thoughts, habits, and feelings about anything and everything. These responsibilities were also Joe Esposito's, and Rick became his protégé.

"We had fun together," continues Rick. "If he had a chick in LA, I had one there; if he had one in Memphis, I had one in Memphis. On many occasions, he said, 'Rick is TCBing; he's ready to go anytime,' and I was, because it was so much fun. The phone would ring late at night: 'Come on, Rick. We're going to the Springs.' And I would just grab my shirt and Levi's and take off. We'd fly out on a Lear jet. Everyone else would come later."

TCB was what life around Elvis Presley was all about. It meant simply, Taking Care of Business—Elvis's business. Anything that ever needed to be done—from the routing, organization, and logistics of a multimillion dollar road show to making sure that the Boss had toilet paper in his bathroom—came under the TCB heading. Essentially this is what Elvis's entourage was there to do—TCB. Rick provides a good definition of what it sometimes meant: "The man would look across the room and just from his eyes you would know exactly what he was thinking; it was your cue. Some of the people that worked for Elvis were that much in tune with him. You were locked into him if you were around for that many years. You became a part of him because you lived exactly the same way that he lived. If you were sitting in a room and a conversation was going on, if he leaned back, automatically you would know that he needed, say, a glass of water. If he leaned forward, you might think that he was fixin' to light a cigar. In a car, you would know exactly what to have and what value was attached to each item, whether the window should be up or down, the radio on or off—you're TCBing *all* the time, constantly alert to his every need."

The letters TCB became a metaphor for almost everything that happened around Elvis. The Boss had a logo designed with the letters and a golden thunderbolt—the symbol of the West

Coast Mafia—jutting through the letters. You Took Care of
Business, but the thunderbolt meant quickly and efficiently,
without questions. Elvis had gold chains that carried a golden
facsimile of the logo made for everyone in the group, and the
logo also came to be emblazoned on the side of his million-
dollar customized 880 Convair jet, the *Lisa Marie*.

TCBing never ceased. It was a seven-day-a-week, twenty-
four-hour-a-day job—taking care of Elvis's food, for instance.
The Boss loved to eat, but his eating habits were easy to handle
because of the nature of his palate, which was either faddish or
uniformly simple, depending on how he was feeling. Elvis was
anything but a gourmet. He never got out to restaurants, but he
knew precisely what he wanted to eat, when, where, and how
he wanted to eat it. For years the staples of his diet were typical
home-cooked southern meals like pork chops, fried chicken,
black-eyed peas, grits, ham, biscuits, turnips, deep-dish apple
pie. Add to this a mania for junk food like bacon cheeseburgers,
french fries, Mexican food, bacon and eggs, and steak, and you
have the classically American, high-cholesterol diet. For six
months the Boss could eat the same thing every day: Spanish
omelette in the morning (his Vegas recipe), toast, orange juice,
and coffee, and for dinner it would be ground sirloin, baked potato, salad with Thousand Island dressing or Roquefort, and
iced tea. Elvis's eating habits were one of the most rigid things
about him. He remained devoted to burnt bacon and peanut-
butter-and-banana (fried in butter!) sandwiches, and he was renowned for his late-night binging. "Whew," Rick sighs, "if
Elvis wanted pizza with everything on it but anchovies, you'd
better get it for him! It wouldn't matter if it was six in the morning; you went out and found a pizzeria and you got it opened,
somehow. That's what you did."

TCBing also meant getting the Boss's room ready whenever
the group pulled into a new town. Clothes were laid out, the
Boss's bookcases were opened, phones were immediately discon-
nected, and all services referred to the adjacent room. The ice
bucket off to the side of the bed was stocked amply with Mountain Valley Spring Water. The humidifier was plugged in and

116 whirring. There were a million things to do, from the largest
right down to the cotton for the Boss's ears when he went to
sleep. They had better be done quickly and correctly.

Rick also did most of the Boss's talking for him on the telephone. Almost everyone who knew Elvis Presley also knew that
he did not like to use the phone; its impersonality bugged him.
When people from out of town wanted to talk to him, they
usually flew to Memphis and came up to the house. Of course,
many people tried to call, and Rick was responsible for putting
them off.

"Sorry," he would say, as diplomatically as possible, "Elvis is
sleeping and doesn't want to be disturbed."

Rick was always aware of who had fallen from grace and into
disfavor, because he was usually the one who somehow found
himself with the task of making sure that the people the Boss
wanted to see were there when he wanted them and that those
he didn't want to see were far away. "There wasn't much that
got around me," he says. "One of the expressions that we used
was 'I've seen a lot come through that gate, and I've seen a lot
more go out.' "

The faces of the people around Elvis Presley since the sixties
had indeed changed, but the inner nucleus of the TCB group—
those few faithful friends who went to work for Elvis after his
discharge from the army in 1960—had remained constant.
These were the men that the Stanley boys spent a great deal of
their time with on the road and back home in Memphis.

The press dubbed Elvis's entourage the "Memphis Mafia"
sometime after the completion of *G.I. Blues* in 1960. Elvis was
going through a "kick"; he wanted his boys to look professional
and insisted for a short period that they all dress in dark mohair
business suits with white shirts and ties. One morning they all
showed up in Las Vegas in their sunglasses, like a squad of
drawling hitmen. For the boys the name had been more of a
lark than anything else, but it stuck, and for good reason: Elvis
ran his inner circle very much like La Cosa Nostra, insisting on
the same loyalty, secrecy, and military efficiency as one finds in

the Mafia. Also, within the hierarchy of power in his group, he was indeed the Don.

Within the group each individual had a special area of concern for which he was responsible. For services duly rendered, each received a salary, went where Elvis went, lived like he did, and were also entitled to all of the fringe benefits (the official ones were expense accounts, new cars, gifts, and the Christmas bonus). Most of the boys were familiar figures of Elvis's past, and they were around much of the time. Billy Stanley tells why: "First of all, if you had millions floating around you'd want your friends working with you—people you could trust. But Elvis wanted his people around not so much to work, but just to be able to talk to them sometimes. He needed to be able to relate to somebody in the normal world, someone who could make him feel, you know, 'I'm not a superstar, I'm a person.' "

Even so, it was sometimes very difficult being both friend and employee of Elvis Presley. The very fact that his friends called him "Boss" illustrates this. The fine line between being a friend and being a worker often blurred. Depending on Elvis's mood, there were times when you were expected to be both at the same time or either one or the other. For the very same reasons, Elvis could go from displaying all of the sensitivity, emotion, and concern that he felt for his friends to the "I don't give a damn—you work only for me" attitudes of being the Boss. Everyone got fired and then rehired at one time or another; when it happened, Elvis was mad and didn't really mean it, and his interests as a friend would supersede his ire as the Boss. He always asked you back unless he truly did not want you around anymore, in which case he could get rid of you as quickly as an old shoe. Marty Lacker was a perfect example of that. Lacker had worked for Elvis for years as his bookkeeper and personal aide and was one of the co-best men at his wedding. He was a pudgy, nervous type with a tendency to stick his nose into others' business, and Elvis began to tire of him. Says David Stanley, "Elvis told him to stay away from him. He told him not to even come up to his car when he saw him on the street."

Elvis did have a whole crop of former employees who left for

118   a variety of reasons but remained close: Alan Fortas, Gee Gee
Gambil, and Richard Davis among them. If you worked for
Elvis Presley and remained true to the fold, there wasn't much
he wouldn't do for you, and if you left his service for personal
reasons (if, for instance, your marriage was going down the
tubes, or you tired of the life-style or had professional aspirations of your own), he would stand behind you all the way.

Elvis was unquestionably the Boss—the Capo di Tutti Capi
in Mafia lingo—but, in Rick's words, "There were about three
or four guys in all that you always paid attention to when they
told you to do something—Elvis, Daddy, the Colonel, and Joe
Esposito. If they wanted something done, you took care of it;
you didn't ask any questions."

While Colonel Parker took care of Elvis's contractual affairs,
Joe Esposito "ran the show." Nobody was more respected or val-
ued by Elvis, his family, or the others in the group than Esposito, and when people speak of him today, the words are usually
filled with glowing praise.

Since their meeting at the Freidberg base in Germany, where
they served together, Joe had remained Elvis's closest, most
trusted friend. During his Hollywood years, he helped Elvis
learn his lines, worked with his scripts, and coordinated his entire life around shooting times, and when Elvis went back out
on the road, Joe was the man who took the pressure off Elvis by
making sure that everything ran like clockwork. If you look at
Elvis's entourage as a work crew, Joe was foreman; if you see it
as a squad of soldiers, Joe was top sergeant; if you prefer the
Mafia analogy, he was the *consigliere* to Elvis's Don.

Nobody knew Elvis better. Joe was, all at once, Elvis's road
manager, bookkeeper, advisor, close friend, confidant, and wet
nurse. During the years of their marriage, Joni Esposito, Joe's
wife, was one of Priscilla's best friends. Joe knew Elvis so well
that he would many times be aware of exactly what was on Elvis's mind and orchestrate things to suit his moods. Says Rick,
"Joe would come to us and say, 'Look, guys, Elvis is thinking
about this today, so don't mention it to him.' "

The Stanley boys looked up to Joe Esposito who, because of
his warmth and professionalism, seemed everything they should

aspire to. Esposito's selfless dedication to Elvis remained unsurpassed by anyone's, and considering his huge responsibilities, he was worth his weight in gold. Dee Presley and the Stanley boys have nothing but tribute for him. "The man was a saint," Rick says simply. "Bless his heart, man, he kept the whole thing together. Whenever Elvis did something wrong, he had to answer for it."

Jerry Schilling was another of the Old Guard whom the boys looked up to. A tall, good-looking, smooth-talking sharpie with dark features and an irresistibly wry smile, Jerry was one of those kinds of guys it's difficult not to like. He was a flashy man, like Elvis, who knew his way around and could usually be seen in the company of beautiful women.

Schilling had worked off and on for Elvis, and when Elvis went off on tour, Jerry became invaluable in many different capacities—security, public relations, transportation, and personal aide. He was, however, very much his own man. A strong identity and outside interests kept him much less dependent on Elvis than some of the others in the group, which sometimes nettled the Boss. "Jerry didn't take anything from anybody," says Rick. "That's the kind of man he was. He always did his job well, but no above-and-beyond stuff because he wanted his obligations known. He always let Elvis know that he was going to be himself, too."

Several years before Elvis died, as the group was celebrating Elvis's birthday in Vail, Colorado, Elvis and Jerry clashed when Elvis insisted that Jerry move to another room in the middle of the night. Elvis was hot and bothered that night, and Jerry quit before he could be fired, but they patched things up later. They parted very amicably. "Elvis always loved Jerry," says David, "but Jerry had plans for his career, and Elvis helped him because he was always so loyal." He went on to become the road manager of the Beach Boys.

Elvis's cousin, Billy Smith, shared a relationship with him that went back to the days when Gladys Presley would ask Billy to sleep with Elvis in case he got up to sleepwalk. "Billy and Elvis were like brothers," says Rick. "Elvis could really relax around him and he loved having Billy around. Billy was one of

120 the few people who could actually kid Elvis and get away with it, and Elvis always wanted to hear his opinions about things— just like Daddy, the Colonel, and Joe." Billy stayed out of the limelight, but he remained a very influential figure in Elvis's life. He was a down-home guy and a typical south- erner—easygoing, good natured, with a temper that could crackle when he got hot.

Nobody in the group worshiped Elvis more than Charlie Hodge, his little rhythm guitarist from Decatur, Alabama. To Charlie, Elvis took on all of the divine proportions of a deity, one that Charlie was always ready to pay homage to. When they were discharged from the army, Charlie followed Elvis to Mem- phis. On the day that Elvis boarded his train for Hollywood, he asked Charlie if he wanted to come aboard. Charlie hopped on the train and never got off.

Charlie's job was to make music. He was a live-in com- panion, rooming in the garage apartment at Graceland or in one of Elvis's California homes. Whenever the Boss wanted to relax by breaking out an acoustic guitar or sit around the piano and harmonize the strains of a good gospel, he was always ready to oblige. "Elvis knew that Charlie could never set the world on fire as an entertainer by himself," says Rick, "but he loved Charlie for his blind loyalty."

When Elvis opened in Las Vegas, Charlie was onstage as his rhythm guitarist, but functioned more as Elvis's onstage valet than anything else. He handed the Boss water, draped his capes, dispensed the scarves that Elvis handed out to his adoring fans at the edge of the stage, and played off of Elvis's stage p. sence. Charlie became so wrapped up in Elvis that he could seem like a "droog" without a mind of his own, who mimicked and agreed with anything the Boss said or did.

Lamar Fike was Ed McMahon to Elvis's Johnny Carson. In rooms full of people, he loved to feed the Boss lines and play straight man, and Elvis loved having him there. Originally from Texas, Lamar had showed up at Elvis's house on Audubon Drive. Gladys had invited him in, and he and Elvis had sub- sequently become fast buddies. When Elvis was drafted, Lamar achieved instant celebrity by accompanying Elvis to the induction center and trying to enlist himself. The newspapers of America reported his 260 pounds the very next day. Lamar followed Elvis to Germany and back again, and with the passing of years his weight went up and up, making him the brunt of every fat joke Elvis or the TCB boys could muster. (He lost a great deal of the weight after a heart attack and bypass operation several years ago.)

Lamar was an intelligent man, keenly interested in making himself useful to Elvis's career, but there was an air of slapstick comedy about him; he always seemed to be slipping on things or falling down, and his immense size, good nature, and willingness to take a joke made him the beloved court jester and "village idiot" of the group. The Boss would love to sit there and laugh with him—more often, *at* him—and the humor could get vicious. In moments of foul temper, Elvis could easily make Lamar his whipping boy.

"Lamar had been around Elvis for so long," says Rick, "that he wanted to be like him, too. He wanted to be recognized as a big wheel in his own right, as an executive." Eventually the Boss put him in charge of his music-publishing concerns in Nashville, and Lamar became an endless repository of music-business statistics on album sales and publishing copyrights. He was the man who searched catalogues and the music scene in Nashville for Elvis's new material. Like Joe, Jerry, Charlie, and Billy, he remained one of Elvis's most steadfast friends and associates right to the end, and the Stanley boys remember him fondly from their very first days at Graceland.

There were other individuals who did not spend quite as much time around Elvis but figured very prominently in his life. Since the Boss's moviemaking days, Larry Geller had been Elvis's hair stylist and kindred spirit in the pursuit of knowledge. Larry was Elvis's connection to the California culture and the world of esoterica, bringing him interesting books to read about meditation, psychology, philosophy, eastern religion, para-psychology, and all of the interests that Elvis so ardently chased during the last decade or so of his life. The two of them would

122   sit for long periods of time, talking. A handsome man with brown hair and piercing eyes, Larry was another of Elvis's closest personal friends.

George Klein, short, dark, swarthy (before he got the nose job that Elvis paid for, he resembled the actor Jamie Farr, television's Corporal Klinger on the *M*A*S*H* show), was the president of Elvis's graduating class at Humes. During the years of his early success, George and Elvis became good friends. Elvis affectionately called him "the world's oldest teenager" (next to himself, of course), and he became quite popular as the DJ at Station WHBQ in Memphis, a job that Elvis helped him to get.

Dr. George Nichopoulos—"Doctor Nick"—was a successful practitioner in Memphis before becoming the Presley family physician and eventually Elvis's personal physician, traveling with him on tour. He became a very familiar figure in the TCB group. A pleasant man with a headful of thick, graying hair, he too was devoted to Elvis, and there wasn't an ailment that the Boss, his family, or friends had that escaped his attention.

Security required another contingent of individuals, and Elvis gathered a small but effective phalanx of bodyguards to surround him. His oldest was Bobby "Red" West, one of his high-school acquaintances. Ex-football player, ex-marine, born roughneck, hothead, redneck, fearless stuntman, actor, songwriter, karate expert, Red West isn't hard to understand—good ole boy, Tennessee style. He and Elvis had been through a lot together, and Red spent many, many years dedicated to Elvis until they had their falling out. Stocky, barrel chested, and bull necked, Red, with his cleft chin and menacing glances, is one formidable-looking fellow. Like Elvis, he had a temper, and within the TCB group he was the group tough guy, known for his violent antics. His cousin, Sonny West, who went to work for Elvis in the early sixties, was a variation on the same theme, except louder and more obnoxious. Eventually both would be fired. They retaliated by publishing a book—the sensationalistic, first look at Elvis's "inside" life called *Elvis: What Happened?*

The incident that first made Elvis realize that it would be wise to have bodyguards around continuously occurred in the backstage corridors following a performance at the International, in Las Vegas. Somehow a young woman managed to get backstage. "She was just trying to touch him," remembers Billy, "but she had long fingernails and ended up scratching his face. She grabbed at him, made one swipe, but that's all it took. Elvis didn't get mad at her; he just wished she wouldn't have done that. Chances are he would have put his arm around her and talked to her. That's when we started getting really tight because he really jumped on us about it."

The problems of protecting him from fans at concerts were huge. The Boss loved his fans and insisted that his road crew treat them with respect, but they had a job to do, and the enthusiasm of the fans bordered on dementia. "Girls would come out at you like wildcats," says Billy, who also worked stage security for a time. "All of a sudden you would see fifteen or twenty coming at you at once and it was your responsibility to stop them; you can't do it just by holding your arms out! We would say, 'Stand back please,' and if they got a little pushy, then we would get a little pushy. Some of the ladies would take cheap shots at us by conking us over the head with their umbrellas or purses, and man, that gets old after a while!"

All of the boys have memories of concert security that are as humorous as they are harrowing. David shudders when he remembers one mountainous blond woman who charged the stage one night like a stampeding water buffalo. The stage was a scant three feet off the ground (unusual for an Elvis concert), and the only thing between her and the object of her determined assault—the spotlit, jumpsuited figure of Elvis Presley, singing "Love Me"—was David. She had fire in her eyes and her nostrils were flaring with anticipation when Elvis caught sight of her out of the corner of his eye and said, in the middle of the song, "Get ready, David; here she comes!" David stopped her charge with a firm body check.

"Oh, I wasn't going to do anything," the woman said, her eyes fixed dreamily on Elvis. But just as the Boss was singing "Treat me like a fool, treat me mean and cruel . . ." the woman suddenly brought her knee up into David's groin. Elvis fell to his knees onstage, laughing hysterically.

124   "Did it hurt?!" he asked David at the edge of the stage, tears rolling down his cheeks.

"*Did it hurt!*" gasped his brother, his knees pressed together and his head spinning.

"Go ahead," the Boss motioned, still laughing. "Deck her one for me."

But it was too late for revenge, sweet though that might have been. Uniformed floor police were already leading her away.

"Man, droves of people used to hit that stage at once," says Rick. "You had to be quick on your feet to catch them before they got to Elvis or somebody was going to get their butt chewed out. It was up to you to protect whatever side of the stage you were working that night."

David became renowned for his quick eyes and nimble-footed response-time when it came to plucking fans off the stage before they reached the Boss. Once he noticed one girl in the middle of a performance sneaking onto the stage from the opposite wing. He dashed the full width of the stage to nab her. Elvis, poised in one of his dramatic singing positions, saw him coming out of the corner of his eye. David had to sidestep around him to get to the girl, and just as he went by, the Boss whirled like Fran Tarkenton, faked a handoff with the microphone, and faded back for the pass, which he threw and David caught in pantomine. Touchdown! "Ladies and gentlemen—David Stanley, Cleveland Browns!" shouted Elvis, who returned graciously to center stage to accept the ovation of an auditorium of screaming people.

Security did have its lighthearted moments, but on the whole it was deadly serious. Since his return to live performing, Elvis had been the recipient of a steady stream of threats: Bombs, extortion, assassination, and the possible kidnaping of his daughter or another member of his family hung constantly over his head.

The first death note was delivered in January of 1971 to Colonel Parker's home in Palm Springs. Elvis was playing Vegas at the time, and the Colonel handed the affair over to the FBI. From that moment on the TCB boys were on constant alert. That night Elvis shunned the use of a bullet-proof vest under his jumpsuit and walked out onstage shaking, not knowing if that would be the night he stopped a bullet. The boys spent the entire time scanning every face in the crowd, searching for the possible assassin. "He just couldn't understand someone wanting to kill him," Ricky remembers. "It really hurt his feelings more than anything else. Elvis always felt that he was just showing a talent that God had given him; why would someone want to kill him for it? Hell, he knew that there were nuts out there, but he also knew that I would have gone right out in front of a bullet. Everybody in the group would have."

From that night on the Boss became more and more haunted by the image of a Sirhan Sirhan suddenly stepping out of a crowd somewhere to point a gun at his head and end it all right there. "We were always ready for some crazy sonofabitch to come up and start shooting," says David. "If we ever suspected someone, we'd walk out into the crowd and check it out before Elvis would even come out. If we saw anyone suspicious, we'd call the police. He was never confident that it couldn't happen, but we did a goddamned good job. Nobody got to Elvis, and he knew it."

But even with the mobilization of the TCB group closing their ranks around the Boss, he still took personal precautions. On any given night, if you frisked Elvis onstage, you would have found a four-shot derringer either in his boot or behind his belt buckle, and if he was just going out for a ride, you might find a .357 magnum under one arm in a shoulder holster and a .45 automatic tucked in his belt. "Sometimes when he went out," Billy remembers, "he looked like he was ready for war."

One night during a Vegas performance, five men suddenly rose from the audience to mount the stage. The Boss seemed uncertain of their intentions at first, unable to determine whether they were friendlies or hostiles, but something in their eyes answered the question for him. The incident received much press, and accounts as to what really happened vary greatly. As Billy remembers it, Elvis lashed out with a roundhouse kick that disabled one of the attackers. The audience couldn't make out what was going on in the commotion, but Elvis had pushed his mechanisms for self-preservation. Bodies flew into the equipment, and the stage was suddenly swarming

126   with bodyguards and police. In the wings Vernon Presley had all but collapsed in fear. All five men were arrested (they later claimed to have only wanted to shake his hand), and according to Billy, one of them was discovered to have had a sword inside his cane. Others in the audience were also held for questioning.

To run security, Elvis hired Dick Grob, an ex-air force pilot who had served many years on the Palm Springs police force. The two men met while Elvis was honeymooning with Priscilla at his home there and Grob was assigned to look after security at the house. The Boss knew that he needed a real pro to organize his protection, and after they got friendly by shooting together at the pistol range, he decided that Grob might fit the bill. His bodyguards may have been diligent and faithful, but, says Rick, "Red and Sonny just didn't have the talent to set up security. Grob was the most efficient man Elvis ever had; he knew his stuff, he didn't have to talk big about what he had done."

Frequently Elvis also had his karate instructor and friend, Ed Parker, on hand to help out. Elvis had met Parker in Hawaii, and when Ed moved to California and opened up his karate studio, Elvis and his friends worked out there. Blond, soft spoken, and articulate, Parker was a well-known practitioner in the small but highly elite world of the martial arts. Ironically, through Ed, Elvis met Dave Hebler, another of the bodyguards who turned on him to write *Elvis: What Happened?*, and Mike Stone, who never worked for Elvis but fell in love with his wife.

David wasn't aware of it, but the Boss had designated him to be his personal bodyguard. Elvis had been watching him closely. He knew that David had all of the raw materials to make a bodyguard par excellence: He was big, quick, intensely loyal to Elvis, and eager to learn. The profession would come as naturally to him as if it ran in his blood. As his own father had once protected General Patton, David would protect Elvis Presley, and from the time David was seventeen, Elvis began molding him.

One day when they were riding in Elvis's limousine, the Boss told him.

"Bodyguard?" David was astonished at the possibility. He had

always preferred the creative, musical end of Elvis's life. "Man, 127
you've got to be kiddin'!"

"We're groomin' you, David," was the Boss's reply. "You're
gonna be the best bodyguard I ever had."

Red West undertook David's training, which began with
karate, extended to weapons, and covered all aspects of security
on tour. It didn't take long before Joe Esposito gave him the
word.

"You're off baggage," he said. "From now on, you just worry
about Elvis."

By the age of eighteen he was packing a .357 magnum, and
was prepared to use it; by twenty he was a black belt in karate.
For a young man constantly striving to prove himself in the
company of very tough, older men, it was heady stuff. "I had to
build my reputation for being fearless," he says.

David moved quickly from a trainee to competition with Red
and Sonny, becoming the Boss's "headhunter"—the man who
always walked out in front of him in crowds of people, coming
out of doors, in hotel lobbies, searching the faces of waiting fans
and probing for lurking malice. In those situations he was Elvis's lightning rod, designed to absorb and handle any jolts
meant for Elvis. The job required guts, intuition, and a perpet-
ual capacity for violence. Elvis was putting his life in David's
hands, and the responsibility was mind boggling.

"He wouldn't go anywhere without me," he says. "He knew
how I felt about him. There was an emotional bond between
us, and Elvis knew I would never hesitate to put my life before
his." That, apparently, was part of the arrangement, and Elvis
even asked David how he felt about it.

"David, would you die for me?" he asked.

"Yes, sir," was the reply.

Elvis was coming out of a hotel in Chicago to a waiting limousine. David recalls leading the way when a man approached,
his hands buried in the pockets of a bulky overcoat. There was a
distant and strange glint in his eye that David didn't like.

"Hold it right there," said David, coming up against him.

The man's speech was garbled and drunken, but it sounded
like "I'm gonna get 'im."

128   "Just keep goin', Elvis," he said, turning to the Boss as he
swept by. David's gun was out and pressed against the man's
ribs. It was a nine millimeter, its barrel gleaming in the afternoon sunlight. The safety was off, his finger caressed the trigger,
and his adrenaline pumped.

"Mister," he said into the man's ear. "I'm warnin' you. If you
want your fuckin' guts blown all over this sidewalk, just keep it
up."

David turned him over to the police after Elvis drove away.
Later, when he told the Boss about the incident, Elvis just
stared off into space for a few seconds, then slapped David hard
on the back. "God*damn*, David, that's how you do it!"

Petty jealousies and rivalries were also a part of the texture of
the TCB group and played into the picture of the dynamics of
life on the road. Usually, when they began to annoy Elvis, he
managed to squash them. The Stanley boys, for instance, irked
the West boys, particularly Red, who was forever trying to tell
people what to do. Ricky and David didn't take kindly to being
ordered about by anyone but Elvis, Joe, Vernon, or Colonel
Parker. David's cocky self-confidence didn't help matters. Red
got so mad at him once that he smacked him and knocked him
out. Vernon told Red to hit the road after that, but Red was
rehired after David requested that he be forgiven. The Boss
always supported his brothers in these disputes. "Red would try
to get on our case," says David, "and Elvis would say to us,
'Hey, I don't care what those guys say; *I'm* the bottom line
around here. Whose name is at the bottom of the checks?
Those guys give you a hassle, you just come to me. Just remember that.' Elvis was hip to the jealousy. He could smell it."

One of the reasons that Ricky and David occupied such a
special place in Elvis's life was their readiness to undertake any
of Elvis's spur-of-the-moment voyages with him. Whereas most
of the other TCBers were older, married, more settled, the
brothers were always ready to jump. The same nervous energy
of Elvis's youth which propelled him inexorably toward his goal
of stardom had not waned in his maturity. The time off that the
boys had from the tours was divided between Memphis, Palm

Springs, Los Angeles, Las Vegas, Hawaii, Vail. "Damn," says
David, "Elvis was always itchy: 'Let's do something!' That's why
somebody was at his house twenty-four hours a day; he never
planned to go anywhere. He might be sleeping and get the bug,
and you could be laying in bed, making love to your wife, when
the phone rings. Some of the older guys would bitch. Elvis
would say, 'Let's go,' and their reaction would be 'Ah, shit . . .
come on, Boss.' That's something that me and Ricky never did.
When he'd call, we'd say, 'OK, Let's get it there!' and we'd be
off."

Nosy reporters seemed to be everywhere on the road. Official
TCB policy to the press was clearly spelled out: "We just never
paid attention to them," says Rick, "that's how we handled it.
We weren't rude because Elvis didn't like that. They would ask
us questions about him, and it would be 'Sorry, I'm busy now.'
Man, you just didn't give interviews." Kissinger or any other
government official ever plagued by security leaks would have
been green with envy at the wall of secrecy that the Boss managed to weave around himself. Nothing was ever spilled to the
press because tight-lipped silence was an essential part of TCB-
ing. And what if they had? "Whoo!" exclaims Rick. "I'd leave
town!"

Once in a while one of the group would bring a potential
new member around for the scrutiny of the Boss and the others,
or Elvis would take a liking to someone and ask them around,
but the presence of a stranger among the tightly knit fraternity
almost always changed the chemistry of the TCB entourage.
"When a stranger came in you could just feel it," David says.
"Elvis was the first to know; he always was aware of it. He could
talk to somebody and know right on the spot if it was going to
work or not. Maybe they would last a day."

When the tours extended to grueling thirty-day stretches or
six-week engagements in Vegas, things either got frazzled,
burned out, or just flat-out boring. To keep Elvis loose, David
would offer himself for roughhousing. Their relationship turned
into a series of running encounters, like Cato the oriental
houseboy's surprise assaults on Peter Sellers's Inspector Clou-

130   seau in the Pink Panther movies. (David was Cato.) Lying in ambush for the Boss, he would pounce on him with a hair-raising scream, and the two of them would go flying across rooms, bounding off walls and onto beds, rolling on floors, laughing, struggling. Furniture was broken, but spirits weren't.

"Back in those days, when he was married," Rick says, "it could get pretty rough because you just didn't have a day off. You never knew when he wanted to go somewhere. All the time we got on each other's nerves, and you felt like decking one of the guys or quitting. But there were two rules when you worked for Elvis: You don't hit and you don't quit."

"There was a certain part of touring that wasn't good," David says, looking back. "You had freedom, but if you were married, it was bad. Sometimes when Elvis wasn't sociable, it was a drag. Sometimes when he was too sociable, it was a drag."

"It cost you," says Billy.

David agrees: "Hey man, it gets lonesome on that road because you live it. You live like he lives."

When loneliness or boredom set in, there were always chicks to take up the slack. Natalie Wood once remarked about Elvis that he was sexier onstage with one "pop" than Tom Jones was after two hours of sweating, bumping, and grinding. Elvis Presley's sexual effect on women was hypnotic—supernatural is more like it. The TCB group became a sexual excursion, an erotic soap opera, and the pleasure boat left the docks every time the Boss revved up the engines of his jet and cranked up his road show.

Women were definitely a fringe benefit of working for the Boss. After the sob stories and bribes were refused, one of the ways that women tried to get to Elvis was by offering to perform any and all acts of sexual derring-do for the boys as long as they could meet Elvis after all was said and done.

David was known as a wolf on tour, but the Boss christened Ricky "Slick Rick, the Raven from Whitehaven" for his smooth manners, sweet talk, and the ease with which he handled women. He had them in every city, every port, and if he didn't, Elvis would let him fly them in.

Today, when they reflect back on the women in the life of the group, the boys shake their heads and recognize that those years could not have but adversely affected their attitudes about the "real" world. "Man, I did things with that group that I never thought I'd do in my life," comments Rick. Billy agrees: "Yeah, we saw a lot of kinky shit at a young age." Most of it happened in Vegas, during those slow moments in the life of the town when the action was down and Elvis would be lying low.

Elvis: What Happened? purported to "expose" the whole can of worms of Elvis's sex life, and the boys feel the need to set certain things straight about what happened and why—specifically those "scenes" that allegedly took place up in his Imperial Suite. According to Rick, "Red and Sonny made a big deal out of the fact that Elvis hired hookers for the boys and then liked to indulge in voyeurism." The boys think that's unfair and bristle at the hypocrisy. Rick lays it on the line: "Elvis didn't need a hooker," he says. "He would never be with one; the man had a woman whenever he wanted one. Those guys were dingbats enough not to be able to hustle their own women, so Elvis would have to get *them* hookers, otherwise they'd get pouty and act like kids. And Elvis would give them money so they could pay for it themselves and not have to feel bad about it. Now, sometimes he would pay for four or five to come up and make it with the guys, and there were times when we would pull a chain, you know, four guys on one chick, but Elvis would always split. He never instigated it; it was never his idea to do those things. He just wasn't interested in that kind of stuff. He did walk into some wild scenes, though. I won't say that he didn't watch sometimes, but he wasn't into group sex and he wouldn't sit there transfixed like some kind of voyeur. The whole thing was just to keep a little excitement going— everybody gets a little kinky once in a while."

Elvis liked Rick's taste in women. Part of TCBing was to know his tastes. "He was basically a one-woman man," he says, "but if he met a fox and felt like it, he just might knock her off, and man, they got everything—cars, jewelry, homes, you name it." The Boss liked women who were classically feminine—not too small, not too big, with perfect features, but with an empha-

132 sis on that well-proportioned and unbeatable combo of beautiful, rounded ass and long, tapered leg. Movement and grace
were also important; the Boss liked women with poise. "Elvis
loved dancers," adds David. "I think that was the ultimate:
'God, what those women can do with their bodies. . . .' "

As a Sex Symbol of the First Magnitude, the Boss had
women waiting for him around every corner. His sexual
charisma appealed to every conceivable type of woman of every
age from the middle-aged ladies who threw their panties and
keys at him onstage to the pert groupies who tried to attract his
attention everywhere he went. The Boss was aware that women
often wanted him simply because he was "Elvis," to sleep with a
Genuine Living Legend. Sometimes he found the situation
more amusing than anything else. Other times it seemed awesome or plain tiresome. And sometimes his libido was equal to
the challenge. When it was, there was LA Talent, Vegas Talent, Road Chicks, but he loved Local Talent the best—those
down-home types from Memphis, Tennessee.

"He really wasn't much into the starlet-actress-model type
after awhile," says Rick. "Elvis liked a wholesome, refined type
of woman. He liked women with class who knew how to handle
themselves but who weren't uppity. Clean appearances were
very important, no cigarette smoking, bad language, drinking,
anything like that. That's what he looked for. If he saw a
woman with a beer can in her hand, no matter if she was the
most beautiful woman in the world, he would just cringe."

In a way Elvis was caught between the image of the mature
worldly woman that men find so attractive and young, innocent,
beautiful girls who epitomized cheerleaders and beauty queens.
Says Rick, "Elvis liked a 'woman'; most of the time he wasn't
into really young chicks, and I've seen him with some of the
best. Sometimes we'd be sitting around and another girl would
come along and someone would say, 'There's no way he's
gonna get this one,' and someone else would say, 'Just you
wait,' and sure enough, he'd slap a Mercedes or a home on
them and . . ."

According to Rick, when it came right down to sex itself, the
Boss was, if anything, remarkably old fashioned and traditional

in his attitudes. "It was very, very straight," he says. "There was 133
nothing kinky about him. Elvis was very proper. I have different
standards when it comes to sex, but Elvis had certain ideas. He
was very private; he wasn't into nudity. He liked mystique; he
liked to use his imagination. That's the way he was."

Elvis also never allowed himself to be seen in the nude. Billy
remembers a skinny-dipping party out in California, held at
Tom Franck's home in Palm Springs. All of the guys and their
dates were around the pool, lounging casually, nude, when the
Boss came out to make a token appearance—a towel tightly
wrapped around his midsection. As he was standing there talking to a few of the ladies, Red West came up behind him and
ripped away the towel, leaving him standing there in his birthday suit for all who cared to see. The Boss glanced down at
himself: "Oh, excuse me, ladies," he said, unflustered, diving
into the pool—the very picture of modesty.

The Boss was not the kiss-and-tell type, either. "He wasn't
the sort to sit around and tell war stories about women," Rick
says. But if it was just a one-nighter or a lark, he might emerge
from his room in the morning, bemused and grinning sheepishly, and say something like "Man, she turned me every way
but loose" or "Get me some oysters, protein, anything!"

The worst thing that a woman could do if she wanted to have
a lasting relationship with Elvis Presley was to throw herself at
his feet, for it was always the women who were the easiest—
those ready to tumble into his bed—whom he respected the
least in the end. He treated them well, say the boys, but they
rarely lasted longer than a week before he would let them down
easy.

Any new woman brought into the group was immediately
subject to an unspoken one-to-ten rating on the TCB Richter
scale. The Boss never settled for less than a seven or an eight;
anything less than five was considered, well, canine. The
women were also treated according to official TCB jungle rules.
With women around, it could become a jungle, but it was the
Boss's jungle, and that was jungle rule number one: Never
make it with Elvis's chick. "God! It was an unwritten code!"
Rick says. "That's one thing you never did!" Sometimes Rick

134 and Jerry Schilling had to tread softly on the Boss's ego because they introduced the girls to Elvis. The problem was that the women they brought around sometimes liked *them* too. "I never fooled with any of his women," Rick says. "If he was finished dating them, I would ask if I could date her, but I never brought her around because it would be uncomfortable."

The group often brought their girl friends around for the Boss's approval. If he liked one enough, he was also known to swoop in for the kill. He wasn't beyond putting his arm around his brothers and saying, "Hey, if you let me date your girl friend, I'll get you a new car," but this was a rarity because the knowledge that a woman had already been with one of the other guys almost automatically disqualified her from his consideration. He had enough of his own—so many, in fact, that he would ask Rick to "keep her on ice for a while" or "tell her to stay in a holding pattern until I'm ready."

"Usually he would see the sharpest woman and find out where her head was at," Rick says. "He'd just sit there and rap with her." The Presley manner with women was irresistible—respectful, natural, gentlemanly, never pushy, always attentive, never contrived—no caveman routines and easy on the macho; just country boy sincerity, and it worked every time. "Elvis never tried to be 'cool' with women," says Rick. "There was an aura around him. You could feel his presence when he walked into a room."

Another jungle rule: no "dogs" around the Boss—just quality women. Some of the TCB boys were known to date "heavy fours" or even "threes." "We ought to send her a box of heart-shaped Gainesburgers for Valentine's Day," the Boss would joke.

Smart-assed, pushy, wise-cracking women were to be kept away at all cost; Elvis had little patience for them. If they got under his skin, the Boss was sometimes known to tell them to quit the premises, and those who refused to leave were bodily ejected (though gingerly). Billy remembers an incident: At a small Hollywood party one particular woman seemed bent on giving the Boss a hard time. He lit a match to light a cigar and she blew it out. He ignored her and lit another and, yep, she blew it out again. Everyone watching who knew Elvis winced when this happened, seeing the signs of impending eruption brewing. When Elvis Presley was getting mad, his face looked unperturbed for a second, like the calm before the storm, then his features would suddenly perk up and his eyes flash a steely blue. But Elvis was determined to remain nice. Nobody knew what the woman's problem was, but when Elvis asked for a glass of water, she picked it up and threw it in his face. The room was deathly silent as the water dribbled down his face and onto his shirt. The Boss looked like he just might tear her limb from limb. "I'm sorry but you'll have to leave my house now," he said, slowly and softly, probably hoping that she would give him one more excuse to throw her out himself. She left.

Everyone had their moments on cloud nine around Elvis, when they were flying high and sitting on top of the world, but moments in the mudhole were also a part of TBCing. Within the TBC group everybody had his little nickname and the Boss's was "Crazy." Elvis's moods set the tempo for group life. The nature of being "Elvis Presley" dictated that he establish a comfortable space for himself in order to simply relax, be himself, and let it all hang out. It meant never leaving his side.

"Elvis would let us know what a drag it was to be confined," says Rick. "He'd say, 'Hey . . I'm not like you guys. I can't get out to a nice restaurant and do simple things like that.' That's why Elvis needed companions, not just employees. He needed somebody that could stick around and hang out with him and not gripe about it. Hell, sometimes I really wanted to get out by myself, but I spent a lot of time around him."

When the Boss was feeling up, everybody was up. When he was down, watch out! Elvis gave his volatile temper free reign within the confines of the group. Any number of things could get Elvis ruffled, and there wasn't an individual in the group who did not become the target of his wrath. Usually it was caused by any number of things building up inside of him, tightening up, creating intense pressure which would then be touched off by something seemingly insignificant that someone either did or failed to do. Rick was witness to every mood the

136   man could conjure, and he illuminates his character better than anyone: "He might get angry about the way his food was served—like if it wasn't cooked properly, or cold," he says, "but you had to realize that the sound may have been bad that night or maybe he got a bad review or had a hassle with a girl friend that kept him up all night."

The Boss also did not like to be taken lightly, and when he thought that he was—particularly if the endless grind of the tours was beginning to get him—chances are that you would know about it. The moods of the people around him also affected his state. Rick explains: "If Elvis was out on the road busting it for twenty-eight days, some of the guys would come in with long faces after only two weeks. He didn't need to see people like that. The environment affected him. He needed to see people up and feeling good; if he saw somebody down and bugged about something, it would pull him down too because he would want to know why. He cared."

It was precisely because he cared that Elvis would invariably apologize after shooting someone down, and shoot them down he did. "Ooooh, boy," whistles Rick, "he could ride an ass! Elvis could get downright cruel. Man! He could get so cruel and come down on somebody so hard that you'd have to start laughing. But it was only for the moment. If he got down too hard, he'd come to you later on and say, 'Hey man, I'm sorry. . . . It's been a rough tour.' "

Elvis only got physical and struck someone in anger once. According to Rick it happened when a fellow who worked with the group only a short time forged some checks in Elvis's name, ripped off some of his jewelry, and—the clincher that really cooked his goose!—started prying into private affairs. Elvis discovered the theft in Vegas and went after him at the airport. When they found him, he was apprehended by the TCB boys with all of the ceremony that the FBI reserves for only the most heinous criminals and fugitives from justice. The guy was dragged back to the hotel to stand trial in Elvis's suite. The Boss just couldn't understand the whole thing because it seemed so unnecessary in the first place. Elvis's policy was to let the boys know that if ever they needed money or had a problem, he was

always there. He was hurt and outraged, and when they returned, he smacked the man in the face, twice.

"Man, what kind of person would *steal* from the person who
is feeding him?" he demanded emotionally. "I gave you a good
job and treated you right; I paid your expenses and did the best I
could for you, and you turn around and *steal* from me! What
the hell is that, *boy?!*"

"Ten minutes later," remembers Rick, "Elvis was crying,
apologizing to him. He said, 'Hey man, I'm sorry . . . I'm not
a bully who hits people.' " After the guy went home to Memphis, Elvis called him up and apologized once again for losing
his temper. "You hurt my feelings," he said, "but I want to
know if you'll come back to work for me."

"That's the type of man Elvis Presley was," says Rick. "He
never did things to willfully hurt people; he was quick to
forgive, and he didn't hold grudges, either. Mostly, he inflicted
his pain on himself."

The existence of yes-men around the Boss never made it easy
to know who was true blue and who wasn't. To a degree, everybody subordinated his identity to Elvis and bowed to his will.
But for the person being 'yesed,' sychophancy always has pitfalls. At the root of the problem was that agreeing with the Boss
was part of your job, part of TCBing. "Not everybody was a yes-
man," says Rick, "but you tried your best to keep the man in a
good mood, because it could be rough if he got into a bad one."

The Boss expected some things of you. When people were
around, for instance, it was very important to show him "respect." In any roomful of people, he was the center. "If Elvis
was talking," says Rick, "he had to be the focus. Usually everything around him was informal and relaxed unless he really admired somebody and wanted to impress them. Then you really
had to be on your toes. We always knew who he admired or
liked, whether it was a celebrity or not. Elvis would want everything to go well, but he never had to tell us. We always kept
alert and made the man look good. That was the main thing—
making *him* look good."

It was one thing to make Elvis look good, it was quite another
to laugh when he laughed, hang on his every word, and agree

138   with everything he did, right or wrong, which is the inevitable result of such an arrangement. Some around him did exactly that; others managed to retain a fair degree of individuality and to influence his thinking, but only to a degree, for there were times when Elvis would make his mind up about something and become as immovable as the Rock of Gibralter. It was this scheme of things that would ultimately allow Elvis to believe many of his own most self-destructive lies.

Dee Presley never spent time with Elvis's entourage on the road. Her observations are thus those of any outsider but nevertheless right on target. "Elvis would always like for people to believe and see things the way he did," she says. "Nobody saw things differently. If they did, they didn't have the nerve to tell him. People who worked for him rarely took a firm stand."

Ricky and David were with Elvis much of the time. The fact that they were family sometimes allowed them more of a latitude for honesty around him in their relationship, but they are inclined to agree with their mother. "It was just a different world around Elvis," Rick says. "It was *his* world and *his* ballgame, and if you didn't like it, just don't let the gate hit you in the butt on your way out!"

For the TCB group—Elvis's closest friends and confidants—it was sometimes extremely hard to put their fingers on just exactly who he really was. One minute he was a lawgiver, a wise man like Solomon, mature, compassionate, down-to-earth; the next, he was the little boy from Tupelo, Mississippi. "He was like a little kid in so many ways," sighs Rick. "If you ever hurt his feelings or if he couldn't get his way, he was like a petulant child, brooding and pouting."

Another reason it remained so hard to pin down his identity was because he parceled himself out, telling different things to different people, laying down smokescreens to "cover his ass," keeping the total picture away from one individual. Intimacy made him uncomfortably vulnerable and more uneasy as the years passed. In Rick's opinion, there are only a select few individuals in the world who can claim that they actually "know" Elvis Presley, and many who have either written or are presently writing books about him aren't among them. "Joe Esposito

knew him," he says. "He knew it all. Priscilla knew the man
very well. Vernon, of course, and a couple of the guys like
Lamar. Linda Thompson did. I felt like I did, too. In the end,
nobody really knew more than anybody else; it all depended on
what was going on. I feel like I had the total picture of Elvis,
but there will always be questions in my mind about him. He
was that kind of a man. He was a fascinating but complicated
man, the kind who could do something that would make you
think he was one of the lowest people in the world and then
turn right around and pull something that could make you cry
and think he was the most magnificent, finest, biggest-hearted
person on God's earth. You've got to look very deeply and consider so many aspects of his life before you can even begin to
understand the man and what happened to him. . . ."

CHAPTER 8

ROCK ME, LORD

A life as important, extraordinary, and highly publicized as Elvis Presley's will always lend itself to every imaginable cliché. It's so difficult to even categorize Elvis because that's the way *he* wanted it. In life, he was an enigma—a walking, breathing paradox that mixed the simple with the profound, the banal with the extraordinary. In death the real man has been even more obscured by his snowballing legends and myths.

The country boy may have seemed easy to grasp but the superstar certainly wasn't, for the superstar provided a little something for everybody. Elvis Presley combined an irresistible and purely American combination of images and influences into one grand concoction of his own making. Like America herself, he, too, was a melting pot; his influences were like ingredients going into an astonishing blender, the mixture that resulted was his life. He reflected the uniqueness and contradictions of the diverse, vast country and people that loved him and made him what he was. Truckdrivers, farmers, singers, athletes, soldiers, movie stars, lovers, dreamers, sinners, and

142 saints found their way into his soul to become a part of him, and yet he could be all of them at once or none of them at all. Elvis was Elvis. He was like his songs, taking what he wanted from something and making it so entirely his own that what emerged was his and nobody else's.

Onstage, in front of his adoring masses, the Boss was most truly in his element—belting out a song, moving, working, sweating, dramatizing himself in front of the colorful extravaganza that showcased the image, making people happy by riding it to the hilt for all of its glories and pitfalls. This, then, is where we begin.

"He was *the* showman," muses Rick. "He knew *exactly* what to do when he was up there, everything—how he looked at the people, how he smiled or frowned, all of the expressions he would hit on different notes in different songs. He knew exactly what the public wanted to see and he gave it to them. When he got on that stage, it was his domain. You can reveal his personal life, and people will always be interested in that, but what it all boils down to is that people acknowledged him for what he did up there, for the magnetism, power, and control he had over his audiences. Hey, I don't care whatever else he did in his life; when he got on that stage, he owned it, and nobody could touch him up there. Nobody could tell him what was good or bad either, because he *knew*."

Elvis often called the stage his "life's blood." It was his emotional release, his reward, his high, his very identity, and there was nothing more important to him than being able to walk out in front of his fans and say, "We're here to entertain you, ladies and gentlemen—just leave the driving to us!"

No matter how many times he did it or how old the routine, there was still a jolting thrill for him to get out there. In David's opinion it was most obvious during those unforgettable moments backstage, in the wings, just before he stepped out to the wandering spots and the blinding glare of thousands of flashbulbs popping and that deafening, almost frightening roar that the mere sight of him walking across the stage was sure to unleash. "He was always nervous before he went on," he says. "It was really a trip to be standing next to him in the wings with

the theme from *2001: A Space Odyssey* playing. He'd look
around and say something funny but he was shaking like a leaf.
I'd go up and grab him by the shoulders and lock my arm
around his arm and he would pull hard on it to relax some of
the tension in his body. Sometimes I'd even hit him. Everybody
would be back there psyching him up, saying, 'Go out there
and get 'em, Boss!' "

"As soon as he got out there," continues Rick, "he would
turn back and look at us with one of those sly grins because he
knew he was cool out there once things got going. Man, he
could do anything with a crowd, and he had fun. He'd kid
David and I and give us a look like 'hey, watch this . . .' and
he would get ten thousand people to scream really quick and
then stop and he would look back at us as if to say, 'Pretty good,
huh?' "

"People were not disappointed when they saw him," adds
Bill, "and that's what he was all about. He never walked out
there and did a half-assed show; he pushed himself to the limit,
and when he came off that stage, man, it was like he had been
playing football for hours." As part of the "wrecking crew" that
got Elvis ready for the show and helped undress him after it,
Billy saw him prepare for the show and helped him recover.
The name "wrecking crew" was an appropriate one, he says,
because the Boss was usually wrecked after the show.

Elvis liked to arrange his performances so that they eddied
and flowed with different kinds of meaning and energy for his
audiences. He sandwiched the stock numbers everybody associated with him—rockers like "Hound Dog," "That's All
Right (Mama)," and the medleys—in between bits of country-
and-western, gospel, romantic ballads, and a few novelty numbers. It was audience manipulation, Elvis style: "He would love
to get the audience up on their feet with a certain song so that
the chicks were surging against the stage," says Rick. "Then
he'd put on a love ballad and just get them right back down in
their seats." The desired effect was that the fans—all very familiar with the man, his image, and the material—would be tanta-
lized by the anticipation of what was coming next. Elvis would
control them at will, getting them into his mood. That way the

144   audience would be able to empathize with the man on the stage and receive satisfaction—get everything they came for. For Elvis, performing was like making love to a woman and making sure he pleased her.

Some audiences were harder to seduce than others, but the Boss always rose to the challenge. "The bigger billings like the Spectrum, the Omni in Atlanta, Madison Square Garden, the Nassau Coliseum, and the Cow Palace in San Francisco would be more of a challenge for him," says Rick. "He'd just kick in that much harder and really go after the crowd."

Elvis's body movement was an integral part of his image, one of his most surefire stage mechanisms and a trigger that always set the audiences blasting off as soon as he squeezed it. The shaking, emphatic gesticulations of the preachers in the little church on Adams Street in Tupelo had taught Elvis one important lesson about body language: If people know how to speak with their bodies, they can get people to listen with their bodies. The relationship that he felt between music and physical energy can be thus traced back to his years singing spirituals, which take their complex rhythms from the very complexities of the body. Elvis never lost sight of the physicality of his music, and how that physicality could be used to put himself across onstage. From the moment he walked out onstage, it was as if he patched his body right into a high-voltage wire. He crackled with energy, and the music resonated throughout his body.

When he strolled out to the opening strains of "See See Rider," all studded with stones and shining, it would be that one pose that Elvis would cut when he stopped at the mike stand—legs spread far apart, one in front of the other, the knees bent, the guitar slung at his side (now more for showing than for blowing)—that would let the people know that . . . yes, folks, *Elvis Presley*'s here. Get ready for some fun!

In the wake of the explosion set off by his comeback, the critics had nothing but the most glowing words of praise for Elvis. *He* has resurrected himself, they seemed to collectively say, and everywhere he brought his show, Elvis was lauded. Within several years many of them began to point out—some

quite savagely—that he was no longer growing as an artist; they
criticized him for being content to parody himself and what he
once was, for presenting nothing more than his myths and
legends onstage and thus not taking his art to higher levels of
risk and achievement.

Well, the Boss just didn't see things that way. Onstage he *was*
his myths, and the performance of those myths was, to him, a
legitimate form of musical theater, complete with all of the necessary polytechnics. Elvis considered himself to be an "entertainer," not a "rock star," not even "King of Rock 'n' Roll," and
his integrity as an entertainer was all wrapped up in giving people what they wanted, in courting them amorously, and in
being able to say that he never left a crowd feeling short-
changed, as if he and the Colonel just took the money and ran.
In the singular endeavor of just "doing his job and doing it
well," critics were irrelevant. As most people who were around
him well knew, he was by far his own worst, most uncompromising critic.

Elvis's numbers may have become "locked in" by the demands of his public, but when it came to the show itself, he was
a consummate perfectionist. Everything—music, lighting,
sound quality, his appearance, and the organization of the concert itself—had to be just so, *his* way. Elvis had a natural ear for
music that had always allowed him to serve as his own producer. When he was up on a stage, he could immediately tell
what was lacking in his sound. That's why he wanted everything
perfect *before* he even got out there, and if it wasn't, he considered it to be a serious breach of professionalism on the part of
his group and a bad reflection on himself. For that reason he
had Ricky, David, and others walking around to all parts of the
concert halls and stadiums, checking acoustics, making sure
that everyone would get a clear earful of what he had to offer.
Feedback unnerved him, as did most other technical mishaps
that occurred during the course of a performance. "I've seen a
mike go out," says Rick, "and he would just take it in disgust
and throw it clear across the stage." In the event of such displays
of temper, the Boss would turn apologetically to his audiences:
"Ladies and gentlemen, I'm sorry about this but we seem to be

146 having a little problem with the sound system, but I'll be *damned* if we don't get it straightened out!" Then he would storm off to the wings, fuming. "If you guys can't get it together, I'll just have to get some people who can . . . tomorrow!"

He did leave a slight margin for error, but only with the musicians. If the bass was too loud or the rhythm guitar slightly off, it would be corrected onstage or brought up after the show in the dressing room, where several people usually lingered to hang out with Elvis and critique the evening's performance. Ricky, David, Charlie Hodge, Larry Geller, Joe Esposito, and others would take it up with Joe Guercio, his musical director. In the end, say the boys, Elvis could be very sensitive to the reviews: "When a show was just popping," says Rick, "and everything was going really well—the crowd was warmed up and Elvis was really hooking and moving a lot onstage with a lot of different moods—he became totally locked into the show. If he got a lousy review after putting himself out that way, he could never understand it. We'd blame it on the town."

North, south, east, or west—it made no difference: "Man, these bunch of country bumpkins don't know what they're talkin' 'bout!" said the boys whenever the Boss got what they felt was an unfair review, or "bunch of smart-assed northerners. . . ."

The Boss always felt confident about the singers and musicians who accompanied him onstage. The original band that he had put together for his first series of Vegas engagements had stayed on and jelled beautifully over the years into one of the finest, most versatile bands in the business.

On lead guitar James Burton, an old-timer from Shreveport, Louisiana, who began his career with Rick Nelson way back in the early sixties, was the man who injected the decorative flair into Elvis's live sound. An excellent rock guitarist, Burton punched in all the frantic leads that Scotty Moore had once provided for Elvis's early recordings. James gave his guitar a distinctly modernized tone, however, and you can hear it in his wah-wah pedal in Elvis's live version of "Polk Salad Annie"— he sounds like a hard-rock guitarist there—but then he could

come right back to embellish a country tune with riffs that 147
twanged and skipped like a fresh-faced country boy visiting New
Orleans for the first time. Burton's guitar wizardry dazzled
Elvis, who, as a guitarist himself, could appreciate his touch:
"Man, those licks were X-*rated!*" he would marvel after Burton
played a blues.

Elvis's bassist was another studio musician, Jerry Scheff, who
also hooked up with Elvis for the Las Vegas engagements and
who worked well with Burton because he was essentially the
same kind of musician—a refined, highly competent stylist capable of breaking loose on an uptempo number. Scheff's playing also synched in nicely with Ronnie Tutt's drumming.

Next to Elvis, Tutt was perhaps the most important person on
the stage. To see him slouched behind his wall of tom-toms and
high-ride cymbals between numbers, it seemed hard to
believe that the bearded, good-natured Texan was the same
man who pounded all of that life and rhythm into Elvis Presley's shows, but as the strings and horns trailed off after the dramatic crescendo of *Also sprach Zarathustra,* Tutt cut loose, and
it was the energy released from his drums that found its way into
Elvis's hips on the more rousing, uptempo numbers. A superb
"technical" drummer, Tutt, like Burton and Scheff, was also a
man for all seasons, but deep down he was a rock drummer—
plain and simple—and his technical versatility combined with
his rock 'n' roll instincts to make him the perfect drummer for
the "big" sound that Elvis built around himself. David Stanley,
also a talented drummer, always tried to watch Tutt closely to
pick up some of the tricks of the trade: "I think Elvis loved that
hard-rock drummer more than anything," he says. "He loved it
when he was kicking so hard it would almost throw him off the
stage."

Off to the right, in a row up front, were Kathy Westmoreland
and the Sweet Inspirations, and behind them or alongside were
J.D. Sumner and the Stamps Quartet. Together they took the
place of the famous Jordonaires on all of Elvis's old numbers
and formed a richly textured, soulful cathedral of voices around
Elvis's. The Stamps and the Sweets were very carefully arranged
by Elvis so that he could either blend his own baritone magnifi-

148 cently with them on gospels or just step out in front of them while they filled in rhythmic vocal spaces in the background. Elvis got exactly what he wanted: The Stamps and Sweets could bring the full feeling of a choir and congregation and all of the fervor of a revivalist meeting to Elvis's stage, or they could surround him with the bopping a capella and finger-snapping harmonies displayed by some of the best vocal groups during the early years of rock 'n' roll.

Behind all of this—the musicians up front and the vocal back-up off to the side—was a full-piece orchestra conducted by Joe Guercio, veteran of the Hilton and master of the Vegas extravaganza, whose strings and horns put the crowning touch of class on the whole setup. The sight of the full assembled band onstage—all multicolored and dancing with glitter and sparkle in the stage lights—was a spiffy enough sight even without Elvis's presence, but when he stepped out in front of them, they became like one living organism behind him, growing and contracting to maximize his effect, blending the style of Vegas with the substance of Nashville. The Boss loved his band with all of the enthusiasm that a little boy would have for a wonderful toy, and you would see it in his face—that sense of fun and power—when he would be sliding into an uptempo number that put together all of the components. His rhythm section was always keyed on his every move, and with one swipe of his hand or quick cut of his hips he would drop everyone onstage right into overdrive. Tutt would be crashing ahead furiously, the guitars would be wailing, and the Stamps and Sweets would turn up a grand, multilayered AAAAAH! in perfect harmony, then a syncopated DOOOOP! right before the horn section kicked in like a crisp slap in the face. At that moment you could again see Elvis most truly in his element, perfectly at harmony with himself and his world, when everything in his life would intersect for a brief musical interlude and create an energy so boundless and vital that he could gather it in the palm of his hand and hurl it out at his audiences like a thunderbolt before suddenly ending it with one vicious thrust of his fist.

"You know," Rick says, "your adrenaline got going every bit as much as his. It was the best band, man, they were just so tight

and that stage was rocking! It was really exciting to be up there
when everybody was pulling like that to tear the roof down."

Sometimes Elvis would be just as awed by his band as the audience was. David remembers Elvis featuring Joe Guercio's Hilton Hothorns in Vegas during one of his engagements. The
Hothorns would come out playing a snazzy horn arrangement
of Chuck Berry's "School Days" ("Hail, hail rock 'n'
roll . . ."). "The guitar player would really kick out the lead,"
he says, "and Elvis would just stand there amazed and watch
them and say, 'Wow, do that again!' and they would just take it
from the top. It was crazy, man. He was really into that band."

Onstage he kept himself and the whole TCB operation loose
with his unpredictable pranks, jokes, stage antics, and that irresistible banter about himself that poked fun at the very image
that the fans found so overwhelming. He also had his special
"treatment," which nobody escaped. David might be leaning
down in front of the piano and Elvis would sweep by, grab him
by the hair, take a glass of water from Charlie Hodge, and pour
it over his head without missing a note: "What could you do?"
he laughs. "You'd just look at him like 'Wait till I get you backstage, motherfucker!' "

The Boss also loved dragging people out onstage (those that
didn't want to go, that is). After finishing a song, he would get
that puckish smile on his face and say, "Ladies and gentlemen,
I have somebody with me tonight that I want you all to see.
This is the goofiest person I've ever seen in my life . . ." and
the unsuspecting victim would be dragged out by those who
were hip to the conspiracy. Joe Esposito was a favorite target
because of his dead fear of the spotlight. Whenever he knew
that Elvis was up to his tricks, Joe would start heading in the opposite direction, but to no avail. After catching him, Ricky and
David would carry him out, kicking, to the Boss. But then it
would be "All kidding aside, folks . . ." and Elvis would go on
to praise whoever it was on the spot. It was one of his ways of
having fun as well as taking his hat off and acknowledging his
gratitude.

Elvis's hottest performances, say the boys, came during the
period 1969–1972, but it wasn't until as late as 1972 that Elvis

150 felt he had the stage show perfected. That's when he came to New York and blew out Madison Square Garden, which they remember as among his most special, dynamic performances. David feels that Elvis's most spectacular performance came in 1974, at the Los Angeles Forum. "I've never seen Elvis or the band better," he says, "and I'm not being prejudiced. They just took the place apart."

The engagements in Las Vegas and Lake Tahoe gave that elite community of Elvis's fellow entertainers and celebrities a chance to show up and catch the show, and they came in bunches. Elvis had a stellar reputation in the entertainment world, and almost everyone passing through made it a point to stop in. "A lot of the people in the business really loved him," says Rick, "because he was a friendly man who had the reputation of wanting them to come backstage to visit him."

The list of people who came by reads like a *Who's Who* of American show business. Singers like Glen Campbell, Leon Russell, Vicki Carr, Ann-Margret, Barbra Streisand, and Wayne Newton were longtime admirers and friends who often came by. Liza Minnelli, Gregory Peck, Kirk Douglas, and Rod Steiger were also ardent Presleyphiles, among many others.

Rick recalls what often happened during those backstage visits: "People would come backstage to tell him what a good show they thought he did, and Elvis would turn it around to talk about something he'd seen them do, about what a good job they did in a certain movie; he could always quote specific things. He would remember the exact setting and quote the lines and do it just the way they did in the movie. Man, they loved it. Elvis would give them gifts, too; he was always the giver, always the host. People would offer him compliments and awards and he never knew how to behave."

The backstage area and Elvis's dressing room became the site of many meetings and reunions. A wide-eyed Muhammad Ali would stride in after a show and cuff the Boss playfully. "Gawd!" he would shout. "We *got* to be the two best-looking sumbitches in the world!"

Alice Cooper might suddenly appear out of nowhere, or

George Harrison might pop in. Even Linda Lovelace once stopped by. Now, the Boss didn't exactly like to rub elbows with porn stars (bad for the image). He didn't want to have his picture taken with her, say the boys, but he was polite and sociable. "The big question running through everybody's mind," chuckles Rick, "was can she *really* . . ?" Nobody found out.

The Boss tried to repay these visits, but his presence at someone else's show always created problems. It was unfortunate because Elvis was a great respecter of talent and would have liked to visit some of his colleagues more often to see what they were up to. "It would be hell for him to go listen to somebody else," says Billy, "and all of a sudden be introduced or noticed because everybody would start crowding around his table instead of listening to who was singing. He hated to take anything away from anybody's performance. That's why we would always walk in just before the entertainer came on, when the lights went down."

Sometimes, at the end of his performance, Elvis would pay homage to the music in his life. He would be standing there in a lone spotlight, exhausted, his hair mussed and the sweat glistening on his forehead and chest, still and serious. "I'd like to say that I learned very early in life," he would say, "that without a song the day would never end, without a song the road would never end . . . when things go wrong a man ain't got a friend without a song . . . so I keep singin' the song. Good night!"

And with that he would suddenly disappear into the wings to be whisked away in a limousine, leaving the tens of thousands of people standing there to digest it all.

Music was the glue that held together all of the disparate elements in Elvis's life. It was the most powerful and enduring truth, the foundation upon which he built everything and the anchor that held it down and kept it from floating away.

When he began to put together his repertoire for his comeback, Elvis was able to draw upon some thirty years of American popular music, of his own making and of others', and it became apparent that although he had the range and instincts to sing just about anything, he needed to be as comfortable with

152   his material as he was around the boys that worked for him. His songs had to suit him like his cars, his guns, like Graceland. Elvis knew that he had a public to please, but if he wanted to do something different, he pleased himself, too, as long as he did it his way. All of the crowd-pleasing Elvis Golden Oldies would remain—"That's All Right (Mama)," "Can't Help Falling in Love," "Love Me Tender," "Don't Be Cruel," "Heartbreak Hotel," "All Shook Up," "Hound Dog," "Trying to Get to You," "Jailhouse Rock"—many of them now cut into abbreviated versions and put into convenient medleys.

The new material that found its way into his act says much about his life and image. Elvis needed a purely personal "hook" in anything new that he did; something that might come from the style of the music itself, but was more likely to come from something in the lyric through which he could convey himself, a personal handle that he could grasp and fuel something in the audience with.

Elvis knew that the only thing that would keep the music fresh, alive, and meaningful was its emotionality, and he went for this openly. He was not a composer and didn't have the benefit of the personal relationship a singer maintains when he performs his own compositions. He, rather, interpreted others.

"He never sang a song unless he felt it," says Billy, referring to Elvis's extraordinary ability to emote his music. "He had to feel it in his heart, because that's where he sang from, that's what made him a superstar."

"The song had to fit him perfectly," emphasizes Billy. Most of them did. You can run through the songs that Elvis plucked up over the years and look for the personal connections. At Hill and Range, Lamar Fike kept a sharp lookout for new material to try out on the Boss, as did Elvis's producer, Felton Jarvis. Ricky and David also kept their eyes and ears open, and oftentimes Felton tried to pitch songs to Elvis through them to lend the song the appeal of the youth market before Elvis even heard it.

When the boys heard James Taylor's "Steamroller," they knew it was destined to find its way into his repertoire. "What do you say we throw this one in Elvis's face and see what he says?" David asked Rick. They did. Elvis listened once and knew it was all there—the lowdown sexiness that he loved in blues, the sudden outburst of brass, the sly fun of lyrics like "I'm gonna inject your soul with some sweet rock 'n' roll and shoot you full of rhythm and blues." The next day he was rehearsing it, three days later he did it onstage, and two weeks later it was recorded. That's the way it was with Elvis. He reacted the same way when David and Ricky brought him Simon and Garfunkel's moving epic, "Bridge Over Troubled Water," a song that he found immediately challenging and ripe with emotion.

Songs that evoked the South were also naturals. Creedence Clearwater Revival's classic, "Proud Mary," fit right in not only because the song was commercially hot and allowed for the kind of vocal arrangements Elvis loved but because the rousing theme of life on the river excited him so much that it churned like a riverboat when he sang it. Tony Joe White's "Polk Salad Annie" affected him the same way. When Elvis did it, the song reeked of the Louisiana swamps.

Then there were songs that were there for special reasons. Marty Robbins's "You Gave Me a Mountain" expressed his need to persevere, hang in there, and remain strong after his divorce, and the pain of being separated from his daughter. "American Trilogy," which Elvis put together, was nothing less than his showy, flag-waving tribute to the grandeur and majesty of his country and its heritage. Only Elvis could have pulled it off.

In the end the Boss's material remained a very commercial mixed bag of his past and present which served to satisfy a hungry public and reflect his own musical tastes. That personal taste in music—what Elvis preferred and why—is perhaps best illustrated by the kind of music he listened to privately. Of his own recorded music, he leaned heavily toward the dramatic numbers with choral backup. "The attraction for him was the eleven voices hitting at one time," says David, "from the lowest bass to the highest tenors and sopranos hitting that same note. He loved the impact of that." Thus he listened to "Crying in the Chapel," "Unchained Melody," "Bridge Over Troubled

154   Water," "You've Lost That Lovin' Feelin'," and his favorite gospel, "How Great Thou Art."

Mostly, he listened to gospel. In Elvis's opinion, there was nothing more powerful or challenging than good gospel music. Wherever he went, he carried around a case of a hundred or so albums—most of them gospel—for the simple reason that he needed them around. Rick says listening to gospel music was a means for Elvis to get in touch with his roots, and for "giving a little praise to the Lord when he was feeling humble and thankful, which he did do. People don't really know that. It tells you in the Bible to sing praise and lift your voices to Him. That was Elvis's way of doing it." Small wonder that Elvis could move mountains when he sang "How Great Thou Art." "That's because he felt it in his soul," Billy says. "He could make you feel religious just by listening to it." If you walked into one of Elvis's hotel suites or visited him at Graceland, you would have heard Mahalia Jackson on his stereo system. To Elvis, she was the Queen of Gospel. He wore her records out over and over.

And what of rock 'n' roll? Elvis's relationship with the music that would be forever identified with him was, like many other things, supremely ironic. He became less and less interested in rock 'n' roll, even if he would never lose his rocking spirit or shun his rock 'n' roll roots. His comeback proved that he could still rock an audience to its knees, but his career in the movies, the Colonel's direction, and his contract with RCA (as well as his own personal tastes) were pointing him right at the heart of the musical mainstream as exemplified by the American pop song. At his press conference after being discharged, when reporters asked him who his favorite singers were, he replied, "Mr. Sinatra."

It was more than good public relations for his upcoming TV special with Sinatra; Elvis was letting America know that Tin Pan Alley and Broadway were as much a part of him as Memphis and Nashville—that he wanted to croon ballads and love songs as much as he wanted to rock.

The one song that signaled Elvis's departure from rock 'n' roll

_____

during the sixties was "It's Now or Never," released after his
discharge from the army. A recycled, pop version of the Nea-
politan song "O Solo Mio," it was his first great chartbuster
since his induction, and it sent Elvis chasing after Frank Sinatra, Dean Martin, and Tony Bennett. The song was recorded to
melt many a female heart, and it succeeded.

Apart from the meaty middle-of-the-road slice of the market
Elvis was shooting for, the song makes sense if you consider
how much Elvis loved Enrico Caruso and other singers of opera
like Mario Lanza and Robert Merrill. While Elvis never became an opera enthusiast enough to attend opera and learn the
librettos of his favorite arias, he would love to play them, sit
back, and marvel at the purely technical vocal abilities of the
great opera singers—at their range and power. To him there was
nothing more beautiful than a well-trained, multiple-octave
voice that could become a song as naturally as a dress becomes
a beautiful woman.

For those who grew up idolizing Elvis as the rebel, as the underground hero and the "boy who dared to rock," it was hard to
swallow him doing "Love Is a Many Splendored Thing," and
"What Now My Love." Many people during the sixties felt that
Elvis had traded the power of his talent for the slick commer-
cialism of his stardom, which is why his comeback to the stage
was so electrifying, why so many critics wrote of Elvis's "finding
himself" after being lost. Rock 'n' roll needed a monarch, and it
was immensely gratifying to see Elvis once again become its
spiritual and emotional figurehead.

But snowed under, first, by his movie contracts and then by
the pace of his tours, the Boss never really had a chance to keep
pace with the unfolding music of the sixties and seventies. The
boys say that he greatly admired the Beatles almost from the
first; he loved their singing styles and their ability to pen great
pop songs and felt a genuine kinship with them. He also felt
they were the first musical "phenomenon" to come along to
rival his stature. Their manager, Brian Epstein, took many of
his promotional cues from Colonel Tom Parker, seeing how the
Colonel, through the years, had "cleaned up" Elvis's act, legiti-

156 mized him, and made him palatable to the entire world. Yes, the Beatles were competition, and Elvis, ever the prankster, sent them a toy water pistol when they were first breaking in America with a note that invited them to play Russian roulette.

Elvis respected each of the Beatles individually, but it was very characteristic of him, David says, to lean toward the McCartney influence in the band—beautifully stylized pop compositions, catchy love tunes, and rock 'n' roll. He went on to incorporate "Hey Jude" and "Yesterday" into his repertoire. David wanted him to record "The Long and Winding Road" backed by Joe Guercio's strings, but it never happened.

It was also characteristic of Elvis to admire the Beatles but still object to their psychedelic era. According to David, Elvis felt that "Lucy in the Sky With Diamonds" and "Magical Mystery Tour" were irresponsible messages that exhorted too many young people to turn on to drugs.

Bob Dylan was another story. Elvis could recognize Dylan's lyric genius and enjoy the power of an epic like "Blowin' in the Wind," but, on the whole, Dylan was alien. His rasping, unusual voice with its atonal inflections was obnoxious. It took Dylan's "Nashville Skyline" to bring the Boss around. Elvis recorded the one Dylan tune that he found irresistible: "Tomorrow Is a Long Time."

When it came to much of the heavy metal sounds of the late sixties and seventies, Elvis drew the line and kept his distance. Billy and David were great patrons of hard rock and constantly tried to get Elvis to listen to things and make him "understand," but the long-haired heirs to the rock traditions Elvis helped to establish were even more ridiculous to him than he had been to the parents who vilified him during the fifties. He never denigrated them or tried to put them down; he just wasn't interested. David particularly tried to turn him on to Led Zeppelin. When they showed up at his concert at the LA Forum in 1974, David hurried back to Elvis's dressing room to tell him that this time there were "real" celebrities out there. Bemused, Elvis just stared at him. "Led *who?*"

"I'd be wearing a Led Zeppelin T-shirt," David laughs, "and

just to harass me, Elvis would grab me and put me up against a
wall and say, 'Man, just what the hell do you think your doin'
wearin' a Led Zeppelin T-shirt on an *Elvis* tour!' "

Boarding the *Lisa Marie* for a tour, Elvis saw a Kiss sticker on
David's briefcase and called him to the back of the plane.

"You know, David, I hear Kiss has a new album out," said
the Boss.

"Oh yeah? What's it called?" David asked, taking the bait.

"It's called *Kiss My Ass!* David, I just don't understand how
you could ever listen to that shit!"

Jerry Schilling once brought Eric Clapton to one of Elvis's
movie nights in Memphis and the Boss didn't even know who
he was. He liked Eric very much; the boys had to tell him that
Clapton was one of the finest blues and rock guitarists in the
world.

Leon Russell was another story. His voice was strange and
offbeat, but Elvis dug it. Besides, to Elvis, Leon was an Oakie
with real style, even if he always was a bit of a freak. There was
a soulful, funky quality to his music that Elvis liked.

While he may not have kept on top of the contemporary
music scene, Elvis never stopped playing music and retained a
passion for fine instruments and the recreational pleasures of
music in his life. Graceland became the scene of many an
impromptu jam session, which might start with Elvis and Charlie on guitar or around the piano and end up with a roomful of
people happily cooking away. The boys say he was a much better musician than people ever suspected, displaying a profi-
ciency for the drums, bass guitar, and keyboards, and he loved to
sit and tinker with his baby grand piano on the second floor of
the mansion or fill the entire house with the mellotron or
organ. If you ventured by and sang with him around the piano,
he just might use you on his next album, as he did Rick on
"How Great Thou Art."

"Come on, Elvis," Rick said, his face reddening when Elvis
told him he wanted him to sing on the gospel album. "I can't
sing, man."

158   "Don't tell me who can sing and who can't," snapped the Boss. "I'll be the judge of that."

Sure enough, he sang on the album.

Elvis and David both maintained a yen for beautiful acoustic guitars. For its fine action and rich tones, Elvis loved the craftsmanship of the Martin D-45. Once he sent David to Nashville to pick up several for "around the house." David returned with news of the special Bicentennial guitar that Martin had manufactured. Only a limited number were available as collectors' items for the real guitar freaks. Elvis's eyes lit up like those of a little boy about to be taken to the ice cream parlor. "Get me one!" he said. "I want one!"

The stores were closed in Nashville and David couldn't reach the dealer at his home. But Elvis wouldn't take no for an answer. Hours later David finally reached John Rich, who used to sing with Elvis. He managed to put his finger on one.

"Well, I've located one," David said when he returned to Elvis. "What the hell should I do now?"

"Don't just stand there!" the Boss said, exasperated. "Go get a Lear jet and get me the damn thing!"

Hours later David returned with the guitar, which had cost fifteen hundred dollars, the jet another twenty-five hundred dollars. Elvis was looking disdainfully at his four-thousand-dollar guitar.

"You mean to tell me *this* is what you got me so excited about?"

"Elvis," David exclaimed, defending the purchase, "it's a collector's item!"

"I thought you said there was an eagle on it," the Boss inquired suspiciously.

"Right there." David pointed proudly to the small cluster of gold stars and the tiny eagle on the guitar. "On top."

Behaving as if he had just suffered the great disappointment of his life, Elvis took the guitar upstairs to get acquainted and slowly fell in love with it. When David wanted to take it on tour several months later, Elvis looked at him as if he was a stark raving lunatic.

"No way, man, not this guitar. This stays here, right in the case, right here in my room!"

David will never forget the night that Elvis took James Burton's guitar away from him during an impromptu rock 'n' roll break and just started wailing, leaving the band, his entourage, and his audience stunned. He did it more to give David a thrill than to prove anything, but there stood Elvis Presley, out of nowhere, riffing away like Chuck Berry as Burton picked up another of his guitars, plugged in, and the two of them started trading off run after run.

"I can rock with 'em, huh, David?" Elvis giggled in the limousine riding from the show, delighted with himself. "I can play 'em!"

"No shit!" was all that David could offer. "No shit, Elvis!"

Underneath everything else in Elvis's life was a steadfast belief in his own destiny. "He knew exactly what he was supposed to be doing," David says. "He didn't even think about it. Elvis believed that he had a guardian angel that was responsible for what happened to him, and he talked about it quite a bit."

Destiny, kismet, guardian angels—Elvis Presley felt that he was the expression of some divine plan, that certain forces had guided his life and watched over him; that he was, simply, born to do what he did in the world. "I was raised with a guitar in my hand and I was born to rock," he sang in "C'mon, Everybody," that rocking number with Ann-Margret in *Viva Las Vegas*. That's the way he really felt.

CHAPTER 9

U. S. MALE

Elvis Presley's life and southern background can tell you much more about him than the fact that he enjoyed good fried chicken with black-eyed peas. His own personal notions of manhood were deeply entwined with distinctly southern American cultural traditions—romantic and magnificent, dangerous and frightening.

"He always went all out," Rick says. "He didn't buy one car, he bought a bunch. He didn't buy one airplane, he bought the biggest, and a lot of them. He didn't date one good-looking chick, he dated the best looking and several of them at once. He didn't have a good-looking wife; he had the best-looking, and the most beautiful kid. That's the way Elvis Presley was."

Southerners are known for their passionate natures, for their zeal and fervor. W.J. Cash, in *The Mind of the South*, calls it "the tendency toward unreality, toward romanticism, and, in intimate relation to that, toward hedonism." Elvis Presley knew no moderation in anything he did because moderation, caution, and restraint simply were not part of the game he played to become who he was. The way that he had managed to step

162 beyond the limitations of his poor beginnings and realize his dreams was through the burning ambition he displayed as a young man trying to make it as a singer. It was the one highway that led from the humility and powerlessness of his youth to a place where he and his family would no longer be poor outsiders but top dogs who belonged on their own terms.

Go for it. Take it to the max. Give it hell. The many such expressions that Elvis and those around him were so fond of are the articulation of how he managed to realize his dream in the first place. Elvis achieved success through extraordinary talent, hard work, good luck, and the turning wheels of history, but raw ambition was always at the root. *Don't let nothin' stop you. Take it to the limit.* There is passion and desire in these sayings—a determination tempered strongly by the excesses and extremes of a man whose entire life grew out of a dream that came true as a direct result of action and impact.

But ambition and drive did more than butter Elvis Presley's bread; it gave him an identity, making him "Elvis Presley." "Elvis was a superstar even when he wasn't onstage," says Billy. "He *lived* his part and everything about it. He had to be a showman in *everything* he did." The show went on even after the stage lights dimmed and everybody went home. In style, substance, identity, and consciousness, Elvis became "locked in" (his words) and guided by what he became. He *lived* his myths and legends, creating a role so natural for himself that he never had to "act" to play the part. Staying within his characterization, he could use his conflicts and contradictions to make himself great.

This crucial characteristic runs through his manhood, his career, his image, and his art, producing his most glorious moments and accomplishments and his ugliest, most self-destructive faults. It also produces the most stinging and important irony of his life and his most profound contradiction: What gave him life, beauty, and power, what singled him out and most excited his fans, is also what would destroy him.

Elvis Presley saw his life as an adventure, and nowhere is the essence of his manhood and his relationship with the public

better expressed than in James McBride Dabbs's *Haunted by* 163
God, a religious and cultural history of the South:

"The need for honor, for a visible glory, is the need to keep alive within society . . . the ideal of the wild, the free, the adventurous. The attribution of honor to a leader is the tribute of the average man, a highly social, accommodating person, to the one who stands alone, who is willing to go on an adventure. This is the sense of the wild within the tame, the looking upward of the barnyard fowl to the honk of the passerby. This is the call of the horizon, the frontier, of which a whisper still lingers in the heart of every man."

The Wild within the Tame was the fulcrum in Elvis's manhood upon which so many of his characteristics had to balance and revolve: the wildness and spontaneity of the man onstage, a man who drove women to a frenzy and touched off a national dialogue on morals, was always sharply contrasted with and contradicted by the man offstage—polite, humble, religious, perfectly mannered, the simple country boy who loved his mom, apple pie, his country, and the Lord, who didn't drink or smoke and behaved like the charming southern gentleman. It was a devastatingly effective combination, one that brought Elvis fame, fortunes beyond his wildest imagination, and problems galore.

The first problem was that while Elvis was expected to be wild onstage, his fans expected him to be tame at home. "I reckon I'll have to start worryin' if they ever *stop* screamin'," he often said about the hysteria of his fans. "That'll mean they don't want me anymore." Elvis's public paid the bills and was therefore to be catered to, his image kept sacrosanct. His fans had expectations of him based on a "good" image that Colonel Parker had been very careful to cultivate over the years, using it to sell Elvis Presley to America. This isn't to say that Elvis wasn't all of the good things always associated with his image, but that he wasn't *only* the good things. For some sixteen years after his discharge from the Army, America fed on that image and a vast gulf developed between who the public thought Elvis was and who he really was.

Nowhere is this gulf better illustrated than by Dee Presley. In

164   over a decade of knowing him she never heard him say anything off color—nary a single cuss word—until one day in Las Vegas, Elvis blew his cool and started swearing like an irate truckdriver. It was outlandish. "He could have told me anything in the world and I would have believed him," she says. "The slightest bit of gossip or rumor would make me indignant because I thought 'God, Elvis would *never* do a thing like that.' And then when he got mad it was like, My God! The Idol! The all-American boy! The person that everybody loved and admired! He just couldn't do that. He saw how shocked I was and he said to me, 'Dee, I'm not like that at all. I do quite a few things that you don't want to hear about.' " The public had expectations similar to Dee's.

So Elvis "covered his ass" (his words) in order to keep the wild hidden well away and to present the tame; he covered it very well with the help of his entourage and his manager. "There's two ways you can be with people," he said to Billy. "You can tell them how you feel or you can tell them what they want to hear."

His fans also had their own schizophrenic expectations. Even though the good things he did—the charitable donations and the gifts to the underprivileged, the philanthropies and favors for friends and his love for children—would always be recognized and appreciated, Elvis still knew that he would have sold far more newspapers with news of a drug bust or a fight. He knew that reporters constantly tried to dig up dirt about him and that women photographed with him slapped him with paternity suits; he knew that pictures taken of him with menacing expressions would appear in newspapers like the *Enquirer* with news of his latest temper tantrum.

The arrogant savvy that he developed was what allowed him to stay on top. This trait was another integral characteristic in Elvis's life and a vital component in his manhood. You can see it in the famous sneer captured in so many of his photographs and in so many of his sayings: "Go look for fools in another village—there's been none around here for a long while," or "Don't hand me no boogie woogie, friend, 'cause I'm the King of Rock 'n' Roll."

But Elvis's graciousness and sense of responsibility to his public always reflected more than the awareness that his fans had made him rich. "It was because he really cared," says Rick. "He always recognized his effects on the standards of morality for his fans. As a Christian and an American, he cared."

Elvis was thus careful to contain the wild within the tame and became the most natural sinner ever to be canonized by his public as a saint, causing him to fear his public at the same time that he loved it. "He was the first one to say that it could all be taken away from him," David says. "Just as fast as he got it."

If he felt his public at his feet, he also felt them at his throat, for he could never go anywhere in broad daylight without a caravan of cars riding along with him to keep people from following and ogling him.

It was a very lonely life. "The only time I can really be me," he once said, "is when I walk through that door and lock it on the inside."

There is a deep tradition of individualism and personal freedom down South that was part of the heritage of the frontier spirit of self-reliance. Wrapped up in it are a natural disrespect for authority, an impulsive nature, and what W.J. Cash called "the tendency to violence." "The generally impulsive nature of the southerner, white and black, permits him to fall easily into violence," Dabbs also observed about southern manhood. "When he is moved, he acts." When something ticked off Elvis Presley, he was also a hothead. The mystique of violence, an important component of southern masculinity, was as much a part of Elvis's concept of manhood as emotions, romanticism, compassion, gentility, and freedom to do what he wanted and to be himself.

"You know the lyrics he did to the song 'Trouble'?" Rick asks. "I saw him do it. It goes: 'If you're lookin' for trouble, you've come to the right place. If you're lookin' for trouble, just look right in my face. I was born standin' up, talkin' back.' That's him. I can just see him now—the way he was. Elvis was a man, by all means. I can't stress that enough. There could never be

166   anything sissy about him. People thought he was weird for being so masculine."

Elvis's notions and beliefs about behavior and honor pulsed with his own secular concept of manhood, and the tendency to violence was as much a part of it as his strong sense of individualism. At times it could make him seem like a fistfighting, gunslinging maverick or vigilante. There is an ethos down South about fighting in which a brawling capacity for violence becomes a vital part of self-respect: Fighting is a natural part of life, but you do it only when you have to.

Elvis wanted the boys to be aware of their limitations. "Don't let your BB ass load your forty-five caliber mouth, son," Elvis would say, "or you're gonna get your ass kicked!"

There are instances, however, when honor requires action, no matter the odds. Women are the touchiest subject going with southern men. Elvis expressed it in his song "U.S. Male": "Mess with my woman, and you're messin' with the U.S. Male; that's M-A-L-E, son, that's me!'

"I've only had two fights in my life," David says, "but when I get in one, it's nasty. I learned everything I know about fighting from Elvis—fighting, attitude, everything. Now, if somebody fucked with Elvis, he'd always try to be a gentleman first and talk to them. He'd say, 'Come on, what did I do?' But if they pushed him, he'd take action."

Elvis was ready to fight when people behaved distastefully in public and failed to show him respect. David remembers taking a ride with Elvis in Los Angeles. As they passed a service station in the Cadillac, several people standing in front flipped the car the bird. Elvis wasn't sure if they recognized him or not and didn't know if it was a personal insult, but the action itself incensed him. He brought the car to a screeching halt, backed the car up, and pulled into the service station, much to the surprise of the group of men. As usual Elvis was carrying his gun. He popped out first, followed by David. Elvis approached the man in front, obviously the ringleader. "Did you shoot me the bird, buddy?" he asked menacingly.

The man contemplated his answer for a moment, then smiled smugly. "I sure did," he said.

Elvis almost pulled his gun on him, but caught himself in   167
time. His rule of thumb was never pull a gun unless you in-
tend to use it. Coming up behind him, David took his gun
and held it concealed. Elvis then turned back to the man, composed and soft-voiced.

"Look, man, I don't like people talkin' to me like that."

On the last word, the fellow made his move. He said, "Sonofabitch . . ." and launched his body toward Elvis's head. A
bad move on his part—the rest of his words were cut short by
one vicious kick that seemed to come from nowhere but spoke
very clearly to the side of his head. The next kick, right to the
man's can, laid him flat out on the ground. The others only
stood by silently and Elvis got quietly back into his car. Then he
drove off down Sunset Boulevard—a swift, terrible angel of vigilante justice.

David remembers another similar incident in Los Angeles
(Elvis always cautioned his brothers about LA: "Man, there are
a lot of nuts out there!"). Elvis was stopped at a red light, it
seems, sitting in the back seat of an Eldorado, singing, when a
women in an adjacent car spotted him and asked for his autograph. She stepped out of her car, and the Boss was about to
oblige when the car that was stopped in back of them started
honking the horn obnoxiously as the light turned green,
before Elvis was finished. But that wasn't what set him off: "We
were just driving down the street after that," continues David,
"and that same car came up to us and tried to run us off the
road. Man, they were cussin' and raisin' hell, and Elvis was so
pissed he grabbed his gun, rolled down the window, and yelled,
'Come on over! Come on over here!' He pumped three shots
into the air and then yelled, 'I'm serious!' I was right next to
him, man, and I said, 'Y'all better listen to him or he'll blow
your brains out right here,' so they pulled up to the next light
and we got out with our guns. As soon as they saw him, they
said, 'God, Elvis, we didn't know it was *you!* We're sorry . . .'
so Elvis put his gun back up. He said, 'Well, you just don't start
honkin' and yellin' like that.' "

There were about six people in the car, and Elvis chastised
them all like an angry traffic cop before he went along his way.

168   "Instant in resentment, and bitter in his animosities," Judge Joseph Glover Baldwin once said about the southern temperament, "yet magnanimous to forgive."

"You can write about the cars, stars, chicks, fighting, and all that stuff," Billy says, "but what impressed me so much about the guy were his down-to-earth qualities. Elvis was the highest-paid entertainer in the world but in other ways his head was in the same place as anybody else who came from the South."

There was a down-home kind of tenderness in Elvis Presley that is hard to communicate. He was a man with a powerful sense of kin and a family man at heart, always intensely concerned about his people and how they were doing. He revered women and was capable of an unfaltering politeness toward people if he felt comfortable, displaying kindly courtesies and the homespun hospitality of the typical southerner. However much he may have felt the need to guard and conceal his inner life, he could cry at the mere sight of his grandmother.

"That was one of the ways you could really see the other side of Elvis," Rick says, "was in the way he treated the people closest to him. He called his grandma 'Dodger.' Before he would go on the road for his tours, Elvis would always go downstairs and talk with her awhile 'cause grandma was getting old and you never knew what would happen. She was a great lady, the type of woman who would say, 'Now sonny, don't work yourself too hard on this trip—you get to losin' weight, son, and I just worry about you.' Elvis would get real choked up and pat her on the head and hug her just like he would have with his mom. He'd say, 'Now, don't you worry, Dodger, everything's gonna be okay.' "

Elvis Presley may have believed that manhood required strength, but he never forgot that strength was nothing without grace and compassion.

The money in Elvis's life typified his strength, power, and compassion and became an important part of his self-image as a man. The American imagination has always obsessed itself with great wealth, and very few people in the history of show

business—even the greatest stars during Hollywood's Golden 169
Era, even the most ragingly popular singing stars of the previous
generation—made the kind of money Elvis did. Elvis Presley
had money magic.

"Man, you can say it and say it but it's still amazing: Elvis
spent money like nobody you've ever seen or heard of," Rick
says. The Boss's wealth was something that neither he nor the
people around him even had to speak of; it was just something
that was *understood.* "You knew it was millions and millions,"
David says. "Nobody doubted Elvis's money. All you had to do
was just look around you and you could tell how loaded he was.
He never even discussed money with anybody except his
daddy."

The actual amounts of his money mattered less and less to
Elvis over the years, says Rick, and the less he cared about it,
the more people like Joe Esposito and Vernon Presley had to
look after it. Elvis spent money for fun, to make other people
happy, because he was bored, to freak people out that he was
doing it, because someone (usually his father) told him not to,
or simply because it was *there.* He was grateful for his money,
loved it, and, even though he worked very hard for it, he was
also capable of losing all conception of its meaning, taking it for
granted, or holding it almost in contempt.

Much to the chagrin of Vernon Presley, a man much more
inclined to know the "value of a dollar," Elvis would give
money away if he was in the mood, but sometimes the differences between "giving" it away and "throwing" it away were
minuscule. With the eight-thousand-dollar cape sewn with precious stones that he tossed off to a fan during his 1973 TV
special *Aloha from Elvis in Hawaii,* he seemed to be saying to
the world: Take it, it's only money and there's always plenty
more where this came from. Rick offers, "He didn't want to
think about it. He felt he deserved it and sometimes he felt
guilty about it, too. He knew he had bounds of what he could
and couldn't do, but he always knew that he was rich enough so
that if he felt like it, he could do most things. What is a TV set?
What's a car? What's a home? He could always get another one.
That's the way it was."

170   Stories and anecdotes about Elvis's indulgences, whims, and moments of generosity with his money seem infinite; the rings, cars, clothes, and cash he gave away to friends, relatives, associates, and total strangers could easily fill a thick book by themselves and become almost meaningless after retelling only a few.

One very noticeable thing about Elvis's spending was the progressive patterns by which he bought things. He liked to buy in sequences, pairs, and patterns—almost creatively, and purchases would set off chain reactions that led to other, larger purchases. It was almost a Domino Theory of Purchase: The horse that Elvis wanted to buy Priscilla, for example, led to the purchase of the Circle G Ranch. And what farm is complete without livestock, tractors, mobile homes for his entourage, more horses, trucks, trailer homes, etc.?

Elvis defined money not only by what it meant in his life but also by what impact it had on the lives of those around him and the potential it had for doing good in their lives. He squandered, wasted, and spent madly and extravagantly; he also gave lavishly to charities, and, in the end, the philanthropist and humanitarian in him were as strong as the spendthrift. Behind this was a biblical belief in the karmic quality of money. "Elvis *gave*," says Rick, "and the Bible says that what you give you get back tenfold. He stayed on top so long because he was a generous man and didn't hoard his money." Elvis built a church for his Aunt Nash in Wallis, Mississippi, and, says Billy, "He was the kind of guy who would see someone in a wheelchair and start crying because he felt so sorry for him. Like the colored lady he gave that Cadillac to in Memphis. She was just standing there looking at his car and he told her to go inside the Cadillac place and pick out any one she wanted. I'd say that Elvis was his happiest when he was giving people stuff. That's what he really got off on."

Don't think that people didn't hear about it, either. Scores of Elvis's fans and other hopeful opportunists sent him letters from all over the world, trying to enlist his aid for operations, mink coats, college educations, or that home of their own they had always wanted. Given Elvis's poor beginnings, they somehow felt that he would understand. His generous reputation got them thinking, "Well, why not me?" Similarly, the merchants that Elvis dealt with, some for many years, would automatically jack up their prices whenever he threw a little business their way. "If the car dealers knew that Elvis wanted a car," says Rick, "they always knew that he would buy six to a dozen. You think they would give him a deal? Hell, no, they would sell it to him for a hundred dollars over what it should have been. Car dealers and jewelers that would charge him outlandish prices did business with Elvis for years. It was ridiculous." Sometimes Elvis would complain, but even if his feelings were hurt, he just paid the price. If he knew he was getting shafted, his usual reaction would be "Well, they're just trying to make a living." If Vernon Presley found out about it, however, all hell was sure to break loose.

No sooner would Elvis acquire something than he would tire of it and move right on to something else, discarding as quickly as he bought. He could afford to be fickle that way, just as he could afford to destroy something for the most whimsical of reasons.

Everyone now knows of his antics with television sets. If he wanted to startle somebody or provoke a laugh, or if something came on that displeased him and he was in a bad mood, he might pick up a loaded .357 magnum and just blow it away. It wasn't only TV sets, either, says Billy. He offers a typical example: It is breakfast in Vegas. The TCB group is sitting around the table in Elvis's suite, looking glum. Elvis, fiddling with a gun, nonchalantly takes aim at the crystal chandelier overlooking the table and cuts loose. Pieces of crystal go flying about the room as shots echo and everybody takes cover. "Well," he shouts in the silence that follows: "Ahm glad Ah finally got some 'tention 'roun' heah!"

Such instances were more an expression of Elvis's humor than of malicious destructiveness, but boredom and frustration also caused them. Whatever it was, the hotel management got hip quickly, as the people at the Hilton in Vegas did, keeping in mind that their celebrated guest in the Imperial Suite had a propensity to shoot things that he didn't like. Billy also remembers a particular painting that somebody did of Elvis. A

172   bad, unflattering likeness, the painting just stood in front of the Boss for several days before he looked at it with that peculiar mischievous expression on his face. "That's the ugliest painting I've ever seen in my life," he said. "Billy, go over and put that up against the wall over there." BAM!

One morning Elvis got up to go somewhere, went outside, and hopped into his yellow Pantera. Unfortunately the car just wouldn't turn over. Elvis was in a hurry, and you could see the pained look on his face the longer the car wouldn't cooperate. He got out, whipped out his gun, and BAM! BAM! BAM! like shooting a sick animal. "At least that horse won't suffer no more," said the Boss, getting into one of his pickups.

Elvis could also be very peculiar and unpredictable about money. If you asked him to buy you something, chances are he would look at you as if you were out of your mind; but admire something—"Man, Elvis, what a beautiful watch!"—and he would probably slip it off his wrist and hand it to you. He surrounded himself with possessions and "things" appeared to play an important role in his life; at times he seemed like a crazed materialist. Yet the Bible told him that it was harder for a rich man to enter the Kingdom of Heaven, and Elvis thought about that quite a bit. He tried never to love money or things for their own sake, and often thought of the biblical adage "He that trusteth in his riches shall fall," or this from *The Prophet:* "You give but little when you give of your possessions. It is when you give of yourself that you truly give."

More than anything else he could own, cars expressed Elvis Presley. They symbolized his manhood, his success, fit his moods, told the story of his life and seemed to him the most accepted, visible American expressions of completeness and accomplishment. When he felt restless, bored, unhappy, or hemmed in; when he wanted to get out, unwind, think things over or have some fun, Elvis did what millions of other Americans do—he took a ride.

The role of cars in Elvis's life goes back to the eternal fantasy of the fifties teenager—wheels, big, fast wheels—and it was fitting that Elvis ran out to buy his mama a pink Cadillac as soon

as he could. Cars meant money, comfort, motion, mobility, 173
power, and freedom to Elvis, all of which he wanted for his
mother. No matter how many he had, he never tired of them.

The Boss spent time in his cars cruising with his friends. You
could see him glide by in long, impressive, official-looking limousines that glistened, in gleaming Eldorados, elegant Mercedes, stately Rolls-Royces, Bentleys, and Stutz Blackhawks.
Then he'd come tearing by in a Dino Ferrari or a Pantera 351,
looking like a playboy or a secret agent with his shades. If he
was feeling down-home, he just might roll by in a four-wheel
drive Chevy pickup. But the love affair extended far beyond all
of his cars and the big, quick Harley-Davidson motorcycles he
loved. Elvis Presley loved virtually anything with a motor and
wheels that *moved*—dune buggies, trikes, go-carts, tractors,
buses, mobile homes, even slot cars.

Accordingly, cars played an important part in how Elvis related to people and how they related to him. On the whole, if
you did Elvis a favor of some kind, or if he was feeling good or
thinking about you that moment, you just might find yourself
with a spanking new Mercedes; but then in order not to hurt
somebody else's feelings, he would go out and get ten more.

Behind Elvis's attachment to cars was something else, something very special they provided him. Thomas Wolfe, in *Look
Homeward, Angel,* called it "the dark storm . . . the mad devil's hunger which all men have in them, which lusts for darkness, the wind, and incalculable speed." Elvis Presley loved the
exhilarating, gut-shaking burst of speed on a dark highway with
his hands fixed on the wheel of the car, his eyes transfixed on
the road, the gas pedal floored, and the speedometer buried.
You can call his driving machismo, thrill seeking, racing adventure, or just plain madness; for Elvis Presley, the ultimate challenge was to be able to look death right in the chops and grin.
"He would take it to the limit," says Rick, "just to see if he
could do it."

Billy illuminates this side of Elvis very well. As resident mechanic and kindred car freak (not twenty-five, he has had
twenty-six cars since the age of fourteen), he and Elvis often
shared those moments together. "He would let me work on the

174 car and then he would get out and just run the hell out of it," he says. "That's what it all came down to—the speed."

Elvis was a good driver, says Billy, but those moments doing more than one hundred and sixty miles per hour with the countryside whizzing past in a blur were still unforgettable.

Elvis and Billy almost bought it one night in Elvis's Pantera. Roaring down the highway outside of Memphis at max speed, they suddenly came up on traffic that was blocking the lanes going in both directions at once. Elvis swerved, went around the right side with hardly any room, then almost lost it into a spin. "Oh, shit, I kept saying to myself; he knows what he's doing!"

Elvis also liked to "take it to the max" on a chopper, and Billy often went along. "It was a very hairy feeling, man," he says. "I'd always get on my bike thinking 'Well, am I gonna die this time or what?' We'd be going down the damn expressway at a hundred twenty miles an hour, and that's pretty damn fast for two wheels. Elvis would take his hands off the handle bars— doin' a hundred twenty—just let 'em go and start flapping his arms up and down real slow like a bird! If you were behind him it looked like he was flying."

How did the police react when they saw Elvis streaking down Highway 55 at the speed of light? It didn't happen that often, says Billy, because the joy rides took place at night. "When they would pull him over and see who it was," says Bill, "they'd wave and say, 'Oh, that's just Elvis. We let him do what he wants. If he wants to kill himself on the highway, that's *his* business.' " Sometimes, Elvis would be pulled over by a well-meaning cop: "Y'all like to slow down a bit?" "Okay, officer, sorry," would be the Boss's response. "Then we'd start busting ass as soon as they left," says Billy.

David remembers Elvis's dune-buggy rides along the silvery beaches of the California coast. Elvis would go full blast up the side of a large dune, shooting the buggy straight into the air at an almost ninety-degree trajectory before it would come crashing back onto the sand and racing off, spinning wheels and spewing sand everywhere. He was just as wild on his snow-

mobiles, gliding across pastures and down mountainsides high
above Vail, Colorado.

Elvis was also wrapped up in the American traditions of
power and patriotism. Like many southerners, he had a great
fondness for anything military—history, uniforms, discipline,
and organization. His own years spent in the service left him
with a great respect for the armed forces and a belief in their
role as watchdogs of freedom, and his enthusiasm for anything
martial was like a little boy's fondness for playing "army" or for
toy soldiers. In truth, the military tradition runs very deep in the
South, and Tennessee isn't called the "Volunteer State" for
nothing; the ranks of the armed forces are usually swelling in
both peace and wartime with crewcut recruits from the southern
states because, among other reasons, there is a special romance
and respectability attached down South to soldiering.

Many of Elvis's heroes were soldiers, particularly the great
American generals of the Second World War. General Omar
N. Bradley lived close to Elvis in Los Angeles for a while, and
Elvis was in awe of him. He also admired Ike and General
Mark Clark. Douglas MacArthur was the classic American
hero, and Elvis learned his farewell speech to Congress by heart
("Old soldiers never die . . . they just fade away."). He thought
of Harry Truman as the feisty little man who had the "balls" to
drop the atomic bomb, but his strongest and most moving war
hero—the image that most captivated him—was the man that
Bill Stanley had been charged to protect those many years before: General George S. Patton.

When Elvis first watched George C. Scott's brilliant portrayal
of Patton in the movie of the same name, he was stunned.
From the moment Scott walked out in front of that enormous
American flag in the film's first scene and began delivering his
brutally honest soliloquy about war, killing, and country, Elvis
was riveted to the screen, entranced by the power of the performance and the character. "Elvis just sat there," Davis remembers, "saying, 'God! I mean, tell it like it *is!* '" He ran the film
over and over and memorized every scene.

176   Elvis's Americanism was an important part of his masculine self-image: He had very strident opinions about America and her "mission" in the world—her unique destiny as the last bastion of freedom against the rising tide of communism. In his interpretation of the biblical notion of Armageddon, says Rick, the strong power from the East would surely be the Soviet Union: "Elvis said, one thing that you gotta remember is what the Pledge of Allegiance says—'One nation, under *God*, indivisible, with liberty and justice for all.' And he said, 'We're the most important free country in the world; God's on *our* side.' He was really into that; totally locked in and dedicated. You know, 'Communism *will not* win; Russia *cannot* win.' Elvis also thought a lot about what the communists mean when they said, 'Give me your youth and we'll take your country,' so he stressed to us how important we were: 'You guys are important in this world.' "

Though the Boss hardly ever came out for the record with political statements that would alienate fans of any persuasion (except card-carrying commies, of course), there were parts of his macho image that were pure redneck-hardhat-rightwinger-badass. His fascination with cops and police work, for example, was lifelong.

Elvis had more than just respect for cops; P-I-G to him meant Pride, Integrity, and Guts. Cops not only performed the most vital function of all public servants, but they got to drive fast cars, they busted criminals and kept America safe, they wore uniforms, badges, and *guns*—hell, sometimes they even had to use 'em! They were noble, courageous dudes who had important jobs to do.

Much of the support Elvis gave police in the way of donations was a genuine expression of his social concerns, but, says Rick, "It was also the little boy in him coming out that made him want to be a crusader against evil, like Captain Marvel, as well as the whole macho mystique surrounding police work." He boned up on law enforcement tactics, criminology, ballistics, undercover work, and the handling of firearms. He was fascinated by the series of assassinations that rocked America in the sixties, and by Mafia hitmen and the elite of the underworld. ("Elvis would have been excellent in organized crime himself," says David. "He had the planning skills and the balls to do anything.") When the Zapruder film of John F. Kennedy's assassination was first aired, Elvis videotaped it and ran it over and over, analyzing it, engrossed by the intensity and impact, awed by the cold ruthlessness of the conspiracy. "He watched that sonofabitch and watched it," says David, another assassination buff: "He was so freaked out that anybody could pull if off; with him it got beyond the killing of a human being and down to the science."

Thus Elvis began his incredible collection of police badges from across the nation. Everywhere he went on tour, TCB security worked closely with the local police force and Elvis always met the officials of the police department. "Come on in! Sit down!" he would say to every captain, sergeant, or patrolman who made his way backstage to meet him. The officers would soon find themselves engaged in serious shop talk about police work; invitations and gifts were exchanged, and, sure enough, Elvis would become an honorary member of the department with a shiny new badge to proudly display in his collection. David recalls when Elvis attended the funeral of a Denver policeman who had been killed. Elvis showed up in police captain's uniform, complete with stripes and special tie pin, and David, who accompanied the Boss as bodyguard, wore a dark pinstripe suit and a large trenchcoat. "Elvis looked like the perfect police captain," he laughs, "and I looked like a Mafia killer."

There were times when the badges came in handy to keep himself and the boys out of trouble. David recalls a beautiful wintry day when he and Elvis were ripping around on snowmobiles, high above Vail, Colorado, at least four miles above where people were allowed to go on the mountaintops. David was stopped by one of the officials supervising a snowplow: "What the hell do you think you're doin' up here!"

"I said, 'Man, I'm just riding around,' " says David. "Just then Elvis pulled up behind me and jumped off that sonofabitch. He was standing there and he had a cigar sticking in his

178 mouth and a helmet and face mask on, but he was staring a hole right through that guy. Elvis told him that we lost our girl friends up there and were looking for them, and the guy said, 'You're not supposed to be up here!' Elvis ripped his face mask off and says, 'Well, look, man, I'm *just* riding around!' The guy was being a real smart-ass though. He wanted to give Elvis a hard time. 'Goddamnit,' he said, 'you're not supposed to be up here!' Elvis threw his helmet down on the ground and says, 'Look, motherfucker, you don't tell *me* what to do . . .' and he whips out his chief of police badge from Denver and shoved it right in the guy's face and said, 'Can you *read*? Now, you better get your ass outta here before I get one of my boys to beat the shit out of you!' He left us alone after that."

Somehow, cops who had not heard of his reputation seemed thoroughly surprised by the unlikelihood of his affiliation with police. When the chief of police in a small town came after David on the suspicion that he had been involved in the sexual assault of a woman (it was a case of mistaken identity, says David), Elvis was there to handle it. "Sorry, Mr. Presley, but we'll have to take this boy," said the chief solemnly. "You ain't takin' this motherfucker *nowhere*," said the Boss, pulling out his federal badge and showing it nonchalantly, "or I'll have you replaced." "Yes, sir! Yes, sir!"

Other times, says Rick, it didn't work, blowing the Boss's ego in the process. He recalls cruising out on the expressway with Elvis in the Ferrari when they passed a wreck on the side of the road. They stopped, and Elvis, being the concerned-citizen-covert-cop that he was, approached the arriving policeman, introduced himself, and offered his assistance. "The cop just said, 'Man, I don't care *who* you are; just get in your car and get out of here!' " says Rick. "And that's all he said. It blew Elvis's image when the cop told him to split, because he *had* to, but man! did he ever get mad about that! 'Tell me what to do,' he kept muttering, 'and me a federal narcotics agent!' After he got all those badges, he actually thought he was a cop." Rick attributes all of this to Elvis's unquenchable fascination with power and his boyish love of heroes. "Too many Clint Eastwood movies," he grins. "He thought *he* was Dirty Harry."

The Boss's badge collection was complemented by his gun collection. "He was really a gun freak," says David, a kindred spirit with firearms. "He was really good with guns, too. You know, you have to learn how to be comfortable around guns to like them, and Elvis was." Billy agrees that Elvis maintained a certain "thing" for his guns: "He didn't go around flashing them all that much," he says, "and they were more like showpieces to him than anything else—he was proud of his collection. He didn't keep them loaded that much unless he kept them with him—*those* were always loaded."

While it's quite true that guns certainly provided Elvis with more of a sense of security, his "thing" for guns was really no different from that of any gun-loving member of the National Rifle Association. Elvis didn't hunt, he liked target shooting. Southern boys grow up around guns and become accustomed to them. Out in the country just about every boy's daddy has a shotgun or a rifle of some kind, and learning how to shoot is like learning how to swim in the lake. Elvis could never afford any as a boy, but once he had money, he began indulging himself. Over the years his collection grew steadily, and he displayed them in game-trophy rooms throughout his houses, in racks and cases that always blended nicely with the darkly masculine feeling of leather furniture, giving certain rooms in Graceland and Palm Springs the air of a sheriff's office.

To Elvis, owning a good gun was like owning a beautiful, vintage guitar, or a car—old ones were fun to have as antiques, the new models were always good acquisitions, and curiosities were interesting to admire. Elvis had them all. His favorites were the regular U.S. Army issue .45 caliber automatics. He liked the commemorative ones the most—those that had been used in the war, which he kept well-oiled and in tip-top condition, and his matching set of gold .45's with ivory handles. He liked .357 magnum Colt Pythons and .22 automatic pistols. His four-shot derringer was small enough to be kept in one of his boots onstage or behind a belt or in his pocket. His rifle collection boasted everything from submachine guns (a World War II Thompson) to BB guns. "He had an M-16," says David, "and a twelve-gauge machine gun specially built for him. He had a

180   .300 magnum assassination rifle broken down in a briefcase, over-and-under shotguns, .22 magnum rifles, 16 gauge rifles—all beautiful guns worth outrageous amounts of money."

The Boss was never without a piece. In fact, his affiliation with the Federal Bureau of Drug Enforcement made him a licensed gunslinger with official permission to carry a handgun at all times, and he was, according to David, a pretty good shot: "He could get a grouping of six shots shooting with a magnum load in about a three-inch span from about twenty-five to thirty-five yards away."

Whatever desire Elvis may have harbored to experience a real shootout was channeled into other things. "We'd buy thousands and thousands of dollars' worth of Roman candles," recalls David, "and turn the tables over in the backyard and put on air-force jumpsuits with gloves, helmets, and masks. There was a red team and a blue team. We'd pack twelve of them in each hand and then really go at each other and have these crazy firework wars. The place looked like Vietnam or something. Elvis got burned on the neck real bad once, right before he made *Speedway*, but the makeup fixed it up in the film."

Karate was the ultimate physical activity in Elvis's life. From the first lessons with Hank Sanaski during his tour of duty in Germany, Elvis took right to it and worked to the ninth degree of the black belt, which he earned right before he died. It was a perfect pursuit for Elvis because it had a distinctly male mystique: "Elvis felt that he had to prove his manhood to us," says Rick. He became an assiduous student over the years, improving, enjoying the impact and controlled power of the movement and the concentration, and also relishing the fact that there was something "different" about karate, something eastern and esoteric for those who practiced it seriously and elevated it to a "discipline" and a way of life. It taught him composure and other ways of collecting and utilizing his energies onstage; it helped his breath control in singing, and became an important part of his stage choreography. Best of all, it utilized instincts, perceptions, self-reliance, and, once again, the question of limitation—all central concerns in Elvis's life. "He who hesitates," Elvis would say, "meditates horizontally."

How good was the Boss? Word certainly got out about his 181
karate, but he himself publicized it because he knew it would be
good for the art and also because he hoped to discourage any
would-be glory hounds from messing with him. He was no master, says David, but he knew his stuff. One of the forms of
karate that he studied, *tae kwon do*, was an aggressive form of
Korean street fighting that demands tremendous use of the feet
and legs for aggressive kicking and counterkicking. Ed Parker
got Elvis into the *kem po* style, which is the more widespread
form of the art. According to David, Elvis worked out every day
until he slacked off toward the end of his life, and when David
took up the art to train as Elvis's bodyguard, the Boss spent a lot
of time personally instructing him along with Parker and Bill
Wallace. David will never forget his first full-pad confrontation
with the much more experienced Elvis. "I was only a yellow
belt," he remembers, "and I came up to Elvis and he just
kicked the shit out of me. God, I thought he was going to kill
me!" Long hours of practice and instruction followed. "We
sparred and I got floored, thousands of times, but I always
had to stand right up to him and say, 'Let's go!' He would
jump on me: 'God*damnit*, David, you're not doin' it right—
you're not holding your hands right and controlling your
movement!' Then when I got my black belt we sparred again
and he was thoroughly surprised. That's when I beat Red and
Sonny."

The martial arts was another subject that Elvis was always
ready to drop whatever he was doing and discuss. He collected
books on the subject, but the man who could really get him
going was his good friend and personal instructor, Ed Parker.
Even though Parker introduced Mike Stone to Elvis and Priscilla, which made Parker self-conscious, Elvis never held it
against him or let it stand in the way of their friendship. "Elvis
always loved Ed Parker," says Billy. "He always had these great
little things that he would say when he was explaining karate.
He would tell you that karate was like a writer's experience.
The first thing that a writer would do would be to wait to hear a
story to get his material, right? Parker would explain how when
you're fixin' to get into a fight, that's exactly what your oppo-

182 nent is going to do—tell you a story. As soon as he moves he starts his story and that's where you stop it."

Besides karate, Elvis loved many other forms of athletics, but he was particularly devoted to boxing and football. Though he never participated in boxing himself, he reveled in the mano-a-mano spectacle of two men pounding each other. The violence of the sport attracted him but the sport also has a rich lore and tradition, which he admired. Strength and guts are essential, but it is also a sport of speed, finesse, stamina, strategy, and (depending on the boxer) sportsmanship. Elvis saw boxing as a very exciting and graphic metaphor for the competitive struggles that all men face in the world; he recognized that all men, in that way, are pugilists. Rocky Marciano was his favorite fighter, say the boys, because he was a tough, bruising fighter who could take a punch and then come back smoking. He also admired Muhammad Ali, who backed up all of his loudmouthed braggadocio with pure skill and power, representing to the world the will to come back to win, and still stand by his beliefs.

Elvis found excitement and meaning in boxing, but football was the sport of the gods. You couldn't have found a more passionate aficionado of the game than Elvis, whose boyhood desire to play never diminished. The Memphis Mafia-TCB operation doubled as his private football squad and the games they played were rough tackle football, played oftentimes without protective equipment, in Bel-Air or Memphis, against other teams composed of Hollywood roughnecks like Robert Conrad and others who loved to be thwacked around on the field.

The games during the sixties were fast, fun, and sometimes brutal, but as Elvis grew older and more involved with live engagements, they slacked off considerably. Even then he was never adverse to the idea of getting out and having a quick game, but you had to curtail the rough and tumble: "Every once and a while," says Rick, "whenever I'd see Elvis not looking, boy, I'd smack him . . . blam! I would be waiting on him, and I'd come in full blast. He would be so shocked that I'd do something like that! I'd laugh, man, but then he'd always do the same thing back to you."

There is a ritualized kind of violence in football that attracted

Elvis, and speed, willpower, strength, grace, and guts involved, but football is also a very military game, a territorial contest waged almost like warfare with the specific goal of penetration and advance—aggression in the purest sense, in which coaches like Vince Lombardi become the Pattons of the gridiron. It is a game that is inextricable from notions of manhood and manliness in America.

Weekends would find Elvis glued to a television set, watching the games along with millions of other Americans. He had a long-running love affair with the Los Angeles Rams, since Memphis was not a football city. He loved the Fearsome Foursome, attended Rams workouts, and even engaged in some on-the-field antics with some of the Rams, whom he invited to play in his own games, but when the abortive World Football League opened in 1974 and Memphis entered the league with the Southmen (Grizzlies), the Boss went bananas. He attended every home game he could, watching from the press box.

As Elvis became less and less physically inclined to play tackle football with the reckless abandon he had shown as a young man and relied more and more on activities like karate and racketball for exercise, his level of football mania only increased. Jim Brown, the legendary fullback with the Cleveland Browns, was his true idol ("Man, that sumbitch can play football!"), and he enjoyed fleet-footed running backs and ends who could run like gazelles—Walter Payton, O.J. Simpson, Gayle Sayers, Mercury Morris, and oh, yes, Elvis Peacock (!) who played for Oklahoma. He also loved those hardnoses on the football field like Dick Butkus and Ray Nitschke, who earned reputations as "bad motherfuckers."

Michael Novak, author of the penetrating *Joy of Sports*, recently did a column on football for *The Washington Star* in which he pointed out that poor boys have always played the game with particular ferocity, perhaps because of the element in football which requires running for daylight. He also made an observation about the game which is worth quoting: "There is something in the male character that demands risk, demands exposure to danger, needs to face death (metaphorically) every single day. It is as necessary to the male organism as adventure.

184   The male cannot triumph over death by bringing life into the world. The male substitute for bearing a child is to face death and wrest life from it. There are many deadly things males would try were rituals like football not available. Motorcycles, drugs, gang fights."

Elvis Presley felt compelled to try them all.

CHAPTER 10

NEVER BEEN TO HEAVEN

If Elvis Presley saw life as an adventure, he also saw it as a search for knowledge, and religion was one of his central and most consuming interests. From the very beginning he maintained a poignant awareness of the death of his twin brother, Jesse Garon, and was fascinated by the questions of life and death as they related to the scriptural teachings of the Bible. The experience of fundamentalist Christianity in his youth, which was strongly reinforced by his mother, had instilled in him a powerful feeling that he could go far in life if only he had faith in the Lord. If the meek could inherit the earth, then Elvis Presley, poor country boy, could be among the heirs.

When Gladys Presley died, Elvis's religious feelings took on an even more pressing importance, and while he would veer away from a conventional, churchgoing practice of religion, he always remained close to its meaning and power. The spirituals and hymns of his youth had imbued him with that power, and he came away from his early religious experience with all of the rudiments of Christianity intact—the traditional beliefs in the

186   Trinity, the power of prayer, clearcut notions of heaven and
hell, and the promise of eternal grace and salvation. Many
times, when discussing religion with Rick, he spoke of having
prayed often and fervently on his way up. "Elvis always gave
credit to the Lord for his success," he says. "He'd say, 'I just
thank the Lord for what happened to me.' "

When Elvis was queried about his religion and his feelings
about churchgoing, his stock response would be that going to
church was simply too impractical because of the disturbance
his presence would create. The more accurate reason, however,
was that as he grew older, his own interpretations of religion
may have left him in tune with the basic tenets of Christianity
but out of tune with the typical minister's interpretation.
He was a Bible-toting, Bible-quoting man who probably never
would have toted his Bible to church even if he could have.
Elvis had his own ways.

"Elvis was not what you'd call a gung-ho Christian," says
Rick, who often discussed religion with Elvis and prayed with
him in later years. "In the situation he was in, it was pretty hard
for him to lead a Christian life." Religion in a conventional
sense seemed to be a commitment to things *not* to do which
Elvis, in his refusal to accept any limitations for himself, was
unwilling to accept. The stern, authoritarian tenets of the "old-
time" religion preached so emotionally throughout the South
always dwelled heavily upon the promise of a better life in
heaven after the troubled life on earth, of the need to control
oneself in order to achieve that reward. Religion as Elvis knew it
in his youth was preached through rules and maxims invoked
from the Scriptures and handed down from the pulpits; the Lord
often seemed a God of wrath and vengeance, terrible in his
judgment when inveighing against the sins of man. Religion
could easily seem an empty echo. It preached grace, salvation,
and evoked universal brotherhood, but often stood for things
like temperance, chastity, and maintaining the status quo.

In his position it was easy for Elvis to take what he needed
from his religious experience and discard what was inconve-
nient. "Elvis had seen a lot of religious phonies in his time,"
Rick adds, looking back on some of their discussions. "He was

dependent upon himself when it came to interpreting the Scriptures and his relationship with the Lord." He could always
maintain his religious fervor and the sincerity of his beliefs
without worrying that they clashed with the life-style of the
"King of Rock 'n' Roll." He was a true believer who made his
own rules so that his beliefs could blend with the way he lived
his life. "I think Elvis would have given anything to have been
even closer," says Dee Presley. "He would have given anything
he had for the peace of knowing God and living closely with
Him. He really wanted that and admired that strength."

He was fascinated by the image of Jesus. Apart from the
Christian belief in Jesus as the Son of God and the Savior of
Man, Elvis was intrigued by Jesus as an historical figure, as a
philosophical concept, as a force in people's lives, in every conceivable way he could perceive Him. "He had pictures of Jesus
everywhere he went, which he carried," David says.

It was the *power* of Jesus that bowled Elvis over, says David,
and it was the power that religion evoked in the lives of men
that was at the root of his personal fascination. All of his favorite
biblical passages, for instance, were the most vivid expressions
of power in the Bible. "One thing that he liked to talk about was
the parting of the Red Sea," says Rick, "or the plagues. He was
really into the miracles, you know; the five loaves of bread and
the two fishes to feed five thousand. Elvis thrived on impact.
Strong things. That's why he liked the Book of Revelations. It's
the Lord's testimony, the prophecy that tells what's going to be.
Elvis locked into it because of its impact, because of the effect it
had on people. See, that's what his claim to fame was; that's
what he'd relate to."

"Raised up," as he was, to occupy such a position of magnitude, Elvis saw his own life as a miracle of true biblical intensity, and he sought religious knowledge to help him understand
it. Within the confines of his sheltered and extraordinary life,
he remained a passionately spiritual man. His world made it remarkably easy to set up his own rules of right and wrong, yet no
matter what he did, he was still subject to the reproach of the
same moral conscience instilled by his mother and the ways of
his youth. "From the experience of his whole life," Rick says,

188 "he knew the right way. That's why even when he did something that he knew was wrong and never let anybody know he felt guilty about it, he was his own worst enemy. He inflicted his pain on himself."

Religion demanded that he distinguish between right and wrong, but just as it sometimes filled him with guilt, it also allowed him to fall back on his Lord whenever things got rough. "Why me, Lord?" he would sigh in his many trying and painful moments.

Elvis Presley was also interested in other religions, in spiritual powers of all kinds, looking for answers, knowledge, experience, and insights into himself and the world, for "self-awareness." "The last twenty years of his life," says Rick, "Elvis was searching—constantly searching, trying to find himself through books and self-realization."

"He asked me once," remembers Billy, "there are so many religions, which one do you think is right? Now, that was one of the heaviest questions he ever asked me. I said, 'The only thing I can say is that I believe in God, Elvis.' And he said, 'Well, you've got your head screwed on right; that's the most important thing. You don't have to go to church or one certain church to prove that you believe in God.' "

"We were walking through the Hilton one time backstage and Elvis had a cross and a Star of David on the same gold chain," recalls Rick. "Someone saw it and asked him why. Elvis just looked at the guy and said, 'I don't want to miss out on heaven because of a technicality!' "

Ultimately Elvis's success and the fulfillment of his dreams had opened up many more troublesome questions than were answered. He began to think about the meaning of his life, about the universality of religion, about man's place in the cosmos, the question of life after death, and the relationship between God and man. He consumed ideas and information along with cars and jewels, and everywhere he went, he traveled with a couple of large portable bookcases in which he carried his favorite volumes along with his newly acquired books. His exposure to the sophistication of Hollywood had made him aware of what he lacked in formal education and of not being well read, but it was a highly personal and specialized education that he now wanted to pursue.

"He would read all the time," says Billy, "whenever and wherever he had free time. He'd read before he went to bed; he'd read during the day; he was always reading something and underlining it, making sure he got the meaning." Sometimes Elvis would then turn the whole TCB group into a seminar, discussing the ideas in his latest books, getting reactions from the group, holding forth with his own opinions. "He was also really into *words*," notes Rick. "Elvis knew they were the building blocks for ideas." He gave dictionaries to his friends and soaked up any new word to cross his path—technical words, slang, everything. Even his well-known pride and ego were overpowered by his thirst. "If someone sprang something new on him, he'd inquire," Rick says. "It wasn't beyond him to say, 'Hey, I don't understand that.' "

Though he dabbled in many fields of interest, most of the subject matter had to do with what might give him an edge of enlightenment by teaching him something about himself or other people. He delved into the teachings of the Far East, particularly Buddhism, and looked into meditation and yoga, and the place where he came to be buried on the Graceland grounds—the area out in back of the mansion known as Meditation Gardens—was designated by Elvis to be a quiet place of contemplation and prayer. Medicine, psychology, and philosophy also fascinated him; he endeavored to find out as much as possible about how the human body and mind worked and how human thought had developed over the centuries.

In Kahlil Gibran, the great Lebanese poet, philosopher, and artist, Elvis found some of the most beautiful expressions of wisdom anywhere and a universalistic philosophy of life that blended many different religious ideas harmoniously. Islam was another religion that he wanted to learn about, and he enjoyed reading about the great mystics, spiritualists, and psychics. Psychic potentialities intrigued him, bringing about an interest in the questions of psychokinesis, telepathy, mind control, and other forms of extrasensory perception. The relationship be-

190   tween character and destiny sparked him to explore the meaning of numbers and the numerical vibrations in numerology (Elvis was a number "eight," known to be "alone at heart," to hide their feelings in life but do as they please) and to discover the astrological implications of having a sun in Capricorn.

The teachings of various gurus also found their way to him, although the only one he considered with any degree of seriousness was Yogi Paramahansa Yogananda, the founder of the Self-Realization Fellowship, with which Elvis carried on a correspondence. He did not see any of this as conflicting with his basic Christian beliefs, but rather as a way of "getting to know where your head is at," and of learning how to utilize that self-knowledge to more fully realize one's potential on many different levels. He also looked into dianetics and Scientology, and many of the other offshoots of the Human Potential Movement, having been introduced to many of these ideas through his longtime buddy and hair stylist Larry Geller, who brought him literature and shared many of the same interests.

There have been reports to the effect that Elvis himself was known to manifest certain "special powers." In truth, anyone who has ever seen him work his magic on an audience would be a fool not to recognize that Elvis was a uniquely powerful, charismatic person (charisma is used here as the "special quality that gives an individual influence or authority over a large number of people"), but the reference here is to powers psychic, spiritual, even "otherworldly."

Rick says, "Elvis believed that people have mental power which is just as real as spiritual or physical power. He believed that his was pretty well developed and I do, too, but he wasn't a psychic by any means. He felt that he had mental power, mostly; he felt that he could read your mind, that he'd know what you were thinking. Hell, sometimes he could! I mean, Elvis was very, very hip; he would blow me away with some of the things he would know. Sometimes, a second before I would ask him something, he would know my question, but it was more because of an 'in tune' relationship we had from being around each other all the time." Rick is using the word "hip" here to mean "perceptive," and one thing that mostly everyone

around Elvis will agree on is that he seemed to have been uncannily perceptive about people and about human behavior,
which is why so many people have called him a genius when it
came to just talking and being with people, at picking up a person's "vibrations."

Sometimes Elvis would like to play games with his "powers"
just to see what he could and couldn't get away with. But no
matter how perceptive he was, says Rick, he wasn't a mind-
reader: "I just didn't believe that he could do it," he says, "and
I'm being honest about it. Sometimes he was right but sometimes he was in left field, too; a lot of people would go along
with it even if it was a clear miss, just to keep from embarrassing
him. They didn't want to blow him down in front of a bunch of
people. You know, if anything continues for so long, it's like
living a lie; you keep it up long enough, and you'll sincerely
believe it. That's the way it was with him. It got to where he
sincerely believed that he could. We had so much love for the
man that we let him get away with it. It was just a kick, though
he got away from it after he knew that some of the guys were
just going along with him. See, occasionally, when he wanted
some recognition or something, he'd do something like that."

Still, there was that certain something about Elvis—a quality
that seemed almost palpably, well, *supernatural*. People around
him picked up on it, and it's what enabled them to even
seriously entertain the notion of his "powers" in the first place.
"I've never doubted Elvis," says David. "If he said he could do
something, man, it seemed like he could do it. I've doubted
him very, very rarely; as far as *I'm* concerned, if you just looked
at Elvis, you could feel his power." Truly, weird things seemed
to be happening to him and around him, and stories abound of
incidents that seem too frequent and too graphic to be merely
coincidental. David recalls a particular karate exhibition in
which he and Elvis were to put on a demonstration. In the
karate studio there were chains from which dummies were suspended as kick bags to practice with. When David and Elvis
were introduced, they walked out onto mats and squared off,
but one of these particular chains seemed to be dangling down
in between them. In one graceful, slow-motion movement,

192   Elvis reached upwards to punch it, and at the precise second that he made contact with it, says David, "lightning struck and it sounded as if the whole earth was enveloped in thunder! Everybody was freaked out, man. Things like that were happening all of the time. I remember driving out to Palm Springs once with him from Vegas. It was me, Elvis, Mindy Miller, and Steve Smith. We're driving along and we come right into one of those hellatious storms—you know, one of those godawful West Coast storms—God! So we're driving along and the storm is coming right for us. Elvis looks up and says, 'Don't worry; it's not going to get us. We won't even get one drop.' Minutes later it's pouring rain right next to us, raining like a sonofabitch, but *not* where we're driving! Man, the sky looked like a holocaust, just all black and lightning, but we were cutting a path right through it! The whole way there it was like that, man, I swear. It was wild."

Similar to Elvis's interests in telepathy and the psychokinetic exertion of his will was a fascination with healing. Like most fundamentalist Christians, Elvis believed that men could heal by the laying on of hands through which the spirit of the Lord can work His power. The impressions conveyed by Red and Sonny West in *Elvis: What Happened?* were of a man firmly convinced that he had these powers and was imbued with special psychic knowledge. Well, say the boys, that's because sometimes it was hard to tell the difference between when the Boss was kidding and when he wasn't. However, Red and Sonny, they say, were among the worst at being able to tell when Elvis was bullshitting and when he wasn't.

What is true is that Elvis was interested in the relationship between mind and body, in how the state of mind can affect the state of the body. His reluctance to be sick for a tour, for example, got him thinking about how the exertion of the human will can affect the health. "If you think sick, you'll be sick," he would say. Whatever it was, say the boys, he could put it into practice to a certain extent.

"I don't know what anybody else thinks," says David, "but I personally believe that Elvis *could* heal. Elvis was the most spiritual man I've ever seen. Now, I don't mean he could heal you

if there was something radically wrong, like cancer, but he had
a way of getting you to relax and stay calm and feel better. Dean
Nichopoulos hurt his knee in Vail once—a real bad sprain—
and he was in a lot of pain. Elvis just talked to him and put his
hand on it and you could almost see the vibration. He just
helped Dean bring himself down to where he was feeling better."

Rick elaborates on this: "To a certain extent, Elvis believed
that if you have enough faith, you can be healed by the laying
on of hands. See, the Bible tells you that you can. I've wit-
nessed healings by hands and I know Elvis believed in it, but I
don't believe that Elvis thought that *he* was the one, that it
could be the Lord working through him. He believed that
through the Lord he could do things like that if it was the Lord's
will."

The Boss believed in reincarnation: The déjà vus in his life
convinced him that he had not only been around many times
before, but was surely returning, as he told Billy, "in the spirit
and body of somebody else."

Many of these interests were outgrowths of Elvis's preoccupa-
tion with religion, but they also reflect, once again, the question of limits in his life. Reincarnation was the ultimate expression of eternity to him. Elvis loved the idea of being able to do
something extraordinary, to test himself to see if perhaps he *did*
have the ability to transcend the norms of human existence. If
anyone was "special," it was he. "Elvis's mind was so far advanced and different from the everyday person's," David says.
"He was almost like an alien—the closest thing I've ever seen to
a true 'leader.' He could have been a leader in any field."

Finally, Elvis Presley had a deeply ingrained fascination with
death, which became the underlying curiosity for his search for
knowledge about life. He wanted to "understand" it and turned
to thanatopsis—the contemplation of death—as a natural interest after his own mother's death, which was the key emotional
experience of his life. His curiosity led him into mortuaries,
where he learned about embalming, and through volume after
volume on the subject.

The evangelist Billy Graham has called death "the most dem-

194 ocratic institution in the world" and something to look forward
to because when we die we go into the presence of the Lord.
The promise, inherent in Christianity, of peace and salvation
in death removed much of Elvis's fear of dying.

"Only when you drink from the river of silence shall you
indeed sing," wrote Gibran in *The Prophet*. "And when you
have reached the mountaintop, then you shall begin to climb."
Reflecting on his own life, Elvis contemplated those words very
carefully. "He read about the cases of people dying and being
brought back to life, and how beautiful it was to die," says Billy.
"He called death the best thing that could happen to you."
"Elvis often said how glad he'd be to see his mom when he got
to heaven," adds Rick.

Death was the last, most powerful and pronounced expression
of the driving individualism that inclined Elvis Presley to follow
his own road, to be free to do things his way, no matter the
cost. Somewhere in those moments thinking about it or when
he came closest to it, Elvis must have recognized that the one
place he hadn't been to held the most answers for him, that
death was the riskiest risk, the most challenging challenge, the
final definition of limits and limitlessness, where the limits he
could never accept in life rubbed against the limitlessness of the
ultimate unknown.

The more boring, lonely, unhappy, and meaningless life
would seem in the years to come, the more he felt that he had
done everything he wanted to do, the closer Elvis would come
to the experience.

"Well, I never been to heaven," he sang so passionately when
he did Hoyt Axton's "Never Been to Spain," ". . . but I've
been to Oklahoma. . . ."

PART THREE

FALL FROM GRACE

1972·1975

He doeth according to his will.

Daniel IV:35

CHAPTER 11

I CAN'T STOP LOVING YOU

Elvis Presley often spoke to his brothers about the special emotional needs of women and how they never got enough credit for the wonders they bring to the world and the struggles they face. He believed that God put women on earth to be, well, *women*—to be put on that golden pedestal where they could best be respected, exalted, and loved. How he managed to lose the most important woman in his life will always remain a painful irony to all who knew him.

If the men around Elvis were there to TCB, the counterpart for the women in their lives was TLC—Tender Loving Care. In Elvis's mind, that was what women were all about. The ideal went something like this: While the men were out on tour, busting it and bringing home the bacon, the women—beautiful homebodies, stolid mothers, and loving wives—remained at home. When the men returned, it was TLC time, which meant good home-cooking, relaxation, time for the children, and good loving. In short, TLC was the very best that the traditional world of domesticity had to offer. The idea of women's libera-

198   tion around Elvis was about as out of place as a Marxist revolutionary in a Baptist church, but the whole scheme was founded on a deep mutual respect, and somewhere along the line of the division into TCB/TLC, the respect fell by the wayside, it seemed, and the women started getting fed up. The TCBers wanted the best of both worlds: girls at their convenience and mates at home. For this reason, not only Elvis's marriage went down the tubes, but others followed suit.

"Elvis was always very protective of the women in his life," Billy observes. "That's how he loved and took care of them. Vernon and Elvis were both like that—really strong southern gentlemen—no cussing in front of their women, and everybody around treated them with respect. If they didn't, they weren't around too long. They had to do everything in the world for their women; the women never had to ask for anything because it was given to them before they could even ask for it. The main thing was that the women never did a lot of striving for themselves—there was always somebody there. That's the way Elvis treated Cilla, that's the way Daddy treated Dee."

Elvis wanted to "build a house" for his woman, and an important foundation for that house was a sense of security. "That's what Elvis liked about the whole arrangement," Billy says. "He always loved the idea of having a woman back home waiting for him." Then there was respect: "When Elvis and Priscilla were first married," Rick remembers, "she used to love to call him 'my husband.' She really enjoyed being Mrs. Elvis Presley, and Elvis loved her in that role. They both felt very privileged to have each other." Privacy and a feeling of exclusivity also was a part of the bond, as was a tender and compassionate ability to empathize with each other's feelings and positions.

At the root of the problems that developed between Elvis and Priscilla was the simple fact of Elvis's life-style as an entertainer. Other women were as much a part of that life as his music and the money he made; they came naturally and seemed an integral part of his world. Elvis had not been able to shake that freewheeling sense of bachelorhood he enjoyed for so long in Hollywood but he also considered it to be his prerogative as a man to have time alone to do what he wanted. "A man has got 199 to be a man, Rick," Elvis would say to his brother whenever woman troubles beset them. "Let's head for the Springs. Guys only."

"One thing Elvis always told me," Billy says. "Never leave a woman mad if you're going out of town." Such is the philosophy of a man who always wanted the best of both worlds and always expected to return when the romp was over, who wasn't going to change for any woman, no matter how much he loved her, and so ran the risk of losing everything. "Elvis was the same when he wasn't married as when he was," Rick says, who was usually there to see how he juggled both worlds. "The only difference when he was married was that he would behave differently when he was home. He *had* to; his wife was there."

Priscilla Presley is a perceptive and intelligent woman. She never had to look very hard to know what her husband was up to, never had to hire private investigators because the telltale signs were everywhere. "The guys used to come through the gate to Elvis's house and talk to some of the girls, who would be waiting there," Rick remembers. "Every once in a while somebody would get loose and try to pick up one of those girls and start talking big. Then the girls would go to Cilla to tell her things to get back at the guys. If it got back to Cilla, she'd talk to Elvis about it and Elvis would can whoever it was that was talking."

Then there were instances when the wives would show up at Elvis's Palm Springs home on Chino Canyon Road, sending the women there partying with the group scurrying for cover and setting off an avalanche of excuses from the husbands. Rick had to become a master of the defensive maneuver on the Boss's behalf, but whenever he had to cover for Elvis to Priscilla, he hated himself for it. "Oooooh, boy," he exclaims, "the job made you a habitual liar. That was the hardest thing for me to do because I always loved Cilla like a sister. It was never lying for lying's sake—you were doing it to prevent a hassle and you had to think fast. You might be escorting Elvis's wife and out of the blue here comes a chick that you know is dating Elvis, looking for him, about to say something like, 'Where's Elvis? He

200 told me to meet him here.' You'd just veer her away and stop it somehow."

Rick recalls one weekend when everybody was surprised at Elvis's Palm Springs home. "Man, everybody got caught," he says in astonishment. "There were too many women around! Elvis had an abili, though. He had nine other guys covering for him. It was up to us to go down with the ship and accept the fact that we were caught, but save the Boss! Don't let it get to where Cilla gets on him. Sometimes we would be completely lost for words and he would look at us with an expression on his face that said, 'Come on, man, say something! Help me out!' "

Other times, if Elvis was feeling contrite, he would admit his sins, leaving the boys who had covered for him standing there with egg on their faces. "Elvis would tell you, 'Whatever you do, don't tell so-and-so that I went out with such-and-such a chick!' " Rick remembers. "Then the girl would come to us and ask about it and we would just stand there stonefaced and say, 'Who, *Elvis?* Shoot no, not him . . .' and then later on he'd turn right around and admit it. No wonder the girls lost complete trust in us."

"Now that I look back on it," reflects Dee Presley, "everything had to be cleared. They never wanted us just popping in. Cilla was smarter than I was. She never missed a thing."

"Elvis was just not a fair husband," concludes Rick. "Anytime you're out screwing around on your wife, that can't be fair, especially the way Elvis would 'lock' his women in. It was rough for her because Elvis was a pretty jealous man, too, and with a woman as beautiful and fine as Cilla, you could see why. Elvis knew how men were and didn't trust them when it came to his wife." Hence the double standard that developed in Elvis's treatment of his wife. "He did feel that men needed time away," says Rick, "but not that much time. When we went on the road and to Vegas, she would only fly in on weekends. You just can't see your wife that way—maybe Elvis Presley thought he could. I'll tell you something: Nobody ever pulled the wool over Cilla's eyes. She *knew*; she knew the man better than anybody and was aware of the situation. She knew Elvis had other

chicks and that he was an entertainer and that was part of it, but 201
I could see that she couldn't accept the fact."

Rick's opinion is that despite Priscilla's pride and dignity, it
was not the other women that destroyed the marriage but the
need on her part for the kind of love that she wasn't getting from
Elvis. "I talked to her after it was all over," he says, "and she
said, 'Ricky, I'm a woman. I need somebody there.' Man, if
there was ever a woman that walked the face of God's earth that
fit the description of 'woman,' it's Cilla! She needed love and
affection. She also needed a home where she could be the boss
without a bunch of guys always hanging around."

After his marriage Elvis still wanted to keep the boys around
him and the clubhouse atmosphere often made intimacy impossible. It was also no secret that Priscilla didn't like some of the
guys that worked for her husband; there was a tension that
usually went unvoiced when she wanted to be alone with Elvis.
"You've got to realize how difficult it was to handle those guys
all the time," says Rick. "Guys would come in late at night
bringing strange women. We had to let her know what was
going on." Dee Presley agrees: "Everybody thought it was ridiculous for Cilla not to be able to have more time alone with
Elvis."

Elvis was no ogre, but he did have certain ideas about marriage and women working. Had Priscilla pursued a career of her
own, she might have had a healthy outlet for her creative energies and time, but she wanted to be a good mother to her
child, a good wife to her husband. "She was having to stay in so
very much," Dee says. "Her life was like mine—very sheltered—just getting up, going to the dance studio, and coming
home. Elvis slept during the day when he was home so they
never got to go out."

It was rumored that Hal Wallis, who produced many of Elvis's films, wanted to cast Priscilla in movies. She also had
numerous other opportunities. Nobody knows exactly what happened to these opportunities, but it is assumed that she
disregarded them at Elvis's command. With time Elvis began to
realize how limited her life was and became more encouraging

202   of her outside interests, and when Priscilla professed an interest in one of Elvis's passions, karate, he was overjoyed. It was his encouragement that led to her private lessons, and the private lessons that led to her romance with her instructor, Mike Stone; and it was the romance that would finally break up the marriage.

Elvis had met Mike Stone years before at a competition in Hawaii, where the native-born Stone was, like Ed Parker, a well-known instructor and competitor. Later, when he moved to southern California with his wife and two children, Stone became affiliated with Parker and Chuck Norris. An attractive man with bright blue eyes, a pleasant, kindly smile, and a headful of thick, dark, curly hair, he started giving Priscilla private lessons after Elvis set it up with Ed Parker. Mike and Priscilla became romantically involved and started seeing each other, and when they fell in love, they soon decided to leave their marriages. Some of Elvis's closest buddies, aware of what had been going on, were forced to keep mum and wait to see what Priscilla was going to do.

For millions of women who fawned over Elvis, it was difficult to understand how Priscilla could ever have left Elvis for Mike Stone. Dee Presley, who met him after Elvis and Priscilla had separated in Los Angeles, puts it this way: "Mike was an extremely beautiful person . . . it's as simple as that. I could understand how she could be in love with him. He was self-assured, quiet, friendly, and very handsome; most important, I think, was that he really made her feel like a woman. She felt a real commitment from him which she felt lacking with Elvis and the chance to lead a more down-to-earth, normal life."

Priscilla is anything but a devious woman. Charades, facades, games with people's emotions, and clandestine love affairs are not her style. She cared far too much for her husband to continue deceiving him and subject him to public ridicule or controversy; she also had a young daughter to think about. Straight-shooter that she is, she came right out and told Elvis what was going on and that she was leaving him—plainly, honestly, as painlessly as possible. "That's just the way she was," Rick says. "Cilla never cared about what other people might think when she did things as long as she truly believed in what she was doing."

The period of separation was to last eleven months. In February of 1972, when Priscilla moved out of their California home, the mood within the TCB group changed quickly, but nobody bothered the Boss with questions. "He was crushed when he found out," Ricky says. "You can call Elvis anything you like— foolish, selfish, naive not to expect his wife to go out and do the same thing he did—but however you look at it, man, he was hurting bad."

Everybody around them was secretly pulling for a reconciliation. The Stanley boys were distraught because of their closeness to both Priscilla and Lisa over the years and would approach Vernon Presley, knowing that Elvis didn't want to discuss it, to ask him how things looked. "Not so good, boys," Vernon would mutter, shaking his head sadly, "not so good." Rumors kept taking off like flocks of wild geese, flying between California and Tennessee. Phone calls were made constantly, but a reconciliation wasn't meant to be. "Elvis and Priscilla were not the types to play with each other," Dee says. "It must have been decided right at the time of separation that they would divorce. I think Elvis would have gladly taken her back and tried to make the marriage work if Cilla would have gone back, but I don't think she felt she could ever go back after what happened. Elvis called her every day for a while: I know how much he had to love her and missed her, especially that first Christmas she was not at Graceland. It was so empty. They never were the same after Cilla left."

On January 8, 1973, on his thirty-eighth birthday, Elvis filed for divorce. For the most part it was to be a very civilized one, not one of those bitter affairs that seem to plague the lives of show-business people. With the interests of Elvis's public image at heart and the offer of what first appeared to be a generous settlement, it was kept discreet and low keyed. The divorce would bear many similarities to Dee's divorce from Vernon Presley in the years to come: Women who married Presleys always wanted to be settled as quietly as possible during the divorce proceedings.

204   The divorce was granted on October 11, and Elvis emerged arm-in-arm with Priscilla from the Santa Monica Courthouse with amicable smiles on their faces for the whirring, clicking cameras of the assembled photographers. Priscilla, dressed casually, looked quite beautiful and somehow content, her hair—now its natural soft brown color instead of dyed black—parted in the middle and falling down to her shoulders. She was a woman of twenty-eight with the custody of Lisa Marie Presley, then five years old. Looking at her, it was hard to believe that she was once the impishly beautiful teenager that Elvis Presley had fallen in love with in Germany, thirteen years earlier.

The Boss had put on weight. Although he carried it well, the strains of the past months were evident in his eyes. Still, he smiled the smile of the sphinx and looked serene for the world.

Several months later Priscilla filed suit against Elvis for extrinsic fraud, claiming that he had failed to disclose assets before the divorce settlement. The new settlement was for two million dollars, and Priscilla went into partnership with a friend and opened Bis and Beau, a posh Beverly Hills boutique.

Elvis seemed resilient in the aftermath of his divorce, but he had a way of concealing his true emotional and psychological state. Rick's impressions were that he was dazed at first but then found release in his work, throwing himself headlong into a series of thirty-day tours. "Elvis seemed like a cat," he says, "who would come back and land on his feet, ready to handle it. He didn't express guilt, but he *knew* that he blew it, because he did. But he was a man: His attitude was, 'You've got to go on—you can't sit around and feel sorry for yourself.' There were moments when it played heavily on his mind, but as far as letting you know how he felt, he controlled it. He let very few people in on what was really going on inside."

As when he had suffered the loss of his mother, Elvis turned once again to the one person he confided in during a time of inconsolable emotional loss—his daddy. "Don't ask questions," was the order of the day. "Just keep rolling." "Sometimes he'd wake up thinking about her and you could tell how he felt,"

David says. "But Elvis and Priscilla were sacred. If Elvis was
upset, you knew why."

The breakup seemed to impose a pattern of failed marriages
on the TCB group. Husbands stepped out on wives and wives
walked; husbands stole other women, and the bereft men turned
right around and stole others; those men, in turn, got bored
after a while and succumbed once again to that peculiarly male
and deep-cutting need to revel in that intangibly exciting sense
of anticipation and escape that comes from the whos, whats,
whens, wheres, whys, and how-am-I-gonna-get-hers of the Next
in Line. And in TCB-land the Next in Lines seemed to stretch
forever.

But somewhere down the road of life the instincts and experience of most "mature" men will tell them that a "strong" man
or a "complete" man is most able to realize his manhood not
through the pursuit of the big buck or the perfect lay or by tests
of guts and fearlessness on Harley-Davidsons, but through the
love and caring in a relationship and by meeting the special and
sensitive needs of those they care most about. This was, in the
end, the most painful failure expressed by Elvis's divorce—that
reproachful, inescapable sense of having hurt people he loved,
which would plague him no matter how hard he would try to
anesthetize those seared emotions with drugs or anything else.

"He had it all within the palm of his hand," reflects Dee
Presley. "He had a beautiful wife and a beautiful little daughter
that he couldn't be with and I think that hurt him tremendously; he couldn't spend more time with her even though she
was his life. Elvis Presley wasn't going to change for any
woman; he had to be accepted the way he was. You know, in
his heart, Elvis was a man capable of great emotions and very
deep love. He knew that all of those girls didn't mean a thing. I
believe that he would have given just about anything to make
just one woman happy—without needing to prove anything to
anyone."

Elvis was the sort of person who didn't readily allow people
into his life to begin with, but once he opened to a person to a
level where love was possible, that person became a part of his

206   soul—a permanent part of his emotional life. This is what made the loss of Priscilla so hard to take. Like the tree that is cut down and dragged away, she may have left him, but the tap root still remained. The realization that his wife had left him for another man was shattering to his ego, but the emotional effects of the divorce went far deeper than that. Elvis's dreams for a family and for being a complete father to his daughter had also vanished.

Many people have asked, if he loved her so much, how could he have taken her for granted? How could he have defeated himself? Elvis's divorce can only be understood within the context of the devastating effects of his mother's death on his emotional life. Gladys Presley had been the one person whom he'd offered his unfettered love to, and her death had taught him the bittersweet truth about love between people, whether they be man and woman or mother and child: There can be no love without pain and loss. When Elvis sobbed, "Oh, God, my whole world is gone!" at his mother's funeral, propped by friends as the newsmen of the world vied for his statement, he meant it much more literally than one might think.

Gladys's death left Elvis with powerful questions normal enough for a child to feel after the loss of a loving parent, but Elvis lived the rest of his life wary of the vulnerability necessary for true emotional intimacy, afraid to love as fully as he knew he could because he neither wanted to lose that love nor have it rejected. With all of his money, his career, the Next In Line, and his boys to do his bidding, it became all too easy for him to evade this problem and substitute "things" for feelings. He became, in plain truth, a deeply emotional man who became emotionally impaired, constrained, and stopped up. He learned to impose his own needs and standards over others—sometimes intentionally, sometimes unintentionally—he hurt many of the people dearest to him *because* they loved him the most. Being the basically good and intelligent man that he was, he could run but he couldn't hide from himself.

"They were both like that—Vernon and Elvis," Dee says. "They could hurt you so bad one minute and it was only because they loved you. The reason that it sometimes seemed that

Elvis only cared about himself was that in his heart he was so miserable that he had to do things to make himself feel good just so he could go on. Some of it was because of his career, but not the way he hurt Priscilla. He was bound to have hurt her, and she was the beautiful little girl that married him and a fine mother to his child."

It wasn't that Elvis didn't think about these things, either. He was always in tune with the feelings of the people around him. It's difficult to fathom how he ever expected to "fool" his wife; he knew she was too smart, too observant, and too inquisitive for that. Knowing full well that his actions ran the risk of hurting and alienating her, he went ahead and did them anyway. Though it was the last thing in the world he really wanted, he all but invited the course of events with Mike Stone to occur. The experience of her leaving him only confirmed all of his fears and suspicions about love being a very risky business indeed.

Priscilla Beaulieu Presley was a down-to-earth, stable woman, young (Elvis always wanted young and inexperienced women because he felt that if they knew only the experience of him, they would be less apt to stray, reject, or compare him), growing all the time, flexible, giving when she wanted to be, selfish when she had to be, and devoted to him; in fact, she was so "right" that his marriage intimidated him into behaving like he did with any other thing in his life that he wanted and then tired of—he threw it away.

The experience of divorce entrenched Elvis more solidly in some of his most basic attitudes about life. Things seemed more transient and expendable than ever to him, but his romantic advice to his brothers smacks of his true feelings. He cared about them and wanted to spare them the same kind of pain. "Protect your heart," he always told them when they sought his advice. "Don't get so wrapped up in one person so that if she leaves you, your whole world crumbles."

Elvis then put his guards up and hit the road, business as usual; no respite, more adamant than ever before in his devil-may-care determination to always be himself and do what he wanted, no matter the cost; he insisted on being accepted on

208   those terms. "If he couldn't be accepted," Rick says, "his attitude would be, 'The hell with you—don't flatter yourself and
think you're such a hot item that you'll crush my world if you
put me down, because I *will* bounce back!'"

Sometimes his deepest feelings would come bubbling to the
surface. His anger and bitterness at Mike Stone, so grotesquely
portrayed as blind, homicidal rage in the book *Elvis: What
Happened?* was an example of finally letting it out. The very
first chapter of that book pictures Elvis in his hotel suite in
Vegas, waking up in a drug-hazed rage and deciding like some
bloodthirsty Mafioso to have Stone killed. The scene had all of
the trappings of a cheap gangster movie. "That was all talk,"
says Rick. "Elvis was just blowing off steam. Elvis Presley was
human. To a certain extent, he did feel that his wife was stolen
from him, but he also knew that he'd messed up and accepted
the consequences. Sure, sometimes he'd get angry as hell, as
much at himself as at Mike Stone, and he'd say things like,
'Man, I'd like to blow that guy away!' Now, you're talking about
a multimillion dollar organization that was armed to the teeth.
Anything could be done, no questions asked. The proof that it
was all just talk is that Mike Stone is alive and well today. A few
minutes later Elvis said that he could never do anything like
that."

With all of its concomitant publicity, people have become
used to considering Elvis's divorce as the crucial turning point
in his life, as that point when his life and career went into a
tailspin and started going to pieces. While it may have removed
restraints on his self-destructive behavior, it is unfair and untrue
to blame his decline lock, stock, and barrel on his divorce, no
matter how convenient it may be for purposes of biography or
journalism. It wasn't a precipitous fall, for one thing, but a
gradual decline rooted in many complicated factors, done as
only Elvis could have done something.

Understanding "what really happened" to Elvis Presley
requires looking far beyond and much deeper than the sensa-
tionalized outbursts reported by his discarded bodyguards and
into his internal life, which he guarded more carefully than
anything. Such an awareness, facile as it may seem or sound, is

the only thing that can even begin to explain how Elvis Presley, a man who appeared to the American public as the have-not who grew up to have everything, a man of boundless spirit, depth, talent, dignity, and compassion, could spend his last years in unspeakable emotional loneliness, taking drugs, hurting many of those that loved him most; a man who didn't care, as Rick puts it, "if snuff went for nine dollars a dip."

CHAPTER 12

LISA MARIE

Elvis Presley knew that broken marriages play most heavily on the minds and hearts of the children involved, and it was the separation from his daughter that made him realize how lamentable the divorce really was. The only moments of domestic happiness he had known were now gone from his life, and though he would see his daughter often, it would never again be as a family.

From the very first moment that Lisa opened her eyes and peered at Elvis through the glass partition of the maternity ward, Elvis wanted nothing more in life than to love and protect his daughter and make her life wonderful. She had been born into a very special world. "A man shall be known in his children," proclaims Ecclesiastes: The proverb clearly spoke to Elvis Presley and Lisa was always to be "Daddy's little girl." She brought out a side of Elvis unlike any other and the very wonder of her existence could make him meek as a lamb. You would see his passion for her rise up in his expression when she was an infant and he would return from Hollywood or Las Vegas and dawdle

212 lovingly over her bed to recite prayers, or when he would sing her lullabies and envelope her with the love of his voice. Sometimes the mere sight of her could make him cry.

Elvis was a doting father, amused and delighted by his child, particularly when she grew past the infant stage and could be seen tooling happily and adventurously about Graceland, mouthing words, surprising Elvis at the piano, or riding in golf carts with Elvis or any of his buddies. Elvis loved her so much that he was a typical "easy make" as a parent—he could easily lose all sense of proportion with her and he spoiled her like a little queen.

"He just didn't get to take her to the zoo and to the park and do the things that normal daddies do," remembers Dee Presley, "so Elvis had a tendency to let Lisa have her way much more than Cilla did." The older she grew, the more she looked like her daddy and displayed his expressions, particularly in the way she would cock her head to one side coyly, in her glances and gazes.

Lisa was five years old when Elvis and Priscilla were divorced. What played on Elvis's mind and conscience in the aftermath of divorce were the possible long-range emotional effects that the split might have on his daughter. He worried about Lisa growing up "too quickly" because of the divorce and his way of life. "He knew that Cilla was doing everything to bring Lisa up right," says Ricky, "but Lisa was around Elvis's guys and things could get pretty rowdy. She got hip quick. You've also got to realize the effect that it might have had on Lisa when she would visit and her dad would have different girl friends—to know that they were spending the night with him. Then Cilla lived with her boyfriend, Mike. Man, Elvis would think about how that all made her feel, and what kind of effect it would have on her because that was *his* little girl."

Lisa's safety outside of the protective walls of Graceland also became a concern. Potential kidnapers and extortionists terrified him, and the boys always carried guns when they picked her up to bring her to Elvis's house in California or when they flew with her to Memphis or Las Vegas. As with the death threats against his own life, Elvis could never be sure that some well-

planned conspiracy would not snatch her away one day to ran-
som her for the fortune that he would have gladly paid for her
return.

Elvis's time spent with Lisa were the most precious and
meaningful moments of his last years. Whenever Lisa visited
Graceland or Elvis's LA home, for a time they would be entirely alone, sitting, talking, playing together, making up for
time spent apart. "Elvis used to call her all the time," recalls
David. "He'd be just sitting there and up and get the urge to talk
to her and get her on the phone, or if he was in Vegas, he just
might send me to LA to go bring her out for a little visit."

Priscilla was very understanding about these visits. Contrary
to reports that she was fastidious and sometimes stingy with her
husband's visitation privileges, she was quite generous. "When
Elvis wanted to see Lisa," adds David, "he could see her anytime he wanted to unless Lisa had something very important to
do."

Christmastime took on an even greater significance for Elvis
after his divorce because they were all together again at Graceland. "Elvis really felt good around Christmas," says David,
" 'cause he would get off on doin' the whole number for Lisa.
He'd wait up all night long on Christmas eve so he could be
waitin' downstairs first thing in the morning when she got up
and he'd play Santa Claus for her. Those were some of the
closest moments between him and his daughter." And Lisa
quickly learned about her daddy and how he reacted to things.
"She really knew her dad," laughs Rick. "I don't think I've ever
seen Elvis yell at or whip his daughter because he just didn't
have to. All it took from him was a—you know—'Lisa' and
she'd cool it."

Lisa Marie Presley was the one individual that Elvis needed
and wanted most to love. She loved her father with the free,
natural, and unconditional love of a child, yet time and distance made even that love only marginally accessible to him.
Because he spent so much time away, his expressions of love oftentimes had to be reduced to presents like the mink coat he
gave her for her ninth birthday ("Cilla said she was either going
to put it away until she was older or tell her it wasn't real,"

214 remembers Dee), shining golden earrings, and the sights, sounds, and thrills of the deserted amusement parks that she and her daddy would enjoy together after everybody else had gone home.

The intimacy between father and daughter increased as time went on, but Elvis still felt in his heart that it wasn't enough. As his health declined in subsequent years, she was the most important person in his life; when his boredom and unhappiness reached rock bottom, she cast the single beacon of brightness into the descending gloom. If there was one thing in the back of his mind that compelled him forward when he was faltering, it was the continuing need to make his daughter proud of him. The knowledge that his daughter would one day have to grow up to confront the contents of *Elvis: What Happened?* with its shrill hawking of his "wrongdoing" was, according to both David and Rick, the most crushing and desolating effect of that book on his life.

CHAPTER 13

UPS AND DOWNS

"The man was into drugs, for sure, and so was I," Rick admits. "I wouldn't say that I wasn't right in there with him, because I was, and we had a blast, too. I'm not ashamed to talk about it now because I've changed tremendously, but it's still very emotional. It's hard for me to sit here and say he did this or did that. What I want to get across are the circumstances—what was going on and why, what he did and why, and how it affected him. Elvis was a phenomenal man, but he was human—he had a lot of problems. I loved the man—worship is closer to it, I guess—he was my 'all' for most of my life. I've done a lot of thinking about his part of the story and I'm at peace about it now. I think it's important for the public to know the truth and not just the worst of it."

As heartbreaking as it is, Elvis's final years are only understandable through a realization of the destructive role that drugs played in his life. Sooner or later the question must rear its head, and because of his shining public image, the issue is a sensitive one.

216   "Elvis was certainly not on dope," emphasized Hollywood reporter May Mann in her book *Elvis and the Colonel*. Toeing
the Parker line, her statement sought to assure Elvis's loyal fans
of what they themselves were already convinced—Elvis Presley's
perfection. "He never has been, nor will be," she continued.
"His mother so ingrained in him the logic of a clean mind,
clean body, good health, honesty, and integrity."

"By 1971 Elvis was a changed guy," Sonny West revealed in
Elvis: What Happened? "He was no longer the shy, fun-loving
kid from Memphis. No, he was just living for himself and all
that damn junk. He was like a walking drugstore."

Are they talking about the same man?

May Mann was right about one thing: Elvis's upbringing and
the influence of his mother's strict morality made drugs alien to
his world in the early stages of his career. However, when he
served his overseas hitch in the Army, he discovered amphetamines. For a GI at that time, such a discovery was natural and
innocent enough: During the Second World War, Benzedrine
and Dexedrine had become a way of life for many GI's. Pills
were being dispensed by the millions to soldiers on the periph-
ery and in combat to keep them up, alert, and moving
forward. At least covertly if not officially, they were still being
used by the time Elvis was stationed in Freidberg in 1959, when
a sergeant would hand them out before maneuvers, not wanting
his men to fall asleep in the cold. "Elvis told me that he
brought back two huge trunkfuls of Dexedrine when he came
back from Germany," Rick remembers. "He said it was just to
be able to stay up and not for the high. When he had that big
bus for those crosscountry drives during the sixties, he'd use
them for the trips. He enjoyed driving long, long distances—
twenty, sometimes twenty-four hours nonstop, and he'd do it by
himself. That was the beginning."

Elvis was a man of boundless ambitions and mercurial energies. Once he found himself sitting on top of the world, it
seemed logical to him that he could stay up there and keep
going even farther for as long as those energies would last.
There was a nervous current of power that pulsed through his
life and his body; it caused him to tap and drum and pace

about, to want to be always doing something or going somewhere. Onstage, he used to perform his shows like a buzz saw cutting steadily through the trunk of a sequoia tree. It never stopped until his body told him in the plain language of overwhelming fatigue that it had to stop. Then, he would sleep.

"Speed" or "uppers," as amphetamines are known to users both on and off the street, seemed so perfect for Elvis because they dovetailed with his naturally energized personality, taking his high energy levels and just extending them farther. Derived from the amphetamine sulfates and the dextroamphetamine sulfates, Benzedrine ('bennies'), Dexedrine, drugs like Dexamyl (from dextroamphetamine sulfate combined with amobarbital hydrochloride), and the methamphetamines like Desoxyn and Desbutal all work on the nervous system of the body and give the user a feeling of being "up" and of not needing food for long periods of time. Always body conscious, particularly when he was making films in which he sometimes appeared bare chested and in all manners of costumes that revealed his physique, Elvis also took the pills as appetite suppressants—to keep himself trim and looking good for the cameras of Norman Taurog and other Hollywood directors. Tolerance, however, is rapidly built up to the pills, and this characteristic of the drug sets up a cycle of increased dosage to get the same effects. On the old time country-and-western circuits, and in show business in general, amphetamine usage was widespread long before the long-range effects of the drugs were known. People used them to work longer hours at greater output, to hop up their performances, to have more fun, and to stay beautiful. Stars with weight problems were always particularly susceptible to amphetamine abuse. Judy Garland, who kept her weight down for her MGM films with diet pills, was a perfect example.

The stickiest problem with the drugs is a possible psychological addiction; users get so mired in using them because once you have been so "up," everything else naturally looks down, and they begin taking the drugs to feel better. Unfortunately there isn't a worse drug to take for prolonged periods of time, and Elvis took them, in one form or another and for one reason or another, for some sixteen years.

218   When ingested, amphetamines speed up the pulmonary rate and the aging process of the body. The more rapidly pumping blood can produce side effects in the user like confusion, combativeness, hallucinations, panic, hypertension, and arrhythmias (Elvis's death was attributed to cardiac arrhythmia). Moreover, there are also certain psychopharmacological effects of amphetamines.

Hypervigilance is one characteristic of these effects. The user feels a sense of heightened awareness; visual, olfactory, tactile, and auditory responses can become finely honed but erratic. An individual's capacity to feel in control of him or herself is enhanced; so is his sense of religiosity, his "realm of insightfulness," if he is inclined toward those concerns as Elvis was. The habitual user can also take on an air of condescension and superiority. Colors will seem brighter and more sharply delineated from their backgrounds, and the libido is increased. The drugs could make Elvis feel a remarkable energy and sharpness of consciousness which misled him because, after long periods of time under their influence, thoughts become jumbled, the body more and more worn out.

Amphetamines played right into many of Elvis's moods and interests. While he was never a speed freak, uppers affected his displays of temper, his hypertension, and his refusal to accept limitations for himself. According to Rick, Elvis was accustomed to taking two fifteen-milligram doses of Dexedrine to prime himself for a performance when he woke up. While this isn't a dangerous amount of the drug (some professional football players have been known to ingest as much as one hundred milligrams before a game), they couldn't but affect his performances: Some of Elvis's funniest, quick-punching lines, his longest, most rambling monologues, and most inspired stage antics came under the influence of the drugs.

Elvis had become habituated to using amphetamines during the sixties, when they enabled him to meet the demanding output of three motion pictures a year and still manage to fit in his marathon football games, the crosscountry trips, nightriding with friends, dates, and parties. When he began the long tours after his comeback, they became more important than ever, heightening the emotional and creative experience of performing live, allowing him energy and concentrating-potential for longer periods of time. But they also created other problems.

"When we started touring in sixty-nine he had to have something to bring him down after the show," says Rick. "When he was finished he was still so hyped up and tense; he couldn't just walk off the stage and say, 'Oh boy, I'm glad that's over with.' Not with him, anyway. He was so into it that he had to have something to unwind him, to let him mellow out."

Elvis was a night owl to begin with. Insomnia seemed to run in the family and the uppers kept Elvis awake for great lengths of time. When he was home from the road and able to spend his time as he pleased, he never minded being awake. In fact, he loved to just wait for sleep to creep up slowly on him and then descend deliciously into a long, restful slumber. But things were different on the road. He needed to get to bed in order to have his energy for the next evening's performance.

"Sleeping medication" became the accepted TCB euphemism for all of the narcotics that Elvis ingested, and for the very good reason that in the beginning he indeed did take them "to get to sleep." One by one he experimented with sedatives and barbiturates like Tuinal, sedative-muscle relaxers like Quaaludes, and class-A narcotics like Demerol and Dilaudid to find out which ones worked best for him and at what dosages. It began with the "downs" that are marketed in capsule form— short- to immediate-acting barbiturate hypnotics and sedatives. Quaaludes, or "ludes," were perfect for his needs because the next morning's side effects are minimal (physicians sometimes prescribe it for the treatment of insomnia).

The serious pitfall in taking these kinds of drugs to get to sleep is that they can leave a residual effect in the morning, a "down" hangover, which causes the user to feel groggy, dizzy, or weak. When someone has to get right up and cracking, the residual effect can be burned away by taking still more amphetamines, which sets up a vicious cycle of either being up or down, or going from one place to the other, or of counteracting the effects of one drug by the effects of another. Somewhere between the recurrent journey of up to down, hyped up or laid

220 back, the personality and body of the user can get hog-tied, mauled, and drawn and quartered.

Elvis kept a *Physicians' Desk Reference* handy and read up on the effect of different combinations and dosages of the pills he was using. As with anything else he did, he immersed himself in the subject, learning as much as he could, becoming an expert, but the drugs he took to help him get more out of life and to meet his professional obligations were, in the long run, what hastened his deterioration.

Like so many other paradoxes in his life that involved the balancing of opposites, Elvis also took drugs to contradict each other in their effects because their effects were in themselves opposite. He began to have moods characteristic of ups and moods characteristic of downs, and the moodswings that embodied many of his most contradictory traits became dependent upon the effects of the drugs. They also reflected his all-out, if-it's-not-one-it's-got-to-be-the-other attitudes about his life.

Elvis came to look at the pills in his life as just another natural part of what he had to do to be Elvis Presley. While in his mind, the issue and image of drugs never ceased to be anathema to everything healthy and the antithesis of everything good and wholesome, he set up a delicate double standard that helped him to rationalize his own drug taking and still allowed him to condemn drug abuse, to speak out against drugs, even to become a federal narcotics agent.

Getting high, on the other hand, was something that came naturally to Elvis. Music was the great high of his life, and other highs followed—money, women, beautiful cars, karate, meditation, power. His self-image would not abide the notion of drug-taking as a high in itself—he was taking them as "medication." As time passed and his drug taking became influenced by the course of events in his life, he began taking drugs for the same reasons that people usually abuse them—to escape pressure, to get mellow and relax, to have fun, or just to get off, but he still was unwilling to admit that to himself.

"Elvis was the type of man that if it was a lie he was telling somebody," Rick observes, "he would get to the point where he actually believed it himself and didn't see it as a lie. You see, in his eyes, he had been right for so long that he couldn't see somebody saying to him, 'Hey, Elvis, that's not right.' He'd think, 'Well, how would *you* know—you're not in my shoes!' "

Billy, Rick, and David all agree that the drugs in Elvis's life were moving quickly from use to abuse sometime around 1972, after his divorce, after three incessant years of touring, after the initial sparkle of his comeback began to fade. It was then that he began taking stock of his life: He was pushing forty, divorced, isolated from his daughter by his career and the divorce, putting on weight, richer than ever but feeling pain, guilt, emptiness, and, most dangerously, a great deal of boredom. There came to be an element of risk and gambling in his drug taking at that point in his life, as well as a kind of self-flagellation.

"Elvis saw things that most other people would never even dream of," Rick says. "It's not that he was burnt out on life, it's just that he had done everything. There was no real kick left for him to get into. He just wasn't a normal person who would get into swimming or tennis. Entertainment to him was his motor-cycles, twin-engine go-carts that went ninety mph, that kind of stuff. So he got into drugs."

If Elvis wanted to get high, he certainly wasn't about to start drinking after all of those years as a confirmed teetotaler. Rick elaborates: "Elvis *hated* alcohol. Some of his relatives had drinking problems and that really turned him off. I've only seen Elvis drink on two occasions and he just didn't know how to do it. If he had a vodka tonic with lime he would just drink it down like it was Mountain Valley water and set it down. He just didn't seem to know that he was going to get drunk if he kept drinking like that, and that's the way he would drink! He'd drink about two or three and be completely whacked out! One drink or one glass of wine, man, and you could tell that he was off."

The Boss stayed well away from LSD, mescaline, psilocybin, or any other psychedelic or hallucinogenic drug. He expressed curiosity about their spiritual effects, but, as with the other drugs that became part of the countercultural lore of the sixties, he shied away from them. His burning curiosity about the LSD experience was satiated by querying a member of the group who once took the drug. Appropriately, the most important thing

222 that Elvis wanted to know was not how high he was or the psychological, emotional, or psychic dimensions of the drug, but whether or not Red could "see God" while he was tripping.

Elvis's feelings about the social ills of drugs also prevented him from smoking marijuana, which his brothers smoked frequently. He frowned on pot smoking as a symbol of moral lassitude to be avoided and saw it as a shibboleth of the counterculture.

"Don't do it on tours, Rick!" he would chide his reefer-smoking brother. "Not if we're on tour! When you're home, you do what you want on your own time. The only thing I've got to say about it is that it's illegal. That's the only drag."

He felt the same way about most of the other drugs associated with street use. According to Rick, he tried and liked cocaine, another "natural" drug for Elvis because it offered a curious, hard-to-pin-down euphoria that fell right in between being high on a mild, pleasant narcotic and the speedy feeling from the heightening wave of energy of an amphetamine.

"He went back to the same old thing," Rick says. " 'You can't fool with it, Rick. It's against the law.' In my opinion, if Elvis would have smoked a little reefer or gotten more into coke instead of the other things he did, he would have been much better off. I don't mean that he should have done it a lot; I tried to tell people that, but they wouldn't listen. See, I had a bad reputation for staying high and drinking because that's what I was into for many years on the road with Elvis. I did drugs because I was bored, too, just to break the monotony. Nothing excited us any more, man. We were all jaded. Elvis and I related more because we were both into drugs. He would ask me what I thought of certain amphetamines and sleeping medications and every once in a while we'd do a couple of downs together in his room, away from everybody else, just for the hell of it. Elvis was like a typical head when he got high; he'd love to sit around and rap and listen to music."

Rick's reputation as TCB head and resident group druggie was well earned. He smoked with the relish of a Rastafarian, hooked down pills to get him through long days, french-fried himself on hallucinogens, snorted long, snaking lines of coke, and could then wash it all down with beer, wine, Jack Daniel's, or (ay caramba!) tequila. His TCB years were an endless high and he was never without his shades to hide the glint of stoned beatitude that perpetually glossed over and dilated his eyes. His brothers Billy and David weren't exactly slouches when it came to getting fucked up on the road, but they trailed far behind Rick, particularly when he started toying with heroin.

Eventually Elvis reached a point where his drugs got out of hand, but the drugs he took were always the same ones he used to either pump himself up or bring himself down. "Unfortunately, he didn't know moderation," says Rick. "Not just with drugs but with anything he did—with cars, homes, trucks, motorcycles, guns—he was just completely locked in, dedicated, never half-ass. On the one hand he would be telling me, 'There's such a thing as use and abuse,' and there he was, just going nuts."

Determined, as ever, to do what he wanted to do, Elvis would tell those around him that it was *his* business. "If he wanted to take nine thousand Quaaludes, he was going to do it and nobody was going to stop him," explains David. "That's just the way Elvis was. His attitude was, you know, 'Fuck you—it's my fucking life and I'll do what I want with it.' "

Elvis's narcotics and amphetamines were all legally prescribed for him by a whole slew of doctors, and this seemed to provide him with a sanction, a further rationale that they were justified. Rick explains: "He had about four or five doctors that he could get anything he wanted from. All they cared about were the cars he'd give them. See, Elvis gave them Mercedes and other stuff for writing prescriptions for him, and one of the things that he tried to do was to keep them separated so that they didn't know anything about each other. They knew about each other, but they just didn't care; they'd write him out anything he wanted. Dr. Nick was different. He knew what was going on and what we were all aiming for in those last years was to get it where Elvis would have only one physician to go to who would supervise everything."

224 "I can't name any names," echoes David, "but they will all know who they are if they read this. Those doctors would do anything for a buck and that's the best way to put it."

With his own private stash Elvis could take whatever drugs he wanted, in his own preferred ways. Usually, say the boys, his drugs remained one of the most private rituals in his life; he felt most comfortable doing them before he went to bed, when he could be assured that he wouldn't have to function, go anywhere, or be seen in the entourage. After being up for several days or at the end of a days' traveling and performance, he would take something powerful and slide away from the pressure. Moment by moment, as the drug worked through his bloodstream and pelted his nervous system and nestled, finally, in his brain, with his cares dissolved and problems benumbed and neutralized, his body would descend like a Boeing 707 coming in for a smooth landing after being caught in turbulence, until it was finally prone, and a rosy, warm euphoria circled his head. Within the room, surrounded by music and a large television screen, his eyelids would look like they were weighted down with lead, but he would keep them open for one last glimpse of the TV, one last bite of food, or just to crack that last joke before succumbing to the drug and slipping thankfully, like a child, into the oblivion of sleep.

Then, depending on whose night duty it was or if there was a woman with him that night, a familiar figure would watch over him until morning, putting him to bed, covering him, making sure that no harm befell him and nothing disturbed his precious sleep.

In Elvis's mind, his drugs were legal, necessary, on the up-and-up; Rick's weren't. When the Boss saw his brother delving further into hard drugs, his fatherly-brotherly feeling for Rick emerged and he laid down the law: Cut it out or get out!

Rick took one look at the Boss's medicine cabinet and drug cache and saw the hypocrisy in his big brother's admonitions. "I just wasn't going along with the way he was," he remembers. "We were on the out-and-out because he was telling me not to do something and then he was doing it himself."

In 1975 the conflict came to a head, and Rick found himself   225
walking out the gate. In the Boss's mind he had been banished
from the court; in Rick's, it was self-imposed exile.

For close to eight months they didn't see each other—the
longest time that either of them had been apart since Rick and
his two brothers had come vaulting up the Graceland driveway
and into Elvis's life for the very first time. Rick's drug habits
continued unabated during the exile, but he no longer had free
access to either the Boss's stash or his many contacts and sources
on the road. Instead, he now had to resort to illegal means of
procurement—namely, forgery.

On the night of August 7, 1975, he entered the pharmacy of
the Methodist Hospital in Memphis with a bogus prescription
for Demerol, a strong painkiller. The prescription had been
forged by a friend, and Rick gave it to the clerk on duty, who
then disappeared into the back. He reappeared with two police-
men, who read Rick his rights, handcuffed him roughly, and
dragged him away. Once again he was in the back of a police
car; his heart pounding against his chest, all of his boyhood
fears about bringing disgrace to Elvis's name haunted him, and
he saw the headlines clearly in his mind: **PRESLEY'S
BROTHER BUSTED FOR DRUGS, FAMILY IMPLI-
CATED.**

During his interrogation Rick was unwilling to reveal his
name—the detectives slapped him around to make him remember. Several hours after he revealed his identity, they took him
downstairs in the elevator, still handcuffed, with a patrolman on
each arm. It was sometime around dawn. Rick had no idea
where he was heading—he assumed that he was being transferred to another jail—when the elevator door opened to the
most welcome sight of his life.

Elvis Presley was standing there, dressed impeccably in a
powder-blue suit that Rick had once picked out for him. There
was a look of pained concern on his face, but the sight of him
was so reassuring that Rick had to fight back the tears.

"This is gonna kill Dee," the Boss said sternly. The words
and reproach in Elvis's expression were enough to bring on the

226   tears. Elvis rushed to Rick, threw his arms around his shoulders, and hugged him like a bear.

"Don't worry, Rick, I'm gonna get you outta this," he said tenderly, looking Rick in the eyes. "Don't worry, man."

He then bent to Rick's ear. "What were you doin'," he whispered. "What were you trying to get?"

Rick just sighed disconsolately. "Demerol."

Elvis stepped back and looked at him, as if to say, *You asshole—you had to go and get arrested for some lousy Demerol!*

"Shit," he said, shaking his head. "I'm not mad at you, Rick. I'm just hurt that something like this had to happen."

His eyes then wandered down to Rick's handcuffs. "Take those things off him," he said to the nearest patrolman. The cop looked away, not acknowledging the request. Elvis stood patiently for a few moments, the emotion reddening his face.

The words that thundered out of him were like bullets being spit from his mouth. "Maybe you didn't hear what I said, *man!* Take those damn cuffs off him or I'll buy out this whole city block!"

The cop looked around for support from his colleagues in the room. When he saw that none was forthcoming, he rolled his eyes helplessly and complied. The cuffs were off and so, before too long, was Rick.

Elvis put Rick up at a Memphis hotel, hired a team of lawyers, and told Vernon to inform Dee, who had been out of town.

As expected, Dee was crushed. For the first time she began to realize how completely in the dark about her children she had become. "When Vernon told me he said, 'We've got a little problem,' " she remembers, "and when he told me I almost fell on the floor. I was so afraid that he was going to become a drug addict. I just didn't know what to do—it seemed that I didn't even know him anymore."

The district attorney wanted to nail Ricky for three to five years on a fraud rap, but he managed to skip away with only a year's probation and was released in Elvis's recognizance. In such situations it doesn't exactly hurt to have a stepbrother who

is a model citizen, a generous supporter of the police department and many other public works, a renowned philanthropist, a national figure, and a world-famous superstar. Rick
was given permission to go back on tour with Elvis even though
felons on probation are rarely allowed to leave the state. The
day after his arrest Elvis asked him back to work.

"You're gonna come back and work for me," he said, "but,
hey, man, you *really* need to dry out, and I'm gonna see that
you do."

"Yeah, you're right, Elvis," promised Ricky.

"So I walked the line after all that happened," Rick remembers. "I didn't mess up for a while and we went back on tour.
Elvis and I got closer than ever. The only thing was that while I
stayed clean, at least for a while, Elvis didn't."

CHAPTER 14

SING AWAY SORROW, CAST AWAY CARE

The *Lisa Marie*, all gassed up and ready to roll, glistens beautifully in the late afternoon sunlight. Perched boldly on the runway of the Memphis airport like a lone eagle on a mountaintop, she collects the TCB principals as everybody gathers to await the Boss. It's time to get back to work.

Fresh from the southern California sunshine, Joe Esposito has a lot on his mind but looks hearty and is sorry to be back in Memphis. He seems everywhere at once as Lamar waves and waddles up the steps to the jet, looking like the fattest cowboy ever to roam the prairie. Felton Jarvis, Elvis's producer, follows.

In the conference room of the jet Charlie Hodge, as usual, is nervous, pacing around the table as he talks to Ed Parker. Charlie is glad to be hitting the road again and is looking forward to the tour with the same zeal with which a long-distance runner primes for the Boston Marathon. Parker relaxes, taking it all in stride, his feet up on the table and his hands clasped behind his head.

Vernon Presley and Dr. Nick arrive together, looking avun-

230 cular, somehow out of place with their heads of white hair and the bags they carry. Jerry Schilling, who.follows them up with Myrna of the Sweet Inspirations, thinks the old men lend a certain dignity to the tours and flashes a grin at the two mechanics who are staring at his beautiful girl friend. "Man," one of them says to the other. "If *that* ain't brown sugar, nothin' is!"

Silent, serious, clipboard in hand, Dick Grob is thinking about linkups for airport security with local police forces. He is sitting in a chair when the Wests make the scene. Red is bearded, putting on weight like the Boss, and losing his hair. Sonny plops down next to him, quiet and withdrawn. He's just had an argument with his wife and his mood is as foul as the Buffalo winter.

Slick Rick appears like a phantom out of the blue. He smiles that stoned smile of his, exchanges pleasantries, and begins readying the Boss's room at the back of the jet.

Billy Smith is behind the wheel of the long black limousine that pulls onto the field. He draws up before the stairwell, stops, and turns to Elvis as the people begin spilling out. "Well, give 'em hell, cuz," he smiles. "Take care."

David is the first out, garbed, as usual, in his jeans, a tee shirt, and an *Elvis* Windbreaker that bulges underneath the left armpit where he packs his piece. Various lanky lovelies then scurry out—a melange of locals mixed with LA talent—dressed in clingy-chic boutique dresses, fingers ablush with diamonds, necks agiggle with pearls, stockinged legs stretching out after the ride from Graceland, heels clomping and clattering excitedly on the pavement . . . followed by Linda Thompson, the loveliest . . . and lo and behold, the Boss emerges, slowly, puffing haphazardly on one of his little Dutch cigars, bedecked in a magnificent full-length leather coat that glares in the light, wearing a pair of those slightly tinted shades that do little to hide his swollen-looking eyes. He pauses for a moment and takes it all in, lost in a private moment and transported somewhere else, then shakes his head quizzically. "Helluva way to make a livin'," he says to Linda.

The others are all aboard—TCBers and TLCers alike— lovers, strangers, hangers-on who can't take a hint, would-be honchos, the whole kit and caboodle. They mill about the passenger area or hang in the lounge, the dining room, or conference area, awaiting the man whose steps are measured and resigned as he climbs up to the jet that bears the name of the little girl he adores. "Damn!" Elvis exclaims once inside, snapping it all together by the sudden audacity of his presence. "Let's get this show on the road!"

For the last eight years of his life, through periods when his health and his emotional and psychological state could least afford the strain, Elvis Presley worked harder than ever before. Everywhere he went, vast gatherings of his fans thundered their approval, and their roaring din and enraptured expressions confirmed to him the purpose of his life, making it seem that he could do no wrong even as things went to pieces. Money rolled in like water filling a tidal basin, and the Colonel kept setting up the dates.

A day ahead of the main TCB body in Elvis's jet, the Colonel and the crew from Concerts West are traveling in the smaller Jetstar, the *Little Lisa Marie*, setting up radio spots and advance promotion and seeing to remaining accommodations. Colonel Tom Parker knows he controls an intricate, beautifully crafted mechanism. As many as five tours in advance booked, everybody sprints for three straight weeks, takes one week off, then gets back in the starting blocks to wait for the gun to sound.

The patterns of the tours crisscross and zigzag, sometimes blanketing one area of the country and then leapfrogging to a short string of far off engagements (the *Lisa Marie* has a threethousand mile range). The tour of June 1974 pops off at the Tarrant County Convention Center in Fort Worth, Texas, where Elvis rips off four shows in two days, then skips over to the LSU Assembly Center in Baton Rouge, Louisiana. From Baton Rouge it jumps to the Civic Center in Amarillo, then up to the Veterans Memorial Auditorium in Des Moines, Iowa. Cleveland is close by, so the Boss knocks off the Convention Center there before heading over to Providence, Rhode Island, and then to the Spectrum in Philadelphia. Then the *Lisa Marie* heads due north and makes for that great honeymoon capital,

232   Niagara Falls, where Elvis again squeezes in two shows (the last two dates have been deuces, with one show at two thirty and the other at eight thirty P.M.). By the time he floats back south into Ohio again (the St. John Arena at Ohio State, this time), Elvis is beginning to run out of gas himself, but the next night he steps out on stage at Freedom Hall in Louisville and doesn't want to disappoint the down-home folks, so he gets out there and shoots it all before climbing aboard, exhausted, for the trip to the Indiana University Assembly Hall in Bloomington. The TCB group knows that he is tired the following night at the Milwaukee Arena, but the audience has no idea as they watch him cutting up onstage and having a good time.

Like any good long-distance runner, Elvis has tried to pace himself, but now must take a deep breath and reach back for that something extra to punch him through the four successive shows he performs in the following two nights, two at the Municipal Auditorium in Kansas City, and two at the Civic Auditorium in Omaha, Nebraska. There is one final show the next evening in Omaha, and then he's off for the final date of the tour—the Salt Palace in Salt Lake City, where he crosses the finish line. In eighteen days, he has performed twenty-six times, and now that he is already in Utah, he roosts in Vegas where his suite awaits him and his name up on the Hilton marquee proclaims the beginning of an engagement slated to begin in several days.

Everywhere, the show has run approximately fifty-five minutes to an hour and ten; by the time he was preparing for his last number, and the houses were all coming apart, the well-lubricated TCB wheels already were turning toward the following night's performance.

Joe, Dick, Ricky, David, and Ed Parker silently slip onstage behind the equipment and in the wings during "Can't Help Falling in Love." Elvis removes his rings and hands them to Charlie so that he can shake hands without having his fingers crunched by ovetzealous well-wishers, and then he croons the number, a favorite romantic ballad, and has the crowd swooning and sighing rather than charging. With the last bars of the song, Elvis slowly raises his arm aloft, pointing his fingers forward and bringing his body slowly forward into a deep bow, then springs into the karate horse stance. The eyes of everyone backstage are focused on the two fingers of the right hand which are pointing above his head, for when they are completely straightened, everybody springs into action like a SWAT team and the Boss—rock 'n' roll apparition that he is—steals away. Moments later he is whizzing away in a limo, surrounded by the boys, a towel around his neck, en route to the airport.

In Vegas the routine is different.

Rick enters Elvis's darkened bedroom at around three thirty P.M. and begins gently waking the Boss. Elvis is sleeping soundly from the previous night's sleeping medication and the long weeks on tour. He shakes him gingerly until he begins to stir. "Boss? Boss? Hey, Elvis, man, time to get up."

Draped diagonally across the plush bed, Elvis groans and rolls over, still asleep. Rick persists, nicely, standing over Elvis with an ice-cold pitcher of orange juice and a pot of steaming hot coffee. "Boss," he repeats.

Elvis stirs, opens one eye, sneers contemptuously at everything in general, and begins sitting up in bed. Silently he takes his first glass of o.j. and sloshes it down. Then another. The process of getting him out of bed takes a minimum of a half hour and requires several cups of coffee. Still in bed, Elvis pops two caps of Dexedrine.

Elvis is up now and into his robe, washed, alert, ready for breakfast. Conversation is light. After all of their years together, Rick waits to sense Elvis's mood. He adeptly gauges which way the winds are blowing and then goes with the flow. If Elvis is down, he is careful not to touch upon the downer he thinks may be on his mind unless the Boss brings it up first, in which case they commiserate. If he is feeling up, the conversation is sprightly, elevated and animated, punctuated with Elvis's humor. The signs are easy to read.

"If he was in a bad mood, you could tell as soon as you walked in the room," Rick says. "If he didn't say anything when you said good morning you knew it. Other times you'd say good morning and he'd say, 'Yeah? What's so fucking good about it!'

234 You'd have to go in there with a mellow spirit, ready to talk to him about anything, give him enough time to wake up, and go from where he was at. I would have to stay one step ahead of him because waking up affected his mood for the rest of the day. I'd also have to keep some of the people that worked for him out because he sometimes wasn't in the mood to see them. That was his quiet time to himself, when he didn't want noise or commotion. You could really see the man when he first woke up because when people would start coming in he would have to be 'Elvis.' He was like that just before he went to bed, too. The problem was that there was usually something to distract him. The man worked a helluva lot. I've never seen anybody work like that."

A leisurely breakfast follows, sometimes so leisurely that the food will get cold quickly; Rick orders three or four rounds of cheese omelettes, toast, bacon, sausage, grapefruit, and coffee. Elvis likes to eat a little bit, talk for a while, eat a little bit more, then stop again. By the time breakfast is over, he has packed away a hearty meal.

At five thirty Elvis either reads or watches television before Rick begins rubbing down his shoulders and legs to get him loose for the show. Shortly after the rubdown Elvis does a few stretching exercises to loosen up for the evening's dips, then prepares a nasal douche by mixing warm water and salt, which he snorts and gargles to clear out the phlegm in his throat. Rick takes out the jumpsuit that Elvis will wear that evening and checks to see that no sequins or stones are missing. It is ironed with the collar standing up; the white patent-leather boots are checked for scuff marks.

Rick next serves hot tea with honey, which coats Elvis's vocal chords and loosens up the throat. At approximately eight fifteen, David, Jerry Schilling, Joe Esposito, Dick Grob, and Rick accompany the Boss downstairs in the elevator, through the corridors, and into the backstage dressing room, where he spends the remaining forty-five minutes before showtime. Rick is careful to make sure that the humidifier is working because Elvis spends so much time indoors in air-conditioned rooms that he needs several around.

"Five minutes, five minutes," comes a voice through the door and an anxious rapping.

"Jesus, I'm gettin' tired of that guy every night," says Elvis. "I *know* what time I go onstage. Ricky, go tell that asshole not to bother comin' 'round anymore."

Rick leaves the dressing room to convey the message. Someone has apparently found his way backstage to talk to Elvis, a guy who seems determined, but Dick Grob has him cornered. Grob is a master at cooling people out and putting them in their place just by talking to them, without having to get physical like Red and Sonny. He patiently explains that Elvis isn't exactly in the habit of seeing strangers before his shows, and when the guy persists, he steps back, gives him one you'd-better-listen-to-me-buddy look, and says "Look, I told you once—now beat it!" No threats, no pushing or shoving, but the man knows that he means business.

Elvis rarely talks about the show until it is five minutes before showtime. Even then, though it is clearly on his mind, he may only ask a question like "Hey, what kinda crowd's out there to-night?" just to prime himself. The two-show schedule at the Hilton produces a total of five thousand to play to in a single night but the moods of the two shows are decidedly different in one important respect: The dinner-show people have to wait as much as an hour and a half for Elvis and by the time he takes the stage they have stuffed themselves on rich hors d'oeuvres and piled themselves full of Baked Lobstertails Internationale or Breast of Young Capon Souvoroff. Bloated, lethargic, and impatient, they are much less responsive at first than the good old cocktail crowd that soaks up a sea of martinis and is roaring like a brushfire before Elvis even hits the stage. While Elvis never slacks on the dinner crowd (he has always been the sort of performer who feeds off the energy level of his audiences) the cocktail crowd has him jumping in no time flat.

The show begins on time. As the familiar strains of his intro fill the showroom and the lights dim, Elvis issues forth from the wings, grabs the spotlight at center stage where his mike rests, looks sly and callow, and cuts his pose. Like a new guitar string, his voice needs to be stretched and played before it can roll and

236   resonate to its full strength and bend into all the dynamic qualities that allow Elvis to overtake and command the music that he performs. Falling quickly into his groove, he lashes the songs out, one after the other, for an hour. The only notable incidents this night are one loud squelch of feedback that sends him into a tizzy and the twenty-thousand-dollar diamond ring that he slips off his hand to a crazy elderly woman fan at the edge of the stage, sending a loud and simultaneous gasp through the entire audience. Elvis just chuckles at the sweet old woman's incredulous expression and strolls offstage to ear-splitting applause.

Rick is there in the wings to wrap a towel around the Boss's neck and hand him some Bayer to stave off the tightening that is steadily creeping into his throat. This is Elvis's most serious problem during a two-show day: His voice is one of the most special in the world, but on certain days it won't cooperate for the second time around. He's drenched in perspiration after the performance; large beads of sweat scatter quickly down his forehead and onto his neck like droplets of rain on a windowpane and the jumpsuit must be changed immediately. Shivering and stiff, he heads into his dressing room for his nightly postshow checkup with Dr. Nick. "How do you feel, Elvis?" asks the good doctor, listening to his heart and peering intently into his eyes. The Boss is feeling stiff and edgy that night. After checking him thoroughly, Dr. Nick hands him two Valiums to remove the rough edges.

Elvis showers and changes and psychs himself up for the second show.

The boys come around to Elvis's suite after the second performance to offer a "Good show, Boss." Elvis's responsibilities for the day are over and the three hours that usually remain before he gets to bed are entirely his. If he feels like having company, the boys may linger to talk about the evening's performances or just shoot the breeze. If he wants solitude, they leave almost immediately and somebody like Charlie, Ricky, David, Joe, or Larry will remain to look after things.

Normally, Elvis just wants to relax, read, or enjoy the com

pany of a woman. During his close to five years with Linda Thompson following his divorce, she would often be with him during this time. Of all the women that he spent time with during those years, she was by far the closest to him. Her awareness and sensitivity made her much more than his girl friend or lover, but a trusted companion, confidante, and, if necessary, a nurse. When Linda was around, the boys were always confident that the Boss would be well taken care of and could relax.

Approximately an hour before he plans to be asleep, Elvis takes his sleeping medication. Before he does, Rick makes sure that the ice bin next to the bed is well stocked with Mountain Valley Spring Water. He also makes sure that the list of TCB rooms with their phone numbers is there in case he wakes up and needs anything.

If it is a new girl who has never been with Elvis before that night, Rick or Joe has already held a discreet, informal briefing with her to let her know a few things about Elvis. "Just be nice," Rick says to her. "Just be yourself—don't be a smart aleck. Show the man respect and he'll do the same for you. If you spend the night and he gets up to go somewhere, keep an eye on him. If anything happens or he needs anything, don't hesitate to call one of us. Have a good night."

If Elvis is alone that night, Rick or David will often sleep in the room with him the same way that Billy Smith did when he and Elvis were young. When three thirty rolls around again, it all begins anew.

"The show took a lot out of his body," says Billy in retrospect. "Two weeks out of every month, sometimes more than once a day. He'd kick himself in the ass to get going."

Looking back, Rick also agrees that the pace of Elvis's professional life during the last few years of his life exacted a terrible toll. "He was really getting tired," he says, "but somehow, he'd always manage to get out there and do it. There were times when we didn't think he was going to make it."

Why didn't he slow down? Or backtrack and come up with a different formula and format that would have been slightly less demanding? Well, the reasons are multifold. For one, in the

238   entertainment business, the winds of favor are notoriously fickle, blowing hot and cold unpredictably. True, Elvis was in the most elite bracket, but the instincts were still to "get out there while the gettin' was good." Wealthy Japanese promoters were offering him as much as two to three million for a *single performance*, and the Australians, in April of 1974, had also put up a cool million for two shows down under. Europeans (especially the British) had been clamoring for an Elvis tour since the fifties and were also chiming in with extravagant offers; Elvis and the Colonel planned to pluck that fruit when it was its ripest, slating an international circuit tentatively for the year following his death (the Boss had even ordered a brand-new customized jet for his intercontinental voyages: It was to be a jet-black Viscount with a gold TCB on the tail).

Elvis also had personal reasons for putting up with the grueling pace. He felt a responsibility to the great many people that he employed—his entourage, the musicians and singers in his show, the roadies, all of the other behind-the-scenes people that helped to put the Elvis Presley Show on the road. The realization that many of these people had families who depended on him for their livelihood spurred him on.

Work for Elvis had also become like an anodyne, a panacea for his ills and problems, which ironically reflected them all right back at him when the quality of his shows started to decline. The satisfaction and sense of accomplishment that the love and admiration of his fans provided him in those last years was so great that it's difficult to measure. To slow down would have gone against the grain of everything in his character; it would have been an admission of defeat, of not being what he once was, of playing it safe. Almost as if to leave himself no choice in the matter, he spent his money more recklessly than ever, as fast as he seemed to make it. The Colonel set up the dates, and for Elvis not to fill each and every one of them would have been unthinkable. Work meant life to Elvis and too much was never enough. Refusing to set limits for himself, he would die before slowing down.

"If only Elvis could have gone into a kind of semiretirement," Rick conjectures, "he would have had it made. You

know, he could have just laid back and recorded a good album   239
once in a while and filled a couple of important dates a year like
Frank Sinatra. He was getting to that mature age where he
could have changed his style, but to him, that wouldn't have
been 'Elvis Presley.' "

With his colorful and sometimes piquant personality, the
Colonel was older, more doublechinned, but as spry and sharp
as ever. He was, as usual, doing what he held to be the most effective planning of Elvis's career, discerning which way the
winds were blowing and letting out Elvis's sails to go full speed
in that direction for as long as the trip seemed worthwhile.
Their relationship had its stormy moments. "They didn't see
eye to eye on everything," Rick says. "Most of the differences
had to do with timing and style." After such a long period in
show business, Elvis felt self-educated in the business end of his
life. He understood that he was the showhorse of the relationship and that all profits were contingent upon his own energies and talents. One of the points of contention, Rick says,
was the long-postponed European tour, which Elvis would have
undertaken much sooner had it not been for the Colonel wanting to wait, as was his style, for maximum opportunity to knock
on the door. "Elvis might get hot at the Colonel and something
he did and say, 'Man, that asshole doesn't know what he's
talkin' about!' But by the next day everything would be worked
out. Their disagreements were very hush-hush, kept behind
closed doors."

But the Colonel could never have committed Elvis to tours
that Elvis himself did not want to do. According to Rick, Elvis
always had his veto over the Colonel's plans. "Elvis was his own
man and would do what he wanted to do," he says. "The Colonel would present things to him, and if Elvis didn't want to go
along with it, that would be it. Elvis's attitude was that the Colonel was not a selfish man; he felt that he always had Elvis's
benefit in mind in his business decisions."

No one around Elvis said, "Slow down, Boss." Elvis's health
had been good for so long that his decline seemed as remote to
Elvis's inner circle as it did to his public. There was something
indomitable and eternally young about Elvis that made his de-

240 cline unreal, as if he could do what he wanted to do and still keep coming back, like Muhammad Ali.

The public received its first jolt to Elvis's perennial image when his weight started to become an unmanageable problem. Elvis had knocked off fifteen pounds for his comeback and appeared in Las Vegas looking better than ever. For the next three years he had stayed reasonably trim and toned. Then he put on weight, which had to be stripped off for his 1973 television special *Aloha from Elvis in Hawaii*. Elvis conjured up his will power, took himself in hand, and lost the weight. Then he put it right back on.

Uppers kept his appetite curbed, but as tolerance is built up to the drugs, they become less efficient as appetite suppressants. Elvis's lack of self-control began to apply to his eating habits, and many of the foods he loved were brimming with calories and cholesterol—banana puddings, ice cream, cakes, peanut-butter-and-banana sandwiches (fried in tons of butter), eggs fried almost to a crisp and covered with black pepper, King Cotton bacon by the pound, burgers, cheese, and Spanish omelettes, french fries, and the great staples of southern cooking like fried chicken, pork chops, roast beef with gravy, plenty of hot rolls, black-eyed peas, and mashed potatoes.

"Elvis loved to eat and he just didn't think of food as doing him damage," Rick says. "He just thought of it as necessary for his strength, and he was right, but he would go overboard. Dr. Nick tried to put him on a limited diet but you just can't limit Elvis Presley—he was going to have what he wanted. Dr. Nick, Esposito, and Jerry Schilling all tried to get him to cut down on things. We tried to limit his orange juice because the acid was no good for him and he drank too much of it, and we once almost got him to the point where he was eating dried fruits for snacks instead of the fried foods and pizza and ice cream and stuff that lays heavy in your stomach, because he liked to eat before he went to bed. He also drank a helluva lot of milk, which he was allergic to and was bad for his vocal chords. His eating habits bothered all of us because we wanted to see him stay in shape and knew how good he would look if he wanted to, but it was tough. Like when he would eat Mexican food, it wouldn't just be a meal; he loved it so much that he would almost eat himself to the point of being sick."

The lack of regular, concentrated exercise became a problem because it guaranteed that the added weight would stay on and make Elvis more susceptible to muscular aches and pains from his stagework. The karate workouts decreased in frequency and intensity with Elvis now observing and coaching more than actually participating. Racketball was good for him and the TCB boys concerned about his health were overjoyed when the sport became one of the Boss's latest kicks, but he became less and less inclined to play vigorously. Whenever Rick became fed up with and critical of Elvis's eating and lack of exercise, the Boss's retort would be testy: "Ricky, me going out there and doing a one-hour show is the equivalent of working an eight- to ten-hour day," he would say. "I *have* to have food so I can keep going. I'm not like you guys, you know—you can go out and exercise. My exercise is done onstage. Besides, man, the weight's fluid. It *won't* stay on."

With his acute vanity, Elvis couldn't have made himself any unhappier than by getting fat. Nothing drove home the reality of his age or dragged down his self-image more than his expanding gut, the loosening muscle tone of his body, and the extra flab he carried. It hampered his stage image before the public, making it hard for him to indulge in the same kind of fun-loving, sexy preening he was renowned for. With a lean bone structure to begin with, Elvis had weighed approximately 170 pounds for a large part of his adult life until he started getting heavy. Slowly but surely he put on fifty extra pounds, some of which he tried to take off with fad diets that caused the dysfunction of his digestive system.

"His weight really bugged him and you could tell that he really cared about it," says Rick, "but he wouldn't acknowledge that much. Except for a few personal aides, he never let people see him with his shirt off and even around us he would try to hold his stomach in. He was worried about what the public would think of him, too. We tried to cover it up as best we could—we had the jumpsuits let out and tried to fit them dif-

242   ferently. We also hung the big belts he wore so they wouldn't drop down on the hips and the gut."

With his jumpsuits getting tighter, one would think that Elvis would have switched to something more becoming to a heavier man and less revealing than the black-leather outfits or the all-white jumpsuits slashed down to below the navel with the wide belts and capes. "Elvis wouldn't even consider that," says Ricky, "because that wouldn't have been 'Elvis Presley.' Anything less sharp or more comfortable wouldn't have fit the image."

As the drugs increased, the weight climbed, and the performances became more erratic, other health problems arose. Recurrent vision problems had culminated in a diagnosis of glaucoma when Elvis was recording in Nashville in 1973. The condition never went away, but was exacerbated by his reading, which he sometimes did in poor light, and by the sweat that ran into his eyes onstage.

Everything that might have adversely affected Elvis's image or remotely indicated that he might not be able to fill his dates was hushed up by the TCB group. When Elvis started forgetting lyrics and slurring words, he pulled out sheets onstage with the words written on them. His fans didn't consider it a lack of professionalism because it made him more accessible to them, more human and fallible—"Hey, he forgets lyrics too."

It wasn't until Elvis was overweight and looking bad that ugly rumors about his drugs started circulating and people began whispering that maybe the King was done. Ignoring them at first, Elvis got mad one night in Vegas and blasted them onstage. "If I ever find out who's been sayin' I'm strung out on drugs," he said menacingly, "I'll knock their goddamned heads off!"

Then he sang "Unchained Melody," his voice irrepressibly potent and rich. Deeply moved, his fans understood that anybody who could sing a song like that couldn't possibly do wrong. They couldn't see what was really hurting because that was all inside, in his soul.

CHAPTER 15

FIGHT AT THE AIRPORT LOUNGE

"Here," Rick said, digging into his breast pocket. "This'll prime ya."

He handed Billy two Roer 714's, which his brother popped and swallowed with a gulp of Busch. Rick did the same.

"Looks like it's gonna be one of those nights, Nub," he then said, grinning conspiratorially at his brother.

The boys rarely got much of a chance to hang out in Memphis after they went to work for Elvis Presley. When they breezed back into town after a tour, they loved to get out, see friends, and have a party. There was a good band playing out at the Lounge that night—a shitkicking country-rock affair—so the two of them headed out there in Rick's white Trans Am, passing a joint of whacky weed back and forth, laughing, talking about some of the crazy things on the road with Elvis. By the time they reached their destination, the ludes had kicked inside their heads like temperamental mules. Tingling-numb, they walked through the door slack-jawed, glassy-eye, rubber-legged, hot to trot, feeling no pain and not much else for that matter.

244   The place was filled with thick clouds of bluish smoke that hovered like smog over the dance floor jumping with college kids, bikers, rednecks, local freaks, and plenty of the Local Talent.

The pedal-steel player in the band was fleeing up and down the neck of his guitar like Cool Hand Luke on the run from the chain gang as they broke into "Six Days on the Road." Standing up there in a rockabilly pose like Elvis, his legs apart, bashing his guitar and looking like he was carrying the weight of the world on his shoulders, the lead singer was having a good old time: "Six days on the road and I'm-a gonna see mah baybeeee toonnaht!" he bawled, as the people stepped and kicked up.

The first shots of tequila that the boys stood at the bar went down smooth and rose hard. Billy grimaced and let out a rebel whoop—"YEEEEAYEAOW!"—and the night spun in searching glances, dances, and constitutionals out to the car where more numbers were fired and everybody did some angel dust, getting higher, laughing, playing pool, their heads like cauldrons about to bubble over.

Rick knew that the run he was enjoying at the table had to be lucky because he was having trouble seeing. He lined up the next shot, saw the nine ball in a faraway haze—but the two honky-tonk angels who were looking at him from across the room he saw clearly enough. My, my, two sweet young things dressed to kill and doin' a good job of it too, he thought, sizing up the situation. The blonde, mmm, pretty, built like a brick shithouse . . . the brunette sultry, a sprinter like himself.

"Howdy, girls," the Raven said, dazzling them with a stoned Cheshire cat grin. "You see the damnedest things in Memphis these days."

People would catch glimpses of the Stanley boys, who were always in and out of town, but the boys were never around long enough to get to know anybody. The girls had seen Rick around, there was an aura of mystery about him. His come-on was like Elvis's—not too strong, warm, friendly, like a gentleman; then just lay back and let them hit on *you*. He bought them a round of drinks and continued to shoot pool, aware that

every lean and hungry eye in the joint was now fixed wolfishly 245
on Josie and Billie, the two ladies with him. By the time he
asked them out, Rick could barely see. With one on each arm,
he squired them out the door, gallantly but sideways.

His destination was the Trans Am parked on the other side of
the parking lot. Rick knew that something was coming down as
soon as he saw the five bikers lined along the pathway toward
his car. Three of them leaned on big black choppers that glistened satanically in the street light, the others leaned against a
pickup, forming a gauntlet that he would have to pass through.
Bloodthirsty-looking suckers, he thought. They were Tennessee's answer to the Hell's Angels or something, with all of the
necessary accoutrements: long, stringy hair . . . missing front
teeth . . . ratty leather jackets . . . hobnailed engineer's boots
. . . bottles of beer in hand . . . probably switchblades handy,
stilettos and razors, or maybe chains and Jesus what if they
have shotguns in the truck . . . mocking, sadistic eyes that
seemed to say, "Prepare to get fucked up, son, 'cause your time
has come!"

The bikers leered at the girls, saying nothing. Hoping that his
passage would be unmolested but knowing better, Rick could
only think about how far away his car looked.

"Well, now," the tall one in front taunted like a hoodlum in
a movie, flexing his fist for effect, "jes' look who's heah. If it
ain't little Elvis hisself thinkin' he's shit with his cars and chicks.
He ain't *nuthin'* but a candyass motherfucker to me."

The goons tittered. The others were off their bikes now,
hands at their sides. The girls looked terrified, like horses being
trapped in a stable fire.

"Look, you guys," Rick garbled amiably, hoping to pull it off
with a little friendly reasoning. "I'm so fucked up I can't hardly
see. You guys could for sure nail me if you wanted to, but I
don't want no hassles—"

The one in front turned to the blonde, Josie, and cocked his
head. "I sure would like a piece of *that*," he said to nobody in
particular, then turned to Rick. "An' if Ah can't, Ah jes' might
take somethin' outta yo' hide, boy."

246   "Well, I ain't fightin' nobody," Rick said, trying to walk through. He felt a sharp pain at the back of his scalp. One of them had him by his hair and was yanking him down to the pavement.

On his back like a turtle, Rick covered up as it started raining blows. He felt a kick to his ribs and knew that he'd better get up quickly. He who hesitates, meditates horizontally! as the Boss would put it.

The girls ran back into the bar but people in the window had already noticed the commotion outside. Billy came running out with a friend before too much damage could be inflicted on his brother's prone body.

"Hey, man, who's been kickin' the shit outta my brother!" he shouted, before a punch that seemed to come out of the night sky caught him flush on the cheek, knocking him backwards. A biker was on him in a flash.

People were pouring out of the bar as if somebody had yelled, "Fire! Run for your lives!" Rick was on his feet and swinging an empty beer bottle after the biker who was on Billy. It shattered against the side of his head with a sickening crash. Glasses and mugs were flying everywhere, punches were being launched, too, some missing wildly, others splitting lips and making cauliflower out of unlucky ears.

Back up on his feet now, Billy, one fiery little package of vengeance, jumped a biker, wrestled him down, and stomped his face with his boot heel. At that second he saw one of the others staggering away from the pickup wielding a shotgun, homicide in his eyes. He dived behind a truck as the errant blast ricocheted loudly off the pavement and shattered the window of the bar. Somebody inside was screaming bloody murder.

The brawl had escalated into a knock-down, drag-out, free-for-all with everybody knocking whoever was closest. Rick got scared when he heard the shotgun, and when he heard the police siren wailing shrilly and eerily in the distance, he managed to find his brother in the melee.

Bleeding, sore, but basically intact, they limped into Rick's car and left rubber in the parking lot, glad to have escaped before the arrival of cops and press.

The Boss was enraged, pacing back and forth in his bedroom, standing over them like a police interrogator while they sat on the edge of his bed.

"*Goddamnit!* Who the hell started it!"

Elvis Presley made the quarrels of his family and his friends his own. When people messed with *his* people, it became a family affair; if it was bad enough or persistent, he would dispatch a posse of TCB deputies to Take Care of Business. Sometimes he went along to do it himself.

"Elvis, they were just a bunch of dumb bikers that had nothin' to do," Rick said, trying to mollify him. "They've been seein' us around and one thing led to another, I guess."

Rick and Billy's presence there at that hour in the morning told the story. When trouble knocked on the door, Elvis wanted to know about it. Sometimes it was more trouble to keep things from Elvis than it was to tell him, but if you told him, things had to be settled *his* way.

"Well, we'll just have to take care of this. We'll get Red and some of the boys to pay these motherfuckers a little visit and then you have it out with the one that's been givin' you a hard time."

"Man, I don't want to fight, Elvis," Rick said. "You know fightin' ain't my thing."

Elvis looked him squarely in the eyes. "Ricky, listen to me. I always told you never to start a fight or go lookin' for trouble, but I also told you never to back down from one, 'cause if you do, you're gonna feel like shit for the rest of your life. Don't worry, I'll take care of everything."

The Boss often delegated these responsibilities to Red West because of his loyalty, fearlessness, and predilection for violence. Elvis always believed in settling differences "fairly." But Rick's account of the bikers led the Boss to believe that "fair" fights weren't exactly their style, so Red, Sonny, Jerry Schilling, and Bill Wallace (a Memphis karate champ) were dispatched as "equalizers."

The houses of the gang had been reconnoitered before the posse pulled up in front of the home where they hung out. Rick

248 was to wait on the lawn with Billy. Before entering, Red removed his pistol and handed it to a startled Billy. "Here," he said. "If anybody comes out that door and it isn't one of us, you stop him, understand?"

Billy just looked at the gun incredulously. "Man, Red, this is gonna be some heavy shit here. I hope nobody gets hurt."

There were three of the gang in the house waiting when Elvis's delegation entered, and it seemed as if they were expected. Several uneasy moments passed in the living room when they entered and Red announced, "Which one of you guys has been beatin' up on Ricky Stanley?"

"Maybe I did," said the one who had challenged Rick in the parking lot. He reached quickly into the other room and Red found himself looking down the barrel of a cocked hunting rifle. "I'll kill you right here," he threatened nervously, "if you take just one step."

Everybody stood silently as the possibility that one twitch of a finger would splatter Red West all over the wall seemed too real to be true. The TCBers breathed long and hard as the seconds passed like an eternity. Red gambled that the man on the other side of the gun wanted to survive as much as he did.

"Go ahead," he said as confidently as he could, "but there's a young man outside with a .357 magnum pointed right at your head who's gonna blow your brains out if you make one move to do it."

Standing guard outside on the lawn as he was told to do, Billy Stanley was nowhere near that window, but the man with the gun couldn't have known that. To emphasize the bluff, Red nodded over at the window. "Kill him if he makes one move," he said to his imaginary ally.

Sweating, his eyes darting nervously around the room, the biker made up his mind. Slowly, as the gun shook and swayed and everybody stood perfectly still, he dechambered the ammunition round by round from the rifle. Red was on him in a second, slapping him all over the room.

When it was all over, Billy and Ricky rode home in silence, thinking about Elvis's law, breathing sighs of relief.

"Man, I'm glad that's over with," said Rick. "We're so lucky 249
nobody got his ass shot 'cause of us!"

"Yeah," Billy agreed, as they drove down Elvis Presley Boulevard toward Graceland to report on the raid.

CHAPTER 16

GOING DOWN THE TUBES

Charlie Hodge was in a nasty mood after the show at the Spectrum because David had ended up with the girl he wanted. It wasn't the first time, and Charlie was back in his room, drunk, badmouthing David to several people when the accused woman-stealer passed in the hall.

"Man," complained Charlie, "that motherfucker's been married only two weeks. When I get back to Memphis I'm gonna tell his wife that he's been fuckin' every chick in sight!"

David stopped dead in his tracks and peered darkly at him through the doorway. "If you do what I thought I heard you say, Charlie, I *swear* I'm gonna whip your ass."

Word by word, slowly and with provocation, Charlie Hodge repeated the threat. David's temper, drawn dangerously taut in the first place, snapped like a twig. Charlie got up to charge as David picked up an ashtray and hummed it across the room. It hit Charlie in the chest and felled him with a groan, but he then charged anyway, like a wounded rhinoceros. David stopped his momentum with a side kick, but when Charlie

252 came on swinging, David lost it, tearing into him with a blind fury.

Red West came running out of his room and Vernon Presley was screaming, "David! David! You'll kill him!"

Dick Grob was cuffing his hands behind his back as they held him to the ground and he was dragged, kicking and snarling, from the room. Charlie's face was a bloody, pulpy mess. The boys rushed him to the hospital for suture of the deep lacerations over his eye and inside his mouth.

Vernon Presley was so enraged by the outburst that he considered having his stepson thrown in jail for assault just to teach him a lesson, but then David hadn't even meant to *hurt* Charlie. When Vernon learned that Charlie was talking about David's marriage, he decided to let Elvis handle the matter.

The next morning David had to tell the Boss that he had beat up one of his best friends. He knocked on the door uncertainly, and walked over to Elvis, who was reading in a chair.

"Elvis, I gotta tell you somethin'."

The Boss looked up from his book, annoyed at the disturbance. His expression seemed to say, "Come on—what is it *now*, David?"

"I beat the shit out of Charlie last night."

Elvis's eyes opened wide and his face fell two stories. "You *what?*" he asked in a soft, trenchant voice.

Just then the door opened and Charlie entered, his head swollen like a watermelon and covered with bandages and nasty black-and-blue bruises. Walking right over to David, he hugged him like a long-lost brother. No hard feelings.

David, not knowing if he was serious or going to plant a knife in his back, hugged him back insincerely and the gesture left him looking very bad in front of Elvis, who exploded like a stick of dynamite.

"Damnit, David! What the *hell* did you do! You beat the hell out of Charlie and now you can just get the hell out of here!"

Crestfallen, David withdrew. Elvis didn't say a word to him for two days. When Elvis Presley was angry at you, boy, his cold-shoulder treatment was as frosty as they come. On the

third day he knocked on David's door. It was time to discuss the 253
matter.

"Elvis," David jumped in, trying to explain his actions, "you know I didn't want to hurt him—I've known the guy ever since I've known *you*—but if it had been Cilla, if somebody said somethin' like that and you'd only been married two weeks, *man*—"

The Boss cut him short. "Forget it, David. I've been thinkin' 'bout the whole thing. You were right all the way."

"There were a lot of emotional things that I went through when my responsibilities with Elvis started getting heavy," remembers David. "It wears on you—walking out there and packin' the gun, checking the crowds—but I loved every minute of it. The life was great, and I decided that I was just gonna *do it*, regardless of what it cost or what it did to me, 'cause I knew I wasn't going to be doing it forever, man. Elvis used to love to show me off to the police chiefs everywhere we went, and my attitude was the more responsibility, the better. I really didn't start losing it with Angie until I started putting all of my attention into the job. That was the most important thing: that responsibility to keep Elvis healthy."

If David was swept up in the power and prestige of his job, he also loved the life on the road. When work was over and he could let down and stop thinking about the bullet with Elvis's name on it that he would step in front of, it was party time.

He knew that his pretty wife languishing at home would have been hurt by his philandering. Angela Stans was a slender, blue-eyed Nashville belle David had met when he worked for Sunberry-Dunbarr. She was a sweet, sensitive girl, attractive and very young. They had been married before David roared off with Elvis. Since then, she had stayed in their apartment in Nashville, waiting for him at home like the rest of the TLCers.

"Maybe I did her a favor," he says in retrospect. "I loved her to death, man, but we were all crazy on those tours. I didn't deserve her. I was insane; I'd chase any woman, but we never even had to chase them, because you would walk into a room and there was chicks, chicks, chicks. . . . 'Work's over, let's

254 go!' Everybody was saying, 'David, you're gonna lose your wife,' but I was too high, havin' too much fun."

Whenever David got fed up, he went home to his wife, convinced that he was home for good. Once, when the boys had been cloistered up in Elvis's Imperial Suite in Las Vegas for four or five consecutive days, Elvis pushed him to the breaking point.

The Boss was in one of his all-time worst moods, not allowing anyone to leave his domain for days on end. The boys had to just sit there and take it as he brooded, harangued, and ranted about the room, disappeared into his bedroom, then entered to vent his spleen once more.

Each paroxysm of anger seemed to be worse than the last and the boys could only look at each other, roll their eyes helplessly, and wonder, "Man, when is this bummer going to end," knowing that only time brought Elvis out of such moods and curtailed the abuse. Everybody was getting it: "Joe!" he would start, and then tie into Esposito. "Lamar!" he would follow, and, one by one, he would work his way around the TCB circle.

"David, you bastard!" he thundered, hovering over David. "All you've been doin' is complainin' around here these last few days! You haven't done shit, man!"

Tired from sleepless days, wired on uppers, burnt out on Elvis's mood, and emotionally frazzled, David glowered up at Elvis, who was pounding the table like Khrushchev at the United Nations.

"Elvis, pleeese!" he beseeched. "Gimme a break . . . let me go downstairs and gamble or *something*—just let me get outta here for a couple of hours and I'll be right back, man—I promise!"

"Nobody's goin' nowhere 'till *I say so*, motherfucker!" fumed the Boss, who turned and stormed out of the room.

He slammed his door hard right at the moment the Stanley temper snapped again. David rose, smashed the glass table, and cracked it.

"Fuck this shit, man—I've had it!" he spouted, kicking furniture out of his way. "Lamar—tell Elvis to fuck off! Tell him I've got just a little pride left and that he's not gonna talk to me like that anymore! I'm goin' home, man! I've had it!"

Feeling free as a bird, burning with righteous indignation, he went downstairs, booked his flight, and flew home to his wife, thinking how crazy he must have been ever to have left in the first place.

Upstairs in the suite, Elvis returned for another bout. He looked quickly around the room. "Where the hell's David, god-damnit?"

Lamar delivered the message.

In Nashville, Angie was surprised and happy to see her husband at the door. "Oh, I quit, Angie," David said, his voice pure sincerity. "From now on, it's just gonna be us, settlin' down. Gonna find a job and everything."

So, there he was, back home. He settled into a chair, opened a beer, put his feet up. What now? He thought about Elvis back there in Vegas, bumming out, and he began to feel contrite. Hell, maybe he'd acted too rashly. Elvis didn't mean anything *personal*. He thought about the tours and the guys and the girls and how good he felt whenever the Boss complimented him on his work. Slowly, over the next few hours, as he drank beer and shifted uncomfortably from room to room feeling out of place somehow, he tried to fight the irresistible urge. Giving in, he picked up the phone to call Las Vegas. He *had* to get it off his chest. Billy Smith picked up the phone.

"Billy? David. Has the sonofabitch settled down any?"

"Naw, not really," said Billy. "He's still pretty hot."

"Well, I don't want to quit like this, Billy, but that was a bunch of shit, I gotta tell ya. I just don't have to take that shit."

Billy said he would tell the Boss that David had called. He hung up the phone, feeling a little better. At least if Elvis understood why he'd walked, he might learn something from the experience. He smoked a little dope, relaxed, but as the hours passed, he still felt guilty. Damn that Elvis, he thought. Once he's in your blood, there's no gettin' him out.

Several hours later the phone rang. It was Billy Smith.

"Well, he's here," he said. "You can talk to him."

"Where?"

"We're in Memphis," Billy said. The phone changed hands. The Boss sounded mellow. "David," he said. "What the hell ya doin'?"

"What're *you* doin'?"

"Oh, nothin," Elvis said. "Just sittin' here havin' a good time. What're *you* doin'?"

"Just sittin' here havin' a shitty time," he said.

"Well, hell," said the Boss. "Come on back, then."

"Do you *really* think I should, Elvis?"

"Look, man," Elvis said apologetically, "it took a lot of balls to walk out on me like that and I felt bad about it. I'm sorry, man, I didn't mean to treat you like that. I was feelin' lousy—"

"Elvis, *I'm* sorry," David said, cutting him short. "I should have known you better than that."

"Well, come on, boy, get your ass back here just as soon as you can."

David managed to bring Angie on several tours and to vacation spots like Vail and Hawaii with Elvis, but she began to tire of being alone. When she met someone else and told David she was leaving him, it seemed a carbon copy of Elvis and Priscilla. As responsible as he knew he was, David took it hard, trying frantically to patch things up and somehow make it all up to her before it was too late. Having been through the whole thing himself, Elvis offered his help. The Boss often advised his brothers and friends about their personal problems. His advice was usually sound; somehow, he just never managed to take it himself.

One afternoon at Graceland, Elvis sat with David and Angie for six hours. It was a marathon marriage-counseling session— the Boss was the counselor. "If it's God's will, you'll get it together; it'll be the way it's supposed to be," Elvis told them. Then they prayed, cajoled, discussed, accused, and made promises. Angie went downstairs after it was all over. She had said she would stay, but nothing had really been resolved.

"David, I wanna tell you, she won't stay," Elvis said know-

ingly. "She's sayin' that she will, but she won't. I don't think 257
she'll ever come back to you."

Knowing in his heart that Elvis was right, David hung his
head. "Elvis, what am I gonna do? I *love* her, man. I never
even knew how much."

Elvis gazed distantly out the window for a moment. He
looked solemn, as morose as David. Then, suddenly, his expression changed—his eyes twinkled mischievously, his grin
was irreverent and ironic.

"Just remember one thing," he then said, gesturing theatri-
cally out toward Elvis Presley Boulevard and smiling the smile
captured for posterity by so many cameras. "Somewhere, out on
that street, there is always a beautiful eighteen-year-old shot of
ass just waitin' for you, man . . . waitin' right now."

Astonished, not knowing whether to laugh or cry, David
found himself laughing anyway, knowing that they were the
same. Elvis knew.

"What the hell kind of off-the-wall thing is that to say at a
time like this?" he laughed, the tears streaming down his
cheeks.

Rick saw it coming a mile away but he didn't know what to
do. Every time Billy's new wife was up at Graceland, she was
coming on to Elvis. Ann Hill was an attractive girl—auburn
haired, blue eyed, with alabaster skin, and a manner much
more mature than her eighteen years would suggest. She was
using every opportunity to strut her stuff past the Boss's idle
eyes. Rick was in a quandary: Billy loved his wife and had no
idea what was going on, but it was only a matter of time before
she got what she wanted.

Billy knew Annie was his girl almost from the beginning. She
was the first love of his life—the first serious woman apart from
the life on the road, the woman he wanted to come home to.
She was young, which Billy liked, because that meant she
would "respect" him. He brought her home to meet Dee and
Vernon and introduced her as his fiancée. Dee was convinced
that her son wasn't ready for marriage, but she saw how happy
he was. Billy was always the most insecure and sensitive of her

258 sons and she didn't want to see him hurt; he was very trusting, and despite his time on the road, still quite naive. She begged him to wait, but when he professed to be so much in love with the girl that he threatened to elope, she consented. They were married in the house on Dolan Street.

From the moment they met, the chemistry between Elvis and Annie was evident to everybody but Billy. She was so consumed by his mystique that she couldn't take her eyes off him, but that never bothered Billy because Elvis was a star and women always reacted to him like that when they first met him. What pleased him and made him truly proud was that Elvis *approved* of his wife. The Boss had high standards when it came to women, and the fact that Elvis liked his wife only reaffirmed the wisdom of his decision to marry her. First, they went up to the house together to visit Elvis. Then, Annie started going up alone.

"At the time Elvis was laying out by the pool every day," Billy remembers, "and now that I think about it, it was strange because he would call over to the house and ask Annie to come over there and then call me up and send me out on an errand. I never thought it was a big deal because it was like Ricky or David asking me to do them a favor. You don't think those kinds of things about your brother."

What Mike Stone did to Elvis, he, in turn, did to Billy, with the exception that the affair lasted only a month. They spent afternoons in Elvis's bedroom at Graceland but more often would ride down to Elvis's Circle G Ranch, just across the Mississippi state line. Elvis felt less guilty there.

The knowledge of the affair played heavily on Rick's mind. For the first time in his life he had been truly shocked by Elvis Presley, and as the weeks passed, his usually unshakable allegiance to his Boss was nullified by the hurt that he felt for his brother. He had to tell somebody. Finally he confided in his mother.

Dee Presley was beside herself, faced with the task of telling her son that not only was the woman he loved unfaithful and unloving, but that the third party was Elvis Presley, whom Billy loved and trusted more than anybody in the world. She simply couldn't bring herself to do it. As things took their course and the stress increased, she fell ill and was hospitalized. Billy and Rick visited her on her first day there, and brought flowers for their mother.

Dee was curious to see if her son's suspicions had been aroused. "Billy, where's your wife?" she probed.

"Oh, she and Elvis went ridin' motorcycles for a while," he said.

"Oh. Well, how do you feel about that?"

Billy shrugged his shoulders. "Hell, Mom, if you can't trust your brother, who can you trust?"

By the end of the month Elvis was tired of Annie and immersed in guilt. He couldn't abide the sight of her in his house because every time he looked at her, his deeds only seemed more reprehensible to him. He insulated himself from the unpleasantness by dropping her like a cold potato and banishing her from the house.

Shocked, hurt, confused, angry, and feeling that her rejection from Elvis's life had made her vulnerable with Billy, Annie vented her frustration on her husband. Billy, still unaware of the affair, couldn't understand the sudden change in his wife. The arguments got worse, her complaints more cutting. Once, in the heat of an exchange, something slipped out.

"What would you do if I told you that I made it with Elvis?" she asked defiantly.

Taken aback by the question, Billy stared hard at her. "I'd get up and get the fuck outta here so fast you wouldn't know what happened," he said. "Why, *did* you?"

"Of course not," she lied. "I just wanted to hear what you'd say."

Billy held on doggedly even as his marriage worsened. This grieved Dee Presley, who still couldn't bring herself to tell her son the truth. "Look, I know it takes two," she says, "and I kept in mind that she was throwing herself at Elvis, but she was just a child. I didn't blame her as much as I did Elvis. There were a lot of people getting very expensive things up at Graceland and that girl just hadn't been around anything like that. Young girls

260 were getting cars and diamond rings; it could have happened to
any child. I wondered how she must have felt knowing that the
whole family knew except for Billy—and Elvis, he knew that I
knew. When he walked in and looked at me, I didn't even have
to say a word. There are your answers, right there: Everybody
has to live with their deeds, and Elvis had to live with what he
did to Billy and what he did to that poor girl, and he couldn't.
He'd try to make it up, but it stayed with him."

Even though it was clearly time to tell Billy, Dee couldn't
until a strange turn of events forced her hand. Billy went to
Elvis to talk about the problems in his marriage, expecting the
kind of compassion and advice Elvis always offered. He told
Elvis that he was on the verge of divorce and why. Elvis was
cold and evasive, avoiding his eyes.

"Well, I guess divorce is about the best thing you could do,"
he said dispassionately.

Then, unexpectedly, Billy was laid off. Elvis had decided that
his presence in the group disturbed him, so he was purged. One
night on tour in Florida, Vernon Presley told him. Billy headed
back to Memphis, feeling shaken, confused, but strangely liber-
ated.

"Mom, I just don't understand it. All of a sudden Daddy gave
me my walkin' papers, just like that. When I saw what was goin'
down, I just quit and walked out. I don't know what's been
goin' on."

Dee Presley told him.

"It began to dawn on me that she just married me because I
was Elvis Presley's stepbrother and we had money," he says
plainly. "I felt like such a fool, I guess, but I was just a kid and I
really thought I was in love. That's what hurt. It took me a long
time to get over it because the first time you fall in love is so
heavy—it stays with you. Once I realized she was just hangin'
in until she found out that Elvis didn't give a damn about her,
we got a divorce. I couldn't believe Elvis would do something
like that. I realized it had a lot to do with her and that she never
loved me like I thought she did, but the only thing I could think
about was that *he* did it to *me*. Why *me?* I took it very per-

sonally. It was the lowest sonofabitch thing to do. . . . I just
had to get the hell away from him."

It was the beginning of an estrangement between Elvis and
Billy that lasted for the rest of Elvis's life. As the years passed
and Elvis became sorrier for his actions, Billy's exile became
self-imposed rather than decreed. "I was just never around that
much because the whole thing bothered him," he says. "Ricky
kept saying, 'Tell Elvis that you have forgotten and that you
forgive him,' and I was going to and to a certain extent I have.
Once you go through something like that you can almost sit
back and laugh about it, you know; I really didn't see what he
even saw in her. She was good lookin' but she was no ravin'
beauty or anything, but always in the back of my mind I would
think, 'I *still* can't believe he did that to me.' I didn't want to be
around that much because I knew it bothered him. He couldn't
look me in the face."

Everybody had his own personal phrase to accommodate the
initials TCB, "Taking Care of Business." The group defined
it as everything from Tennessee Choir Boys to Two Colored
Boys; for Billy, it became Taking Care of Billy.

The estrangement meant that Billy would always remain the
odd man out among the brothers, and the feeling that Ricky
and David could play such key roles in Elvis's life while he was
excluded bothered him greatly, but at the same time it also gave
him a chance to evaluate how he really felt about Elvis and the
group. "There was just too much competition around him," he
says, "you know, who's gonna be closer to Elvis, who's gonna
ride in the car with him—that's bullshit. I just didn't want it
anymore."

Elvis's advice and wisdom also became suddenly suspect to
Billy. "When he would start preachin' after that and telling people how to do things, he might as well have been talkin' out of
his ass as far as I was concerned," he says, "because there he
was gettin' fucked up just like everybody else. That's why I
didn't listen to him."

What Elvis's affair with Annie led to was, all bitterness aside,
Billy's emancipation from Elvis's legends and myths and from

262   the need to see him, in his own mind, as anything different from what he knew he was or wasn't. His big brother's fallibility, faults, kinks, and wrinkles all became suddenly apparent, and while he would never blurt out any unsavory truths about his life to an unsuspecting public, in his own mind he was being released from the restrictions of having to live Elvis's lies. "Everywhere we went," he recalls, "somebody would always introduce us as Elvis's stepbrothers, you know, and we would get the best tables and everything would be on the house. They'd ask us, 'How does he treat you? What are your lives like?' and we'd have to tell them, you know, 'Oh, man, he's the best guy in the world, he's the King,' and that really gets to be like hell after a while. I just wanted to tell the truth one time. If people asked me how I felt about him after what happened, it was hard for me to say what a terrific guy he was or what a good brother he was, but I always did. I had to do a lot of acting."

Time passed and Elvis tried to make it up to Billy, but the damage was done; the wounds healed slowly but they left noticeable scars. The real tragedy was that the two men truly loved each other. "I didn't like it when he tried to give me cars and money after that," Billy says sadly. "I was saying to myself, 'You don't have to give me nothin', man, just let me be around you and let's forget it.' It bothered me that I couldn't be around Elvis because I loved the guy as much as anyone, even if he did hurt me. I especially found that out after he died, when it was too late. Whenever we were together, it was only for a few minutes and it was a strange feelin'. I don't want to make it seem that the guy was a low life or anything for what he did 'cause he made a lot of mistakes, or that I'm tryin' to sell the guy down the road, which is something I'd never do, but for us to do a book about him honestly, I could never feel right unless I told my side of what happened between us."

So, for the rest of Elvis's life, Billy kept his distance. "What I really was after was to get his respect instead of just being somebody that worked for him," he points out. "That's the main thing I wanted to get across to him. I wanted him to be able to say, 'I've got one stepbrother that's out doin' it on his own.' "

Billy landed a job as a jet mechanic and stayed pretty much

out of sight. It took him a while to understand that Elvis, at one
time or another, hurt *everybody* he loved, and that adultery was
just one of the hazards of being related to him.

"Elvis, that's got to be the lowest thing I've ever heard of,"
Rick told Elvis when they finally were able to discuss the incident openly. It had left a bitter taste in his mouth. On the one
hand he knew how badly Elvis felt and tried to persuade Billy to
help expiate the Boss's guilt by forgiving him. But now he was
laying it on the line. "Man, I just don't see how you could have
done it!"

"Rick, it was *her*," complained Elvis. "*She* was the one.
What was I supposed to do?" His expression pleaded total innocence and begged for acquittal, but the tone of his voice offered *nolo contendere* to the charges.

"Elvis had a really good way of justifying his actions," Rick
remembers. "He was one smooth talker, man, and I had always
looked up to him because of the age difference between us. If
he did something wrong, he could have me pretty well snowed
to where I would be thinking . . . well, I can see why he did
that now. We had so much love and trust in him that it just
seemed impossible, but the incident gave me a whole new outlook on people. That's when I started thinking that maybe it *was*
the look-out-for-number-one world I'd been hearing about. I
just stayed on my toes from then on. He knew that it bothered
me."

It was the first time in his life that Rick was angry enough at
Elvis to think about "covering his ass," but in all of their years
together, he only had to resist Elvis once. Elvis wanted his girl
friend, Jill, one of those elegant, fetchingly beautiful society-
model types born and bred in the South. She and Rick had
lived together for several years, and Jill helped Rick through the
most difficult period of his life—his days as a junkie. Besides
Priscilla, Lisa, and his own mother, she was the only woman in
the world who meant anything to him. He was determined to
stand his ground. Elvis broached the subject one afternoon up
in his bedroom at Graceland.

"Look, Rick, I want to go out with Jill. Do you mind?"

264   "No, Elvis," he replied. "*Not* her."

"Come on, man. I just wanna ask her out. I think she's nice."

"*No.*"

"Tell you what," Elvis said, trying another track. "How would you like a new car—anything—"

"Look, man, if it comes down to that, I guess I'll just have to find me another job."

The Boss backed off at that.

The entire burden of Billy Stanley's devastated emotional state fell back on his mother, who slowly helped him restore his self-confidence and make him realize that he was better off for the experience. He continued to stay away from Graceland, and everyone knew the meaning of his absence.

After several years Billy met another girl. She was young— the boys took Elvis's advice about eighteen-year-olds more seriously than one might think. He never even told her he was Elvis's brother, wanting to be sure that it was Billy she was interested in. It was, and they were married.

One afternoon Billy decided to take Diana up to Graceland to meet Elvis. He really didn't know what to expect, but he felt compelled to. The boys brought their women to Elvis like a ritual, and Billy recognized that in a strange sort of way he was still seeking his older brother's approval. He also wanted to share his happiness and show Elvis that he still loved him. He went through the gate uncertainly. "Trust ye not in any brother," said the prophet Jeremiah; "If thy brother trespass against thee, rebuke him; and if he repent, forgive him," said St. Matthew. Billy's emotions were caught somewhere in the middle.

Elvis came out of the door, a typically scornful expression on his face. He always looked at his brothers that way; it meant, "So, you little shit, what kind of trouble have you gotten yourself into *now?*" It was his way of joshing you when he knew you were serious about something.

"Elvis, this is my wife, Diana. Diana, this is Elvis Presley."

Elvis looked at Diana pleasantly but critically, then looked back at Billy, expressionless, then he looked at Diana again, then looked back at Billy, a broad smile on his face that said, "Well, all *right*. Looks like you haven't been doin' too bad for yourself after all!"

"You know," Billy says today, smiling ruefully at his own honesty and thinking about that moment, "don't you know that just made my head shoot up ten feet in the air just to see him smile at me again, just like I was a kid again and the whole thing never happened."

CHAPTER 17

SOUTHERN BELLES

"She couldn't have come at a better time in Elvis's life," Rick says fondly. "He was hurtin' from the divorce, needing someone, a kind of woman who could be a lot of different things."

Beauty-queen tall (5′8″), with long, shapely, strong-looking legs and the classic 36-23-36 proportions of the Girl Next Door that Hugh Hefner had in mind when he prepared *Playboy* magazine for the hungry eyes of the American male (she, of course, never posed for the publication), Linda Diane Thompson generated enough force to register a ten on the TCB Richter Scale. A junior English major at Memphis State, she became the 1972 Miss Tennessee in the annual Miss Universe pageant and then met Elvis Presley; needless to say, she never went back for her diploma.

For close to the next five years, she was Elvis Presley's girl friend, traveling companion, lover, confidante, comedienne, co-conspirator in practical jokes. If ever a woman deserved to wear both the TCB and TLC logos on a single chain around her neck, it was Linda.

268   She is, of course, a beguilingly beautiful woman. Her neck is long and elegant and the face is that of the model-actress with a touch of the farm girl; the cheekbones are high and prominently chiseled, the mouth wide with sensuous, ample lips and perfect rows of pearly teeth; the eyes are a warm, smiling brown and the hair, which has been honey blond at times, is a natural soft brown. With her skin a movie-star tan and caparisoned in gossamer blouses or leggy pants and high boots or haute couture dresses with heels, *watch out*.

Beauty may have brought about her entrée into Elvis's life, but beauty alone was never enough to sustain a woman's presence in his life for more than, say, a month. Linda also had a beauty of the soul and spirit, humor and compassion. Best of all to Elvis, she was a real southern lady, a Memphis belle with an accent as sweet as honeysuckle who begins sentences with things like "Well, bless his little heart" and turned her nose disdainfully away from the unpleasantries of foul language. Rick, who has seen all of them come and go, explains what made her so special: "She was by far the closest to Elvis besides Cilla," he says, "because she was a southern girl, you know. High morals, but easygoing, and she had a very big heart. That's why Elvis respected her so much. You know, a lot of girls down South still won't go to bed with you unless you promise marriage, and Linda was a virgin when she met Elvis. I really don't know if Elvis promised to marry her; I don't know anything about marriage discussed between them. I'm sure they did, but I don't know what the deal was, but you know, Elvis was brought up in the old school and he felt very lucky to have somebody like that."

Marriage proposals notwithstanding, Linda moved into Graceland with Elvis and became his steady, live-in girl friend. For quite a while, the relationship suited them both perfectly. Linda had aspirations of her own; she wanted to break into the movie and television labyrinth of Hollywood. Elvis, of course, showered her with credit cards, cars, clothes, a home, anything else that she may have wanted. Linda was certainly aware of the benefits afforded by her relationship with Elvis, but unlike scores of other girls who have known him (carnally or other-

wise), her opportunism and knowledge of how he could open
doors for her was always tempered by a very deep love that she
developed for the man. Like all of the other women in his life,
at first she aroused the suspicions and mistrust of those around
Elvis whose first inclination toward any new woman in his life
was to see her as an empty-headed, gold-digging chick with
plenty of looks but only a credit-card mentality who was using
Elvis—"going for a buck"—and would be discarded in several
weeks' time like a used Kleenex tissue. Linda was very different
and she proved it.

"She was a fantastic woman and still is," observes Rick,
"loved and respected by my family, by Cilla, by just about everybody. Linda stayed with Elvis even more than his own wife,
and it was a good thing because she was really good for the
man. You know, she could have had what she wanted and
pulled out long ago, but she hung in there because she cared,
and let me tell you something, being Elvis's girl friend is *heavy.*
You do what he does and that's it. She did it for five years—
traveled with him, took care of him, and a lot of credit has to go
to that girl because she would have done anything for him."

Linda was a Gemini lady like Priscilla, Dee, and Grandma
Presley, but her personality was markedly different from Priscilla's in that she was more easygoing, less strongwilled (Dee's
opinion), had more of a sense of humor (David's), and was, on
the whole, much more flamboyant in dress and appearance.
She came along at a time in Elvis's life when he needed a
woman who could play many different roles as determined by
his mood of that particular moment, and she fit the bill; she
could cheer him up when he was down, mother him when he
needed solace, indulge him, sit and discuss books and religion,
share his interests, and then, like a chameleon, transform herself from a buddy into a sexy, mature woman to become his
lover. Her awareness of his drug problem caused her to guard
him when he took his sleeping medication at night. If he got
up, she got up, and if something was wrong, she was always
there. Linda also loved Lisa and they got along beautifully
whenever she visited; the feeling was quite mutual on Lisa's
part, and Linda and Priscilla became good friends.

270   Aside from being with Elvis, which was sometimes as much a
job as a pleasure for her, the most obvious reciprocation of all
that she put into their relationship was Elvis's offer to buy her
parents a home in Whitehaven, which he did, and his invitation to her brother Sam to become one of his personal bodyguards. She was also written up and photographed, traveled,
vacationed, bejeweled with beautiful stones, and outfitted with a
wardrobe that rivaled any woman's. But was she happy? When
it came to the emotional bottom line of their relationship, Elvis
bridled at commitment and sought safety, once again, in numbers. He felt most comfortable leaving their relationship in that
ill-defined state between a commitment and a more "open"
relationship. "Elvis told me that he wanted to start dating other
chicks," says Rick. "He was going to get Linda her own home
so he could have whatever chicks he wanted over to his house
in Memphis. I think he really loved her in his own way, but
you know, one of Elvis's theories was that you gotta get away.
Women can't understand things like that, and I don't think
Linda could either."

Whether she could or couldn't, she swallowed her pride and
sometimes came along on the dates as his friend with other
women before she too began to stray. After so many years the
relationship began to meander. "Linda really loved Elvis,"
offers Dee, who also harbors a strong love for her. "I think she
would have loved him even if he hadn't been 'Elvis,' the great
star. I think the reason they split up is because she saw that they
would never get married, and after all those years, she gave up
hope."

"Linda was getting into that same cage that Elvis was in,"
elaborates Rick. "You know—withdrawn, not getting out much,
just falling into the same thing as the guys. She's a young,
beautiful woman—twenty-six, twenty-seven years old—and she
needed to get out and see what was going on in the rest of the
world instead of getting locked in by Elvis. She'd been around
for five years and she really cared, but she had to get out, and
you know what? It's a good thing that she did, because nobody
can live like that. No woman could live up to the standards that
Elvis wanted; they'd go nuts. They'd get to that point where

Top: Elvis and Priscilla in Las Vegas, April 1968. Middle left: Vernon and Dee at Elvis's Circle G Ranch, May 1968. Middle right: Minnie Mae Presley, whom Elvis called "Dodger," Dee called "Mother Presley," and Billy, Rick, and David called "Grandma." Bottom: Vernon Presley returns to Tupelo to show Dee the Elvis Presley Center.

ELVIS PRESLEY CENTER

Top left: Elvis in black leather as he appeared in the live segment of his 1968 Christmas special. (Wide World) With Vernon and Bill Miller *(top right)* of the International Hotel, perusing his contract for his first Las Vegas engagement. (Photographer unknown) Above: The family in their booth for opening night, Las Vegas. Right: Elvis opens the three-thousand-seat Showroom Internationale of the Hilton. (UPI) Opposite page: Profile of the mature Elvis Presley, taken sometime between 1969 and 1970 at the zenith of the great comeback, before his divorce. This is the "Boss" that the boys like to remember. (Printhouse Ltd.)

The Vegas years. The quintessential Elvis Presley, onstage. (Wide World)

Backstage in Elvis's dressing room in the Las Vegas Hilton, with Dee, Vernon, and Billy *(opposite page, top)*, and Rick and David *(middle)*.

Mr. and Mrs.
Vernon Presley,
at their happiest
before the storm
(bottom two).

Elvis working out at karate with Chuck Norris *(above)* and riding at Graceland *(right).* (Photographer unknown) Below left: Elvis leaving Trinity Baptist Church in Memphis after Sonny West's wedding. Elvis was best man at the wedding —what he was doing with the flashlight is a mystery. (UPI) Below right: "Pleasure to meet you, Guvnuh." Elvis was always courted by politicians who sought his support, but Elvis remained reticent, feeling that public displays of political partisanship might alienate fans. Here, he shakes hands with George Wallace (Dick Grob and Sonny West are in background). (UPI)

Scenes from the Circle G Ranch *(left and middle)*. Elvis bought the ranch after Priscilla got him interested in riding.

Below left: Elvis's 1973 television special, *Aloha from Elvis in Hawaii,* telecast via satellite to nearly forty countries around the world. (Wide World) Below right: The Boss deplanes for a show in Charleston, West Virginia. Red West is in foreground, Dr. Nick in the doorway, and Charlie Hodge is peering behind him, in the shadows. (Wide World)

Elvis and Priscilla *(above)* are granted a divorce and leave Superior Court in Santa Monica, California, followed by Vernon Presley. (Wide World)

Dee Presley blowing it all away for a photographer *(right)*. Ironically, Elvis's divorce would affect her marriage adversely, too.

What he lost: Priscilla Beaulieu Presley and Lisa Marie Presley, photographed for the family sometime after the divorce.

Takin' Care of Business: Rick and David relax with Al Strada *(at left)* during one of Elvis's engagements in Vegas *(top)*. Portrait of David when he started working as Elvis's bodyguard *(left)*. He became Elvis's headhunter *(opposite page, middle left)*, and Elvis started calling him "Starsky." Rick and the Boss *(above)* in Palm Springs.

TCBing at an Elvis concert meant stage security once Elvis hit the boards. Sometimes you'd find yourself in the damnedest situations. Rick comes up with a random leg *(top left),* probably belonging to a zealous fan making a break for the stage. Slick Rick, the Raven from Whitehaven *(top right),* in his white Trans Am. Diamond Joe Esposito *(middle right),* Elvis's road manager, personal bookkeeper, and closest, most trusted friend. Elvis shakes hands at the close of a concert *(right)* as David keeps a sharp eye out for trouble. Notice: He isn't wearing his usual assortment of rings, which have been removed and handed to Charlie Hodge before the ritual.

Dee Presley during the years of Elvis's decline and her slow, painful estrangement from Vernon Presley. Portrait of the southern lady in her garden *(top right)* and in the studio *(top left)*. With Jerry Lee Lewis in Nashville on his birthday *(above left)*. Dee and Vernon *(above right)*, as painted in their booth in the Showroom Internationale. Left: With the fans.

Top left: Linda Diane Thompson — actress, southern belle, and Elvis's traveling, live-in girl friend for close to five years. (Globe) Ginger Alden (top right) posing with a painting of Elvis after his death. (Wide World) Right: Elvis's magnetism never diminished for his most adoring fans, even with his weight problems and the declining quality of his shows. (© 1977 photography by Harry Siskind)

The Boss at the very end. (© Doug Bruce/Camera Five)

Vernon Presley *(right)* being helped from the mausoleum at Forest Hill cemetery by Joe Esposito and Sandy Miller. (Wide World) Memphis police salute the hearse bearing the casket as it passes *(below)*. Elvis Presley had been their loyal supporter. (Photographer unknown)

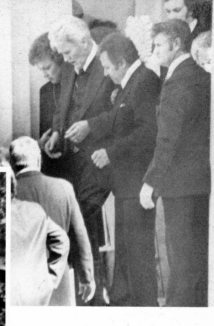

Dee Presley at the mausoleum *(below)*. (Photographer unknown)

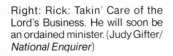

Billy Stanley. (Martin Torgoff)

David Stanley. (Martin Torgoff)

Rick marries Robyn Moye.

Right: Rick: Takin' Care of the Lord's Business. He will soon be an ordained minister. (Judy Gifter/ *National Enquirer*)

Dee—in a satisfied state of mind. (Martin Torgoff)

they didn't know what day or city it was anymore, where they weren't able to even get out for a walk."

Gradually, though they remained the best of friends, Linda and Elvis phased each other out of their lives. "It was no real big traumatic breakup thing," says Rick. "They both just kind of bowed out gracefully." But with Linda gone, Elvis seemed more alone than ever before. Another very special woman, she ended up being taken for granted just like Priscilla. The friendship, warmth, and understanding she added to his life were gone, abandoned for the Next in Line. She had no choice but to move on. Had she stayed in his life as his girl friend or maybe even his wife, she may not have been potent enough to turn his life around (he was already falling into the bad patterns when they met), but David and Rick both think that she would have made a big difference on that fateful August morning when Elvis rose from his bed and stumbled into his bathroom to meet his Maker.

The Boss seemed to age more rapidly after Linda's departure, which also seemed to coincide with an upswing in health problems and drugs. There were still women to occupy his time, but they lost meaning quickly and rarely held his interest for too long. It was as if someone had pulled the plug on his libido.

Sure, there were still brief flings, affairs galore, flirtations and encounters both during and after Linda. Elvis was spotted with the likes of blond and willowy Cybill Shepherd and a gorgeous model from Chicago named Sheila Ryan, who later became Mrs. James Caan. Then Ann Pennington and Mindy Miller waltzed forth, performed a brief fandango with the Boss, and twirled away, as did many others. "He was lonely," says Rick. "He tried to kill it with companionship. He may have been forty, but he was pushing seventy and just wanting to relax. If there was any way he just could have lived comfortably, it might have added years to his life, but you've got to realize how much he loved his work."

Right around this time the excitement and intrigue of the Next in Line went flat. The smiling faces and beautiful bodies of those eternally available women no longer seemed to matter.

272   Elvis realized that even with his double chin and girdled midsection, the women would still have queued up outside his bedroom door had he let them: It wasn't his vanity or lack of self-
confidence that flattened his interest in women. Sex just seemed
to lose its mystique, its pizzazz. "He just wasn't that much into
it anymore," Rick says. "Hey, when Elvis was twenty years old
up until the time he was thirty, he was with different chicks
every night, constantly. Woooo! You know, he got to feeling
that 'enough's enough!' When he was thirty-five, thirty-six years
old, he started to slow down a little. I guess he burned himself
out with all of those women, so he became more interested in
companionship than anything else. There were many times
when he would be dating a girl and never make it with her, and
it got to the point where the chicks that he did make it with
were the exception. It got frustrating for the women because one
of the reasons that they would be dating him was because they
wanted to make it with him! They'd start coming to me asking,
'Hey, what's going on here?' "

In these situations Rick's function as "public relations" in Elvis's life became more important than ever. "I'd make up
things," he remembers, "like 'Oh, he's just got a lot on his
mind tonight,' or 'It's the pressure and all of the shows—he's
tired,' which *was* true. I'd do the best I could there but then
they'd start coming to you for services . . . and you knew that if
you were to make it with Elvis's chick, you were in for big
trouble. You'd see a very elegant chick, man, dying to be with
you and you always had to say 'no thanks,' knowing that
chances were he'd never find out."

The women still kept trying to stay in Elvis's life even after it
became clear to him that they didn't fit into the companionship
scheme. "They'd get bummed out," he says, "because the
women would still be flipping for Elvis and he would date them
for a month or so and fly to another city. He'd tell them that he
would see them the next week and never call back. They would
try to stay in touch with me to know what he was doing, but it
was no use."

In the light of Elvis's fatigue, his health problems, and the effects of narcotics, it isn't hard to understand why he wasn't feeling randy, and the state of affairs continued until he met Ginger Alden—Miss Memphis Traffic Safety of 1976. The year he met her, many people around Elvis were incredulous at what transpired, and rumors began to fly that he was once again in love—that he had found the Real Thing, and the nineteen-year-old Ginger was his newly betrothed.

The meeting occurred during one of Elvis's Vegas engagements. Rick and George Klein both knew the Aldens in Memphis. The family was in Las Vegas that night, so Rick and George invited the three Alden sisters, Terry, Rosemary, and Ginger, the youngest, up to his suite. Rick actually expected Elvis to be much more interested in Terry Alden than in her two sisters. "Terry is not beautiful," he says, "but she's a pretty girl, and if you just sit down and talk to her for five minutes, she becomes radiant. Rosemary is a really nice kid. Ginger was more pretty faced than her sisters, but man, if you sit down and try to talk to her, you can't get anything out of her. She's not smart." Much to everyone's surprise, Elvis "locked in" on Ginger.

Yes, she was pretty, with long, dark, thick hair swept up off her forehead and falling down past her shoulders, smoldering brown eyes, and a youthfully voluptuous figure, but there was something lacking in Ginger that was always noticeable in his women—that element of polished class and elegance. With Ginger it never mattered. Elvis was looking for and seeing something different because she represented to him the one that might keep him Forever Young. Elvis Presley—"fat and forty," as Walter Cronkite characterized him on the night of his fortieth birthday—somehow hoped that Ginger might restore to his life his youthful vigor and the beauty and innocence that was slipping away from him with the passing of each day.

"I think it was mostly infatuation," says Rick, "because she was a young and innocent type of girl who didn't have a bad name and hadn't been around much." The very fact that Ginger had the distinction of not having been around much made the idea of a relationship with her very attractive to Elvis

274   because it enabled him to feel more secure in the knowledge that she hadn't known many other men and was more adaptable to the life that he would show her.

In all fairness to Ginger, who has received much criticism from Elvis's friends and family who found her relationship with Elvis to be incomprehensible and their plans for marriage bordering on the preposterous, she should not be faulted for her opportunism in the relationship. When he met her, Elvis's state was becoming more melancholic and the general attitude was that if she could make him happy . . . well, all power to her. Everybody kept their mouths shut as Elvis would have demanded of them, but as time passed it became more evident that the whole thing would never have been possible had it occurred at a different point in his life. It seemed to many a last-ditch effort on Elvis's part for the happiness that he had always avoided, with precisely the sort of young girl who was least equipped to provide it.

Rick says, "She's kind of a sore spot with me because I think Elvis was being deceived by Ginger. I thought it was sad. I don't want to blow the girl down. She's an all-right kid, but she just didn't know what was going on. She was just trying to play the role of Elvis's girl friend."

According to David she didn't play it well. "She was freaked out, to say the least," he says. "Hell, she was under a lot of pressure because she just didn't know how to act. She didn't know what to do. All of a sudden she was brought into Elvis's life and the man's telling her that he loves her—wow! That had to be blowing her away! I sympathize with her because I understood her position."

Elvis's fans, and particularly the gossip columnists, were having a field day, even making false comparisons with Priscilla. "She resembled Cilla during the sixties, but only a little bit," observes Rick. "Man, she doesn't look anything like Cilla," disagrees David. "Cilla outclasses her a hundred percent." "I could see what she was trying for the brief moment I saw her," says Dee, who *understands* these things. "She may have been trying to look like her but I saw no resemblance. But don't you know that it must have made her happy anytime that anybody said that? But then there were other women in Elvis's life who had tried to look like Cilla too."

Elvis's feelings for Ginger came as a surprise to everyone in the TCB group. "We wanted to know if she was for real," says David. "We always suspected Elvis's women and then we see him fall head over heels for this girl." What made it unlikely was the age difference between them, which gave them little in common and even less to talk about. But there was no doubt about the fact that Elvis wanted her around because he was afraid of losing her, and he once even suspected David of trying to steal her. "The reason that Elvis suspected me was because Ginger was so young that we could relate," he says. "She was twenty and I was twenty-two, and we could sit down and talk— you know, 'Did you see McCartney last week, did you hear this, did you hear that . . .' and I used to do it just to be nice because she was Elvis's chick. He just got that impression because I used to flirt a lot on tour." Vernon Presley even approached David and Dee to ask if Ginger and David were having an affair. Whether he himself was curious or was inquiring on Elvis's behalf isn't clear, but there was no doubt about the fact that her youth and his age made Elvis uneasy.

But even if the relationship was irrational or misguided, would he have married her? "I don't think so," is Rick's opinion. "He may have been engaged, but he made the statement to me that he wasn't ready to get married. David thinks that Elvis really dug Ginger, whereas I just don't think so." "He didn't say when," states David, "but he said to me, 'I'm gonna marry that girl.' I personally don't think that he would have gone through with it, but who am I to know? I have to say one thing, though; that girl was taking advantage of Elvis. She was going for a buck, and she proved that after he died."

Whether he would have or wouldn't have is now completely irrelevant, but one thing is clear: Elvis Presley would spend the last, most tragic year of his life with a girl who could scarcely have understood what was happening to him, very likely deceiving himself into thinking that she might rekindle the vitality he

276   needed to keep going and give him a more optimistic outlook on life. Whatever his motive with Ginger, be it love or otherwise, it didn't work. When the chips all fell that August morning, she would remain in bed, asleep, while Elvis had his moment of truth.

PART FOUR

FOUR

THE FINAL CURTAIN

1975-1977

Lost, yesterday, somewhere between sunrise and sunset, two golden hours, each set with sixty diamond minutes. No reward is offered, for they are gone forever.

Horace Mann,
Lost, Two Golden Hours

CHAPTER 18

TAKING IT
TO THE LIMITS

Rick understood the step up from capsule to ampule and hypo-
dermic needle better than anyone else around Elvis Presley. By
the time Elvis started seriously abusing his sleeping medications, he had already run the gamut himself—pain killers,
opium-based drugs, Dilaudid, Demerol, morphine, finally
heroin. By the time it started getting bad with Elvis, Rick had
already kicked, and it hadn't been easy. He became frightened
when he saw how Elvis was using drugs, knowing where it was
heading. "I've never seen anybody who could take it like that,"
he says. "You just don't do dope like he did and live through
it."

Rick's time in the rehab hospital taught him how hard it was
to get rid of a habit. "I was very lucky, man," he says, looking
back. "I really enjoyed getting off on the drugs and I was getting
more used to it, but I wasn't all the way to the point of my body
craving it if I didn't have it, so I wasn't totally addicted yet. But
it was starting. I knew it because I would be pissed off and irritated more often when I didn't have it. When I started to get
strung out my girl friend Jill put it to me. 'It's either the dope or

280 me.' She was right. I committed myself to the drug rehab program at the hospital. Nobody talked me into it; I did it of my own free will. But I was lucky."

The power and nature of Elvis's drugs was what worried Rick. "It was all prescribed narcotics, no black-market stuff, and he was heavily into it for about five or six years, but it started getting bad in nineteen seventy-two to seventy-three. That's when he started getting into needles. Wooo, man, that's when I really started to worry—when he became a needle head. His body began to look like a pin cushion. He never stuck anything into his veins because they were too shallow—he'd go into the muscle, and it wasn't only drugs. Sometimes he'd shoot vitamin B-12, but mostly it was the same drugs I did—Tuinal, Demerol, and Dilaudid. He was addicted, for sure. He enjoyed the high."

The World Health Organization defines drug dependence as "a state of psychic or physical dependence or both on a drug arising in a person following administration of that drug on a period or continuing basis." Over the years Elvis had built up both kinds of dependencies. Apart from psychological or emotional reasons that may have motivated the upswing in his drug taking, there was danger in the drugs themselves. If the narcotics user discontinues the intake of the drug he has become dependent on, the effects are unpleasant; if totally cut off, the user can experience anxiety, nausea, weakness, tremulousness, confusion, disorientation, hallucinations, or convulsions. Moreover, if the dosage is decreased in strength or frequency or tolerance is built up and the drugs are not increased sufficiently to bring about the same results, the same symptoms can occur—milder, perhaps, but still very unpleasant, tempting the user to increase oral dosage or to administer the drugs by injection. The result is a vise which only turns tighter with the passing of time. Rick knew the symptoms and tried his best to dissuade Elvis from continuing, to step back and take a look at himself. It was a touchy issue.

"Hey, Elvis," he said one afternoon, broaching the subject, "I gave it up, man, and you're a much stronger man than I am. Why can't you do it, too?"

The Boss's reaction was contingent upon his mood. If he was feeling receptive to the advice, he could say, "I *am*, man. I know exactly what I'm doing," as he did to Rick that day. "That was the one answer you wanted to hear from him," Rick says, "so you wouldn't pursue it any more because he'd get pissed. You just hoped that he meant it, but he never did. I just couldn't see hope for him if he didn't get it together."

Elvis seemed bent on the drugs for many reasons. He searched for rationales and found them when he needed to. Health problems and muscular aches and pains from performances became a convenient excuse. "He was like a hypochondriac sometimes," Rick continues. "He enjoyed the feeling of the relief of pain. If he had a little pain from something, he'd try to get rid of it by taking something strong—every bit of it—and if he thought he might have more pain later on, he'd take more drugs then, before it happened, to prevent it. See, the man actually thought he was benefiting himself by some of the things he did. There were times when he'd realize what he was doing to himself, though. He'd get mad at himself and say, 'Man, what the hell am I doing!' But that last year he just didn't care anymore."

The others around Elvis were as powerless as Rick in influencing Elvis's behavior, because if they tried, he could become incensed, feeling that they had no right to meddle in his personal affairs. Joe Esposito, Rick, and Dr. Nick all successfully infiltrated his bottles of medication to decap the barbiturates and substitute harmless mixtures of vitamins, but that proved ineffective because he usually knew or had too many sources. Rick was in a precarious position because he had been a fellow drug user and Elvis never liked to use a needle himself. He knew all about Rick's experiences and entrusted him with the job of administering the drugs. The contradiction of trying to stop or at least cut down his Boss's drugs and then help him shoot up is evident, but that's the way it was for everyone else around Elvis. The dope became, like everything else, an outgrowth of Taking Care of Business. "Sure," Rick sighs with a straightforward honesty that doesn't hide the sadness and regret in his voice. "I did it for him all the time. David did, too. A lot

282 of people will say, 'Well, if you *loved* the man, how could you have done it? Why didn't you try to tell him?' I'll tell you why: After a while, he just didn't want to hear it. He'd say, 'Cool it. I don't want to hear it.' You could not penetrate. He'd been up there for so long that nobody could talk to him."

The issue of guilt did not enter the picture. "Look," Rick points out, "he was going to do it anyway, whether I did it for him or not. There were times I protested, but in the long run I was devoted to the man—to doing his bidding—and I would do whatever he wanted me to do. Whether or not it was good for his health didn't make much of a difference. People were thankful that I was around most of the time because I knew what was going on and half the time nobody else did. Many times I had to do things to pull him through and keep him alive when we thought he wasn't going to make it. He'd fall asleep sometimes in the middle of eating and nearly choked to death on his food."

Another problem was when Elvis would wake up, forget that he had taken his medication, and then take more. "Sometimes I'd find him on his back on the floor," says David. "I'd carry him to his room. We'd pull the covers over him and stay with him."

As the problem worsened, Joe Esposito became more crucially important to Elvis's life and the TCB operation than ever before. According to Rick he was the one man who could come closest to really reaching Elvis. "Joe would get angry at him whenever Elvis would pull something bad," Rick says. "Elvis would have to answer for his actions more to Joe because he respected him so much. Many times he answered for Elvis's actions, and every time something went wrong, he was trapped in the middle but always kept his head. Elvis couldn't have made it without him because there's no earthly way that the things that went on in that group could have continued without someone like him at the helm. Vernon couldn't have done it—he would have snapped under the pressure."

Still, even Joe only had so much sway with Elvis. In the long run his influence was as limited as everyone else's. When it came down to Elvis having his way, Joe was just another employee like the rest, there to Take Care of Business. Elvis might be completely truthful with him or give him a half-baked reason for an action, or he just might get mad and say, "It's none of your goddamned business!" So Joe would get the axe like the rest. "He would always fire me and Joe so many times," Rick remembers, "but then he'd hire us back the same day. I remember once when Joe got fired the group started falling apart so bad that he had to hire him back and pay him a lot more money before Joe would put up with it again. He was making a fine salary at the time Elvis died and he deserved every penny of it. Hell, the guy was so valuable he should have gotten a percentage."

It was Joe, Rick, and Dr. Nick who convinced Elvis to enter the hospital and dry out. There were two weeks in October of 1973, two weeks in January and February of 1975, and two more weeks in August and September of that year when he was admitted to the hospital in Memphis. Reasons of health were released to the public—fatigue, enlarged colon, stomach inflammation, gastroenteritis. . . . "Every time he went in was to dry out," says Rick. "You can cover it up as much as you want. They would slowly and surely try to cut him off his medication. I thought it was ridiculous because they'd cut him off but still give him small amounts. If they wanted to dry him out, I didn't understand why they couldn't cut him off completely just like they did with me when I went in. Blam! That's it. It's rough, but it's the only way you can do it."

"Drying out" on narcotics and downs is a complicated process that can only be accomplished in the drug-free environment of a hospital and is rarely successful because it requires the complete cooperation of the drug user, who usually has a very strong dependence on the drugs. The psychological and physical withdrawal symptoms range from the unpleasant to the excruciatingly painful; kicking a strong down or narcotics habit is tantamount to a private slice of hell on earth for the unfortunate user, and this is what Elvis faced. At least he was in the hospital, which meant an admission of the problem. The situation would be delicate enough for Dr. Nick and Joe Esposito, who took charge of the operation in the hospital, but they were sometimes confounded by the home troops. "We had to filter

284 some of the employees out when he went in," recalls Rick, "because they would want to bring him stuff in the hospital. They'd get stuff for it, you know, cars."

With all of the doctors and employees involved, it is still both unwise and unjust to blame anybody but Elvis for his drug habits. He was the sum total of his life and times, of his life-style, his psychology, and character, of the world that he created for himself; those that did his bidding were only a part of that world. His efforts to dry out and detox in the hospital were only partially successful. Even if he had achieved one hundred per-cent success, he might very well have gone back to the drugs.

"As he started to do more drugs he became more withdrawn," says Rick: "He only confided in a few people—me, David, Esposito, Billy Smith, Charlie, Larry." "Withdrawn" in this case meant seclusion—"hibernation" in TCB lingo. Elvis would disappear into his room for longer periods of time. "Somebody would always see him, though," says David. "I saw Elvis three times a week on a normal basis, even if he was in so-called seclusion. I was allowed, so was Ricky, Charlie, and Larry Geller. See, Elvis really liked his room. I *loved* his room. I could sit there and listen to music with him all night. He would just read, watch television, relax. He was fortunate enough to like seclusion. Anybody who says, 'Well, I feel sorry for Elvis because he wanted to get out' is off the mark; he liked that way of life. He could always get out if he wanted to and if he did we went to Vail or Hawaii if he felt like it."

Elvis remained astonishingly calm and composed about him-self those last few years. Like always, he still had his emotional moments. "He was into controlling his emotions for sure," David says, "but many times I've seen him break down and cry. We had an expression that we liked to use: 'Your eyes are the mirror to your soul,' and sometimes it's good to cleanse things by just letting go, because that's what a man is." Elvis still be-came angered by bad service at hotels and had fights with his girl friends, but, says Rick, "I think he more mellowed than got angered those last years. The only things that got to him were the really bad things and the pressure, but he started laying back and taking it easy."

Loneliness could set in, unexpectedly. "Sometimes Elvis would want to be left alone," says David, "but sometimes we'd leave him alone too much, and he'd let us know about it. I'd say, 'God, Elvis—I'm sorry—I thought you wanted to be alone now,' and he'd say, 'No, I want you guys to *talk* to me. . . .' I'd love it, you know; I wouldn't go to bed even if I had to be up and goin' at six in the morning."

But even with all of his wealth and the devotion of a few close friends, the one almost constant condition of that last year was an overwhelming, crushing, damnable sense of *ennui*, a total apathy and acquiescence to his condition and life. Nothing could excite him anymore, nothing could hold his attention. "He'd had it all," says Rick, "and it seemed that he was just tired. People will say, 'Oh, if only Elvis could have gotten out and done this, if only he could have done that.' He'd already done what he wanted to do—the women, the bikes, the cars, jets—that was the last kick, and he got three of them. 'Elvis Presley Airways.' He always tried everything and then got burned out on it and just moved into bigger things when it wasn't fun anymore. I guess to a certain extent he felt that he'd done it all."

This feeling of profound apathy and aimlessness rubbed off on the boys. "We were really getting depressed," Rick remembers. "When Elvis got down, I got down; if he had that I-don't-give-a-shit attitude, that's the way I would react and just slough everything off with a *big deal*. If he couldn't get excited about anything, neither could we."

The impression one would conjure of Elvis during this final period of his life seemingly illustrates a man reclusive, paranoid, insecure, and unsure if he had a friend left in the world, a man so whacked out and screwed up on narcotics that he didn't know what was going on anymore. On the contrary, things just plowed right on: business as usual. The Boss functioned enough to work and live his life, although the pace became more difficult when he did work. "He knew exactly what was going on at

286 all times," Rick says. "I never saw him freak out or just lose it. He always kept his wits about him no matter what; it's just that he stopped caring."

To the TCB boys closest to him, Elvis Presley would remain "Boss"—benefactor and manipulator—the most sincere friend and advisor who couldn't follow his own good advice and a man of supreme contradiction to the very end of his life. He lived more and more in a world of I, Me, Mine but stayed a child of hard times, recklessly generous one moment, cruelly selfish the next, a man who would graciously offer you a home and then become furious if you took a french fry from his plate.

His desire for escape and release became evident in his behavior. "He had his finger very much on what was happening to him," Dee Presley says, "and he really had to face it; that's where the hurt and stress was coming in. It began to close in because you can only live a fantasy for so long. I believe Elvis was beginning to face that when his health started going bad."

Dee Presley firmly believes that Elvis's intelligence and sense of morality—as unique and bent as they had become by the powerful forces in his life over a long period of time—created a deep guilt as he confronted the hard reality of throwing his life away. "With Elvis's knowledge of the Bible," she says, "there must have been that tugging—a feeling of wanting to pull back from it all. See, with all of his ways, Elvis wasn't really 'doing what he wanted to do,' and I'm not talking about being a star or entertaining—I'm talking about his life. He would have been good if he had, because he was a good person who wanted to live more. I feel that. Strongly."

Yet his feelings about death remained a paradox even as he flirted with it. By 1976, after his last attempts to dry out failed, he did more drugs than ever before. "I just said, 'God, if Elvis keeps up like this he'll never make it,'" David remembers. "You just don't do barbs like that every night. You know, it's a strange thing about Elvis: I don't think he intended to live long, but I also don't think he killed himself on purpose."

David's last observation puts the paradox of death in Elvis's life more sharply into focus and brings to mind a particular incident. The Boss was sitting in front of his television when the news of Freddie Prinze's suicide came on. Prinze, a young, brilliant comic from New York and star of *Chico and the Man*, had also been catapulted suddenly to fame and fortune at a young age. He was idolized by kids everywhere and a guaranteed sellout on the nightclub circuits, and a hot property for television and movies. While it was all happening, he got married, had a child, and seemed to have become engulfed by his instant celebrity, by the pressures, the money, the drugs. One evening, after his wife left him and took their child, he loaded himself up, as usual, on Quaaludes, coke, and booze, stuck a gun to his head, and blew his brains out.

"Jeez!" Elvis said, turning away from the television in disgust. "That's really the chickenshit way out!"

Prinze's suicide had affected the Boss because somehow he recognized the similarities in the pathology of their despair. Elvis extracted one important lesson from the death, which was a strongly felt religious resistance to out-and-out suicide. "The Lord's way would never be to kill yourself," he said earnestly. Also, his sense of manhood and dignity would never allow him to take the "easy" way out. His intricately constructed mechanisms of rationale, which still allowed him to fall back on the belief that he wasn't doing anything wrong by his actions, helped him to survive whatever impulses he may have had to pull a Freddie Prinze on the world. Had you suggested to him that he was doing with drugs, diet, and overwork over a long period of time what Prinze managed to accomplish with a bullet in a split second, he would have scoffed.

Elvis Presley surely wanted to live, but, on many levels, he just as surely prepared himself for the inevitability of his death. He clung fast to life even in the atmosphere of lethargy and listlessness that pervaded the final year of his life, when he became bereft of his most powerful motivations to live and could feel the specter of his death creeping closer. Like black and white knights, his life and death impulses vied for power over him, jousting on the fields of his conscious and subconscious.

He talked about it more and more. "He told me that he

288 began to accept death right after his mother died," Billy says. "He said, 'Death is the hardest thing for anyone to accept,' and anything hard to accept was a challenge for Elvis."

"Death never scared Elvis because he had to conquer every fear he had of it," says Dee Presley. "Elvis couldn't live with fear. I think the final fear in his life was to walk out on that stage and no longer be 'Elvis Presley.' "

Apart from challenge and the question of exceeding limits, the promise of peace and release in death became more important to him. "I guess in the end he was just as much aware of death as life," Rick says. "A lot of people will get up and think about how the day is going to be. They're really in tune with life itself—thankful and in praise of it. Elvis remained thankful for life, but he became more *aware* of death. It was more on his mind than living."

Sometimes, at night, he would ride south from Graceland on Highway 51 to the Forest Hill Cemetery to visit the grave of his mother. With the vast, empyreal expanse of the night sky stretched above and the moon and stars beckoning to him, he would stand there, somberly and respectfully, his hands at his sides, his eyes turning from the sky to the gravemarker.

GLADYS SMITH PRESLEY
APRIL 25, 1912–AUGUST 14, 1958
BELOVED WIFE OF VERNON PRESLEY
AND MOTHER OF ELVIS PRESLEY
SHE WAS THE SUNSHINE OF OUR HOME

Then he would turn to the figure of Christ with the two angels at His feet, feeling, during those moments of communion with her spirit, closer than ever before to peace, to the answers he sought, feeling the imminence of reunion. He spoke of her more often and reflected on how different his life might have been had Jesse Garon lived and Elvis Aron not been an only child.

People closest to Elvis were still refusing to acknowledge the truth about him even though the signs were everywhere. He now lived the nocturnal life of the bat, never seeing the sunshine, taking the fresh air more rarely, shunning most exercise. Racketball became a travesty. "He'd get out there and just walk over to the ball and take one swing," Rick says. "It was killing us all because we wanted him to do things."

As performance time neared before his Las Vegas shows, the Boss now rode the elevator down the thirty floors from his suite to a golf cart, which transported him through the backstage corridors to the stage so he would no longer have to walk. With cops jogging alongside like Secret Service men around a presidential limousine, the hotel employees would stop and stare at him with their trays in hand as he rode impassively by.

"It got to where he was totally bedridden during the days that last year," Rick recalls sadly. "We'd fly into a city and he'd get right into bed as soon as we got there. We'd have to get him up to do the show. Back on the plane, he'd get right back into bed."

Back at Graceland before a tour, the boys had their hands full just rousting him out to get his circulation going and his energy up. Rick would burst into his room. "Hey, Elvis, we just went motorcycle ridin'! Come on! It's a beautiful day!" Someone else would offer, "Hey, man, have you been doin' your exercises—come on, man! Get up! Get out of bed!"

If they could even get him out of bed, they considered it an accomplishment.

The public was getting hip. Lyrics were slurred more often and forgotten. His puffy appearance, so terribly hard to abide for those who knew how magnetically handsome Elvis had been in his late thirties, began to rankle fans and critics alike. The punch left his stage movement, but usually his superbly gifted voice, which could seem remarkably intact on a good night, and his pure musical canniness were enough to carry him through. On nights when they were failing and when his energy ran out, he subsisted on guts, willpower, and the ragged edges of his emotions. Whatever else he lacked he could always compensate for by simply riding on the coattails of the most mythic and archetypal of his stage qualities. Incredibly, there were still moments of pure brilliance in his performances.

290   Critics savaged him. "That was his livelihood, the most important thing he had done all his life," says Rick. "He was still a
perfectionist. When people said that he did a lousy show, it was
like a slap in the face. See, he stayed confident of himself and
maintained his self-respect. Elvis knew that he was slurring
words but he didn't want to admit it to himself. He knew what
kind of condition he was in but he was trying to instill in his
mind, you know, 'Hey, man, watch this, I'm *still* going to go
out there tonight and do this show and—you know what?—it's
gonna be good, too!' He would get out there and do it, but bless
his heart, man, he just couldn't. He was beginning to realize
that."

Simple problems of health sometimes held him back. "God,
if Elvis was sick on tour, we'd all cry," remembers David. "If he
couldn't give one hundred percent, he was very upset because
he had to deliver."

It was during this period that Elvis began singing "My Way."
"That was his song," Rick says. "He always knew about it and
liked it, but he never started doing it as part of his show until
that last year. Of all the songs he did, that one meant the most
to him. It was so dramatic for us and for other people who really
knew him and understood what was happening to see him get
up there and do it, because he did, man . . . he took the
blows, and he *still* did it his way."

The song became Elvis's statement on his life for anyone who
cared to listen, his comment on the pleasures, pains, price,
glories, and failures of being Elvis Presley. Perhaps Sinatra had
done the song better, but the emotions of triumph and tragedy
that Elvis filled into Paul Anka's lyric—culled from the experience of his own life and replete with all of his ironies and contradictions—made the song, for all who knew him, as poig-
nantly real as an open wound.

"I'd like to do this song for you, ladies and gentlemen," he'd
say into the blinding lights at the end of his shows, mopping the
sweat, catching his fading breath and picking up the sheet with
the lyrics. "Don't know all the words . . . but I'm gonna read
'em off this sheet . . . hope y'all don't mind," while behind

him the slow, wistful piano introduction led him slowly into the song as James Burton haunted the melody with bittersweet guitar notes like a whippoorwill on a lonely, summer night. Elvis sang slowly and simply, without being fancy or showy, concentrating hard on his breath control so he would be sure to deliver the crescendo, carefully mouthing and enunciating the words, sometimes failing. Coming close to the finale of his show, his audiences would sit, drained like Elvis, unusually silent but raptly attentive, aware that they were seeing something special and that somehow Elvis was finally spilling the beans. He sang the words, his breath tremulous, the phrasing unsteady: "And now the end is near, and so I face the final *curtain* . . ." and his voice would quaver slightly on the word "curtain," and when he came to "I've lived a life that's full, I've traveled each and every *highway*," the voice would clog once again with emotion on the final word as Elvis freed himself to tell the world that he could still laugh at it all even if the price he had to pay would be his life, and that he was still his own man, a true believer in himself.

And when it was over, he'd say almost ruefully, "And now I'd like to sing the *saddest* song I've ever heard in my life, ladies and gentlemen," and he'd sing Hank Williams's "I'm So Lonesome I Could Cry."

"If there was one person I would compare Elvis to in his loneliness," Rick says, "it was Hank Williams. Kindred spirits. Men with a lot of pain and a lot of music who died young."

Even at the very end, on those last few tours, Elvis had enough left to dazzle. He would tell his piano player to get up and would sit down himself to perform "Unchained Melody," pulling his audiences into the time machine of his life as he struck the chords, his eyes closed, lost in himself, his voice richly mellow and still feral with anguish, as he burst forth, ". . . Oh! My love! My darling! I've *hung*ered for your touch. . . ."

They didn't call him King for nothing.

CHAPTER 19

DADDY AND DEE

Those last few years were a time of calamity and pain for many of the people enmeshed in Elvis Presley's world and some would get caught in the strong undertow of his decline. For Vernon Elvis Presley, a man who lived for his son, life became a matter of Taking Care of Business. He tried desperately to protect Elvis from an outside world that seemed about to swallow him whole, but the far more difficult problem was protecting Elvis from himself.

Vernon Presley may not have known the full extent of his son's problems because Elvis was always careful to spare him details, but he knew that his boy was in serious trouble. Dee Presley recalls moments when he felt so afraid and frustrated that he would break down and cry. "My God, Dee," he would sob when he felt lost and helpless. "What happened to that little boy I knew."

Almost as soon as Elvis went back to live performing, Vernon felt it necessary to be with him on the road as much as possible. He became a part of the TCB crew, subjecting himself to the

294 same pressures, anxieties, and temptations, but it was his deep fear for Elvis that kept him there even before things started going bad. "He just couldn't sit by the phone in fear all the time," Dee says, "worrying that something dreadful had happened or that Elvis had been killed. That was his son, his only child. I really began to understand then why Elvis had never really grown up. Gladys never let him and Vernon couldn't either: He was going to worry for him. The truth is that Vernon was the one who could always walk into the room and talk with Elvis when he was upset. He could calm him down. He had to stay right there and try to keep the whole thing together, and it literally tore his heart out."

"Daddy was the one person right there, who Elvis could always open up to without worrying," echoes Rick. "There were things that went on between Vernon and Elvis that I couldn't even imagine, and I knew both of them very well. *Nobody* stepped in there—wives, employees, family, *any*one—between those two, man, because if you did, you were in for one big hassle. You know, until Lisa came along, Daddy was 'it' for Elvis. He was the one connection to his mom."

Behind closed doors in hotels, on the plane, or back home, Vernon consulted with his son about everything, guiding, trying to advise, consoling, reproaching, quelling his son's fears, and reinforcing in him a strong sense of family solidarity. The bottom line of this sense of solidarity between Vernon and Elvis Presley was an emotional sense of "us" against "them."

"When you got right down to it," Rick observes, "Vernon really didn't give a flip about anybody but Elvis because he thought everybody was around for a handout. Now, there *were* leeches around Elvis, for sure; everybody had their price, but Daddy was wrong because there were also people around Elvis who genuinely loved him. It boiled down to the fact that the Presleys didn't trust anybody."

On the road Vernon Presley's presence was always a good incentive for his son to "get out there and give it that little something extra," as Rick puts it. There was also friction between them, however, and they clashed when Elvis did things that

Vernon would criticize and object to as not being in his son's best personal interests. When he saw Elvis dabbling in eastern religions, mysticism, and the psychic realm, for instance, he became disturbed and let his son know about it.

Money was Vernon Presley's major concern—Elvis's money. His time on the road allowed him to observe firsthand how Elvis spent his money, and it horrified him. He tried his best to curb it. "Vernon thought it was downright embarrassing when Elvis would do those things with his money," Dee says. "But what really upset him was when he thought Elvis would try to buy friendship. Elvis always knew the difference between true friendship and bought loyalty, but he wanted friends so badly that it seemed he would do anything to have them. Sometimes, when he was feeling insecure or upset, he would say to me and Vernon, 'What would I do tonight, Daddy, if everything went down? Who would be there besides you, Dodger, Delta, Dee, the boys?' See, Elvis had those kinds of fears, and that's what tore Vernon apart."

Elvis Presley disliked restraints to begin with, but it bothered him that even with his millions, his daddy still worried about money. It was as much Vernon's nature to worry about money, however, as it was Elvis's to squander it. "It wasn't just Elvis that he worried about," Dee says. "Vernon kept track of everything—the way Priscilla spent money and her clothes, Linda's spending, my things, things Elvis gave his guys, things he gave away onstage. That's just the way he was."

In part Vernon Presley kept his nose to Elvis's book for tax reasons, working with Memphis accountants to see what could be written off. When he saw the money going out as quickly as it was coming in, he became frightened because he knew how hard Elvis was working.

When they clashed over money or anything else, it was explosive, as it usually is between father and son, but what could make it worse was their similarities in temperament, particularly their intense stubbornness. Elvis clearly didn't need his father's approval for anything he did, but his father's disapproval just as clearly bothered him. Thus it was difficult to call the outcomes

296 of their confrontations. "It kind of balanced out as to who would have final say," says Rick. "Sometimes Daddy would, sometimes Elvis would."

"They had one of the tightest relationships between father and son I've ever seen," adds Billy. "That's why there were times when Elvis would say things to Daddy that he didn't really mean, but every time he'd come right back to apologize and was crying when he did it. He lived for Daddy, man. That was his life—the last person in the world that he wanted to hurt."

When Elvis's mood soured and everything seemed to go wrong at once, there were moments when Vernon Presley had to shoulder more than he perhaps bargained for, even with a pro like Joe Esposito around. Elvis always worried about his daddy's health and tried to keep his more disturbing secrets from him. "Daddy knew about the drugs," Rick says, "but he didn't know the details; he didn't know how bad it really was. Elvis tried his best to cover it up but Daddy was getting pretty hip those last couple of years, and he was worried sick about it. But if Daddy *ever* tried to keep anything bad from Elvis, woo, boy, Elvis would get mad as hell. The one thing that worried him was Daddy getting sick."

As it turned out, Elvis fears were justified, for the life on the road was surely undermining Vernon Presley's health.

"Above everything else, Vernon Presley is a man," says Dee. "He always tried to stay strong and calm, but he was getting tired, too, and he had so many heartaches. Sometimes he would be sitting there with Elvis all night long trying to keep it straight, trying to keep peace with everybody, but there wasn't much he could do and *that* was what was really killing him—his helplessness. He'd say, 'My God, Dee, it seems that my son doesn't care who he hurts anymore.' No one loved Elvis like Vernon Presley. He gave him everything he had. First he gave him our marriage, then he almost gave him his life."

Multifarious is a good word to describe Dee Presley. What happened to her marriage to Vernon Presley during those years was, in part, caused by the same set of circumstances that bent

and destroyed other marriages around Elvis, but the course of   297
events in her life during the years of Elvis's decline was also
deeply rooted in her growing self-awareness as a woman.

Dee stayed home like an obedient wife (TLCer) when her
husband went off on the road with Elvis. As the years passed,
she found herself caught in a vise of conflicting emotions about
herself, her marriage, and Elvis Presley's world. The outcome
was her slow estrangement, separation, and ultimate divorce
from Vernon Presley. The marriage wavered, seesawing back
and forth until another woman appeared, at which point it
buckled but did not break officially until the tragedy of Elvis's
death. By that time lawyers were taking depositions and papers
were being put in order but they settled without going to court.
Both were so shaken by the recent events that they could hardly
speak. Vernon flew to the Dominican Republic for a
"quickie"—everything was as neat, clean, painless, and civilized
as possible. It was Taking Care of Business—the most efficient
legal surgery possible, which served them both. The only thing
it never reflected was their true feelings.

"I'll probably outlive everybody and I have Vernon to thank
for that. I didn't get caught up in what was happening around
Elvis because I could choose to be anywhere I wanted to be and
to stay out of it. I guess I stayed away because I knew it would
have been too much for me, so I filled my life with other
things. Now I understand what Vernon meant when he once
said, 'Dee, there's a certain amount that you don't know and
might never know until perhaps later.'

"I married Vernon knowing that his son would need him. I
would say, 'Elvis needs you more than I do. Go to him.' Elvis
thought it necessary for the men to travel without their wives
and he made a statement once when someone was trying to
bring his wife along on a tour: 'I'm so damned tired of this because
look at my stepmother; she doesn't go! She could be anyplace
that she wants but she allows Daddy and I to have the privacy.'
So I was being held up as the example of the understanding
wife. The whole thing never seemed like a problem until I
started getting restless. Elvis and I both wanted him, I guess;
that's what it boiled down to.

298   "Of course, I realized that there would always be a lot of women around Elvis and that he would have to pay attention to them, so that's another reason I wanted to stay away. The same was true of Vernon; he was a very handsome man and women would be making a fuss over him, too, so I projected the strong and understanding image, but I never thought about what I was doing. I wasn't going to make it any more difficult for him. I'd say, 'Go, everything is going to be fine,' when inside, I was hurting.

"When the car would pull out of the driveway, I had to turn my face the other way sometimes so he couldn't see the tears. He'd call back when he got to the airport and sometimes as much as three times a day. If I would have picked the phone up once, called him, and said, 'Vernon, I need you,' those would have been the most welcome words in the world, but I don't exactly say what I'm feeling inside. It's my pride. I guess Vernon didn't really feel that I was too much in love with him.

"I had mixed emotions about what went on around Elvis, or at least what I *knew* about. In a way, it was a big relief at first when Vernon went on tour, because he had always been there so much that it seemed I would get a chance to do some things on my own. I knew that there was wrongdoing on tour, but I wanted to ignore it. I didn't have respect for men who walked out on marriages and let families break up, so the reason I wasn't there was because *Dee Presley* didn't live like that and *Dee Presley* couldn't just openly walk into any such behavior. Vernon wanted to shield me from all of it, so it wasn't just Elvis that he was trying to protect, and when he was laughing with me on the outside I knew that he was dying on the inside.

"No, I was the selfish one. I look back now and think that I was in love with life. When everything had been fine, I loved Vernon; when things started going wrong (and Lord knows they did!), he was a jackass—as stubborn as he could be, extremely jealous of me. I myself made my own happiness as Mrs. Vernon Presley, with my friends, my church, and my boys.

"But it seemed that everything I had wanted for my boys, all of my dreams and hopes for them, had been taken away. Everything that happened to them only disillusioned me more about what I had done. I never felt that when they were young, but then they grew up idolizing Elvis. I was so shocked when I learned that Ricky was taking drugs and when he was arrested, I almost died. Billy was so hurt by Elvis that it made me cry just to see what was happening, and then my youngest, David, was out there with a gun, ready to die for him. I never forgave them for that. I'd been hurt bad on occasion in my life, but the deepest hurt was when my sons left to go off with Elvis because then they could no longer come home and share their lives with me. They couldn't tell me about the drugs and the women.

"I spent sleepless nights praying to the Lord to send me a miracle. I prayed to God that if they were on that plane or in that Showroom to just touch Vernon, Elvis, and my three boys—to just stop them that very moment and show them that it wasn't all real—the whole thing was just something that glittered—to slow them down because they were living too fast.

"Priscilla and I were both birds in a cage while the men had all the freedom they wanted, and I guess I resented that very much; if I hadn't been filled with resentment, I don't think I would have been as cold to Vernon as I was when I lashed out. I guess we began hurting each other around nineteen seventy-one–seventy-two. The boys were out of the house, everyone had their life, and I felt empty; there seemed to be something missing.

"I lived in my own little world. We hardly ever had guests in our home. I kept my own very private circle of friends and I loved all of them—Pearl and Paul Shafer, Dr. Charles and Gerry Kyle, Wilma and Clyde Sparkman and my minister, C.W. Bradley, and his wife, Roberta. Even when I went to Vegas to see Elvis and Vernon, I stayed in the suite and sometimes wouldn't go downstairs. The shows became routine to me. I liked it much more when I could have Elvis playing the piano and singing at home. I liked the glamor of getting out, but perhaps I had become too used to it and was getting spoiled. You know, I have to be one of the most vain women I know, and Vernon once told me that he thought I'd much rather be admired than loved because everything around me and about me had to be perfect, but I was discovering that life isn't perfect,

300   that life isn't what Dee Presley thought it was going to be, that people weren't going to live up to my expectations.

"The problem was that I was so wrapped up in my own disappointment that I couldn't really see what was going on. Everything was kept from me, anyway. Their lives weren't like mine; they weren't carried around on a silver platter and petted. When Elvis was having problems, it wasn't Dee that everything came down on. If someone even looked at me crossways, I would have run to my room and cried and everyone would have been in there in a second comforting me! My God, *they* were all taking a lot of hard knocks! And there was poor Vernon, whose only goals were trying to protect Elvis and me. . . . Now I understand what he meant when he said so many times, 'Dee, you and Elvis are going to kill me.'

"The house was so empty with everyone gone so much. Everybody had something to do but me. Vernon didn't want me to have a career, and that's when I started writing songs. I wanted to be something myself, to do something fulfilling and have the attention and the focus on me. Lyrics started coming out of me and I wrote a song called 'My Lonely Heart.' Then I wrote 'Passionate State of Mind,' which was my first country-western tune. It was about a woman with an unfulfilled passion just running wild inside of her, but outside she's very meek and mild. . . .

"About four years before we separated, I took my own bedroom. I did it because Vernon would have trouble sleeping and it would keep me awake. He'd come back from a tour and come in late at night and it seemed that the only thing we could talk about was 'Well, how did it go on tour?' I guess that was the beginning of it. When Vernon would want to be very affectionate or want to make love, I had something inside of me that just didn't want to be bothered. 'Just tuck me in bed and kiss me good night on the cheek.' *Dee* couldn't be disturbed. Remember, Vernon had been a terrific lover; it bothered him when things started slacking off. He was sitting there and hurting inside.

"Vernon always told me that it would be impossible for him to live without me. He said, 'Dee, I would love you under all circumstances. I would never leave you. If you lost your eyesight, I would be your eyes.' Now isn't that beautiful? That man poured his heart out to me; he had no pride when it came to loving me, but I didn't say those things to him. It would have taken me years just to be able to say them. Three years later perhaps if I had the same thing to do over again I could have looked him in the eyes and said, 'Vernon, I cannot live without you.'

"Vernon taught me everything I knew about love, and when I turned him away he would come to me and say, 'Dee, is this all there is?' Then I made the big mistake: I told him that if there was ever another woman that he could take to bed, to find her. I said, 'Vernon, as far as I'm concerned, that part is gone.' He said, 'Dee, you're young and beautiful. It's got to be there.'

"I'll tell you what . . . People might say, 'She used her sex as a weapon, but how could she have not enjoyed it?' Well, I did enjoy it, but I knew exactly what to get with it. I used it to get what I wanted, even in marriage. There were times when we wouldn't be together for up to a month and he would ask me if I ever thought about what we had lost. The problem was that Vernon was having trouble with his health then, and if I had been more experienced instead of having to be petted and loved all the time myself, I could have made it different. I didn't realize that you had to do certain things to your husband—had to touch them and caress them—all right, I can't get any plainer than that. I just could not do them. I was too inhibited, and I guess it all goes back to my upbringing. They were *my* hangups. Perhaps that's why many women lose their husbands today— because they do not satisfy, and make love, and do all of the things necessary to please their men. Now I realize those things.

"Vernon was forever loving me and he was the one that did everything, and he always had a fear of not pleasing me. He just wanted to make me happy. But my ways, the ways that I had been taught, was not to give yourself without getting something in return. I could hardly even so much as talk about these things freely and feel comfortable about them; to me, they were disgusting and vulgar, whereas now, I can.

"He never stopped desiring me, but if it wasn't exactly the

302 way I wanted it or was used to it, disappointment would come on my face and I would want to get up and leave. What man can make love to a woman with disappointment on her face?

"I was never the aggressive one. No wonder he was sitting up at night and I was laying there on my bed, feeling sad, wanting to turn back the tide. He knew it, too. He'd say, 'Dee, you don't always say what you feel. You're a born actress. You can pull that little girl act and cry and be so sweet and never open your mouth and I just want to do everything for you, but there's one thing I'd like to tell you about yourself: You know how to kill a man without even opening up your mouth! You just give him enough rope, Dee, and when that rope gets tight enough, you just take it and let a man hang himself.'

"I'll tell you something else that happened which bothered me—he let himself go. He became fat and lazy and not romantic, and I had always wanted to make him over so that he looked like a playboy. That's one thing that a man makes a mistake by doing with me, because I never did it and it bothers me tremendously. Vain? Yes. I had Vernon looking so good that even Elvis was jealous of him! I'm serious—that's how good he looked before he let himself go. If he had done what I wanted him to, he would have stayed in good condition. That was the way I wanted him to be. I wanted him driving convertibles, going out on yachts, doing all the things that I wanted to do.

"Maybe I was trying to hurt him back in some way, I don't know; I didn't understand what I was feeling. I'd say, 'God, Vernon, I wish you could find somebody to excite you!' You don't know what it did to me when he started not being able to make love to me. I let the whole thing happen and sent him away to another woman. Oh, do I regret it!

"First, he started coming home less and less. Right around our thirteenth anniversary he called me from Las Vegas and said that he was going to Palm Springs for a birthday party for Colonel Parker. I could feel then that there must be another woman. He kept asking me if there was anything wrong, and I just said, 'You do what you have to do.'

"I started traveling, going on trips. I remember calling Vernon at his office to tell him that I was going on a vacation

alone. I just said, 'If a plane leaves today, I'll be on it.' At one
time, I would have never said something like that to him because he was in full command. He was my master.

"I didn't find out about Sandy Miller until nineteen-seventy-
four. My own sons knew things about my husband, and they
could never tell me because they were on the payroll. Besides,
there are some things that you cannot tell mothers, and I'm
glad in a way because the hurt would have been so deep."

"You *sonofabitch!*"

The words came hissing out of Dee like an adder, stinging
Vernon as soon as he hung up the phone. The expression on
his face showed that he was just as surprised as she was by her
uncharacteristic profanity, but she was enraged. The phone
calls from strange female voices were becoming more frequent.
First it had been "Betty from Dallas" calling; then little snippets
of information about this other woman. But this was the first
time that Vernon ever took the call in front of her, openly acknowledging the fact that he was involved with another woman.

"I want you out of the house tonight!" she demanded, leaping
to the attack.

"Dee," he said, slowly shaking his head, "that's not like you.
That was so unbecoming; that hurt me more than anything in
the world. If that's the way I make you, you're right: I should
get out."

"Well, I'm sorry if my language offended you, Vernon," she
said insincerely, "but I think I dislike you very much tonight
and it just came out that way!"

Now that it was finally happening, Dee was surprised at how
shocked and scorned she felt—how hurt, and how she felt the
need to hurt him back.

"All these years, Vernon," she said, zeroing in on her anger,
"you took all of your pent-up emotions and threw them at me.
Now you're doin' the same thing you always accused me
of—how should I act? There was a time when I might have
tolerated it, but not anymore. I want you *out* of the house tonight!"

Dee Presley stood there, reddening, rigid, and self-righteous,

304 believing in her anger, resenting him; Vernon Presley, with his guilty, hangdog expression, looked suddenly vulnerable. The words flew like perfectly aimed arrows.

"Vernon, maybe you'd better go to her, 'cause I don't know if I ever want you to touch me again."

"I don't want to leave you like this," he apologized, "but if I don't fly out there now there's a chance she might take her own life."

The gravity of the moment set in during the silence that followed; for the first time the risks they were running and the possibility of losing each other seemed all too real. Dee recognized the threshold of separation, but she also knew that she would let him go without putting up much of a fuss. That wasn't her way: She would let it rest and let him simmer in it to think about what he was really doing. Go ahead, then, she said to herself. Whoever she is, wherever she is. She collected herself.

"Vernon," she said tenderly, searching his face now, "I want to ask you something. Can you ever take anybody else or treat anybody the way you treated me?"

The question was as close as her pride would allow her to asking him if he still loved her.

"Hell, no," Vernon Presley said earnestly, understanding the question. Something in his eyes always told the truth. She would be the only woman in his life no matter what happened.

He went in the bedroom to pack his bags. She went in the kitchen to get a cup of coffee and wondered if she had made a mistake.

"When he was out on those tours with other women," reflects David, "me and Ricky always knew it, man, but how could we say anything to our mother when our careers and positions were at stake? See, Vernon took really good care of us on tour and workin' together. We became sort of like best friends. You know, we started covering for each other—you do this for me and I'll do that for you. Vernon never had to ask me, 'Don't say nothing to Dee,' because he never had to worry about it. I never said anything or never even questioned him."

"Yeah, I'd introduce him sometimes to other women when

we were on the road," Rick says, "because we trusted each other. He met Sandy in Vegas and they started dating and I really didn't know what was happening with Mom but it seemed that she was kind of wanting to get out of the situation. It was her idea for the separation and that's when Sandy was in the picture. Before that, I wouldn't ever go back to my mom, because how could I do that to my dad?"

When Vernon started seeing Sandy Miller, it wasn't a question of divided loyalties or a conspiracy of silence against their mother. The boys felt that Vernon and Dee's marital affairs were their own business and better left alone, and the situation did not begin to put serious pressure on them until they saw the marriage about to break up.

Sandy Miller, the woman that Vernon Presley was seeing, was in her thirties, a divorced lab technician and nurse from Denver, Colorado, a mother of three small children. She was an altogether different woman from Dee Presley. Rick and David described her as a "good at taking care of Vernon," simple, not demanding, without their mother's deeply ingrained standards and expectations, neither fiery nor self-centered.

Vernon moved Sandy and her children to Memphis, into an apartment, then into a house on Old Hickory Road. Since he professed to Dee from the beginning of his relationship with her that he always intended to continue his marriage, Dee couldn't imagine how he expected her to react to the knowledge that the other woman was living right there in town. Vernon felt the need to let her know what was going on, but at first, after they had decided to separate, he told her that she was nothing but a housekeeper. Soon the truth came out. Dee wondered whether Vernon had brought the woman to humiliate her somehow, or because he genuinely loved her and wanted her close to him, or because he was trying to see how Dee would react to it. Did he expect to be able to have a foot at home and a foot at her house? Did he want to see her squirm uncomfortably now that he had taken up her advice and found another woman?

One afternoon, after she had learned that Sandy was in Memphis, she had packed her bags and was preparing to go to Nashville. Vernon appeared at the house right before she was to

306 leave, to say good-bye. Their separation hung in the balance, and he was there to lay the cards on the table.

"Dee, as long as I'm going to have to leave the house, I'm going to need a housekeeper where I'm living," he said, "and I don't want you going by there to surprise her." Then, he told her all about Sandy.

"My," Dee said as nonchalantly as possible after he was finished. "That's very interesting, Vernon. Is she pretty?"

"You know damn well that you don't have to worry about other women, Dee," he offered to her, probing and mollifying. "She's fairly good looking, but she's not beautiful. You know how I feel about you, baby. God gave you beauty of body, Dee, but he also gave you beauty of spirit."

The last words were beautiful and disarming, but Dee was determined to draw him out.

"Have there been others besides this one?" she pressed.

"Noooo!" he exclaimed.

She thought for a second and asked bluntly, "Well, what do you want me to do about it?"

"I had hoped that you would have gotten her out of my life," he said matter-of-factly. She was surprised, but recognized the challenge. He wanted to see how she felt about the possibility of losing him. He wanted to see how much she cared.

"Am I hearing what you're saying?"

"I hoped you'd get her out of my life," he repeated, hurt. "How do you feel about it?"

Dee paused, not really knowing what she wanted to do, but determined to play out her apathy, so as not to let him know how hurt she really was. They were sitting by the pool in their backyard, and she walked over to him and kissed him gently on the forehead.

"Vernon, I'm going to give you time so that you can think about all this. She's already here, isn't she? Okay, then. Go stay with her, but come home when you need to or want to, and I'll call you if I feel the same way."

As always, he broke first. "Please don't hurt me like this," he said tenderly. "I think you're makin' a big mistake, Dee, because when I walk through that door, it's gonna be painful for 307 both of us."

It was Dee's pride speaking now, plain and simple. She believed her words, because she felt that he was "wrong" but still wanted to understand him and allow him the latitude to make his own decision. "You know that one of us is going to have to go, sooner or later," she said, "but I'm willing to give you time, Vernon, to decide."

There, it was said, but so much left unsaid. The car was packed and ready to go. Tears brimmed in their eyes, and there arose a look of desperation in Vernon's face.

"Stay with me!" he pleaded suddenly. "I'll promise to get her out of my life if you don't go! Promise me that I'll never lose you!"

Dee was shackled in her decision. She couldn't open to him while the other woman was still there. Something in her wanted to stay, but she felt that she had to be strong, she had to show him her integrity, her sense of self-esteem, even if it meant the martyrdom of their marriage. Like Elvis, she would protect her own wounded feelings by building a wall around them, falling into the attitude of the "woman wronged." She retaliated.

"You'd better keep her, Vernon," she said tersely and intractably, avoiding his eyes. "I could never promise you that."

She got in her car with her secretary and drove off, leaving him standing there.

"I didn't make the final decision that night; it went on and on. Everyday, he came home and we talked. He sat there and had coffee with me, hour after hour, sometimes well into the morning. Sometimes when we were together, it was so beautiful, just like when we were first married. And when we made love he was so kind and gentle. It's funny that after we were going to split up was when we began to desire each other again."

Vernon was in Vegas with Elvis when Dee decided to "drop by" and pay a visit to Sandy Miller. It was a summer day in

308 June 1974, and she had decided to finally indulge her curiosity to see just who this "other woman" was. She knew that Sandy had just moved into the new home that Vernon had purchased on Old Hickory. Dee had been out at her pool that afternoon, so she was dressed in silver pants, sandals, and a black see-through blouse. She didn't want to frighten her; she simply meant to communicate that Dee Presley was alive and kicking, and that she knew what was going on.

She pulled up to the house, got out, and entered it confidently, as if she owned it. In the cluttered living room she encountered Becky Yancey, one of the secretaries at Graceland who had been helping Sandy get things in order, and an unassuming-looking woman, her hair mussed, wearing old rolled up jeans and a painting smock. She was holding a mop.

Dee first stared stonily at Becky, both surprised and disappointed to see her there. "Well, Becky, what are *you* doin' here?" she asked, leaving her fumbling for a reply. She turned to the other woman.

"You must be Sandy," she said, grinning tautly. "I've been meanin' to come by and meet you. I'm Dee."

Sandy smiled weakly and uncertainly. She mumbled a meek "It's nice to meet you."

"My, my," she said temperamentally, a note of friendly condescension in her voice. "So *this* is where you're gonna live?"

She looked cursorily around the room, not truly interested.

"What a step down," she then pronounced, as if she were sorry for both of them.

Sandy just stood there, very much stunned, trying to keep her composure. "Think I'll have a look around," Dee announced.

Dee knew that she'd held the trump card from the moment she walked into the room (she had, after all, the element of surprise and the legitimacy of being Vernon's wife), but when she returned to the living room, she delivered the *coup de grâce*. She was going to confront Sandy head on, with compassion, sincerity, an element of reproach, and a bit of aloofness.

"Sandy, do you *love* him?" The question was a well-aimed arrow. "I sure hope that you love him, Sandy, because sometimes when you love somebody you just have to open your hand

and let them go—you don't hold on too tight. I want you to be 309
sure because I'm gonna let you have him. He needs you to take
care of him."

Mop still in hand, Sandy was speechless as Dee bent to her
little daughter. "This is your daughter, isn't it? My, she's pretty.
Who do you tell her my husband is?"

The question hit hard. Dee wanted to see what sort of woman
she was, whether or not she felt guilty, but she didn't answer.
Just then her daughter Laurie offered, "You mean Vernon?"

Dee shook her head sadly. "My, Sandy, she's quite young to
be calling him *Vernon*, don't you think?"

Then she was gone, as quickly as she had appeared.

Her phone was ringing when she got home. Vernon Presley
was calling from Las Vegas, and he was agitated.

"What's wrong, Vernon?" she asked innocently.

"I just heard of the dramatic entrance, that's all," he said. "I
told her it would be like that. I said, 'Dee will never hurt you
with her hand but with words she'll probably make you feel like
crawling into the nearest crack so you can get out of her sight.' "

"Well," she said lightly, "that wasn't my intention at all."

When it became clear that there wasn't going to be a reconciliation, the matter of separation and divorce hung in the balance and other parties involved started feeling the shock waves.
Elvis, from his standpoint, couldn't understand Vernon's disclo-
sure of Sandy to Dee in the first place. He knew Dee well, and
he knew that if his daddy was going to have a girl friend, it
would have been wiser to keep her under covers. "Why did you
have to tell her in the first place, Daddy? Didn't you know that
she would deliver the ultimatum?"

Dee's sons were caught in the middle. "What do you do
when your dad wants you to be cool but you love and respect
your mom?" ponders Rick. "The divorce thing almost split the
family, man, because Vernon is Daddy, Dee is your mom, and
you work for Elvis, so there's controversy as to who to be loyal
to when it gets right down to it. I didn't think that it was right
that we be brought into it, and that's what Elvis requested. The
first thing that we had to do was to be fair to ourselves. Elvis as-

310 sured us that no matter what happened, it wouldn't affect our relationship. He said, 'It's their problem, let them work it out. Don't let it bother you guys—we got a job to do here.' "

Billy, who spent less time around Elvis and Vernon and more around Dee, also felt the pull. "That was the most pressure I've ever felt in my life," he says. "It's almost like having to take sides, and that was the last thing I wanted to do. I think Elvis accepted what Vernon did because he was concerned for his father's happiness, but he still wanted Dee to know that she was a part of the family even though they were getting a divorce."

Looking back, it is easier for Dee to understand the quandary that her boys found themselves in. "At times they were more loyal to Elvis than they were to me," she recognizes. "They loved me, of course, but Elvis had been such a big part of their lives. You've got to keep in mind that Sandy traveled with Vernon on the road, so Ricky and David were with them. That was bound to have affected them."

One thing is certain: Neither Ricky or David ever felt anything even close to resentment or bitterness against Sandy, particularly when Vernon's health slipped seriously and she stepped in as nurse as well as girl friend. "Sandy took good care of Daddy," says David, "and that's why we admired and respected her—because we love Vernon. She's a good woman, man. She took better care of him than anybody else could have."

Time passed. Vernon and Dee lived apart, and the moments of tenderness and love they still shared together were interspersed with Vernon's implacable frustration. It seemed, at times, that they were on their way back together. They spent a weekend together in Vegas and Vernon joined Dee and Linda Thompson for a vacation in San Juan that Dee remembers as among their most beautiful moments together. But then there were acidic moments and outbursts. Vernon felt vulnerable because, in the event of divorce, Dee would hold the trump card of his public infidelity. His relationship with Sandy was known throughout Memphis. When Dee tried to make him face it once, there were cruel threats. Dee remembers calling Vernon at a hotel on the Sunset Strip where he was staying with

Sandy, which provoked a tirade of abuse. He had never talked to her like that before.

"What is wrong with you, Vernon!" she admonished. "Is your woman in the room? She can't be getting any pleasure out of this!"

"Go ahead, Dee! Get your lawyers! See if I give a damn! And I'll tell you what—you'd better not expect to get too much out of this because you won't! And you know something else? Something just might be done to that pretty face of yours!"

She was deathly silent, parrying the threat in her mind with the knowledge that Vernon Presley would never do anything like that; but the mere fact that he had said it paralyzed her.

"That don't frighten me, Vernon," she replied weakly.

"Or," he said, adding fuel to the fire, "I just might get some of this bunch that works for Elvis to get up and say they've been to bed with you!"

Dee winced as the words cut deep and burned like dry ice. Her knees buckled and she fell to the floor, weeping, feeling frightened and helpless, wondering if she had ever hurt him that bad.

"If I would have let him," she reflects stoically, "he would have crushed my spirit. But there was never anybody that could do that to me—not Bill, not Vernon. The more cruel things he said, the more determined I was not to let him get me down. I decided that I wasn't going to lose sleep over a man; it wasn't worth it."

Still, as 1974 turned into 1975, Dee and Vernon played an emotional tug of war with each other, keeping all options open, but all possibilities of reconciliation seemed to end on the afternoon of February 1, 1975, when Vernon was stricken with a heart attack at his home on Old Hickory Street. He was rushed to Baptist Memorial Hospital, where he remained for a month. Everyone in the family was devastated by the news, but Elvis, then in the hospital himself to be cut off his narcotic medications, was terrified that his daddy was going to die. He would live the rest of his life with that fear.

Suddenly Vernon Presley was a very sick man who needed constant attention. Dee, for the first time, felt all but cut off

312 from him. They spoke quite a bit on the phone but the one time she visited him in his hospital suite was too much to abide. She went there and was horrified to see how bad he looked. Sandy was at his bedside and there was a thunderstorm raging outside. So many feelings were rising inside her that she could hardly speak. Vernon looked gaunt and fragile, like a man who has been to the edge and come back, and all that she could muster was a "How are you feelin', baby?"

His voice sounded empty and pathetic. "I almost died, Dee," he sighed, and she began to cry.

If only she could tell him how much she loved him and wanted to be with him, to take care of him, she thought; but it seemed that it would all be up to Sandy now. There, in that hospital room, as the three of them remained awkwardly silent, Dee began to grasp the depth of her loss. She could only look away, out the window, and resign herself to the turn of events.

Bad times were coming, and Vernon's heart attack seemed to be the harbinger. He had tried to stand at the core of his son's existence and now that the condition of his health was permanently changed, he would be less and less able to withstand pressure and make a difference in Elvis's life.

For Dee, it meant learning how to be alone for the first time in her adult life, learning how to live with memories, regrets, and her love.

As she stood there in the hospital room, Vernon expressed concern that she would be driving in such bad weather. "You best be heading home, Dee," he said protectively. "Looks like a pretty bad storm outside."

Dee also knew that it was time to go, but for other reasons. "But the storm's on the inside, baby," she said. "It's all on the inside."

"I had a real fear of him not being with me anymore. I was there in his life for seventeen years; thirteen of them right by his side, and there was a lot of feeling there. I really don't think that either of us has ever fallen out of love with the other, and I wonder if it would have worked if we went back. Would he have thought that I went back out of pity? What man could have lived with that?

"I can say honestly that I don't think Vernon ever got over me, the same way I'll never get over him. After things started getting bad between us and we separated, I sold Vernon our house on Dolan and moved into another place and Vernon moved in with Sandy and her children. He said to me, 'Dee, your house is haunting me to death. You're everywhere.' I said, 'Good, Vernon, I hope that in every room of that house you see my face and hear my voice. I hope that I never leave. I never will, but I can never come back there because somebody else was there.' That's the way I felt. I was glad that Vernon had Sandy to take care of him, but I still felt that resentment.

"I pulled the car in one night along the drive. I had the top down and it was a beautiful night with a lovely moon. I thought about the weddings and birthday parties; I thought about Christmases and about where Dee Presley spent her hours waiting for her family, and I thought about the woman my husband was living with. Then I thought about my very first night in Memphis, Tennessee, and I said, 'Lord, thank you for all that was good and all that was bad, and for everything that was bad, Lord, please erase it from my memory.'

Elvis Presley was saddened by the breakup of the family and worried about his father's health. When Vernon and Dee forged ahead with divorce plans, he became petrified that Vernon would not be able to withstand the experience of a publicized divorce, with all of the depositions, testimonies by other members of the family, and other unpleasantness. He was somehow sensing that time was running out, and he wanted desperately to get in touch with Dee.

One afternoon at Graceland, exactly two weeks before his death, he had Ricky get in contact with Billy, for Elvis knew that if ever there was a person who could get his mother's ear, it would be her first-born son. Elvis took the phone as soon as Rick managed to raise his brother.

"Billy," said Elvis, "I want you to do me a favor, OK? This

314   is so important, man. I need to speak to your mother. . . . I'll give you five thousand dollars if you just get her on the phone for me. That's all I want, man . . . just to talk to her."

Jesus, his voice sounds bad, Billy thought; there was an urgency and a desperation in it.

"Hell, Elvis," he said. "I don't want the money. I understand. I'll call her right now."

Billy hung up the phone and called Dee in Nashville. She returned Elvis's call immediately. When he picked up the phone, he was weeping and mumbling his words almost incoherently.

"Elvis, are you sick?" she asked anxiously.

"Naw, I'm OK, Dee," he sighed, "but I'm so worried about Daddy." Then he started to cry again. "This thing . . . this isn't what I wanted for us . . . Dee . . . everything's shot to hell it seems. The family's spread out everywhere. . . . Please, Dee . . . Don't do this to him . . . I don't want to see this happen . . . please. . . ."

Her heart sank as the premonition spread horribly over her, up her spine, making the flesh crawl. She knew that she was speaking to a drowning man, reaching out and trying to put things straight before he went under, and she began to cry, knowing in that instant that it was all going to go up in smoke and that she had to do anything not to hurt him.

"But Elvis," she said softly, trying to make him understand her hurt, "he's in love with her."

"He thinks he is," he said, trying to assuage her.

"If he's confused, Elvis, he's old enough to know better," she said sadly. "He's with her, Elvis . . . she washes his clothes and cooks for him and works in the garden and they go to the country to pick blueberries. . . . He wants her, Elvis—she's not as demanding as I was. He's comfortable with her and he doesn't have to be afraid of losin' her."

There was a silence on the phone before he sighed deeply and began to sob, and it broke her heart to hear him crying.

"Nothin' worked out the way I wanted it, Dee." He seemed to be talking to himself. "I'm losin' everything . . . Cilla . . . and now Daddy's sick and I'm scared . . . soon you'll be gone. Nothin' worked out the way I wanted it."

"Tell me, Elvis. Please, what can I do . . . anything. . . ."

He brightened a little then and she could hear hope in his voice, as if maybe at least he could put something right after all. "Promise me that you'll keep this thing outta court," he pleaded for his father. "It'll be better for everybody that way, Dee— Daddy, the boys, you—we can settle it all outta court. You'll be taken care of Dee, and live in the manner that you're accustomed . . . you know, we all want that. You know how I feel about you and the boys . . . I'll always want to take care of y'all. . . ."

Dee thought about Vernon and her sons and Lisa and Cilla and how she never wanted to hurt any of them by going into court with Vernon and agonizing over a divorce when she would have to bring up things that might hurt him.

"Don't worry, Elvis," she tried to assure him. "I understand how you feel 'cause I feel that way myself—you know what I mean? We'll find a way to work it out. Don't worry."

Elvis sighed. "Bless you, Dee," he said. "I'll never forget you. You'll always be a part of this family as far as I'm concerned, you know. I've always respected you, Dee. You came in like a lady and you bore it like a lady. I love you, Dee."

"I love you too, Elvis." The words warmed her but she was still afraid.

"Will you promise to come up here and see me when you come back home?" he said happily.

"I'll be there, Elvis."

Shaken, she hung up the phone.

CHAPTER 20

ELVIS: WHAT HAPPENED?

The subject of Red and Sonny West and the book *Elvis: What Happened?* is still a touchy one for Billy, Rick, and David. Though all three are outspoken about their feelings, David is still the most bitter. "I don't care what anybody else says," he contends angrily, "I was with him closely all that last year and that goddamned book did more than anything else to kill him because it crushed his spirit. We all saw the effect it had on him."

"It was a Judas act," Billy says simply. "It was nothing but a cheap shot that just happened to be a book. I want everybody to know that those guys were not angels trying to make Elvis improve his life. They didn't give a flying fuck about him, and that's why they did it in the first place."

"Man," reflects Rick with a philosophical tone in his voice, "the most incredible thing to me was that it was a high-school friend that did it to him—a friend of twenty years. *Twenty years!* They didn't do anybody any good except their bank books. I bet Red's sorry he did the book. The man's dead and that helped kill him."

318   On July 13, 1976, Red (Bobby) West, Elvis's bodyguard and companion for close to twenty years, and his cousin Sonny, who went to work for Elvis in the early sixties, were fired by Vernon Presley. Vernon cited a "financial" reason, but as the West boys describe it in their book, they believe the "execution," as they called it, came about "as a whim of Elvis Presley's." Red was particularly incensed because after all of their years together, Elvis simply flew out of town and left the dirty work for his daddy, leaving Red out in the cold with no warning, no income, and nothing to do. Some time after their termination, they contracted to write and publish a book—an "inside" look at Elvis Presley's life—which became *Elvis: What Happened?*

Most people have surmised that Elvis must have been disturbed about the book even though there were reports to the contrary but as with everything else in his life, its effects went much deeper than one might suspect. The knowledge of the book was the most significant final episode in the life of Elvis Presley. It removed the last emotional and psychological barriers between life and his acceptance of death.

Red and Sonny liked the prestige and life of working for Elvis, but neither liked the subordinate nature of their jobs. At the same time they were the group grouches—the most consistently unpleasant and malcontent members of the entourage. Pushy, aggressive, easily irritated, and quick to violence, their frustration levels were usually higher than those of others in the group. They took it out in any number of ways; one of them was by being unnecessarily rude to people. Elvis, over the years, had become disillusioned by the image they presented, and the disillusionment would lead to alienation. "Here you are with a multimillion-dollar organization," Rick points out. "Everybody is supposed to be professional in their jobs, and here you've got a couple of guys who should know better behaving like badass rednecks. That's when you get people coming to you saying, 'Man, what's *his* problem!' That's what was happening with Red and Sonny."

According to David, Elvis had also become disturbed by the

brusque and oftentimes crude attitude that Red West displayed
toward women on tour.

But even with their complaints and strong come-ons, it was frustration that was at the bottom of the problems that developed between Elvis and the Wests. Red was a family man with ambitions of his own. He dabbled in stunt work, acting, songwriting; he also played guitar and sang. Like everybody else in the group, Red had to take his fair share of abuse when Elvis was in a foul mood and became tired of being under his thumb. When Red got mad, he was capable of irrational violence, which precipitated a series of incidents and overreactions in security situations. This resulted in the surfeit of costly lawsuits pending against Elvis (in fact, Sonny even talks about this in their book, referring to Red's need to "control himself," and how he would have to go outside and get into a fight just to let off steam).

"If you said something that rubbed them wrong and they were mad about something," says David, "they just might hit you in the mouth. Our rule was never to react violently unless you saw somebody doing something really dangerous. The whole time I worked as a bodyguard I only had to go after people two times, but they caused about six or seven lawsuits, all for unnecessary things." Rick agrees: "Without them," he says, "there wouldn't have been problems like that. Not a single lawsuit."

The one single incident that most discredited them in Elvis's eyes and convinced him that they had to go came in 1975, at the Sahara Tahoe Hotel. As David and Ricky remember what happened, Elvis was having a small party backstage after a performance. Lisa was visiting him, and a group of people were sitting around playing cards—Charlie, Lamar, Red, Sonny, David, Ricky, Elvis, and several others. Suddenly the lights went out. David and Ricky were dispatched to investigate and see if it was a general power failure or just affecting that part of the hotel.

Outside, down the corridor, they heard a loud drunk and disorderly man intent on seeing Elvis. They questioned him, and

320   he claimed to have switched off the power. Back in the room Elvis had his gun out just in case some conspiracy was afoot, and Sonny went to see what was happening. When he arrived on the scene the man refused to leave. He then got rowdy and pushed David, whereupon Sonny stepped in and drilled him in the face with his right fist, knocking him unconscious. The man's hands were then cuffed behind his back and he was taken to the security room, where he was placed face up on a bed.

By that time he had come to. Livid with rage, he kicked out with his feet (his hands were still cuffed) and at that moment, says David, "Red just dropped down on the bed and smashed the guy in the mouth and the guy started bleeding badly— hemorrhaging. Elvis ran over and cupped his head so he wouldn't choke on his own blood. He felt so bad about the whole thing; he apologized and everything but the guy decided to sue anyway. What Red did was so cheap, man, and that's when Elvis saw those guys for who they really were."

It was no secret that the Wests had become very nettled by competition from new blood in the TCB organization. Elvis hired Sam Thompson to work security, and Al Strada also joined the group. The biggest threat to the Wests, though, was David, whom they had trained. Shortly after receiving his black belt, David was sparring with Red one day as Elvis watched. "Red hit me," he remembers, "and knocked me out! I looked at Elvis after they slapped me 'round to bring me out of it. I had respected those guys because they had a personal interest in training me and they were older, but I was through taking that shit. Elvis saw the situation. He said, 'You're a man, now, David. You're on your own,' so I got off the mats and pro- ceeded to prove to Elvis I could handle myself."

Aside from the disquieting realization that his bodyguards could be like the bullies they were supposed to protect him from, there were still additional reasons for bad blood between Elvis and the Wests. On several occasions Elvis and Red had come dangerously close to violent confrontation themselves. Rick recalls the most dangerous of them:

"We'd been in Vegas for quite a while," he says, "and things had gotten monotonous and crazy and everybody was getting on everybody else's nerves. After being up a couple of days straight with Elvis, you felt like you just had to have a break and sometimes he wouldn't give you one. After several days of this Elvis decided that he had to go to the doctor. Well, we all knew that when he wanted to go the doctor like that it was to get some dope. Red was in his room lying down and I was laying on the couch in Elvis's room when he came out. 'Get up. Let's go, man, we're goin' to the doctor.' Everybody thought it was a drag but got ready to saddle up, and I went in to get Red. He said, 'Oh man, that's a drag,' and slammed his door, and when Elvis heard that, wooo! He got pissed! He went in there and told Red that he would kill him if he didn't listen. He was mad, man! Sure, he was overreacting, but that's the way it got sometimes."

"Elvis reached for his gun," Billy remembers, "but then he stopped himself and went into his karate stance. Sonny stopped Red and Daddy was in there screaming for them to calm down. It was a bad scene."

The flareup had frightened Vernon Presley, a man not terribly partial to the Wests to begin with. "Red had always rubbed Vernon wrong," Dee remembers. "He came in early in our relationship and opened his mouth and Vernon threatened to fire him. He always worried about Red and Elvis clashing one day because he knew that if it happened, it would be bad. Whenever we were away on vacation, that was one of his concerns." Rick elaborates on the cause of some of the tension between Red and Vernon: "Red always resented my mom for dropping Bill Stanley and marrying Vernon," he says. "He knew Bill Stanley in Germany and once said, 'You guys got a really raw deal.' "

Sonny West had also long fallen into disfavor. According to the boys, Elvis always felt closer to Red anyway. "I'll tell you something that Elvis used to say about Sonny West," Rick says. "He'd say, 'That's the only guy on the payroll that I pay to just stay away from me. I have to pay him to stay away!' Sonny just never stopped talking. He was the loudest, most obnoxious guy in the group."

Dave Hebler was the third in line of those guys purged in the

322 Firing of July 13. A floater who had held and lost many jobs before meeting Elvis through Ed Parker, Hebler was a relative latecomer to Elvis's entourage hired expressly to beef up the TCB team of bodyguards with his karate talent. From the beginning he was a mercenary, not unlike a professional soldier who would go where the opportunities were best. He was never really intimate with Elvis, who suspected his loyalty, particularly when he seemed to side with the Wests in disputes. When they were canned, he was also given his walking papers.

One gets the impression from them that the whole thing was pure whimsy and capriciousness on Elvis's part—they use the words "whim" and "execution"—as if Elvis woke up in a bad mood one morning and decided to fire them because he had nothing better to do. All three of them were fired for the same reasons that anyone is usually fired from a job: They had become undesirable as employees, and the truly surprising thing is not that they were fired, but that they managed to last as long as they did!

"When they were gone," Rick remembers, "things worked much more smoothly. We didn't have to worry about Red getting drunk because he'd had an argument with his wife and then hit some kid or beat up a reporter. We never really understood what a nuisance those guys were until they were gone."

Well, as destiny would have it, Elvis hadn't heard the last from his former bodyguards, who were burning with anger at the unexpected termination. If one single emotion emerges from their book, it is a seething sense of bitterness at Elvis for firing them—casting them off, cutting them off from the munificence of their salaries, expense accounts, and bonuses. "There was a lot of anger," Rick says, "and that's the main reason they did the book." "They were trying to get back at him," agrees Billy, "and that's all there is to it." However you look at it, the human emotion of vengeance was what spawned *Elvis: What Happened?*; without it, the whole thing would never have been possible. Personal vendettas are serious business, particularly when they become the motivation for such a book.

It was the World News Corporation that bankrolled the initial contact with Messrs. West, West, and Hebler to cooperate on a

book about the "personal" life of Elvis Presley. The boys would
only have to feed the delicate information about their ex-boss's
drug taking, sexual proclivities, and whatever else into the tape
recorder of Steve Dunleavy, a Rupert Murdoch employee
imported from Australia to write for the *Star* and the *Post*, who
would do the rest.

Elvis: What Happened? was not so much guilty of deception
as it was of the trivialization and sensationalization of Elvis's
life. Here, then, is the indignity and cruelty of the book: It
garishly highlighted the blackness in Elvis's life—the drugs, the
self-destruction, his most selfish, irresponsible, and insensitive
moments—without allowing him the dignity of understanding
or compassion; it pointed out and pumped up his destruction
without recognizing the despair that unleashed it; it robbed
him, finally, of self-respect because it rendered him inhuman
and therefore grotesque since the book was primarily a work of
vengeance that sought to exploit and not understand, to simply
"reveal" and not explain.

One final aspect of the book is worth taking note of before
considering its effect on Elvis Presley, which is the noble and
righteous hope expressed by the authors at the end of the book
to "save" Elvis from himself. The passage in question arrives
after Hebler expresses his one remorse about writing the book—
that his mother, who always believed that Elvis was "God-fear-
ing and a Christian," would now have her illusions about her
hero shattered. "All three," Dunleavy, the coauthor of the book,
observes, "despite their obvious bitterness about the firing and
their realization that Presley felt nothing for them, pray and
hope that Presley will read the book and come to the realization
that his life is leading him on a path to disaster." Then Sonny
West lays down the "challenge" to his ex-boss: "He will read,"
he says, "and he will get hopping mad at us because he knows
that every word is the truth and we will take a lie-detector test to
prove it. But just maybe it will do some good."

"The last time I talked to Sonny," Billy says, responding to
this "challenge," "I kept telling him that I thought the book was
a cheap shot and he was saying that he thought it would make
Elvis straighten out. I said, 'The hell with you, man, you *know*

324 damned well that nobody or nothing would make Elvis straighten out unless *he himself* wanted to!' " "No, you've got to realize why they did it," Rick adds with finality. "There was no love or compassion or anything—they did it for the money."

In truth, there is no reason to believe that the Wests were not as saddened and shaken by the decline and fall of Elvis Presley as anyone around him. They had, after all, spent long amounts of time as part of his life and until their estrangement from his confidence their loyalty had been unshakable. But these hopes were stuck on the front page of the book as if it were the sole justification and prime motive for its existence. In all seriousness, one could think of much better ways to try to reform his life than by publishing a scandalous book that could have damaged his career and did destroy his self-esteem.

To many people who knew Elvis well, this contention of doing the book to "help" Elvis, which the authors clung to when faced with Elvis's sudden death and the questions of the press, seemed nothing more than a nauseating attempt to justify the book and a way for the authors to assuage their own guilt at the prospect of making a large amount of money on someone else's misery—someone who had supported them for years and greatly enriched the quality of their lives. That being the case, Red and Sonny West were boldfaced liars; on the other hand, if they sincerely believed it would help Elvis after all those years of knowing his character, then they were merely fools. Most likely, they were both.

It didn't take the Boss long to know what was going on. "As soon as Joe Esposito heard about the book," remembers David, "he called us all into a room and said, 'OK, boys, this is *it.*' " What followed was a TCB summit meeting to tell Elvis about the book and plan strategy, the kind of meeting that Elvis only held after the most serious events and problems in his life. Ashen faced, Elvis just stood there in complete disbelief. It had never even occurred to him that they would ever *think* of doing something like that to him! "In 1977, when he heard about the book," Rick says, considering Elvis's overall state and the effect of the news, "his whole life went like *that.*" (He snaps his

fingers.) "That was the final blow—the heaviest thing that could   325
have happened to him. How much can a man take?"

The change in Elvis was apparent; it seemed that somebody
had just pulled the plug on him. "He was miserable," says Rick.
"He would relate to me and David and Billy Smith and Esposito and say things like 'Hey man, everything's gonna be cool—
this book's not gonna hurt me,' but you could tell that the man
was just trying to convince himself. We were trying our best not
to let it bum everything out. When he'd really get down, we'd
say, 'Come on, Boss, don't worry about it. Let's not let this
thing bring you down. Those SOB's can't hurt you with literature like that.' You'd find yourself being very, very careful about
your actions and things you said around him. The slightest reference to the book could depress him."

"It hit him so hard," David observes, "because Elvis was
always so private about everything he did for his whole damn
life. He was so freaked out that they would even consider doing
it. That last year when we were back in town and I would spend
the night with him, he would talk about that book every night.
Every single night, man."

According to both Dee and David, Elvis knew the precise nature of the material in the book. "He had his own people watching every move," David says. "I think he had his lawyer out
there, too. . . . He read the manuscript when the thing was
finished and they had a rough copy. He had access to everything." Dee recalls that before the book was licensed to Ballantine Books, Incorporated, for publication, it had been rejected
by another publisher and somehow a bootleg copy of the outline
and presentation was leaked. Dee managed to see it during a
visit to Los Angeles. "I was sick when I saw how it would make
Elvis look," she says. "I was in total shock. I was so upset that I
called Vernon up and said, 'Vernon, this book is going to ruin
all of us! This book is going to *kill*.' "

In Elvis's mind, the knowledge that the book was being steadily prepared for publication was like living with a time bomb
ticking relentlessly away right underneath him, which would
change everything when it exploded.

326   First, he worried about his own family. "He was very concerned about his daughter," Rick says. "Then there was Cilla,
who knew what was going on but didn't know he was that heavily into it. Vernon didn't know the full extent, either. Elvis was
worried that if he did, Daddy might have another heart attack
and die."

Elvis's image had remained unsullied until the final year of
his life, and his anxieties about the public reaction to the book
are obvious. Hebler came closest to recognizing this when he
lamented the fact that his dear old mother—as a typical Elvis
fan—would be so shocked to know the "truth" about him. Elvis
feared that once his fans learned that he was not the paragon of
virtue and goodness, it would crack open his career and allow
his fans to peer into the gaping fissure and see him as a mon-
strous fraud. He feared that the book would besmirch everything
wholesome he had ever stood for in his life.

Greil Marcus made an interesting speculation about *Elvis:
What Happened?* in *Rolling Stone* magazine following Elvis's
death. "The feeling I get, reading stuff like this," he wrote, "is
that Elvis may well have wanted the book to appear; that he
wanted the burden and glory of acting the King removed once
and for all; that he wanted, finally, relief."

"Sure, he wanted to finally be able to let down and relax,"
says Rick. "He wanted people to see that he was human—that's
what it was all boiling down to—that he made mistakes in life.
But the thing about Elvis was he didn't want people to know details about him. He never did."

Elvis built his entire life around his public and stage per-
sonae, where everything came together to single him out and
shape his destiny as "Elvis Presley." Psychologically and emotionally the book actualized what was perhaps his greatest fear in
life—of not being able to be "Elvis Presley" any longer. The process had already begun with anxieties about his age, his looks,
his performing ability—now his public image had been violated
too.

Sometimes his rage would well up inside of him like a poi-
sonous vapor and his temper would get the better of him. Ironically, Red and Sonny had told Dunleavy that Elvis once

thought about having Mike Stone "wasted" after his divorce from Priscilla, and Dunleavy had played that card to the hilt in the book. Neither Red nor Sonny could ever have known that when Elvis's bitterness at what they were trying to do to him got bad, they came far closer to being the victims of his wrath than Mike Stone ever did. The only difference was that Elvis wasn't going to have someone else do it: He almost did it himself.

"Several times he woke me up during the middle of the night in LA, dressed, ready to go, with a couple of guns on," David says. "I was the only one he came to, because he knew how I felt about it. I'd put my gun on and say, 'OK, let's go,' but I knew what I was doing—I knew that he wouldn't go through with it, but I'd still go along. I told Vernon that he was thinking about it and what was happening and he said, 'David, if he says let's go get them, go with him, but on the way there you throw every shot you can think of in there—bring up Priscilla, bring up Lisa, me, anything.' So even before he got to my room, I never thought, 'Well, were gonna get 'em this time'; I'd think, 'He's upset again and I gotta talk him out of it.'

"So we'd be driving over to where Elvis *knew* they were and I'd say things like, 'Elvis, when we're in jail, can I have a color television set in my cell?' or 'Do you think we'll have adjoining cells?' Just to break his thinking. Meanwhile, he's still madder than hell and I'd say something like 'Elvis, what are you gonna do with Lisa? You're gonna be in jail for the rest of your life. What're you gonna tell *her?*' Then he'd cool down and start really thinking about the Bible and the Ten Commandments. 'Man, this is the devil runnin' away with me, making me mean,' he'd say. Once he said, 'I'd like to kill those guys,' and then he said, 'Man, I couldn't do that; I loved those guys.' "

CHAPTER 21

"AND NOW THE END IS NEAR"

Waiting for the appointed moment, Rick languished backstage with the Boss while people pressed like sardines in the front rows up against the stage fixed their eyes on the wings in anticipation of the King's entrance.

The chant escalated—"WE WANT ELVIS! ELVIS! ELVIS!"—taking on the timeless cadences of mass gatherings like great sports events, political conventions, or an Elvis Presley concert. The stage was lit more uniformly than usual by the CBS television crew there to film the concert for posterity and prime-time viewing as per a lucrative contract hammered out between the Colonel and CBS executives. Everywhere large studio lights had been strategically placed to facilitate perfect taping conditions for the cameramen, transforming the stage into a fluorescent steambath.

It was June 21, 1977, and it was muggy in Rapid City, South Dakota. A documentary crew had been feverishly busy all day getting footage of Elvis fans for a special preface to the live performance. Elvis's staunchest and most adoring loyalists would

330 declare their undying love and explain why they had come all the way from such and such a small town in the Midwest just to be at the concert ("I have my little daughter with me," explained one lady fan, "and I've *always* talked about how great he was when I was growing up so she had no idea who he is! And a kid just can't grow up not knowing Elvis, is how I feel! He is *just* the King! He will *always* be the King no matter what. . . .").

Elvis was standing off to the side in the right wing before he would make a specially designated entrance for the cameramen, dressed and ready to go, as usual, garbed that night in a yellowish-beige jumpsuit with a golden sun rising in relief on his chest in an Inca mosaic of precious stones and golden thread, the gold-fringed collar in matching pattern and the gold-studded belt hung tightly on his waist, centered by an enormous rectangular buckle. The same gold-encrusted design adorned the sharply flared pantlegs all the way down to the white patent leather boots.

The Boss seemed completely absorbed as Rick stood by him, the light from the stage dancing off the Martin guitar that hung off Elvis's shoulder. His hair was sprayed and combed back carefully, his chin encroached down into his collar. Everything seemed ready to go, but it seemed somehow different that night because Elvis had too much on his mind. Rick knew that the cameras were making the difference.

It was the first time that Elvis would be in front of cameras of *any* kind in quite some time. The criticism of the tours during the previous year churned in his mind ("*His attempts to perpetuate his mystique of sex and power end in weak self-parody,*" *Variety* had pronounced: "*Elvis is neither looking or sounding good. He's thirty pounds overweight: he's puffy, white faced, and blinking against the lights*"), and what seemed strange as they stood there was that the cameras—friends to Elvis's career for so long—now seemed like cold intruders, even adversaries.

Elvis was tired, troubled, ravaged by drugs, and grossly overweight; he looked terrible, and he knew it. For the first time in his life he had to step out to public scrutiny without the benefit of his good appearance, knowing that the cameras would unsympathetically reflect all that had happened to him and all that he had become. He felt naked.

Vernon Presley sat out front in the audience, knowing how important and difficult the night would be for his son. He looked frail and wan since his heart attack, and Elvis would announce during the show how nice it was to have Daddy back on tour for the first time since his illness. He would also introduce Ginger Alden as "my new girl friend" and she would stand to bask in the exhilarating spotlight of national exposure. Everyone else in the TCB entourage was assembled and deployed, knowing that Elvis would have to rise to the occasion, hoping for the best, worrying.

The band broke into the rumbling barrage of drums that led into *Also sprach Zarathustra* and the introductory strains of "See See Rider" and "That's All Right (Mama)." Rick again glanced at the Boss: He had that faraway, lost look of a man pondering his life and staring into the abyss of himself, when the images and events of a life all seem to blow through a mind at once. Rick had seen that look before, when Elvis would wax philosophical about something. Still, he wondered what was tumbling through Elvis's mind . . . probably Gladys . . . Cilla and Lisa . . . Linda . . . Daddy being so sick . . . the bad articles . . . now Red and Sonny were writing that book about him. He knew how tired Elvis was as the Boss licked his parched lips, took a deep breath, and steadied himself.

Elvis frowned sadly and turned to him. "Know what, Rick? I may not look too good for my television special tonight, but I'll look good in my coffin."

And with that, Elvis Presley stepped out to face America for the last time.

CHAPTER 22

MOTHER AND CHILD REUNION

Come lovely and soothing death,
Undulate round the world, serenely arriving, arriving,
In the day, in the night, to all to each,
Sooner or later delicate death.

> Walt Whitman,
> *When Lilacs Last in the Dooryard Bloom'd*

It was meant to happen.
I sincerely believe that.
He was being called on to go.
There couldn't have been a better way for him to go;
or a better place than where it was
and how it happened.

> David Stanley

The bright lights of Memphis twinkled in the distance and the
Mississippi snaked sluggishly off into nothingness as the roller

334   coaster slowly climbed to a dazzling height with a jerking motion. Preparing himself for the adventure, Rick turned to wink at Elvis, who sat in the car behind him smiling with his arm around Lisa.

Lisa knew something was up because Rick and Elvis always acted like a couple of idiots to make her laugh when they took her out to Libertyland. Rick stood and perched himself on the side of his car and at the split second as the train paused before it dipped, he wailed like a banshee into the night and leapt through the air to clutch onto the rafters and side railing where he hung like a monkey to enjoy Lisa gasping and Elvis roaring with laughter. He stood there chuckling as the train disappeared down the tracks, shaking the rafters and trailing away in Lisa's long and delighted scream. When the train came around again, Rick popped back into his car and Lisa looked reproachfully at him and said, "Ricky, don't *do* that!" before they plunged again. Then they got on the Dodge 'Em bumper cars and rode for what seemed like hours before dawn, when they got back in the car to head home.

Lisa was enjoying her several weeks visiting her daddy and granddaddy at Graceland before returning to Los Angeles to start school. The weather in Memphis that August had been tropical in humidity, blistering under a southern sun that hung day after day in the sky to scorch the city, turning the poorer sections into an inferno and making it so hot that you couldn't even go outside without sweating clear through your shirt in a matter of minutes.

Elvis had returned from his last tour to spend the final few weeks of Lisa's summer vacation at Graceland and was gearing up for an eleven-day tour slated to begin on the sixteenth, when he would fly off to do a show in Portland, Oregon, and finish with two successive shows back in Memphis at the Mid-South Coliseum on the twenty-seventh and twenty-eighth. As usual he avoided the heat, preferring the air-conditioned and dehumidified atmosphere of his bedroom during the day and the cool of the night, when he would take Lisa out to Libertyland for excursions on Casey's Cannonball and the Little Dipper.

The usual contingent was there at Graceland getting ready for the tour—Charlie, Ricky, David, Dick, Billy Smith, with the other principals expected to arrive in town by the sixteenth for the tour. Ginger Alden was spending her nights with Elvis at Graceland and David and Rick were on duty as usual, alternating their nights and days on call for the Boss. Joe Esposito, who usually arrived in town a day or two before the tour to put things in order, was in town by the fifteenth. Things were progressing. Taking care of business as usual.

The Boss got up late the afternoon of the fifteenth and David then came by to talk to Elvis about his impending divorce. He was depressed about Angie, and Elvis counseled him to remain strong and keep on pushing despite his vanishing hopes for a reconciliation. David left and tried to psych himself up for the tour. At nightfall Elvis took Ginger out for a ride in his Stutz and then returned to relax and put some of his affairs in order before the tour.

Anyone passing the mansion on the night of the fifteenth or the early morning hours of the sixteenth would have seen the light burning brightly on the second floor where Elvis stayed. Rick was on duty and he was busy getting Elvis's trunks ready before David was scheduled to come on duty at noon. Rick hadn't had a chance to get his own clothes washed, folded, and packed for the tour, so he was planning to double back to his apartment when David came on. He was no longer seeing Jill, but they were still good friends and she would give him a hand.

Sometime around 2:00 A.M., Elvis wanted to play racketball. Though terribly out of shape, he had been doing a little swimming and racketball to limber up for the tour and that way avoid muscle pulls on stage when he moved. The court, which Elvis had built when he became a racketball enthusiast, is located at the right side of the house, in the left part of the backyard, and Elvis, Ricky, Ginger, Billy Smith, and his wife, Josie, accompanied him down there. In sneakers, shorts, and sweat shirts, Elvis, Rick, and Billy smacked the ball against the wall for some two hours. "Elvis didn't get out there and bust it," Rick remembers, "but he played. It didn't seem that he was overexerting himself or anything like that."

Rick stayed with Elvis until five or six that morning, when

336 Elvis handed him a prescription for Dilaudid. Rick went out and had it filled quickly. The drug was in capsule form and Rick noted that the dosage was no more than usual, certainly not enough to cause any undue concern on his part. "It wasn't any amount that could have even come close to killing him," he says flatly, "but if he had been straight when he had the heart problem, who knows man, he might have survived."

Rick and Elvis spent some time alone after Billy Smith left and Ginger was out of the room. Elvis was in the mood to pray. Rick was one of the few people that Elvis showed his spiritual side to, and when the mood struck him, they often prayed together. That year, with his knowledge and anxieties about Red and Sonny's book, they prayed more often than ever before. Around six o'clock they sat on Elvis's bed, clasped their hands together, and closed their eyes.

"Lord," Elvis prayed aloud, "help me to have insight and forgive me for my sins. Let the people who read that book have compassion and understanding about the things I've done. Dear God, please help me to get back when I feel down like this, and to always strive for good in the world. In the name of Jesus Christ. Amen."

Rick nodded his amen to Elvis.

"Ricky, tell David when he comes on tomorrow not to disturb me under any circumstances," the Boss said. "I don't want to get up until about four. Need plenty of rest for the tour."

"Okay," Rick said. "I'll start gettin' the rest of your stuff down and I'll see you later."

"Good night, Rick."

"Sleep well, Elvis," he said, closing the door quietly.

The morning air was still outside as the sun began to poke its head over that part of the world, sending low, mellow rays over Graceland and casting the estate in summer dawn tones. The horizon was tint-edged a beautiful orange-red; birds chirped peacefully as Elvis slept and nothing disturbed the tranquility of the morning save a random car or two passing the mansion on Elvis Presley Boulevard.

Inside the mansion, silence also reigned. Elvis and Ginger

were asleep in his bedroom and Lisa slept in her bedroom upstairs. Aunt Delta was asleep downstairs in her bedroom; so was Minnie Mae Presley. Vernon and Sandy Miller slumbered in the house on Dolan where Dee Presley had raised her boys.

The others on the grounds also slept soundly—Charlie Hodge in the furnished apartment above the garage and Billy Smith with his family in their trailer quarters. Joe Esposito was in his room at the Howard Johnson's Motor Lodge in Whitehaven. The only people awake were Pauline Nicholson, Elvis's trusted housekeeper, Harold Lloyd, who manned the front gate, and Rick, who busied himself with various chores and waited for his brother David. He would remember to pass on the message about Elvis wanting to sleep for as long as possible.

Elvis woke up sometime around nine o'clock. It was not unusual for him to rise after only several hours sleep (even with the sleeping medication) and sometimes take more medication to get back to bed; other times, he felt like staying up and reading or watching television. These were the moments when the TCB boys would have to be most on their toes in case Elvis needed them or something was to go wrong. If a woman was sleeping with him, they were always instructed to call if anything unusual happened, unless it was Linda Thompson, who was always on top of the situation. Ginger had learned the score, but that morning, after Elvis told her that he was going to his bathroom, she dropped back to sleep. Considering her scant three hours of sleep and that she was anyway probably not fully awake in the darkness created by Elvis's specially lined dark curtains, it isn't hard to understand why.

Located off his bedroom on the second floor was Elvis's outsized and luxurious bathroom. With its walls knocked out to create space, Elvis had transformed it into a combination bathroom-office-study-lounge. One wall is mirrored and fringed with those large, spare lightbulbs that one usually associates with the dressing room of a star. Under the mirror is a large Formica table top with a sunken purple sink upon which were strewn all of Elvis's toilet articles. The shower, a circular one with its walls done in a brown, black, and white tile design, is situated right next to the counter. The room is carpeted in plush

338   purple; books, comfortable easy chairs, a television, and other items of leisure were placed casually about.

The Boss's bathroom was the most private room in the house and the most private place in his life. Nobody ever went in without knocking. It was logical that the most private sanctuary in a life so fraught with publicity would have to be the bathroom, so Elvis made it into the place where he could be alone with his thoughts and most intimate with himself. The distance from the bathroom door (a heavy wooden one) to the bed where Ginger slept is approximately thirty feet.

Very few people know *exactly* what happened next, and that's probably the way Elvis would have wanted it. It is known that he sat on a chair and read for a while and David would later recall that it was *Shroud of Turin* by Ian Wilson, a book about Jesus and the evolution of Christian theology that Larry Geller had given Elvis as a present. It is also known that sometime between ten and two thirty that afternoon, Elvis had a heart attack. The preliminary findings by Dr. Jerry Francisco, the Shelby County coroner, would rule that cardiac arrhythmia and hardening of the arteries were the "natural" causes of death. Elvis may or may not have taken more of his sleeping medication; he may or may not have taken a dangerous amount of that medication if he did take more. If he had taken more and then had his coronary difficulty, the narcotics, as Rick has suggested, may very well have impaired his ability to react and help himself. If he experienced a serious heart failure with an acute chest pain such as that felt during a massive heart attack, he couldn't have lasted for more than three to five minutes, in which case the narcotics would have lessened the pain considerably.

Whatever it was, sometime, some way, before two thirty in the afternoon of August 16, 1977, Elvis Aron Presley, wearing a pair of blue cotton pajamas, alone in his bathroom, dropped his book, kneeled over onto his face, gasped desperately for the vital breath that the sudden lack of oxygen shouted for, and was unable to find it. In an instant as long as eternity, he left his trouble behind, found his final meaning, and took it to the last limit, his body prostrate on the floor before his Maker but his soul—as relatives, friends, and the millions of people who

adored him believe—immortalized, rocked gently once again in   **339**
the loving arms of the mother who rocked and sang him to sleep
into the quietude of the Mississippi night.

The world outside the door of the bathroom had remained
oblivious to the sublimely private moment and drama of his
death.

Waking sometime before two thirty and realizing that Elvis
hadn't returned, Ginger Alden rose from the bed and ventured
toward the door of the bathroom. She knocked several times. A
sense of dread must have crept over her when she received no
answer, for she knew that it was unlikely that Elvis would have
gotten up to go out. She opened the door to find him sprawled
across the floor. What she did next is unknown; she remained
collected enough to call Joe Esposito, who was the next person
on the scene. What she reported to him on the phone is unknown, as is the exact condition of the body when Esposito
arrived.

Rick had gone home by that time and David was downstairs
shooting pool on Elvis's antique Brunswick table with his friend
Mark. He had arrived at Graceland about noon and, in obe-
dience to the instructions left through Rick, had not knocked on
Elvis's door. David and Rick had stayed together for a short
time, helping to assemble some things in preparation for the
tour, and Rick had then gone home.

Upstairs, in the bathroom, Joe Esposito gauged the situation
and sprang into action. If there was one breath of life left in the
body of his boss and even the slightest chance of reviving him,
he knew that every second would be precious. He picked up the
phone and called the Memphis Fire Department's Engine
House No. 29, located at 2147 Elvis Presley Boulevard. Knowing Joe and how his mind works, he probably always knew that
in the event of an emergency that would be the closest ambulance unit to the mansion. He told them, simply, that "someone" was having trouble breathing at Graceland and was in
serious trouble. Thus, when Charlie Crosby and Ulysses S.
Jones, Jr., jumped into Unit Number Six, turned on the siren,
and headed south on Elvis Presley Boulevard, they had abso-

340 lutely no idea of who was "in trouble." This was standard operating procedure and Taking Care of Business: Always publicity conscious, Joe didn't want any news of the incident leaking out before help even arrived. His fears must have been the worst, however, for he then called Vernon Presley at his office in back of Graceland, knowing that if it was too late for Elvis, Vernon should be there. Accompanied by Sandy Miller, Vernon hurried over to the mansion, not knowing what to expect.

As David shot pool downstairs, he suddenly heard much commotion on the stairs leading to the second floor. It was either Vernon and Sandy, Charlie Hodge, or Al Strada, who were all on their way up there by that time. Lisa had one of her friends over that afternoon, a girl named Amber, who then came downstairs into the pool room. "David," she said innocently, "Elvis is sick."

Taking Care of Business shot through David's mind. In crisis situations all outsiders were to be removed from the grounds as quickly as possible. He had to get Mark out of there. He also thought about making telephone calls to inform key people that the tour was likely to be postponed and to wait for further details. Mark lived right in the immediate neighborhood, so he hustled him into his car and sped down the driveway to drop him off. His heart sank as he pulled back in and saw the gate open for the orange and white ambulance unit, which he followed up to the house. When he saw Patsy Gambil, Elvis's cousin and a longtime secretary at Graceland, running from the mansion, screaming, he expected the worst. Racing through the door, he bounded up the steps three at a time, his heart pounding, entered Elvis's bedroom, took the corner into his bathroom, and was confronted with a sight that will haunt him for the rest of his life.

It didn't seem at all real at first; it seemed surreal, like a Dali painting or a strange movie in which everything that was happening seemed brutally real yet cast in another dimension of reality, somehow distorted and bizarre. The paramedics were just arriving in front of him and Joe was hunched over Elvis, giving mouth-to-mouth resuscitation. Elvis was flat on his back now in only his pajama bottoms. Charlie was trying to pump his chest and give him external cardiac massage until the paramedics took over. Ginger was gone, nowhere in sight. David's eye naturally gravitated to Elvis's face. It was blue and purple-splotched. He knew that he was dead. *No*, he tried to tell himself, *this can't really be happening. It can't be happening.* He felt weak at the knees and fell to the floor in shock.

When David then turned to look at Vernon Presley, he was sure there would be two deaths that day. Vernon had collapsed against the tile wall of Elvis's shower, gasping, stricken eyed, with Sandy Miller at his side. Looking at him, David thought that one Presley may be dead, but it was now important to keep the other alive. He looked at Sandy and suspected that God had intended her to be there with him on that day. Vernon then clutched his hand and put it on Elvis's leg. "David," he sobbed piteously, "he's dead! My son is dead!"

"No . . . Daddy, he's not dead," he heard himself say. "This isn't happening . . ." until his own voice suddenly sounded far away and he felt himself receding autistically, only to be shaken out of it by the harsh commanding tones of Joe Esposito.

"David! David!" he snapped. "Help us!"

The effort of the paramedics had been unsuccessful. In cases of cardiac arrest and suffocation, the usual procedure at the site of the collapsed victim would be external cardiac massage. A device is then inserted to depress the tongue in order to run tubes down the throat into the lungs to administer air directly. An intracardiac injection of Adrenalin can be pumped directly into the heart, and catheters can be run into the arms through which drugs can be run to increase blood pressure (mixed, usually, with dextrose and salt solution).

While he was cognizant of what was going on, David recalls seeing no injections or catheters, only massage and air tubes. The efforts of on-the-spot revival attempts can last up to twenty minutes, during which time it can be discovered by checking to see if the victim's pupils are fixed and dilated whether he is taking in any oxygen. If all else fails, there is nothing left but the last-ditch hope of the cardioverter, which is usually administered at the hospital, but more than likely the victim will be dead on arrival. The cardioverting consists of applying two pow-

342 erful electrodes to opposite sides of the heart and sending a jolt of electricity that can resynchronize the electrical impulses of the heart. It was the only hope left, and they would have to get Elvis to the hospital. Joe's command had been to help them get him onto a stretcher.

They lifted him onto the stretcher and carefully but quickly carried him down the stairs. It was during this time, David thinks, that Lisa must have been able to see what was going on, because she had been kept from the room. Outside the front door, they lifted him up into the back of the ambulance. Just as Joe, Al, and Charlie were hopping into the back with him, Dr. Nick came racing up the the winding drive, screeched to a halt, got out, and climbed into the ambulance.

David just stood there for a moment, dazed, still wondering if it was some kind of movie, when Billy Smith came up to him. Billy had been out riding. "What's goin' on?" he demanded.

"Come on!" David grabbed him. "It's Elvis!"

The ambulance had turned out of the gate past several curious onlookers and north onto Elvis Presley Boulevard. Wailing hypnotically, it raced through the hot, humid streets as revival attempts continued in the back, turned left on Union, and sped toward the emergency room at Baptist Memorial Hospital. It was 2:56 P.M. when he was rushed in. Dr. Nick and Joe Esposito quickly managed to have the place closed and the entrance cordoned off by police so that nobody would be able to get through, making the place as security tight as the Dallas hospital that had received the bleeding body of John F. Kennedy.

When they arrived, David and Billy showed their TCB identification cards to the police and were admitted to the emergency room, where they found Joe Esposito, Charlie Hodge, and Al Strada, their heads down, deathly silent. Inside, through the double doors, Elvis was being frantically worked on by a team of doctors and nurses trained in every conceivable means of reviving a dying person.

David looked from face to face. "Have you heard anything?"

They just shook their heads.

When one of the doctors emerged, Joe Esposito looked up.

"Doctor," he said, "how long do you think he's been without oxygen now?"

"Too long," was the reply.

"Then we should pray that he's dead then, shouldn't we," Joe said, his eyes downcast.

"Yes," the doctor said compassionately. "His brain's been without oxygen too long now. Even if he lives, he'd be like a vegetable."

The door then opened and Dr. Nick emerged, his white hair disheveled, his shoulders hunched over. David was the first one to rise. He looked into the doctor's eyes for a glimmer of hope, but he saw nothing. Dr. Nick just closed his eyes and shook his head.

It was three thirty P.M. when Elvis Aron Presley was pronounced officially dead. It was all over.

Everybody just stood there. David, Charlie, and Billy were crying now. Joe stood there perfectly still, lost in thought. Something then seemed to flash suddenly inside of him, and he sprang once again into action. There was too much to do to allow his emotions to get the better of him at that moment. There was Vernon and the family to think of, security, the press, the autopsy, funeral arrangements . . . *the goddamned press!* Somebody was going to have to Take Care of Business. People were already gathering outside and the press was on the scene. Joe stood there like a field commander, barking concise instructions to everyone in the room. Under no circumstance was anyone to say anything to the press without clearing it. . . .

Dr. Nick made the announcement to the press at the hospital and then got into his car to return to Graceland, faced with the task of telling Vernon Elvis Presley that his only son was dead.

Elvis's body was removed to the morgue on the second floor of the hospital, and every important doctor on the premises was called in, as was Dr. Jerry Francisco, Shelby County coroner. Whenever the cause of death is not immediately apparent, the law requires an autopsy, which usually takes three to four hours. During the preliminary stage of the autopsy, Dr. Fran-

344   cisco claimed that cardiac arrhythmia and coronary disease were the natural causes of death. Dr. Francisco also said, according to *The New York Times*, that Elvis also had a history of mild hypertension. "But the specific cause may not be known for a week or two pending lab studies. It is possible in cases like this that the specific cause will never be known."

At a press conference reporters, now familiar with the contents of *Elvis: What Happened?* (released some fifteen days prior to Elvis's death), peppered Dr. Francisco with questions to find out if there had been any indications of drug abuse. Dr. Francisco is reported to have said (*The New York Times* of August 17, 1977) that "the only drugs he had detected were those that had been prescribed by Mr. Presley's personal physician for hypertension and a blockage of the colon, for which he had been hospitalized twice in 1975." Dr. Nichopoulos, in the same article, was quoted by the Associated Press as saying that Elvis had been taking a number of appetite suppressants, "but the physician said they had not contributed to his death."

Much remains mysterious. It would, of course, be irresponsible to point any fingers at anyone (particularly officials of the Baptist Memorial Hospital and the Shelby County coroner) in light of an absence of concrete information, but much would seem to contradict the initial public statements of these individuals. For example, why no mention of the Dilaudid that Elvis took that morning after Rick filled his prescription? That would certainly have shown up during the autopsy, particularly if Elvis had taken more of it when he woke up. Dr. Francisco stated that the only drugs he detected were "prescribed" by Dr. Nichopoulos for "hypertension" and "blockage of the colon"; it is unlikely that Dr. Nick would ever have prescribed a strong narcotic for either condition. At any rate, Dr. Francisco also mentioned that Elvis had been hospitalized for both conditions in 1975, whereas Rick remembers that in both instances Elvis was in the hospital to be cut off his sleeping medication.

Several medical scenarios for the death were plausible, none of which, if they were in fact investigated and pursued, was ever made public because the ruling of "natural causes" at the preliminary autopsy quashed forever the possibility of a public in-

quest into the death and assured that all future findings would
remain within the Presley family.

Cardiac arrhythmia occurs when the heart, instead of contracting and pumping in its normal muscular patterns, begins to
flutter out of synch with itself. If you open and close your fist
slowly to simulate the muscular action of the pumping heart,
you can get a good idea of the arrhythmia condition by opening
the fist and then, instead of closing the fingers in unison, flut-
tering the fingers up and down irregularly, for that is what
occurs to the heart muscle and pumping action. There are
various kinds of arrhythmia, and it is highly unusual to diagnose
it as a cause of death at a preliminary autopsy stage because
most pathologists would consider it to be an antemortem
and not a postmortem factor, meaning that it would be more
likely to in turn cause something else to happen that would
be the cause of death, like myocardial infarction, or the inter-
ruption of blood flow which brings about the collapse of the
heart and the suffocation of the victim. Also, to determine, at
a preliminary stage, that cardiac arrhythmia was a "natural"
cause of the death would have required that the examiners establish the electrical condition of the heart, which would have
been difficult, considering that it is confirmed on the living
heart with an electrocardiogram.

Despite extremely tight security that day, rumors from inside
the hospital were leaking out to gathering reporters who were
hanging around the hospital like circling vultures. Someone
said that nine drugs had been found in Elvis's system. In *Rolling Stone*, an anonymous hospital employee was reported to
have said that Elvis had the arteries of "an eighty-year-old
man." There was also talk of enlarged colon, gastroenteritis,
stomach inflammation, a severe liver condition that was being
treated with cortisone, and even lupus, a rare and chronic sys-
temic inflammation of the kidneys and skin.

One thing is certain: There were enough things allegedly
wrong with Elvis at the time of autopsy to make it extremely difficult for the examiners to determine the exact cause of death.
Moreover, regardless of what drugs may have been detected,
there was also enough coronary damage to make it just as likely

346   that Elvis had succumbed to heart difficulty as to anything else. David thinks there was a "strong possibility" that Elvis over-dosed on his medication when he got up that morning. It had, after all, been known to occur, and he recalls several times when he found Elvis unconscious on his bathroom floor in sim-ilar instances. Then, if he had felt palpitations, his ability to dis-cern them might have been impaired by the narcotics, or, per-haps, the drugs affected his breathing, which in turn set off the heart problem. Again, the possibilities are numerous.

    Dr. Nick was well aware of Elvis's drug problems. At the moment of Elvis's death, in all likelihood, Dr. Nick would have tried his hardest to keep that information from the public in order to preserve the good name of his patient, to spare Vernon Presley any more pain than necessary, and to preserve his own professional integrity as Elvis's known personal physician in the very delicate and controversial matter of his drug abuse. Dr. Nick probably told the examiners the state of Elvis's health as he perceived it before the autopsy, including his cardiac history. One plausible explanation may be that Dr. Francisco found enough initial coronary damage to justify his ruling and knew that the rest of the findings would have to remain private, what-ever they might be. Whether or not Dr. Nick asked him to do it is irrelevant; the responsibility for the autopsy was his and his findings would have to stand in the end. He could have ruled natural causes even if there had been other primary or ancil-lary causes like drugs noticeable at the time, and waited for the final results. That way he would have been doing nothing at all unethical, yet he would have been serving Dr. Nick's inter-ests. His statement that the precise cause in such a case "may never be known" certainly left him enough room to move.

    Whatever really happened, whatever the autopsy ultimately concluded, will probably never be made public. Rick later heard family scuttlebutt to the effect that later findings would turn up some eleven different traces of drugs but still rule that the heart had caused the death. Usually, the examining officials at the autopsy have all the vital organs removed—brain, heart, liver, kidneys. It is also customary for them to be put back in a

bag and placed in the coffin of the deceased before burial, when
the autopsy is completed. In Elvis's case, that didn't occur.
Maurice Elliot, vice-president of the Baptist Memorial Hospital,
has been quoted (in *Rolling Stone* and elsewhere) to the effect
that none of Elvis's vital organs were ever returned but were
kept at the hospital for further tests. Elvis would be buried
without them.

While all hell was breaking loose at Graceland and at Baptist
Memorial, Rick was at a restaurant with Jill, ordering something to eat. Something inside of him told him to get back to
the house quickly. *Something's wrong,* he intuited, *there's business needs taking care of.* . . .
The waitress was standing before him with his salad. "I'm not
hungry, ma'am," he said. "Check, please."
Only an hour or two had elapsed since he'd left Graceland
and a mere ten hours since he and Elvis had sat on his bed and
prayed, but the dreadful feeling grew and grew the closer he got,
and he knew it when he saw so many people beginning to
congregate in front of the music gate. He started to run. They
opened the gate for him and he made for the house, bursting
through the front door.
Dr. Nick had just arrived from the hospital with the news.
Everyone—Grandma, Aunt Delta, Uncle Vester, Vernon, and
Sandy—were all waiting in Grandma's room. Rick seemed to
arrive just as their incredulity passed and the painful impact
began to hit home. He mulled it over and over in his mind
. . . Elvis dead . . . Elvis is dead . . . crying . . . wondering, his arms hung loosely at his sides and his head down, if
life would be worth living now that his world had ended—when
Lisa Marie Presley came up to him. Nobody had told her yet,
but she sensed it. Tears streamed down her cheeks and she
looked Rick straight in the eyes, expecting a straight answer
from him.
"Ricky, what's wrong with Daddy?" she asked boldly, trying
her best to disguise the fear in her voice.
"Lisa . . . honey . . . he's sick," he said lamely, choking on

348 the words, "your . . . daddy's uh, not been . . . feelin' well . . . lately . . . and . . ." Paralyzed by his love for her, as he looked her in the eyes, he was unable to utter the words.

She cut him short, not taking her eyes off him. "Then why are *you* cryin'?"

"I'm concerned, baby," he lied, trying to fight back the tears. She looked so much like Elvis at that moment and he cursed the fact that it's always worse for people who are left behind, when he heard Vernon Presley in the next room, broken, crying, "Oh, God . . . no. . . . It can't be true . . . God, no . . ." and something snapped inside of him and he bolted from the room, not knowing where he was going, out the front door, down the drive, out the gate where the crowds were growing steadily larger, running faster, faster, seeking release in the purity of the pistonlike motion of his legs, startling those he passed by the look of wild-eyed desperation on his face, wanting to sweat it out of him and run till he dropped because if he stopped he was afraid he too would want to die.

People who knew him and passed him as he ran down Elvis Presley Boulevard tried to get his attention. "Rick, Rick!" they called to him. "Where you goin', man! Ain't you heard?" But he heard nothing but the pounding of his heart, the insane rhythm of his breath, and Vernon Presley's voice in his ear.

An eerie hush seemed to enshroud the city as news of the death spread, which then gave rise to commotion and even panic. It seemed that everybody heard the news all at once, dropped whatever they were doing, and made their way toward Graceland. In Whitehaven roads were clogged with cars and people on foot. The crowds in front of the music gate, which were growing into the hundreds when Rick arrived at Graceland, were soon thousands and showed no signs of abating as Elvis's hometown fans began gathering for what would be a two-day vigil. They pressed up against the gate, caught up against each other, not knowing what would happen next but not caring, some silent and hollow eyed, others screaming.

Phone calls were being made from inside the mansion as the news was flashing around the world and newspapers rushed

frantically to remake their final editions with banner headlines.
The Colonel was notified as was everybody else connected with
the TCB operation. Priscilla was in Los Angeles, unable to get
home, when finally the *Lisa Marie* was dispatched to bring her
to Memphis. Lisa, once she found out, apparently called Linda
Thompson herself. Everywhere friends, relatives, and associates
of Elvis Presley were rocked by the news, and if they weren't notified personally, they tried desperately to get through to Graceland.

It was perhaps roughest on those like Billy and Dee who
could not be reached by the family before they learned from
other sources. Billy was at his house in Whitehaven, far enough
removed from Elvis Presley Boulevard so that he was unable to
see the unfolding drama. Aw, it's got to be bullshit, he thought
when the news came on the television. The people over at his
house and his wife, Diana, tried to get him to call the mansion
to find out the truth, and he didn't want to at first, afraid in his
heart that it might be true. He finally relented and dialed Elvis's
number. Someone picked up the phone but he couldn't even
tell who it was.

"This is Billy," he said simply. "Is it true what I heard?"

The voice on the phone said, "Yeah." Nothing more.

He left the phone dangling and went out in his front yard.
Gone, he thought, crying—gone before I could even say it to
him—tell him that I forgave him, that I loved him. Now I'll
never be able . . . at least not in this life. But he probably
always knew.

Off to the west, the sun, which had been merciless all day,
was beginning to set. Billy felt cold and his lips quivered as he
sat there and wondered what had happened. He needed to find
his brothers. Sweet Jesus, this is gonna be bad, he thought.
Poor Elvis, maybe he's better off where he is. . . . All hell's
gonna break loose. . . . There's nothin' left. He wondered
what his mother was doing, if she had heard.

Dee Presley was crosstown, in East Memphis, in her place on
Perkins Road, also far enough from the pandemonium to keep
her completely in the dark. She was watching a late-afternoon

350 movie on television, a love story, when the phone rang. It was a lady friend, one of her neighbors, and Dee thought it was a social call.

"Dee, how *are* you," her friend asked uncertainly.

"I'm fine."

"I heard about Elvis," her friend said, hushed and respectfully.

"Oh," Dee said, beginning to suspect that something was wrong but hoping it was just more idle gossip. "What did you hear?"

"Elvis is dead."

The words fell on her ears like a sledgehammer. She couldn't speak. All she heard was a ringing. "What are you sayin'!" she shouted, suddenly angry and hysterical. "My God! You're not tellin' the truth!"

Silence. "Oh my God," her friend said slowly, awkwardly. "I can see that you haven't heard yet."

Dee hung up and dialed Graceland but her phone was dead. So many people in the city were trying to confirm news of the death at one time that the circuits were overloading and communications were breaking down. Dee felt isolated and frightfully cut off, swept into the fearful anarchy and uncertainty that the phone call had loosed in her mind. She sat in a chair, crying, feeling more alone than ever before in her life, wondering if Elvis had been alone when it happened, hoping that he had had no pain, worrying about Vernon. Images and fears raced through her mind, tormenting her. She stared mutely and uncomprehendingly at the television screen. Finally the official bulletin came on. Though it confirmed the death to her, it was still meaningless as the voice of the announcer said the words.

Finally the phone rang. It was her son David. As best as he could, he related the events of the day. Dee had to get through to Graceland, to Vernon. She kept trying, unsuccessfully. Finally she heard a dial tone, dialed the number, and waited. The phone at the mansion rang. She asked for Vernon.

"Oh, my God, Dee," came his voice, barely audible. "My baby is gone. My *baby*, Dee. Everything is gone."

"Should I come, Vernon? Vernon, I'm worried about you.
Vernon . . ."

"Don't start drivin', Dee . . . I'm afraid you'll have a wreck
. . . the crowds . . . it's terrible, Dee . . . please stay there
. . . the body, Dee . . . it isn't here now . . . wait till an es-
cort comes. . . ."

As the moments passed they found themselves able to speak
more calmly, but neither of them was all there. They spoke
briefly of the funeral arrangements, and Dee suggested their
friend and minister C.W. Bradley for the eulogy. Vernon told
her to go ahead and call Bradley, it was a good idea, and promised to call back when he knew more.

Somewhere along Elvis Presley Boulevard, back in Whitehaven, David had found his brother Rick. It was the first time they
had been together since their paths had crossed that noonday.
With the sun setting over Memphis and the crowds still building in front of the mansion, they held each other there on the
side of the road and cried, knowing their lives would never be
the same.

"We'll *kill* those sons-of-bitches if it's the last thing we do,"
David wept bitterly, the bad blood against Red and Sonny well-
ing up with his sorrow.

Rick wasn't saying much. His blue eyes looked as flat and
deadened as the emptiness that crushed him inside. He knew
his brother's hatred for what it was; a vehicle, a means of getting
away from his own pain. David just looked at him.

"Guess what," he said. "We ain't got nothin' left but each
other, Rick. There's nothin' left."

At eight ten that evening, the body of Elvis Presley was removed from Baptist Memorial and taken by black hearse to the
Memphis Funeral Home for embalming, where Elvis had gone,
on occasion, to witness and learn about that same process.

Dusk found the crowds at Graceland even larger. Headlights
were turned on and the police were doing their best to control
the crowd and keep order. There is something astonishing about

352 the spontaneous gathering of a great many people—something timeless, powerful, sometimes frightening; it conjures up images of riots, revolutions, demonstrations, great and momentous events. This crowd of Elvis's mourners was no different; it was a densely packed human mass of sorrow and respect of every imaginable social, political, ethnic, racial grouping and religious persuasion—a broad cross-section of the America that Elvis Presley had reached for and had been able to put in his pocket —there because they were trying, perhaps, to clutch onto something that had also died in them that day. The knowledge of Elvis's death provoked a response in America that was unprecedented because it evoked the deaths of Kennedy, Judy Garland, Valentino, and James Dean all at once; even the members of his family and his closest friends, after all of those years of his mad superstardom, would be stupefied by it. People tried desperately to keep something of his now that he was gone; they wanted to make sure that they had a memory of their own from his life, and that very peculiar human inclination that makes us more apt to appreciate posthumously an individual and his work in the world exploded across the country within a matter of hours, sending people into record stores, where millions of his albums walked off shelves within the next twenty-four hours. Three days later Ballantine Books would announce that one of their chains had ordered some two million copies of *Elvis: What Happened?* The book had appeared on August 1, with a bust of the singing figure of Elvis silhouetted garishly against the darkness. In Beverly Hills, Sonny West and Dave Hebler would call a press conference, angered by how people were responding to their book (rumors were circulating that they were "bloodsuckers", said Sonny), and blast Steve Dunleavy (their coauthor, whom they now called a "sensationalist"). Dunleavy was hawking the book on television talk shows and calling Elvis a "walking medicine cabinet." Sonny would insist that he did not write the book out of spite or to exploit Elvis, but out of "love and admiration," and profess that he wasn't at all interested in how it was doing. He even ventured to say that Elvis, wherever he was, "knew" he was telling the truth. Ver-

non Presley wasn't so sure about that, however, and made it
clear they weren't welcome at his son's funeral.

The next two days passed in a numbing haze of pain. For the
boys it was time to harness their emotions. There was business
to take care of. The most important thing to them all was that
everything be perfect, exactly the way the Boss would have
wanted it, and in the interests of that, they forgot about themselves. Joe Esposito stood tall and strong; everybody took their
cues from him.

Vernon Presley realized that the death was too public an affair to keep completely private, that the mourners straining their
necks to look over the jagged rock wall surrounding Graceland
had grief that would also have to be mollified, so he decided on
the evening of the death that Elvis would lie in state for one
day, during which people would be conducted in an orderly
manner up the driveway and into the foyer of the house, where
the body of his son was to be placed. People heard the news and
the crowd immediately started to grow, stretching now for miles
in either direction of Elvis Presley Boulevard and moving in ser-
pentine currents and waves. The police had been duly informed
and were on hand to handle things. Vernon had decided that
the gates would be opened between the hours of three and five
P.M., and Joe Esposito, Dick Grob, Sam Thompson, Al Strada,
Charlie Hodge, David, Ricky, and others were to be inside the
foyer while the people filed past the coffin. Floral wreaths were
arriving that day by the thousands from all over the world, and
they were being placed outside in front of the mansion where
they were forming an enormous wall of verdant color. While a
contingent of Air National Guardsmen stood crisply at attention
outside the doors, the boys spread themselves out inside, still
protecting the Boss who lay underneath the crystal chandelier in
the foyer in a stately, copper-lined coffin, dressed in a white
suit, looking noble, tranquil, frighteningly different. It was, for
all of them, the most difficult day of their lives.

People who collapsed at the sight of him were helped to their
feet and then along out of the room. Several people were brazen

354   enough to produce cameras, which were angrily snatched away, but most people behaved with the utmost respect, with the solemnity befitting the occasion. Given the mood of the boys, it was a good thing. "Anybody who would have made a wrong move that day would have died," David says. "They would have been the next to go."

The family stayed out of sight. People who were aware that the funeral would be the following day were pouring into Memphis, and Esposito had his hands full coordinating everything, getting the cemetery ready, hiring limousines, contacting friends and relatives.

By the time the gates were to be closed, there were still thousands of people both inside and outside, undaunted by the soft rain that had begun to fall, determined to get that one last look. Vernon decided to allow the gates open for another hour and a half, after which time they would be permanently closed to the public. Six thirty rolled around. The people who were still waiting couldn't believe it, but the gates were closed like a dike against a flood. There were angry shouts, boos, protests, screams and crying, but there was nothing they could do—the American public had gazed upon the corporeal countenance of Elvis Presley for the last time. Some gave up after a while and went home. Others remained, riveted.

Sometime early Thursday morning a white Ford driven by a crazed eighteen-year-old boy whipped into the parking lot across the street, turned, and went ploughing off into three girls standing on the median strip of the highway. Two of them died almost instantly, the third was critically injured. The assailant was immediately apprehended, but the rest of the night passed fitfully, both outside and inside the mansion.

The morning dawned hazy over Memphis and it looked like the weather would be fretfully hot for the funeral. By afternoon, when friends and relatives started arriving at Graceland, it was hot, but the sky was a cerulean summer blue.

That morning Larry Geller groomed Elvis for his funeral. He was changed into a pale blue suit which Vernon had given him for Christmas and Larry styled and carefully combed his hair for what must have felt to him the most important role in the many years he had been Elvis's friend and beautician. "He told me it wasn't easy for him to do," David remembers, "but Larry always seemed to know how Elvis liked to look." "The Boss looked real good," Rick says. "I was so glad because we owed it to the man that he would be looking real good, just the way he would have been proud of."

Dee Presley was picked up by limousine and drove through the streets of Whitehaven toward Graceland with trepidation in her heart. From almost the moment of the announcement, the press had tried to get to her, and the previous twenty-four hours had been rough. She dreaded the thought of seeing Elvis in a coffin and was beset with worries about Vernon. But as with everyone else, the true feelings and the effects of that day would only make themselves felt in the months to come.

Walking through the foyer she turned right, into the music room and living room where Elvis was laid out. Ricky and his friend Robyn Moye, David and his wife Angela, and Billy and his wife Diana met her at the door and accompanied her toward the casket, which was in front of the rows of gold folding chairs set up for the service. The casket glistened in the afternoon light and she felt dizzy and weak kneed as she approached it. She noticed the Beaulieus off to the right and the Aldens off to the left, but as soon as she caught sight of Elvis's face, she could see nothing else—struck, as she was, by how strangely swollen it seemed, and by the beatific expression.

For those who knew Elvis Presley during his life and attended his funeral, the uniform impression seemed to be that an aura of peace seemed to surround him in death, of that sublime release he had sought in life that now seemed spread over him pleasantly, the way night befalls a countryside in summertime after a day of hot, blanching sunshine. In his face, at least, there wasn't a trace of the tempest that had been his life.

Standing there beside Dee, David couldn't keep his hands from touching Elvis. "Even though he was dead," he remembers, "it just seemed that he was still talking to me, telling me things. I just grasped his hand and tried to listen—he was saying, 'Keep on goin', man, you won't have any problems. You'll make it. Don't worry about me. I'm at home.'"

356   Dee found Vernon in a side room off the living room, sitting on a couch, weeping. He looked shockingly older than he had the last time she'd seen him, the experience of the death furrowed deeply into his face, especially around his eyes, and he looked pitifully frail, as if he himself were teetering on the very edge of life. Sandy sat on the floor at his side and Mother Presley rocked back and forth in silence. Dee began to cry as soon as she saw him.

"Did you see him, Dee?" he cried when he saw her. "Did you see my baby?"

Dee embraced him gently.

He looked at her, not knowing what to say, either. "Do you think I chose the right suit for him, Dee? How do you think he looks?"

"I just can't believe it's really him, Vernon," she fumbled. "I just can't believe it's him."

Then there was a silence between them.

"Do you think he knew? Do you think he knew it?" he suddenly asked.

The question brought back all of those nights alone when Vernon was off with Elvis, trying to protect him, in vain, from the world and himself.

"Yes, I do." She began to cry.

"Do you think he wouldn't tell me? Why? *Why?*" He shook his head slowly, bewildered.

"Vernon, he wanted to spare you," she said. "He wanted to spare us both."

"Wasn't that cruel, that he wouldn't let me know, so I couldn't help?" He seemed so baffled, she thought, like he would never be able to understand.

"It wasn't cruel," she said, wanting to comfort him. "He knew you could never bear the thought."

So they sat on the couch for a while like that, Sandy saying nothing but never taking her eyes from Vernon's face, and they wept. Dee tried to comfort him, but she knew there is no easy solace for a parent who must bury a child. There was so much inside of her, so much she might have said, but she couldn't;

the woman at his side, it seemed, made it so they couldn't be
uttered.

Back in the living room Dee saw Priscilla, and they spoke briefly. If there is one thing that stands out in her mind and in many other minds about Priscilla Beaulieu Presley on the day of her former husband's funeral, it has to be the composed sense of poise that she displayed throughout. Her grief and whatever else she felt that day would remain her own. As the woman who had married Elvis and who had his only child, Priscilla knew that many eyes would be on her that day and on subsequent days, that people would want to know how she felt about it all and be looking for some display or cue as to what was going on inside of her. She was tender and yet impenetrably calm that day, dressed, simply, in black, with her hair tied back and falling loosely down her back. Rick, who loved her as a sister and knew her as Elvis's wife, wondered if her time apart from Elvis and his life since their divorce had opened so many new vistas that she felt removed from it all; more likely, he thought, was that she had *known*, she had known his time was coming, too. Priscilla's major distraction that day was Lisa, who stood in silence at the end of her father's coffin for as long as she could until her mother led her away. Everybody at Graceland that afternoon surely knew that the real tragedy of Elvis Presley's death would lie in the heart of his daughter, the heart of a child. "She knew that her daddy was dead," remembers David, "but she just couldn't figure it out. Only her mother would be able to help her do that."

The organist started playing "Danny Boy," a song that Elvis loved to play when he felt like sitting at home, warming up his voice by entertaining his friends. The rendition was slow and mournful, like a funeral dirge, as everybody sat, lost in his own private thoughts, communing with his own private memories and meanings. Rick sat, lost, momentarily pulled away from his private pain by the spectacle of it all. Rex Humbard spoke first, but the only thing he could hear were sobs, his mother's from one side and Vernon Presley's from another, rising above the words. To him they seemed more expressive of what was really

358   going on there, more literate somehow than the words. Then
C.W. Bradley delivered the main eulogy. He spoke of his first
encounter with Elvis Presley—how impressed he had been by
his humility, how speechlessly excited and overcome his daughter had been to meet him—and of the long friendship he had
enjoyed with Vernon and Dee . . . and it went on eloquently
until he got to the part about the brevity of life, of its transience
and meaninglessness in the face of the larger truths of God, and
that's when Rick began to look around the room and wonder
what it all meant. This life. That life. Elvis's life. What his
death said about the world that we live in. The words were
beautiful but they failed to reach him; he was too lost in himself, in his own emptiness, in the panorama of the room . . .
twenty years of a life to digest, accumulated in that single room,
focused on that coffin. Stories about him, the music he created,
moments of magnificence, entertainers, friends, enemies, girls
he had dated, families he had known, his wife, his daughter,
right there, in his music room, in his own home . . . wow, he
thought, it was *wild*. He glanced around the room at various
people whose whole lives were so entwined with Elvis's and
wondered what they were thinking and feeling. He looked at Joe
Esposito, who had been such a pillar of emotional fortitude and
responsibility those two days, whom Rick had always looked up
to and loved. Suddenly Joe's features seemed to be sagging
under the weight of his now emerging emotions; he looked as if
he had aged ten years during those two days. Rick looked at
Ann-Margret, beautiful, sexy; she was the one woman from Elvis's Hollywood past who simply couldn't stay away, who had to
come, and he wondered about that compulsion and what she
was feeling. Then there was Linda, who had loved Elvis as
much as any woman in his life. If only Elvis had stayed with
her, he thought, maybe he would still be alive. He resolved to
seek her out after the funeral and tell her how much Elvis had
said he really loved her. Colonel Tom Parker was impassively
quiet, almost expressionless. What would the Colonel do now?
Then Rick looked at the guys who comprised the TCB entourage. They were probably taking it hardest because their
lives, which had revolved completely around Elvis's, would be

most changed. Poor Charlie Hodge, he thought, looking at
him; now there's a guy who's known nothing but Elvis Presley
for twenty years. He really felt for Charlie. At least he and his
brothers were still young men, but Charlie? What in blazes
would he do now? God. Then Jackie Kahane spoke briefly—a
man who had always tried to make Elvis laugh. At the end of
the shows it was always Jackie who'd had to deliver the disap-
pointing news to the assembled multitudes that "Ladies and
gentlemen, Elvis has left the building." Elvis could always ask
him for the right words in the event of a special occasion on
tour, but on the occasion of Elvis's funeral Jackie could only see
fit to make the same simple announcement. "Ladies and gentlemen . . . Elvis has left us now . . . but he will go on in the
hearts and minds of those who loved him. . . ." Words simply
failed, in the end. There would always be something ineffable
about Elvis Presley, it seemed, something beyond words. And
then Rick heard Vernon Presley, broken, sighing aloud, "Oh,
sonny . . . just thank God there is a Lord," and he thought
that maybe that was the only meaning, the only explanation.

It was time. Slowly people were rising and moving toward
the casket for a last look before it was closed forever. Dee Presley rose, surrounded by the three boys she'd brought to Graceland so long ago, for one moment of anguished farewell.

The casket was covered, and the pallbearers stepped forward
to remove it to the hearse. Outside, white Cadillac limousines
were lined up to transport the assembled mourners to the Forest
Hill Cemetery. Lamar Fike, George Klein, Joe Esposito, Jerry
Schilling, Dr. Nichopoulos, Felton Jarvis, and Gene and Billy
Smith hoisted their charge aloft and moved him outside.

Crowds had lined virtually every inch of the roughly three-
mile distance from the Graceland gate to the gate of the cemetery. A hush fell over them as the casket emerged, followed by
the mourners. Hawkers stopped hawking across the street, and
all that was audible were the subdued whispers of the busy-
bodies and the voices of little children. All eyes—of people
along the roadway and on the neighboring lawns, on the tops of
cars, perched in such numbers in the trees that the branches
bent and sagged from the weight—were fixed on the hearse as it

360   was being loaded. Seventeen white limousines were lined up to
take the two hundred mourners to Forest Hill, and people silently stepped into cars. The air was painfully still. When almost everybody was in the cars and the procession was ready to
begin, a large bough from one of the trees on the front lawn
broke off and came crashing to the ground, startling all who saw
it.

Dee had decided that she had had about all she could take
and wouldn't be coming to the cemetery, but by the time she
got into her car, she'd decided to join the funeral procession. It
was only right, after all, that she see it all the way to the end.
When she arrived everybody was standing in front of the white
mausoleum. Several brief prayers were delivered and several
people, Vernon, Priscilla, and Lisa among them, got up to go
inside. Gladys's coffin had been placed in the mausoleum as
well, and Vernon spent some minutes alone in there. He
emerged shaken, barely able to walk, assisted by Sandy on one
arm and Joe Esposito on the other. The door was then closed. It
was time for everybody to go his own way.

Dee was thinking about the people that lined the roadway,
and how important it had always been for Elvis to know that he
was loved by them. She flashed back on being in a limousine in
some place like Hawaii or New York with Vernon, Elvis, and
Joe, with the inside of the car so dense with smoke from the
little cigars Joe and Elvis would smoke that she always coughed.
Elvis would peer happily out the window of the car at the faces
of the people who wanted to see him. "Look, Daddy, look at
the crowd," he would say, "they all came today." She also
recalled the ecstatic expression on his face in his dressing room
after a show, how worn and tired he looked, but how he lit up
when you said, "Elvis, you were great tonight! They all just
loved you!"

"Elvis was our life; that's what it amounted to," says Billy
Stanley. "When he died, something in all of us died, and not
because he was rich or great or anything—because he was so
real."

CHAPTER 23

THE LEGACY

The hardest thing for David to swallow was that Elvis no longer was going to just call up on the phone one day and say, in that low-lulling, unmistakable voice of his, "David! What's goin' on? Get your stuff together and get your ass on up here. . . . I'm fixin' to fly out to Vegas." No matter how many times he said it to himself—"*Elvis has left earth! It's time to move on!*"—it wouldn't sink in.

Reeling, bitter, rootless, and uncertain of the future, David left for Nashville the very day of the funeral. "I moved up there because my wife lived there and I wanted to try and stay close to her because I needed something so badly," he says.

In the months following the funeral a voracious industry had popped up in the aftermath of Elvis's death, plastering his image around each and every corner David seemed to turn. Every poster he saw, every street he drove down, all of the faces of Elvis's friends, evoked memories of growing up with him, of working, of the good times. He started taking drugs furiously and drinking, but it didn't help. One night he began taking handfuls

362 of Valium. Five led to ten, ten to fifteen, fifteen to twenty. His own life no longer mattered. He ended up taking seventy Valium. Thinking that he would soon be able to talk to Elvis, he tried, the darkness enveloping him, but something stopped him and he managed to cry for help. He staggered into his mother's room.

"At the time he said he wanted to die," Dee Presley remembers, "and when he came in, I could see that he meant what he said. I just thank God that someone was there with me at the time to help me rush him to the hospital. I was worried that we weren't going to make it, but we got there in time. They pumped his stomach and kept him overnight. I thank the Lord we got there in time."

Lying in the hospital that night, David swears that he felt Elvis in the room with him, reproaching him for his self-destructive stupidity. "It was like he was saying, 'David, look at you. Haven't you learned any lessons from me? You look like me, and I don't like that."

Dee Presley faced her own private ordeal just trying to keep her three sons from trying to go off the deep end after Elvis died. It's no small miracle that any one of them didn't end up buried in Meditation Gardens along with their stepbrother. "I expected them all to go at any time," she says, "but I had to be there so I couldn't live in fear. I could see why their lives were so empty. If I'd lived a life like that with Elvis, it would have destroyed me, too."

Dee calls those critical months following the death the "leveling off" period.

"My sons were deprived of a college education because they went off on the road with Elvis and they gave their lives to him," Dee says resentfully, "and they were not left in the will. Elvis always promised them he would always take care of them, and then there was nothing. Perhaps there were jobs they could have stepped into, but they really weren't trained for anything. So what could they do?"

There were unconfirmed rumors that various people—the Stanley boys among them—had been included in Elvis's will

before he had learned about Red and Sonny's book. After that
he was so shaken that the will was rewritten and completed to
exclude everybody but Lisa Marie Presley.

Dee, Billy, Rick, and David may not have realized it at the
time of the funeral or during those barren months that followed,
but Elvis had bequeathed them a legacy far more valuable than
money.

Billy Stanley would seem to be the victim of the story, the
true casualty of the life around Elvis Presley. All of his inarticu-
lated hurt and love was buried along with Elvis, and the death
left an entire emotional chapter of his life unresolved.

"When he died I took it so hard because I couldn't be with
him when he was alive," he says. "I knew that the guy wasn't
going to be around much longer, and I really wanted to be
around him on those last couple of good days he had. I felt left
out when he died, and I don't know why—like he went off on
tour again and I didn't get to go; I never even had any idea how
much I loved the guy until he was dead. I just got fucked up,
twenty-four hours a day, eight days a week. That's what I do
now, because there's a big void in my life, and that comes closest to giving me comfort."

"The thing that happened," as Billy calls the affair between
Elvis and his first wife, may have poisoned the air between
them but it never diminished the love. "I cried for a week
straight after he died and I just kept thinking that the only thing
I wanted to say to him was, 'Forget about all that, Elvis, because you loved me much more than you can hurt me. The
whole thing that happened is past history.' I wanted him to
know that I loved him to ease his mind so that he wouldn't
worry about me. I guess I feel that me and him are stronger
now.

"You know what always seemed strange to me?" he wonders.
"The relationship that Elvis had with his mother is exactly the
same as my relationship with Dee. Elvis just wasn't the same
after she died because he relied on her for so much. He just had
to go on living without her and that was it. Even Vernon would
talk about how unreal their relationship was. 'Never, never let

364   your mother lose respect for you,' that's what Elvis always told me, which is why I guess that I listened to Mom faster than Ricky or David."

Billy's second marriage was torn apart by the bitter hangover from his first marriage. His wife was young, too young, and it was as if Billy's emotions with her were contained in a hermetically sealed can. Somewhere in the back of his mind was the possibility that a similar scenario might be enacted and leave him heartbroken and lonely. "See, I trusted her," he says, "but I guess I never let her know it. Elvis always told me that if you keep a woman guessing you'll have her around for the rest of your life. He said, 'Once they get to know that, they start taking the whole thing for granted, runnin' all over and doin' what the hell they want. That's when you might as well forget it, son, 'cause once they lose that respect for you, they're gonna hit the road for sure.'

Billy knows that this is the ripest time to reassess his life in light of what was good and what was bad about Elvis's life, to separate the two, then discard the bad and put the good to use. His life is inert right now. He has time to sit home, mull things over, speculate, dream; he feels unfulfilled, sometimes gets tense, and explodes. His job as an apprentice jet mechanic lasted for about a year. "I can always be a mechanic," he says unenthusiastically. "I can work on anything that runs. I can always fall back on that, but I'm not going to."

When Billy confronts his mixed emotions about life with Elvis, he recognizes that his love for Elvis will always be tempered by resentment. He looks back with a hard-nosed sense of honesty and thinks about the Elvis "that didn't give a fuck about anybody but himself, had what he wanted because he was King of Rock 'n' Roll, did what he wanted to do.

"But he also taught me how to be a person," he acknowledges. "The thing that I always loved about Elvis was how he got off when he was giving people things. Elvis really taught me how to feel for people that were less fortunate than you, which was beautiful. You know, even as a kid I always tried to be like him that way. I'd freak people out, if I saw an old man comin' down the street who was poor, and I'd hand him five bucks or something. Hell, if I had his money, I'd be the same with it."

Billy also admired Elvis's steadfast belief in his own individualism. "Elvis was one of the most regular, *ordinary* guys in the
world," he says, "and I'll keep saying that, because that's what
impressed me so much about him, because he was also so *different*, so much himself; and he was determined.

"I know I just can't hang out for the rest of my life," says
Billy. "I want to do something important with it, because when
I'm gone, I want people to know that there was a man named
Billy Stanley around and that he was different from everybody
else . . . just like Elvis."

David Stanley doesn't like to lose. Like Elvis, he abhors being
second best at anything. He stands idly by at the pool table as
you sink shot after lucky shot, a look of painful exasperation on
his face at having to stand so helplessly by and watch the game
slither away, and then when you miss your shot he nods omin-
ously at you as if to say, "OK, motherfucker, you think *that* was
good? Watch this . . ." as he strides up, takes aim, and in one
explosion, runs the table. Then he smiles after killing you—as
gracious in victory as he is pissed off in defeat—and the smile
says, 'Shit, man, nothin' to it!' "

Because of the nature of his personality and his relationship
with Elvis, David is perhaps the most obsessed with Elvis Presley's legends and myths and certainly the most haunted by his
spirit. David drank so deeply of Elvis that many of those characteristics and opinions have been incorporated into his own identity. He sees a magnificent kind of glory in the way Elvis conducted his life and he "locked in" on Elvis's power, glory,
glamor, stardom, art, his professional prestige, on his determination. It's all he's ever known, he wants it himself, and nobody's going to stand in his way.

"When it came down to the will," he remarks, "I never even
thought about being in it. I just never expected anything.
Look—he had a little girl, a father, a grandmother, and a wife.
People were saying that we were cheated because we gave so
much to Elvis, and you gotta realize that Mom may be thinking

366 that. I'm not. Hell, as far as I am concerned we haven't been cheated out of anything. As far as business and teaching are concerned, we've been given the ultimate life."

Taking Care of Business runs in David's veins. "I'm used to all of it, man," he says, "and I like that taste. I've got to stick with it because it's my life. I want to be a millionaire. I want to be creative. One day when I was telling Elvis that I was planning to become an actor or make my mark in music, he said, 'David, you can have what I have, just be cool about it; be skeptical, keep your eyes open, and be yourself.' I've never forgotten that. Whether he was right or wrong, he was still the Boss, so we'll see. But I know I'll never be able to get that life out of my blood—the business, the road, the work, the prestige. I want to do it till I die, even if it's at forty-two years old."

If Elvis Presley was a man cloaked in destiny, then David believes that his destiny was Elvis Presley, which is why David was so lost when Elvis died.

The morning of August 16, 1977, still dogs him, and virtually everything David does seems to be forever pervaded by an acute awareness of death. He is remarkably stoic about the subject for someone his age, even reconciled to it, as if he accepts the necessity to blow his life out in the process of getting what he wants and then check out Elvis in that Great Road Show in the Sky. He has that same "throwaway" notion of life and sense of the inevitability of doom that Elvis began to come to terms with after the death of his mother. "My ideal is to love and take care of those I love and *do* until I'm gone, and whenever that is, it's cool. Sometimes I feel like I'm on death row myself. I've had dreams of dying and that's all I've had since Elvis died. Maybe he wants me that bad. I once told Elvis, 'If I die before you, I'll save you a place.' He said, 'Don't worry, your place will be taken. When you get there, you got a spot.' In that way death, to me, is the most fascinating thing in the world because I know that I'll never know the answers until it happens. I want to know those things that he talked about too; I want to see him again. I get these premonitions that I'm going to die and they scare me because I had a premonition Elvis was going to die and that my wife was going to leave me— If I die, I die, but

before I kick out, man, I'm gonna *go!* When I saw Elvis laying
on that floor, dead, that was reality staring me right in the face.
I'm gonna do it right, and I'll be goddamned if people aren't
going to know where this sonofabitch came from!"

All of the maxims and characteristics David soaked up around
Elvis have transposed themselves into a mystical axis, a spirit in
his life that he seeks communion with, an energizing force so
irresistible and compulsive that he obeys, upholds, and pays
homage to it without questioning its substance or the possibility
of any detrimental effects. He meditates on his memories and
they become his mantra, his vehicle into the future. You can
see it happen when he gets depressed. He simply walks into his
room, opens the window, sits down, and summons Elvis into
his consciousness. Suddenly Elvis is there, startlingly real. "He's
around," David says simply, as if Elvis were only in the next
room and all he has to do is knock on his door to talk to him
again. "Sometimes I don't like going up to his house. I don't
like a lot of people around me when I go up there; when I go, I
go alone. I can't listen to his records, and every show I go to
reminds me of him. But here, in my room, I can talk to him."

Word got out that David was more Elvis-haunted than his
brothers, apparently, and the *National Enquirer* recently invited
him to New York to participate in a seance that the paper was
holding in order to "contact" his spirit. David went along for
the hell of it, not really knowing what to expect, but for those
true believers, spiritualism is no laughing matter. The whole
thing seemed a travesty designed to drum up copy for some half-
baked article about Elvis's ghost. Nevertheless, there he sat, in
the Drake Hotel on Park Avenue, around a table with such paid
paragons of parapsychology as Hans Holzer and Sybil Leek. The
medium went into a trance; Holzer then asked questions, and
everyone in the room, with a melodramatic and chest-beating
sincerity, maintained that contact had indeed been made,
though David felt absolutely nothing. In fact, according to the
medium, Elvis approached David, laughing, during the seance.
"It was such bullshit," he says, "but if he *was* there, I can understand why he would have been laughing! The whole thing
was so goddamned funny! Like he was saying, 'Man, you poor

368   thing, look what you're goin' through!' I just kept thinking to myself, 'Hey, Elvis! If you are here, leave, man! Get the hell out of here!' "

Back in Memphis, David lies low and slowly adjusts to life without the Boss. The process is an ongoing one, but he's sure that when his moment comes, he'll be ready.

Elvis always told the Stanley boys that he would take care of them. "He didn't mean that financially," insists David, "and I knew that; he meant in other ways." The Boss would just never renege on such a promise, and David thinks that it's only a matter of time before he claims his inheritance, whatever it may be.

So much of Elvis Presley has rubbed off on Rick Stanley that even Priscilla Presley and Linda Thompson have told him that they see more of Elvis in him each day. Rick's first reaction to something like that is, of course, positive: He feels overjoyed, flattered, but then he gets to thinking, "Hey, wait a second, that could mean a lot of *different* things. . . ."

If a new dictionary defined some of the most colloquial meanings for the expression "fuckup," it might go something like this:

> **fuckup**—n., a social, moral, psychological, or emotional designation for someone who is constantly getting into trouble or doing things considered by many to be "wrong"; someone who does not live up to the expectations of others and makes a mess of things (i.e., his life) by doing things to himself considered to be "wrong" (i.e., drugs, alcoholism, crime, etc.); an ineffectual, bumbling, untrustworthy, pathetically poor excuse for a human being; someone who is any combination or all of the above, and, to make matters even worse, doesn't even care (in fact, a common characteristic of many fuckups is that they relish the designation).

Rick Stanley, who broke his mother's heart by skipping off to become Elvis Presley's protégé at the tender age of sixteen, would seem, at least, to have fit parts of the definition during his years as Slick Rick, the Raven from Whitehaven (the Boss's nickname), sidekick to a superstar, consummate roadie, druggie, and chickmeister. His would-be detractors in the TCB group even tried to point out to Elvis just in which ways he did fit the definition during those times when he ran amok, but even through his worst periods Elvis always stood behind him and he retained his boss's explicit trust and faith. "Look," Elvis would say, "he's a rowdy young man and he loves to have fun, but he knows how to listen to people. Someday he's gonna have an impact on people." That single comment contains Elvis's legacy to Rick Stanley, one that changed his entire life.

Rick crawled deep into himself after Elvis died. He harbored a deep-seated bitterness at the cruelty of a world that could claim a life like Elvis's and it irked him to see people who were close to Elvis wallowing in self-pity. "I just couldn't tolerate people feeling sorry for themselves," he says. "My attitude was, 'The hell with you—look what happened to the man. He's the one that's dead!' " Rick also wanted to get clear of those people who he felt had somehow given Elvis a "raw deal" both during his life and after the funeral (he prefers not name names), because they could become the targets for his intense hostility. But even the people who were his close friends, who truly understood his feelings, succeeded in bringing him down. "Everybody knew him," he says, "and everywhere you went there was somebody telling you how sorry they were. I had to get out."

After losing close to thirty pounds in a matter of weeks, Rick split for California—wan, wracked, wired, his eyes hollow and ghostly. "My Dad wanted me to stay on and help out at the mansion," he remembers. "He wanted me to ride around on the golf cart and keep people from coming over the walls. I love my dad, man, but it was too weird. It was too much."

Elvis's death had unleashed a rampaging beast in Rick's life, a beast dangerous and hard to control because it preyed upon his slowly unraveling emotions. Los Angeles seemed vacuous without Elvis, a barren wasteland where the beast easily flourished. Rick hoped that if he could find something to do like stunt work or bit parts, he could keep his mind off the pain. People like Joe Esposito heard that he was in town and offered their service— even Red West offered to help, but his emptiness worsened because so much of LA life revolved around the very things that

370 Elvis's life seemed to symbolize, like money, power, glamor, and sex. Rick began to feel more desperate as the weeks passed, leading him to believe that if he couldn't find something to fill the void left by Elvis in his life, the beast would claim him as surely as it had claimed Elvis. He could sense the danger when his drugs and drinking increased.

A woman wrested him away from destruction. Robyn Moye is a tall, willowy blond with soft, friendly brown eyes and a gentle, knowing smile. She was exactly the sort of girl Elvis would have liked—an easy, natural, unpretentiously beautiful woman—tender, warmhearted but emotionally strong and assertive, uninterested in power and power games, graciously and gracefully southern without being timid or demure, intelligent, religious but not old fashioned, free from perfection hangups, aware of her limitations, and very much in touch with herself. In fact, when Rick had brought her up to Graceland to meet the Boss, he had said as much. "That's the one, Ricky. That's the one you can depend on."

Robyn knew Rick from high school. They dated over the years, but not seriously until the last year of Elvis's life. She never really knew anyone quite as wild as Rick, but she more than tolerated his wildness—she understood it.

Robyn knew how wrapped up Rick's life was with Elvis's, and when he died, she was afraid for him because she knew how heartbroken he was. She boarded a plane for Memphis determined to give him something to help him through. "Rick, you're going to have a big, big thing happen in your life," she said as she got off the plane. She was holding a Bible.

"During the funeral," he remembers, "she spent the whole time witnessing to me about the Lord, telling me about Jesus. When you witness to somebody, you just speak of the Lord and not your own way of thinking because it's either black or white, but I just couldn't see it at the time. I was too hurt. My thoughts were, why would Jesus take Elvis away? Why would He do that?"

Thus the seed was planted at the funeral, even if Rick might not have been receptive to it at the time. There was also a man at the funeral who approached Rick out of the blue, tapped him on the shoulder, and said, "Son, do you realize what kind of effect you would have on the young people of this country if you gave all this up for the Lord?" He was a stranger. Rick still doesn't know who he was.

When Rick decided to leave Los Angeles, he didn't want to return to Memphis because, to him, that would have meant being dependent on his mother, which seemed almost like still being dependent on Elvis for everything he had. Robyn invited him to Florida. He realized what a great idea it was, packed, hopped a plane, and arrived almost penniless, but not before Robyn had talked to a young minister named Jay Zinn about him. Jay Zinn has established his congregation at the Fort Walton Beach Christian Center, in Destin, Florida.

Jay's congregation, in a storefront where he has established his church, is also young and numbers about a hundred and sixty. It's a nondenominational, nonsectarian congregation, a kind of unique and easy homogenization of unitarianism, fundamentalism, or anything else that might work, as long as it comes under the guise of the Good Book. In shirtsleeves and a tie, Jay stands in front of the room before preaching and straps an acoustic guitar around his shoulders. The musicians— another guitar, bass, and drums—stand off to his left, awaiting his cue. Someone at the overhead projector turns on the machine and places the words to a hymn somebody has written on the machine to be shown on a screen up front so that everybody can see, and Jay starts to strum. Bar chords for Jesus.

"I met him the second day I was there," Rick remembers. "Robyn asked me to go to church with her and I said OK, but I wasn't really that hyped up about it. Man, I hadn't been to church in over seven years! But I was hyped up when I left, when I felt the Spirit knocking at my heart—'Open up! Let Me in!' You know, you don't really meet many hip ministers, but Jay really knows the ways of the world, and I guess that's why I could relate to him. He's a man of God in the truest sense: He doesn't want anything for himself, no money, publicity, all he's interested in is saving souls. The man opened his home to me, and if there's anyone who helped fill that vacant spot, it's him."

Jay easily reached into Rick because he had been there him-

372   self. He knows about drugs, booze, women, about Existential Despair in Modern Times. He also knows about crime from his days as a thief in Cincinnati, and quite a bit about art, because he'd always wanted to be an artist when he was growing up in Dayton, Ohio.

"I thought it would be better for Rick to start a new life," Jay says, "totally obscure, away from Memphis, to where he could become his own man and have enough time to get his roots grounded so he could stand up to anything. He had nothing when he first came down here, and I was glad about that because love has nothing to do with money. We were in a position to help him, and that humbled him. After being broke for so long, he began to appreciate the little things in life like being able to eat."

But after all of those years on the road Rick's new religious enthusiasm was naturally hedged with skepticism because his whole life was so uniformly programed by the material, the tangible, the physical, the temporal. "It was hard for me," says Rick. "It was fine to love Jesus and everything, but I was still real careful. I'd think, hey, wait a second, man, I want to *see* something! It bothers me that I do that, but that's just the way I am and the way the world is. Let people see a miracle and they demand to see it again: Do that again! Once is not enough. But I've seen evidence."

Whatever cynicism remained was destroyed by the intensity of Rick's baptism. As Jay remembers it, "He had a very unique experience that not many people have. The Spirit was physical; it shook him so much that he had to lay out flat over the floor. He couldn't stand because the Holy Spirit moved over him so heavily, and I believe God needed to do that for the sake of him going away with no doubts whatsoever." Rick also had an ulcer that was bothering him, which Robyn told Jay about during the day. Jay resolved to heal it by the laying on of hands during the baptism. He told Rick to lie back down on the floor, laid his hands on him, "and a spirit voice rushed over him and started speaking in tongues. His stomach went up and down and started to jerk. I could tell that it was God doing that to him, and the ulcer was gone."

Rick's heart was torn between Memphis and the new life that he had found in Florida. "His whole family at the time wanted to stay together because of Elvis's death," Jay remembers, "and lean on each other, but what happened to Rick was that during the period of time he was home, he found himself being dragged back down. Surrounded by people that were not really influenced by the Lord, the principle of peer pressure was upon him; with no one to back up his convictions and him not strong enough yet, you naturally fall back into what you're used to. It's just like a plant that you plant in its early stages and keep in the greenhouse; when it grows to adulthood and maturity, that's when you can start moving it from location to location without worrying, but until then you nurture and protect it. I felt very much like a personal instrument of God in bringing Rick into His Kingdom, and I prayed that the Lord would bring him back."

The change in Rick startled his family and buddies in Memphis, but his own brothers were the most astounded. They couldn't believe it—the radiance, the confidence, the joy. Here was this ex-junkie who had spent a good part of his life flying around in jets and driving flashy cars with Elvis Presley, bedding all manner of women, gambling, boozing, staying high on drugs, lying for Elvis (or doing anything else that he might have asked), suddenly returning home, blissed out on Jesus!

Returning again to Fort Walton Beach, Rick decided to move in with Jay, his wife, and their two infant kids, until he could afford a place out in Destin, closer to his job as a lifeguard. Time passed pleasantly on the beach as his skin turned a golden brown, and you could see him every day sitting on his chair in front of the Silver Beach Hotel with those same mirrored shades on and a dog-eared, well-underlined Bible close by, thinking about his life, about Elvis, learning to discern the mind of God and to see His footprints in the thunderous crash of wave upon shore, in the squeaking of seagulls, the fortifying warmth of the sun, and the happy sounds of the little children playing at the water's edge, which drifted up to him on the Gulf breezes. If you approached him, you would see against the side of his equipment shack a mirror with a silhouetted image of Christ em-

374 bossed on it so that everybody who wanted to use the mirror could look in it and see, superimposed over his image, the image of Christ. That, to Rick, was what the ballgame was about—learning to be like Jesus.

"Man, there are a lot of miserable people out there," he says, "who are completely lost, who need help, and all of the psychiatrists in the world aren't going to do it. If you get into the Bible, into God's words, you can deal with those things because you won't have 'problems' any more, just little valleys that you go through when things aren't going well for you. But that's when your faith is being tested. If you praise the Lord with all of your heart when things are going wrong, you'll see some of the good things that can happen to you. I found that out. There are miracles happening in the modern world."

Today, when Rick looks back on his relationship with Elvis, and thinks about what Elvis represented in his life and to the world, he gets a clearer perspective on the role of religion in his life and in the world. Such expressions as "he was my *all*, my father, mother, teacher, boss, best friend, and there wasn't anything right or wrong that I wouldn't have done for him" illustrate to what degree people need to apotheosize others like Elvis Presley—to make them into Jesus figures. "I believe it's possible that Rick had come to that position just like everybody else who was idolizing Elvis," Jay says.

When his religious awakening comes back to the experience of Elvis Presley, it takes on special dimensions. For all of its good and bad ("the good will always outweigh the bad with Elvis") he feels that Elvis Presley was a blessing in his life. "The Lord blessed me by putting me in that environment with him so I could see what it's like to have everything—to have the world at your feet—and have your soul lost. Until I was twenty-four years old, I always looked to Elvis as someone I wanted to be like, and you can't help but be like somebody if you've been around them that long. But if you're around something like that, you begin to get a complex. You say to yourself, well, if he's so great, what about me? What am I going to do? How am I going to follow him up? In my own way, I'm going to follow him up, but the glory will be for God and not me. Thanks to

the Lord and Elvis, I've got an interesting testimony, and I feel
that all of the things that happened in my life were for a reason.
It was an act of God that I was able to come through without
wigging out. Not many young people have experienced what I
have, and I'm in a unique position to talk to people and share
my testimony with them, to break down barriers and talk to people about problems like drugs. That man took me when I was
sixteen years old and believe me, he taught me more about life
than any college could have, and I'm talking about *his* kind of
life."

Elvis's enduring qualities of compassion and generosity as
well as his pain and turmoil are embodied in the testimony that
Rick speaks of. The congregants were deeply touched when he
first got up there to share it in his church. There's nothing
holier-than-thou about it; it's a simple, wholly personal account
of a great life gone tragically and unnecessarily haywire. "If I
only had more of an awareness of the Lord when I was with
him," he laments, "I really think I could have played a bigger
part in his life. I think he might even be alive today. He would
have seen my peace of mind and how happy and fulfilled I was
and he would have been curious about it. I would have wit-
nessed to him out of love. Either he would have changed or I
would have. He might have fluffed it off, but who knows? So
many people worshiped that man, can you imagine if Elvis
would have directed himself toward the Lord?—if he would
have made a big, monumental move, how many souls could he
have saved?"

Rick sees the constant tension in Elvis's life between what he
knew to be good and what he knew to be bad as the reason for
his affliction of soul. "From the experience of his whole life,"
he says, "he knew the right way. It's pretty hard to lead a Christian life considering the position he was in. For all that, he
handled it well." It was, however, the life itself that dragged
him down and pulled him in opposite directions.

"But who are we to judge?" Rick asks. "That's for God to
judge, not us. We just don't have the right to do that. Who
knows what vows Elvis made to God on his way up, struggling?
Who knows what he prayed for and said, 'Lord, if you'll just let

376   me do this, I'll do that for You,' and how many of those promises he kept?" Rick's time on the beach at Destin allowed him
space to think about right and wrong in Elvis's life because
those rights and wrongs were a part of his own life. He thought
about Elvis's spiritual feelings and the salvation of his soul. He
thought about his philanthropy and the church that he erected
for his Aunt Nash in Wallis, Mississippi. "There's a lot that
people don't know," he says. "All of the souvenirs that came
onstage and the gifts to his home were given to orphanages.
Elvis was always thinking along those lines. He really cared
about his country, his public—their morals, what they thought
of him. He gave so much of himself that he couldn't help but
reap back tenfold. Given his circumstances, he may not have
lived what you'd call a 'Christian' life, but he always accepted
Jesus Christ as his Savior and he acknowledged Him to me many
times. He bore witness on a lot of his decisions because he was
a tender-hearted man. I don't think Elvis ever fell from the
Lord's grace. I think I'll see him in heaven, which is why I
don't get upset now that he's gone. I think that the people who
really loved Elvis should be rejoicing knowing where he's at and
strive to be up there with him."

Rick knows that his particular legacy from Elvis is greater
than anything Elvis could have left him in a will. "Mom felt
like it was a raw deal because we spent a lot of years locked in
and dedicated to the man," he says, "and then it seemed that
after he died everything was slammed in our face. It's true that
nobody was hurt more than Billy, David, and myself when he
died, but everything's cool with us. Still, it makes you wonder,
you know, did he really care that much; it wouldn't seem like
he did. I was told things like 'Just stick with me, Rick, and you'll
be taken care of for the rest of your life.' Nothing ever came of
it and I never looked for anything, either. I just dug being
around the guy."

Sometime after his death, a Memphis attorney approached
Rick and advised him to sue the Presley estate for breach of
promise on the grounds that promises made to him were like an
oral contract. In fact, several suits have been brought against the

estate, trying to hold it liable for things that Elvis Presley said he
would do but never had a chance to do. Rick wanted nothing to
do with that. "I just don't want to talk about my brother," he
says. "He's done a lot for me, and I love the man. I have a lot
of respect for him and I'm still loyal to him. I'm not bitter at
all."

Soon after Rick stopped working at the Silver Beach, the
evangelist Moody Adams heard about him and invited him to
join his team of traveling speakers. Last July, Rick gave his first
public testimony in Pearl, Mississippi, and the response was immediate and overwhelming. In only four months of speaking,
he's addressed over fifty thousand people, fifty-two hundred of
whom have come down that aisle to "make the decision for
Christ."

Rick faced his first crowd when he addressed a packed football
stadium in Jackson, Mississippi. He was met by hundreds of
kids at the airport carrying signs that read *He served the King of
Rock 'n' Roll / Now he serves the King of Kings.* People stood on
car tops to hear him speak and after that the places were overflowing. At his first stop in Memphis, so many wanted to hear
him that he had to speak twice. He just stood up there in Elvis's
hometown and spoke his heart, wearing a crucifix and the TCB
chain around his neck. "The best thing about it," he says, "is
that people aren't looking for a big wheel like Elvis. They're just
looking for someone who loves the Lord."

Thus the Raven became deacon, and Rick Stanley's back on
tour. Only this time, as he puts it, he's "under new management."

They don't make women like Dee Presley anymore. She's
something of an enigma, even to those who know her well.
Somewhere along the way, sometime during the social change
of the last twenty years, they broke the mold. To see a woman
like Dee Presley begin to reevaluate her life, to reexamine values and ways of thinking in light of the unfolding events of her
life, is fascinating and a testimony to the existence of such
change. In some ways she is like a young girl forging a fresh

378 identity; in other ways, she is like a keyhole into a graceful and romantic past, a lovely anachronism outwardly modernized, perhaps, but inwardly self-connected to a time gone by.

She looks great. To see her float by in her white Eldorado with the top down on a sunny day—her hair blowing in the breeze and a scarf blowing behind her—you would think . . . now, *there* goes a real Southern Lady. There is still that sense of distance, a detachment that she exudes, which gives her that highfalutin' air of imperious untouchability. That's Dee, outwardly at least.

"My way of love was selfish," she admits, looking back. "Sometimes I wonder if I was ever really in love or just in love with the idea of love, or maybe just in love with three young men named Ricky, Billy, and David. My concept of love worked only as long as things were going smoothly. I never allowed for mistakes, and life isn't like that. As long as things were beautiful and didn't disappoint me, I was fine. I learned what life is all about for me and I'm a new person because of it, but I couldn't realize it until I sent away the greatest love that I had. Now I feel like I'm discovering myself for the first time."

Freedom is new for Dee Presley, frightening and exhilarating, as exciting in its potential as it seems disorienting for its anxieties. The boys are grown up now. Vernon Presley is removed from her life, and that empty space that she faces with each day is teaching her a great deal. "I can look back at when the boys were small," she says, "and I can see what a tremendous part of my life they were because I always felt needed. There's absolutely nothing to do now; I can spend time anywhere I want, go where I want to go, do what I want to do. You know, that can be a happy time in a woman's life, but it takes time. I don't know if I like it yet."

She worries about her boys, but less than during those precarious months after Elvis died. It may be true that she is more cognizant of what they do and why (whereas at one point in her life her shock and disappointment would have left her incredulous), but she still worries. The Stanleys were a hard-drinking breed, so she worries about their drinking, and drugs, to her, are simply incomprehensible. In her own way she assumed that

their strict upbringing and religious guidelines and the sanction-
ing presence of Presley wealth could have insulated and protected her sons from all things bad in the world, but she never
bargained for the bumpy ride of the sixties, and she certainly
never bargained that Elvis Presley would become the source of
turmoil in all their lives.

The most obvious change is her new role as her sons' bene-
factress, a role that she has had to take over from Elvis. The
Boss had taken good care of the boys over the years ("he spoiled
us rotten is more like it," says Rick, "and we loved every minute
of it"), showering them with cars, gifts, expense accounts, and a
nifty salary on the TCB payroll. Dee's no-fault divorce settlement with Vernon Presley didn't exactly leave them out in the
cold, but she wasn't about to let that kind of life continue.
Financially and emotionally, it was time to sober up, and the
woman who could write a check for whatever she wanted and
never worry suddenly had to balance her budget.

"What bothers me," she says, "is that I think it will be very
hard for them to really work. They're spoiled, and I guess that
as long as I'm alive, they will be. I am to my sons now what
Elvis was, and I can't give them the toys they've been used to.
But I'm beginning to put more responsibility on them now."

Dee doesn't mince her words when the subject of Elvis's will
comes up. When she recalls all of Elvis's sincerely expressed
promises for her sons' welfare and her own experiences during
those last years, she becomes honestly resentful. "We may as
well face it; the resentment's there," she says. "Personally, I
don't feel that I could have been given enough money for what
I've been through, but speaking as a mother, I felt my sons
should have gotten something. I'm well aware how they feel
about it, but how hurt do you think they are? Did he really love
them? I think they're covering up the feeling that Elvis only
loved Elvis Presley when it came to some things. But the show
is over now. The final curtain fell on August sixteenth."

Her life would seem shattered, an exercise in tragedy and fu-
tility in which she was her own worst enemy, had she not been
able to step back from it all, thinking about the unfolding of
events. Dee Presley is amazingly ebullient. Her zest for life runs

380   at high tide. A strong and courageous woman, she's been able to bounce back, glean wisdom from her mistakes, and forge ahead—more youthful, directed, self-confident, and mature than ever. Her unwillingness to allow her life to become the soap opera that it would seem removes the danger of self-pity and fills her with purpose and energy, but takes time.

"Regardless of what I'm doing," she says, "it would be the same. No matter what I do, there would be a certain amount of lonely feeling because I've got so many memories of that life. Sometimes it takes me a whole day to get through something, and I actually feel lonely when there is someone there right with me. That's one of my real fears—being alone. Perhaps in my case more than many women, being alone seems frightening because I was always used to close family ties and that special someone being there all the time; I'm used to being sheltered and protected. After my marriage, I didn't know how to do *anything*, not even drive a car."

Dee is excited about the prospect of reconsolidating her family after so many years of being fragmented and apart from each other. Along with her own sense of self-discovery, this is perhaps the most important part of her legacy from Elvis.

Dee still could not speak to Vernon Presley before his death without dying a little inside. The passing of time allows her a healthier awareness of how and why she and Vernon went wrong, but for all of her coolness, his harshness, and their misunderstanding, she maintains nothing but gratitude, respect, and love for him.

"There was so much pain in his eyes and he was so very thin," she says. "He could hardly walk and he didn't look like himself anymore, but he was still a strong man with so much feeling. Besides my sons, God knows I love him more than anything else in the world. There will never be another like him. Our love was a different love and I'll always have it. He and Elvis made me what I am."

What began with James Elliot and moved to Bill Stanley may not end with Vernon Presley because Dee needs a man to love. One Good Man. "With my first two husbands, it was a physical attraction from the beginning, which is very important, but first

I'm going to see what we have in common. . . . I expect him
to open car doors and and to always pull out my chair for me. I
expect hand-kissing and gentleness, but I expect strength; he's
got to be the strong one. I expect him to watch his language and
not drink too much. I expect him to be faithful. I hope he likes
to read; I hope he likes art, and I hope he likes to go to the theater; I hope he likes to go sailing, boating, and horseback-riding.
I hope he goes to church with me, because I want a real spiritual love with someone, a real feeling that a man shares a love
of God with me. It all boils down to this: I just hope he's perfect! That's what I'm looking for!"

Dee Presley—quintessence of southern womanhood—lives
with her memories, looks optimistically to the future, or looks
back wistfully as a becoming pall of bittersweet melancholia
overcomes her. "I've got to get over it," she resolves. "I really
think it's going to be all right. I'll get through everything
through prayer. God can make a miracle happen in our lives."

Her dreams are the dreams that we all know so well, and if
you looked at her and tried to get her to compromise them by
doing something contrary to her ways, if you criticized her for
being so concerned about future heavens that she forgets to live
and savor the moment, she wouldn't apologize but would smile
that churchly smile and say, "*Dee Presley* has to wake up tomorrow!" And if you looked at her, frowned thoughtfully, and asked
her if she has any regrets, her deep blue eyes would flash with
life and she'd colorfully snap, "Not one thing! I'd do it all over
again!"

The first anniversary of Elvis's death was being heralded as a
major event in Memphis; indeed, in all likelihood, it would
have been, had it not been for blackouts and strikes by police
and firemen during those weeks, which kept a great many people away. The public sector is now deciding how best to accord
Elvis his place in history for future generations. City, state, and
national proclamations and observances are not far off. Before
long a twenty-five-foot bronze statue of some fifty tons will stand
on the bluffs overlooking Memphis and the winding Mississippi
River. Elvis will be cast in classic Greek pose, gesturing out over

382 the city he grew up in, like a modern day Achilles in a jump-suit.

Vernon Presley, of course, had remained very silent since his son's death. He let the Colonel handle business arrangements and contracts with the estate. He remained tight lipped about his feelings because they were so painful, and his life with Sandy Miller was very private. He got out rarely, but Rick noticed him at ringside in Las Vegas for the first Ali-Spinks fight on television. The mansion is empty except for a housekeeper, Grandma Minnie Mae, and Aunt Delta Mae. Elvis's rooms have been locked and everything is as it was on that August morning. Vernon Presley reckoned quite conscientiously with the continuing public need for his son, yet remained resentful of exposures and allegations of his son's "bad side."

On June 26, 1979, almost two years after the death of his son, Vernon Elvis Presley died of heart failure at the age of sixty-two. He had been in and out of the intensive care ward of Baptist Memorial numerous times and had been barely able to walk; his closest friends and relatives, aware of his worsening condition, had long known that it was only a matter of time. "Vernon Presley died when Elvis died," Dee says sadly. "The amazing thing was how long he was able to live with such heartbreak. He was a strong, beautiful man. I shall always love him."

The entire Presley clan gathered at Graceland for the funeral, an emotional reunion of the friends, relatives, and close associates who had comprised Elvis's world. With their heads solemnly bowed before the three graves of Elvis, Gladys, and Vernon, they all stood in the Meditation Gardens devastated by their grief, their tragedy, yet uplifted by the closeness that shared experience brings.

After the passing of time Priscilla Beaulieu Presley has become more comfortable with public exposure but still remains highly private about her life with Elvis. Linda Thompson has also preferred to maintain silence and keep her memories of Elvis her own. She leads her own life in Nashville and Los Angeles. Now a regular on *Hee Haw*, she pursues her career with determination and purpose and remains, of all the women

who ever loved Elvis Presley, one of the most warmly remembered for her charm, humor, grace, and tenderness.

"When you do a book like this," Rick says, "you've just got to
be honest. You can't say, 'Well, I've got to cover this up because I love him too much,' because if you want to get your
points across about him, you've got to be honest with yourself.
You can't pull punches; you've got to lay it all out, and the
good will outweigh the bad. Whatever bad there is, is in there
for a reason. All of those well-kept secrets about Elvis are coming out now, because he did things that have to be answered
for.

"I felt that I had something to say," he continues, "so I discussed it with Vernon. You can't wipe away those feelings after
so long; I love Priscilla and I love Lisa. I know Lisa will never
have to worry about anything financial for the rest of her life,
but I worry about where she'll be at spiritually and emotionally.
I don't want her to be unbalanced or anything like that. I want
her to be proud of her father, but to understand that the man
was so wrapped up in himself that he couldn't see out the window, that sometimes he wasn't a respecter of persons because he
never had to answer to anybody. I want her to understand the
position he was in, how hard it is to have anything you want
anytime you want it, and still stay sane. Just think about trying
to do that yourself for twenty years! Elvis was such an in-depth
man, but he had so much built up on him that he could hardly
keep his chin up. But Lisa will have it together because she'll be
like her daddy and her mother too. But those were the things I
had to reconcile before I could do something like this."

The time has come after months of posturing, self-examina-
tions, and procrastination. Meeting each other for the first time
is awkward because this writer is a stranger to their lives, an
alien in a position to ask delicate questions that seem naturally
prying at first. Somehow it seems that they actually can't believe
it's happening; that it's going to be done.

Nightfall in a small cabin on the Gulf of Mexico. A cool sea
breeze blows through the cabin window and slow, gentle waves
lap rhythmically against the shore. Billy, Rick, and David sit

384 around a coffee table; a bottle of Wild Turkey is opened, ice-cold cans of Busch pop, joints are rolled and fired. The tape recorder sits on the table next to a butt-filled ashtray. Slowly, as the ambience becomes more comfortable, the conversation becomes more animated, touching upon familiar ground.

"—fast with his hands, man," says Rick reverently. "Unbelievable."

Football. Elvis's spiral passes. How he'd smoke you hard on the field. His hands. Mnnn. His hands!

"Well, describe his hands to me," the writer says. "I mean, what were they *like?*"

Silence descends momentarily on the room as the six eyes search the writer wondering what kind of question is *that* to be asking for a book about Elvis Presley, wondering if maybe this writer might be as crazy as they are; he *is*, to be sure.

"Manly," Rick jumps in, his eyes excited now. "Definitely manly. His fingers were long and slender, not necessarily thin. Unique. The kind of hands you'd look at and never forget."

Billy is leaning forward, gesticulating as if he had a mike in one hand and was delivering the Sermon on the Mount with the other. "Remember how he'd use his hands when he did 'How Great Thou Art?' He always knew how to use his hands—"

"Firm," interjects David, "solid as rocks. Couple of his knuckles were bony, kinda *big*, you know . . . 'member when we was real little, Rick? Down there in the basement? He'd get these boards and always be breakin' them with his hands, his elbows, his feet—"

"—expression, power with his hands," Rick is explaining, everyone talking at once, the level rising. "That's what he talked about, man—Jesus, and how he could use his hands—"

"—callused on the fingertips from playin' the guitar," says Billy.

"—soft, though, when he touched you," David adds, "gentle, like when he put his hands on your shoulder when he talked to you."

The image of his hands stops everyone and we stare at each other, stupefied. Excitement passes like electricity across the terminals of batteries and we realize that maybe, just maybe, if we trust each other, we can pull if off, we can do this thing. The hands seem so much of what he was—musician, athlete, actor, lover—and the metaphor is a revelation, a vehicle that can take us anywhere we want to go now, into any subject, any feeling, when the lights suddenly go out and we still feel it in the darkness but nobody dares to move now as our hearts quicken and we listen to the slight, ghostly rustle of the breeze through the curtains, the mechanical whir of the tape recorder, and the distant waves.

"That's *him*, right there," says David in the darkness. "Hey, *Boss*, don't worry, man. We're gonna tell it like it is. . . ."

Alden, Ginger, 273–276, 331, 339
"All Shook Up," 34
Aloha from Elvis in Hawaii, 169, 240
Ann-Margret, 358
Army, 41–42, 60

Bodyguards, 126–128
"Boss," 117, 118
Bradley, C.W., 299, 351, 358
Bradley, Roberta, 299
Brown, Earl, 96
Buergin, Margit, 53
Burton, James, 146–147, 159, 291

Bean, Orville, 7
Beatles, 155–156
Beaulieu, Priscilla, *see* Presley, Priscilla Beaulieu
Berry, Chuck, 9, 36, 96
Binder, Steve, 94
Black, Bill, 23–24
"Blue Moon of Kentucky," 28
"Blue Suede Shoes," 34

"Can't Help Falling in Love," 232
Change of Habit, 96
Clapton, Eric, 157
Colonel, *see* Parker, Colonel Thomas A.
Comeback, 144–154; celebrities attending, 150–151; hottest performances, 149–150; musi-

390 Comeback (*continued*)
    cians, 146–149; repertoire, 151–154; reviews, 144–145, 146
Crafton, Ollie, 6
Cronkite, Walter, 273

"Danny Boy," 357
Daughter, 80–81, 211–214
Davis, Richard, 79, 118
Death, cause of, 343–346; family and friends reaction to, 341–342, 347–351; fascination with, 193–194, 287–288; first anniversary of, 381–382; funeral, 357–360; public reaction to, 348–352; public viewing at Graceland, 353–354; rumors about, 345; threat, 124
Denny, Jim, 29
Diddley, Bo, 36
Divorce, 203–205, 207, 208
Domino, Fats, 36
"Don't Be Cruel," 34
Drug problem, 215–227, 271, 279–284
Dunleavy, Steve, 323, 326–327, 352
Dylan, Bob, 156

Ed Sullivan Show, The, 37
Elliot, Bessie May (Heath), 4, 5
Elliot, Davada, *see* Presley, Dee Elliot
Elliot, James Wright, 4–6, 9, 37–38

Elliot, Maurice, 347
Elrod, Jean, 11–12
Elvis and the Colonel (May Mann), 216
Elvis Sails, 41
Elvis: What Happened? (Red and Sonny West), 126, 216, 352; cruelty of, 214, 323; effects of, 317, 323, 324–327; inaccuracies in, 131, 208; why written, 322
Esposito, Joe, 49–50, 79, 80, 118–119, 149, 229, 232, 234, 240, 254, 281, 282–283, 335, 339, 353, 358, 359, 369
Esposito, Joni, 118

Fike, Lamar, 49–50, 120–121, 254, 359
Fontana, D.J., 26
Fortas, Alan, 118
Francisco, Dr. Jerry, 338, 343–344, 346
Franck, Tom, 133
From Elvis in Memphis, 95–96
Funeral, 357–360

Gambil, Gee Gee, 118
Gambil, Patsy Presley, 77
Geller, Larry, 121–122, 338, 354–355
G.I. Blues, 60
Gibran, Kahlil, 189, 194
"Good Rockin' Tonight," 27
Gospel music, 23, 154
Graceland, 65

Graham, Bill, 96
Grand Ole Opry, 28–29
Grant, Currie, 52
Grob, Dick, 126, 230, 232, 234, 235, 252, 253
Guercio, Joe, 146, 148

Harum Scarum, 64
Health problems, 242, 271, 289–290
Heart attack, 338–343
"Heartbreak Hotel," 32
Heath, Bessie May, *see* Elliot, Bessie May
Hebler, David, 126, 321–322, 326, 352
Hill, Ann, 257–259
Hodge, Charlie, 49–50, 79, 80, 120, 229, 251–252, 353, 359
Holzer, Hans, 367
Hospitalized, 283–284
"Hound Dog," 34, 37
"How Great Thou Art," 157
Humbard, Rex, 357

"If I Can Dream," 96
"I'm So Lonesome I Could Cry," 291
"In the Ghetto," 96
"It's Now or Never," 62

Jailhouse Rock, 39, 60
Jarvis, Felton, 229, 359

J.D. Sumner and the Stamps Quartet, 147–148

Kahane, Jackie, 359
Kathy Westmoreland and the Sweet Inspirations, 147–148
Keisker, Marion, 21–23
King Creole, 40
Klein, George, 79, 122, 273, 359
Klein, Rick, 273
Kyle, Dr. Charles and Gerry, 299

Lacker, Marty, 79, 117
Las Vegas, 96–100, 233–240
Leek, Sybil, 367
Lewis, Jerry Lee, 36
Lime, Yvonne, 53
Live a Little, Love a Little, 81
Lloyd, Harold, 337
Locke, Dixie, 53
Los Angeles Forum (1974), 150
Love Me Tender, 37, 39
Loving You, 41, 53

Madison Square Garden (1972), 150
Mann, May, *Elvis and the Colonel*, 216
Marcus, Greil, 326
Marriage, 79–80
"Memphis Mafia," 49–50, 116–117

392 Miller, Mindy, 271
Miller, Sandy, 303–309, 310, 311, 313
Moore, Scotty, 23–24
Moye, Robyn, 355, 370–371, 372
Musicians, 146–149
"My Way," 290–291

Neal, Bob, 29
Neely, Richard, 20, 61
Nicholson, Pauline, 337
Nichopoulos, Dr. George "Dr. Nick," 122, 223, 229, 236, 240, 281, 283, 344, 346, 347, 359

Parker, Colonel, Thomas A. "the Colonel," after Elvis's death, 358; and Elvis's wedding, 79; and Las Vegas, 96, 100, 238–239; marketing Elvis's name and face, 37; meeting Elvis, 29–30; and recording contract, 32; and TV specials, 60, 94
Parker, Ed, 126, 181, 202, 229, 232
Penniman, Little Richard, 36
Pennington, Ann, 271
Phillips, Dewey, 24–25
Phillips, Sam C., 22–23, 24–25
Pierce, Webb, 27, 28
Pink cadillac, 31
Presley, Dee Elliot, 4–6, 9–13; after Elvis's death, 377–381; calling Elvis, 43–44; and Elvis, 50–51,

66–69; father, 37–38; marital problems with Vernon, 297–315; marriage to Bill Stanley, 15–18, 20–21, 37–39; marriage to Vernon Presley, 61–62, 71, 72–73; meeting and dating Vernon Presley, 45–49; and new house in Memphis, 70; "official hostess" at Graceland, 65–66, 68; pregnancies, 16–18, 74–75; and sons, 20–21, 31, 83–92, 100–103; and Vernon and Bill, 54–59
Presley, Elvis Aron, in the army, 41–42, 60; and bad concert reviews, 290; becoming an image, 33; bedridden, 289; and Billy's estrangement, 260–263; and Billy's wives, 257–260, 264–265; birth of, 7; body movement, 144; bodyguards, 123–128; boredom on tour, 129–130; and cars, 112–115; and chimpanzee, 68–69; and the Colonel, see Parker, Colonel Thomas A.; comeback, 144–154; daughter, 80–81, 211–214; death of, 338–346; and Dee Presley, 43–44, 50–51, 61–62, 66–67; discovering singing voice, 8–9; divorce from Priscilla, 203–205, 207, 208; and drug problems, 215–227, 271, 279–284; and Eastern philosophy, 189–190; on The Ed Sullivan Show, 37; emotionality of, 152; and family breakup, 313–315; and family, sense of, 168; and fans, 69, 123; and fascination with death, 193–194, 287–288; and fascination with police, 176–178; and father, 72, 204, 293–296, 311, 313; and fight at airport lounge, 247–249; and fighting,

166–168, 352–353; and first big audience, 27; and first job out of high school, 21; and first recording, 24–26; friends of, 116–122; and Ginger Alden, 273–276; and gospel music, 23, 154; and Graceland, 65; at Grand Ole Opry, 28–29; and guns, interest in, 179–180; and hard rock, 156–157; and health problems, 242, 271, 289–290; and heart attack, 338–343; high school years, 13–14, 18–20; honor of, 166; hospitalized, 283–284; idea of manhood, 161; identity, 137–139; and karate, 180–182; in Las Vegas, 96–100, 233–240; and Linda Diane Thompson, 267–271; and Lisa Marie, 80–81, 211–214; loneliness of, 285; loud clothes and long hair on, 19; on marijuana, 222; marriage to Priscilla, 79–80; and money, 168–172, 295; moods of, 136–138; and mother, 7–9, 40, 204, 206; and movies, 64; musical taste of, 154–157; as musician, 157, 158, 159; musicians of, 146–149; performance, last live, 329–331; on power and patriotism, 175–176; and Priscilla, 52, 76–80, 202–205, 207, 208; on psychedelics, 221; and raw ambition, 162; RCA recording contract, 32; reaction to Freddie Prinze's death, 287; reading interests of, 188–189; recording song for mother's birthday, 21–22; religious feelings, 185–194; and Rick, 90–91, 100–103, 107–108; and Rick's girl friend, 263–264; and Rick's use of drugs, 224–227; and riot in Jacksonville, 31; and rock 'n' roll, 34, 35–36; separation from Priscilla, 202–203; as "showman," 142–143; singing blues, 26–27; singing gospels, 23; "special powers" of, 190–192; and sports, 182–183; and stepbrothers, 60–61, 83, 85–88, 109–116, 128; success, 32; summer of '69, 100; TCBing, 114–115; tour in '70s, 229–240; TV Christmas special of '68, 94–95; TV special (June '77), last, 329–331; and weight problem, 240–242; "wild within the tame," 163–165; withdrawn, 284; and women, 131–135, 197–200; youth, 7–9

Presley, Gladys (Smith), concern for son, Elvis, 7–9, 34–35; death of, 40, 204, 206; marriage to Vernon Presley, 6–8; move to Memphis, 13–14, 18–19

Presley, Jesse Garon, 7, 71–72

Presley, Lisa Marie, 80–81, 211–214, 334, 383

Presley, Minnie Mae, 71–72

Presley, Priscilla Beaulieu, after Elvis's death, 357, 382; birth of daughter, 80–81; character, 207; divorce, 203–204; and Elvis's friends, 199, 201; exchanging letters with Elvis, 75–76; and karate, 202; leaving Elvis, 202–203; love affair with Mike Stone, 202; marriage, 79–80; meeting Elvis, 52, 53; stay at Graceland, 76–79

Presley, Vernon Elvis, character, 71–72; concern for Elvis during last years, 293–296; death of, 382; and Dee and Bill Stanley, 54–59; with Dee, and Elvis, 50–51; and Dee's boys, 83, 85, 92; divorce, 297, 309, 315; and

394   Presley, Vernon Elvis (*continued*)
Elvis's business, 71; and Elvis's success, 32, 34; and Gladys's death, 40, 204; heart attack, 311–313; jealousy of, 73–75; marital problems, 297–315; marriage to Dee, 61–62, 71, 72–73; marriage to Gladys, 6–7; meeting and dating Dee, 45–49; move to Memphis, 13–14, 18–19; on the road with Elvis during last years, 293–296
Presley, Vester, 69
Prinze, Freddie, 287

"Rag Mop," 23
RCA recording contract, 32
Religious feelings, 185–194
Robbins, Marty, 27
Rock 'n' roll, 34, 35–36, 154
Russell, Leon, 157
Ryan, Sheila, 271

Scheff, Jerry, 147
Schilling, Jerry, 79, 80, 119, 157, 230, 234, 240, 359
Seance, 367–368
Shafer, Pearl and Paul, 299
Shepherd, Cybill, 271
Sholes, Steve, 33
"Showman," 142–143
Sinatra, Frank, 60
Smith, Billy, 119–120, 230, 255–256, 359
Smith, Gene, 359

Smith, Gladys, *see* Presley, Gladys Smith
Smith, Travis, 69
Snow, Hank, 28
Sparkman, Wilma and Clyde, 299
"Special powers," 190–192
Stanley, Bill, 12–13, 15–18, 20, 31, 37–38, 46, 48
Stanley, Billy, 18, 88; and Elvis's death, 363–365; estrangement from Elvis, 200–203; and fight in airport lounge, 243–249; and his wife and Elvis, 257–260, 264–265; leaving home, 100; masculine influences in life, 83; on the road with Elvis, 111–112; relationship with Elvis, 83, 85–88; trying to influence Elvis's musical taste, 156–157
Stanley, David, 88–89; as bodyguard, 123–124, 126–128; and Elvis playing guitars, 158–159; and Elvis's death, 361–362, 365–368; and fight with Charlie Hodge, 251–253; leaving Elvis and returning home, 254–255; leaving home, 100; and life on road with wife at home, 253–254; masculine influences in life, 83; and mother, 84; on tour, 232, 234; and problems with wife, 256–257; relationship with Elvis, 83, 85–88, 128; roughhousing with Elvis, 129–130; trying to influence Elvis's musical taste, 156–157
Stanley, Dee, *see* Presley, Dee Elliot
Stanley, Rick, 89–92; and drugs, 222–223, 279–280; and Elvis and drugs, 281–282, 283; and Elvis testing loyalty of, 107–108; and Elvis's death, 368–377; and Elvis's interest in girl friend, 263–264; and fight at air-

port lounge, 243–249; leaving home, 100; masculine influences in life, 83; on the road with Elvis, 100–103, 109–116; relationship with Elvis, 83, 85–88, 128; and TCBing, 114–115; touring in 70s, 230, 232, 233–236; turning to religion, 371–377

Stans, Angela, 253, 256–257

Stepbrothers, 83–92; *see also* Stanley, Billy; Stanley, David; Stanley, Rick

Stone, Mike, 126, 181, 202, 208, 327

Strada, Al, 320, 353

Suits against estate, 376–377

Taurog, Norman, 217

TCB (Taking Care of Business) group, and Elvis's moods, 135–139; and jealousies and rivalries, 128; people in, 111, 116–122; and reporters, 129; and security, 123–128; "TCBing," 114–115, 137; women and, 130–135

Tchechowa, Vera, 53

Television specials, Christmas ('68), 94–95; last, 329–331

"That's All Right (Mama)," 24, 26, 28

Thompson, Linda Diane, 139, 267–271, 358, 382–383

Thompson, Sam, 320, 353

Tutt, Ronnie, 147

"Unchained Melody," 242, 291

"U.S. Male," 166

Viva Las Vegas, 77, 159

Wallace, Bill, 247

Wallis, Hal, 60, 201

West, Bobby "Red," 30, 49–50, 122, 133, 247, 318–321, 369

West, Red and Sonny, *Elvis: What Happened?*, 126, 216, 352; cruelty of, 214, 323; effects of, 317, 323, 324–327; inaccuracies in, 131, 208; why written, 322

West, Sonny, 122, 318–321, 352

"Wild within the tame," 163–165

Will, 362–363

Williams, Hank, 291

"Without You," 23

Women, 131–135, 197–200; *see also* Alden, Ginger; Presley, Priscilla Beaulieu; Thompson, Linda Diane

Wood, Anita, 53

Yogananda, Yogi Paramahansa, 190